PERSPECTIVES IN VERNACULAR ARCHITECTURE, IV

Perspectives in Vernacular Architecture, IV

Edited by
Thomas Carter and Bernard L. Herman

Philippe Oszuscik
1992

University of Missouri Press
Columbia and London

For the Vernacular Architecture Forum

ISSN 0887–9885   ISBN 0–8262–0792–8

∞™ This paper meets the requirements of the
American National Standard for Permanence of Paper
for Printed Library Materials, Z39.48, 1984.

Designer: Rhonda Gibson
Typesetter: Connell-Zeko Type & Graphics
Printer: Thomson-Shore, Inc.
Binder: Thomson-Shore, Inc.
Typeface: Sabon

CONTENTS

II. Buildings and Regions

III. Buildings and Popular Culture

ACKNOWLEDGMENTS

This volume brings to a close our term as editors of *Perspectives in Vernacular Architecture*. We thank the Vernacular Architecture Forum and its Directors for the opportunity to be a part of this important series. Thanks also go to the people at the University of Missouri Press, and particularly Jane Lago, for their patient assistance. The authors deserve a vote of appreciation too, for they got things to us on time and proved amenable to our comments and suggestions.

The work on *Perspectives, IV* was made easier by the specific contributions of many people. First, there was our editorial board consisting of Carter Hudgins, Gary Stanton, Elizabeth Cromley, Christopher Yip, Pamela H. Simpson, Margaret Purser, Alice Gray Read, Carolyn Torma, Michael Steinitz, Camille Wells, and Fred W. Peterson. The comments offered by the board guided us in making tough decisions and providing advice to the authors represented in this volume.

At the University of Utah our work was aided by the editorial assistance of Susan Deal Anderson and the encouragement and financial support of Carl Inoway, Dean of the Graduate School of Architecture. Additional funding was provided by the S. J. and J. E. Quinney Foundation. At the University of Delaware, the long process of preparing *Perspectives, IV* could not have been completed without the help and editorial insights of David L. Ames, Linda Boyd, Nancy van Dolsen, Gabrielle Lanier, Carole Hermes, and Rebecca Siders. Finally, we thank Catherine E. Hutchins for her careful reading of the introduction.

Note to the Reader

Unless indicated otherwise in the captions, all illustrations are by the authors.

PERSPECTIVES IN VERNACULAR ARCHITECTURE, IV

THOMAS CARTER AND BERNARD L. HERMAN

INTRODUCTION
TOWARD A NEW ARCHITECTURAL HISTORY

One of the main problems with defining the field of vernacular architecture in the United States is the breadth and diversity of the objects under investigation. At any given time and in any given place almost any kind of building can be included within the boundaries of what those of us working in the field call vernacular architecture. Such catholicity has led many observers to characterize vernacular architecture studies at best as expansive and at worst, vaporous. Both viewpoints support the proposition that the materials we study, the sense of what constitutes traditional, popular, and elite culture, and the ways in which we view all aspects of the built environment are innovative as well as diverse. *Perspectives in Vernacular Architecture, IV* exemplifies this. It includes essays ranging from a study of colonial brickmasons to one looking at the process of twentieth-century suburbanization. The expanding array of interests and approaches is even more apparent when one compares the essays in this volume with those found in earlier volumes in the series.[1]

Adding to the definitional quandary is the tendency among American vernacular architecture scholars to focus on the artifact. While we have not avoided theoretical and definitional posturing, our inclination has been toward fieldwork. It has been more important, and more fun, to study old buildings and landscapes than to build academic empires. Such an attitude has been vital to the health of the movement; more than a decade of fieldwork is now being transformed into books and articles that clearly demonstrate the value of vernacular architecture research. Still, the expansiveness of our pursuits proves troublesome when we try to explain—particularly to people encountering the subject for the first time—what we mean when we say *vernacular architecture* and *vernacular architecture studies*. The publication of *Perspectives in Vernacular Architecture, IV* makes us think once again about what it is that we do, for the essays presented here draw on the widest possible range of interests, methods, and theories. As a group they call attention to the difficulty we face when forced to generalize about the field and its practitioners.

Perspectives in Vernacular Architecture as a publication series is nearly a decade old now, and experience if nothing else makes several observations possible. First, while most of us in the field feel comfortable using English historian Eric Mercer's definition of vernacular architecture as those buildings "which belong to a type that is common in a given area at a given time,"[2] we often spend a great deal of time examining quite extraordinary structures too. In this volume there are essays focusing on the houses of California's Mexican gentry, the mansions of New England's emerging nineteenth-century bourgeoisie, and the suburban retreats of urban industrialists, none of which are, within their specific cultural contexts, ordinary buildings. Often this involvement with the architecture of the elite stems from the simple fact that the largest and most substantial buildings are the ones that survive. The *truly* ordinary structures have vanished. We must be aware that vernacular architecture studies are often not the egalitarian tomes we claim them to be.[3]

The same kind of ambiguity surrounds the other main tenet of vernacular architecture research, regionalism. One of the most pervasive and persuasive definitions of vernacular architecture follows a line of thinking based in linguistics: vernacular buildings are localized versions of widely known forms.[4] Many of the best examples of vernacular architecture research adopt a regional perspective by exploring the close link between built form and local culture. It is unsurprising that the bulk of the essays in this volume fall into this category. But there are other studies that fall into the vernacular camp, particularly those dealing with twentieth-century topics such as suburbs. These studies are more diffuse and reflect nationwide trends and values. We include these studies under the rubric of vernacular architecture and have placed them in the section on popular culture, yet it must be remembered that reconciling the intensely local with the more broadly American, or even international, is sometimes difficult.

So what is vernacular architecture if it is not limited to the ordinary and the local? The response to this question posits an emerging paradigm for the field. The theoretical and methodological underpinning of vernacular architecture studies as we know it may be found in two seminal works that appeared in the 1970s, Henry Glassie's *Folk Housing in Middle Virginia* (1975) and Abbott Lowell Cummings's *The Framed Houses of Massachusetts Bay* (1979).

In his study of Virginia housing, folklorist Glassie advanced two key concepts that have influenced scholars in a truly interdisciplinary sense. First, Glassie demonstrated that folk buildings are the products of deliberate and often complex design processes that possess linguistic analogies.

Second, such designs, like language, are strategically situated texts in vast, complex, and fluid discursive contexts. The long-range effect of Glassie's work has been to guide a field increasingly engaged in the discovery of mind and meaning in architecture and architectural systems. *Folk Housing in Middle Virginia,* more than any other single work perhaps, makes us recognize the complexity and significance of vernacular buildings.[5]

Cummings's study of colonial Massachusetts housing set forth a rigorous standard for architectural documentation and artifact analysis. Cummings demonstrated the role of careful recording of architectural fabric and the critical reading of documentary sources as essential to discovering intricate questions about antecedents, diffusion, and regional style. Where Glassie provided an anthropological frame of inquiry, that is, a fundamental concern for understanding human behavior through the analysis of buildings, Cummings introduced an archaeological perspective, a concern for the level of documentation that makes systematic analysis possible. The care with which Cummings considered the physical evidence provided by buildings linked the study of vernacular architecture to parallel research in social history and community studies.[6]

Together these two authors and the proliferating publications of their students and colleagues have provided the methodological and theoretical basis for the study of almost all aspects of vernacular building. And it is at this juncture that the study of vernacular architecture fuses with the larger field of material culture studies. Material culture has surfaced as a field of inquiry that "employs physical objects as primary data." Buildings become, in this light, historical documents—nothing more, nothing less.[7]

This is no great revelation of course. Those who have bothered to think about such things as definitions have always stressed methodology: vernacular architecture is an "approach" to architectural studies, Dell Upton has written; Camille Wells, editor of the first two volumes of *Perspectives in*

Vernacular Architecture, noted, "It is clear that vernacular architecture has become, for many scholars, less a kind of building than an approach to looking at buildings."[8] These observations ring true to the spirit of the vernacular architecture movement. While we treasure our scholarly eclecticism, we hold the line on our rationale of using buildings to learn about people and their functional, aesthetic, and symbolic manipulation of the environment. We do not always achieve these aims, but they are our goals. In actual operation, vernacular architecture is a kind of architectural study with a strong orientation toward historical explanation and as such is both similar to and different from two close relatives—architectural history and the new social history.

What we share with architectural historians, assuming architectural history to be a branch of history, is an interest in buildings. Yet we commonly distance vernacular architecture from traditional architectural history out of a belief that architectural historians are concerned only with the object or the "piece" of architecture rather than with history in general. Art historian Ken Ames promoted this notion when he wrote, "History and art history often seem to move in opposite directions. Put in oversimplified terms, historians use art to study the past while art [and architectural] historians use the past to study art."[9] Ames takes a point of view widely held outside the discipline of art history and one that is particularly popular with vernacular architecture people, yet it is a point that needs redress.

Certainly some architectural historians may be preoccupied with connoisseurship, but such a fascination with the object is not unknown among students of vernacular architecture; think, for instance, of the seemingly endless studies of log buildings.[10] It is also true that architectural historians engage regularly in the pursuit of what art historian and theorist George Kubler has called the "artistic biography," the reconstruction of the life and work of a particular architect.[11] Clearly topological studies, which may be considered arti-

factual biographies, have been and will continue to be a staple of the vernacular architectural diet. Finally, the charge that architectural historians are uninterested in "mind and meaning" is unwarranted. Art historian Donald Preziosi in a recent reassessment of his discipline has observed, "There is a deep sense in which, for the art historian, art has always been a historical event or phenomenon, a sign of the times, an index of historical, social, cultural, or individual growth, identity, change, or transformation. It is fair to say that even at its most formalist or idealist moments, this perception has been a given in the discipline [of art history]."[12] The conflict between connoisseurship and history is found in nearly all fields and disciplines, often translating into an opposition between the text, be it a work of literature, folklore, or architecture, and the context, the circumstances in which the particular text occurs and from which it draws power and meaning. Even we students of vernacular architecture must routinely remind ourselves of Henry Glassie's early admonishment about the "obsessive" treatment of artifacts."[13]

Vernacular architecture in many respects maintains a relationship to architectural history that is similar to the one the new social history bears toward traditional history. The new social history arose during the 1960s and 1970s out of a concern that history had become preoccupied with great men and events. The new historians moved to correct the injustice by bringing the forgotten people of the past—blacks, women, workers, the poor—into the mainstream of history through methodologies emphasizing the joint benefits of textual, quantitative, and ethnohistorical approaches.[14] What began with a radical manifesto to rewrite history from the "bottom up" mellowed in the 1980s into a desire to recover cultural wholes. Historian Cary Carson has written pointedly that "recognition for history's neglected majority follows inevitably from the new emphasis historians are giving to society as a working organism, a community of individuals and groups who are mutually dependent on one another—top to bottom or bottom to top, it doesn't matter. This integrated, all-aboard view of society *is* fundamental to the New History perspective, as are the questions that flow from it: How were historic societies structured? How did their parts work together? What underlying forces eventually altered both structure and function?"[15]

Vernacular architecture studies developed in a strikingly similar way. The first studies spoke out vigorously against the elitism of traditional architectural history, a history of a few white wealthy males. In time the harangue has been replaced by a plea for understanding how common buildings occupied contexts comprising wide social and economic spheres. Like social historians, vernacular architecture scholars have begun to speak of wholes, or in Carson's words, of architectural "communities." Upton has been the most outspoken proponent of what he calls a "landscape" approach to architectural history that includes many "kinds and scales" of buildings, both "vernacular" and "high-style." In the 1980s Upton, Bernard Herman, Thomas Hubka, and Robert St. George took the first steps toward achieving such a broad approach to the study of building systems.[16]

The relationship with social history, however, has its limits. While the two areas of inquiry share certain objectives, their methods and their primary evidence diverge. Historians and their colleagues in American Studies remain nervous about any artifact as evidence. The past decade saw the appearance of a number of studies exploring the social meanings of Victorian-era architecture, including Gwendolyn Wright's *Moralism and the Model Home* (1980), Dolores Hayden's *The Grand Domestic Revolution* (1981), Clifford Clark's *The American Family Home* (1986), and Sally McMurry's *Families and Farmhouses* (1988). These authors have provided fine excursions into the literature of architecture and popular culture, but books such as these are not true architectural studies because they are not based on the field investigation of actual buildings. In their explorations of written culture, these scholars have not pursued the connection between the prescriptive literature and actual behavior. This observation is not intended to diminish the contribution these individuals have made, but simply underscores the very real sense of dislocation that exists between what Americans have historically stated about themselves on paper and what they have written on the land itself through their material culture.

The premium vernacular architecture scholars place on "object-driven" studies returns us to the simple fact that those of us who study vernacular architecture or, better yet, those of us who have adopted the vernacular architecture approach, are at heart architectural historians. For better or worse, vernacular architecture studies "complement traditional architectural history."[17] The kind of architectural history we pursue, however, remains distinctive in its scope. We are concerned with developing an approach to architectural history that emphasizes historical explanation and speaks of architectural systems or landscapes, high and low, both common and elite. In pursuit of these goals we draw on the methods of cultural and historical geography, historical archaeology, linguistic and literary theory, as well as the new social history and architectural history.

It may be useful in the long run to rethink the name *vernacular architecture* itself. Camille Wells intimated as much in her introduction to *Perspectives, II* when she acknowledged that the field had become so vague that "in a literal sense, the term [vernacular architecture] is outmoded or inadequate."[18] The term is inadequate precisely because it suggests a method for studying *all* kinds of buildings, not just a particular type of buildings, that is, common ones. Because vernacular architecture now describes an approach to the study of buildings and because the particular configuration of this approach is innovative, we are tempted to use the term *the new architectural history*. Such a term has several advantages. First, it acknowledges that what we are doing is indeed new. Second, it recognizes our strong affiliation with both architectural history—the study of buildings—*and* the new so-cial history—the study of human communities. From this perspective, vernacular architecture—the common, the local, the regional—becomes part of what we do, as does the study of popular, broadly based architecture—house trailers and mail-order cottages, and the architect-designed houses of the elite.

The essays contained in *Perspectives in Vernacular Architecture, IV* exhibit the chronological mixture, the treatment of elite and common buildings, and the opposition between regional and popular culture that characterize the vernacular architecture paradigm of the 1980s—our new architectural history. Not only are they exemplary statements of current scholarship, but they also reveal a shared commitment to the desiderata of the movement: the rigorous recovery of cultural meanings through careful documentation of actual buildings supplemented by research in primary documents. The organization of this volume respects three major research areas in vernacular architecture studies: builders, regions, and popular culture.

The six essays grouped in the first section, "Buildings and Builders," range in time and topic from colonial brickmasons in southern New Jersey to women homesteaders on the Great Plains. The authors ask a variety of questions challenging old assumptions that folk builders are somehow anonymous and vernacular architecture lacks design. J. Ritchie Garrison, Gabrielle Lanier, and Michael Chiarappa present meticulously detailed reconstructions of the builders' trade that are based on collective and individual artisan biographies. In each of their essays the sense of community context is paramount in understanding the terms of particular contracts, the organization of labor, and the dissemination of ideas. Catherine Bishir and Howard Davis extend the discussion into the area of cultural norms as reflected by common sense and rule of law. Finally, Carolyn Torma and Rebecca Bernstein demonstrate the role women exerted in the design process.

"Buildings and Regions," the second section, acknowledges the continuing influence and vitality of geographical approaches to the new architectural history. Landscape studies and diffusion theory remain elemental to the study of common buildings. Jay Edwards, Chris Wilson, and Charles Bergengren focus separately on the processes of dissemination, selection, acculturation, and invention. William Chapman and Gregg Kimball explore issues in African-American architectural history that broaden our notions of how we might consider black builders in a southern city and plantation housing in the West Indies. Margaret Mulrooney and Annmarie Adams raise questions about architectural values, regional culture, and hegemonic contexts in their studies of corporate housing and the architecture of social reform. Finally, Mark Reinberger, Laura Phillips, and Mark Brack offer detailed treatments of specific regional building traditions.

The final group of essays, gathered under the topic of "Buildings and Popular Culture," addresses an important facet of the American national psyche, the need for housing reform. Believing that the nation's moral well-being is directly related to the strength of the individual household, for two centuries reformers have sought to remedy perceived ills in the social fabric by continually redesigning the American house. Elizabeth Cromley's history of the bedroom charts significant shifts in American sleeping habits, many coming in response to changing attitudes toward health and family structure. Leland Roth provides a fascinating account of Edward Bok, powerful editor of *The Ladies' Home Journal,* and his quest to make his magazine a source of "uplift and inspiration" for American homeowners. Mary Corbin Sies contributes a thoughtful inquiry into suburban culture, the quintessential feature of the modern American landscape.

In the end it may be that all definitions of vernacular architecture fail when compared to the material and contextual complexity of the objects we study. This may not be such a bad thing. The people of the past have been very good at creating their own social hierarchies based on gender, class, race, and religion; we do not need to help them by adding additional categories like elite, meaning "high" architecture, and vernacular, or "low" architecture.[19] High, low, or middle, the buildings may change but the approach and the ethics of that approach remain the same.

I. Buildings and Builders

J. Ritchie Garrison

Carpentry in Northfield, Massachusetts
The Domestic Architecture of Calvin Stearns and Sons, 1799–1856

In January 1811, a thirty-two-year-old carpenter named Calvin Stearns began building a house for Gen. John Nevers in the small rural community of Northfield, Massachusetts. It was Stearns's first significant commission, and, knowing that the house was a statement about its owner and the capabilities of its builder, he probably tried hard not to disappoint his patron. Nevers, a lawyer and recent arrival in Northfield, chose to build a large central-passage, double-pile house with the front door centrally located on a bilaterally symmetrical facade, features that were common to many of the largest mansion houses built by the Connecticut River valley's gentry since at least the 1760s. What set the Nevers house apart from the earlier examples was its elaborate and delicate exterior detailing. The fanlighted door, sweeping blinds that fanned out from the attic windows, large pilasters at the corners of the building, and delicate brackets under the structure's eaves were in the new federal fashion. Without violating the formal architectural etiquette of local social discourse, Stearns and his patron had signaled a shift in what many in town would have regarded as modern architecture—they had created something distinctive that fit in with other houses along the village street but that unequivocally articulated the talents and aspirations of artisan and patron.[1]

What makes Calvin Stearns's work important to the study of building in early America is that fifty years of his account and daybooks, as well as those kept by his son George, have survived to document the working habits of seven carpenters from the same family over two generations. In addition, at least two dozen houses built by Stearns, several barns, and a few outbuildings remain. Like the accounts, they reveal much about the Stearnses in the context of their community, about the position of builders in the antebellum New England economy, and about the process of designing and building.

Calvin Stearns was born in nearby Warwick, Massachusetts, in 1779, to Nathaniel and Elizabeth Stratton Stearns. His father was a mason and stonecutter; his mother was from one of Northfield's oldest and most prominent families. Although Nathaniel Stearns's two-story, central-chimney, lean-to-roofed house still stands in Warwick, little is known about Calvin's childhood. At some point he and his younger brother Samuel learned the trade of carpentry. Like many other young journeymen during this period, he "tramped," moving from one job to the next, relying on family, friends, and kin to help get started. Calvin made the first entry in his daybook in 1799. Most of his work that year consisted of odd carpentry jobs in his hometown of Warwick. He earned a full day's pay of one dollar but was still too young to have much renown. In March 1800, as spring work picked up, he headed north to work on his uncle Ebenezer Stratton's house in Brookfield, Vermont. After the Revolution, settlers moving to Vermont swelled demands for building, and good opportunities were available for able carpenters by the late 1790s. Following several weeks of work at his uncle's, he moved on to another job, beginning a pattern he would repeat for the next several years. Most of the time he helped build or repair dwellings and sheds—framing, roofing, clapboarding, and making sash—but in October 1800 he had the chance to work for Reuben Sanderson on Stephen Conant's house, one of three great mansion houses being built in Windsor, perhaps Vermont's most rapidly developing community (Fig. 1). Work on the Conant house provided an ideal opportunity to absorb some of the new design principles and construction details of the day. While in Windsor, he also saw several houses designed by Asher Benjamin, who recently had come north from Greenfield, Massachusetts.[2]

Benjamin already had a reputation further down the Connecticut valley. In 1795, he worked on the Connecticut State House in Hartford, constructing the first circular staircase in America; between 1797 and 1799 he designed and built two sophisticated dwellings in Greenfield and an academy in nearby Deerfield, Massachusetts; and, before leaving for Vermont, he published a carpenter's guide suited to American craftsmen. Benjamin's Windsor projects were then among the grandest and most expensive dwellings in the state. Built for an elite, they signaled the penetration of urbane and sophisticated architectural design into New England's hinterlands. For young journeymen like Stearns who made their livings by tramping, these elaborate houses were discourses in modern style, house form, and fashionable decoration, a language that could later be interpreted, scaled, and adapted for less wealthy patrons.[3]

Tramping, a term early nineteenth-century craftsmen used and modern carpenters still employ to describe the process of moving to find work, was an important economic strategy for young or unemployed carpenters. There was seldom enough work in country towns for younger craftsmen to settle down and make a living from their trade. Because construction work at different job sites was temporary, carpentry was an inherently unstable form of employment. For journeymen who lacked

Fig. 1. Stephen Conant house, 1800, Windsor, Vermont. (Historic American Buildings Survey)

experience or reputation, men like Stearns, this instability forced them to move where work was available or to take up side occupations to carry them through times when there was no building going on. From another perspective, tramping prepared young journeymen to become master carpenters and provided a conduit for diffusing architectural information. In his years of tramping, Stearns met other carpenters, saw new construction details, and learned different building traditions from several masters and distinguished architects that would supplement the local architectural vocabulary he grew up with. Because it is easier to trace stylistic change through written documents, scholars have emphasized the importance of pattern books, periodicals, and prescriptive literature in changing architectural design. Clearly, these sources were influential, but the Stearns accounts indicate that tramping was probably just as important a means of exchanging information.[4]

Leaving Windsor, Stearns continued to tramp, working for others at one dollar per day. Most of the time he took on small jobs or portions of larger building projects. His accounts detail the charges and the jobs: clapboarding for Nicholas Bragg, Jr., in Springfield, Vermont; finishing three rooms in George Field's house back in Northfield; and repairing sash in one of the town's schoolhouses. By 1805, he had acquired some land near Northfield's main street on the road to Warwick and begun building a house, perhaps for himself, perhaps for speculation. There was little urgency. He had no family and no particular reason to establish permanent roots in town. In February 1806, a carpenter friend, Josiah Oakes, enticed him to leave Northfield and head for Brookline, Massachusetts, where he worked on a structure designed by Peter Banner, an architect who would later become known for his design of the Park Street Meetinghouse in Boston. Banner was born and trained in England. He had worked extensively in New York, New Haven, and now the Boston area, and he took young Stearns with him in April to Boston to work on another project.[5]

In the early years of the nineteenth century, Boston was an exciting place for a young carpenter. Led by a robust international maritime trade, the economy boomed and prominent local citizens promoted a series of building projects that transformed the city's appearance. Neoclassic architecture, much of it designed by Charles Bulfinch, attracted attention and admiration. Work was plentiful and wages were high enough to attract rural carpenters into the city. Stearns earned as much as $1.50 per day—$.50 more than he could have gotten back in Northfield—but the high costs of room and board, which at one point amounted to $4.50 per week, eroded his earnings and prompted him to seek less expensive accommodations. In July, he returned home to Warwick, where he worked for several months on Stephen Ball's house and the Warwick meetinghouse. By February 1807, he was back in Boston working on the India Stores, a massive project designed by Bulfinch. The scale of construction was too large for a single undertaker, and the project's directors divided work into smaller units, contracting with various master builders to erect different sections as if they were separate structures. One of these undertakers was Peter Banner, who hired Stearns as a carpenter.[6]

While in Boston, Stearns usually worked six days a week. Following a practice that continued for the rest of his life, he wrote in his account book once each week, usually recording only the number of days that he worked: "Mr. Peter Banner to six days work." He rarely noted specifically what he was working on but recorded purchases in greater detail: a broad ax, an astragal plane, a saw, a level, books, a handkerchief, and clothing. Probably through a carpenter friend, Augustus Richardson, he also met his wife, nineteen-year-old Statyra Richardson, who was working in a tailor's shop in Cambridgeport. He married her in November and moved back to the house he had started in Northfield to begin family life, for Statyra was already pregnant and commercial business in Boston had collapsed due to the Embargo Act of 1807. With him he brought his new tools and the knowledge he had gleaned from working with a large crew of urban craftsmen on one of New England's biggest building projects. His education as a journeyman was complete.[7]

Despite the carpentry skills he had polished and his experience with neoclassical urban design, it was not immediately clear what Calvin Stearns would do in the slower-paced rural economy of Northfield—an economy that by 1808 was reeling from the sudden cessation of international trade and the sharp depression that followed. New England merchants had reaped enormous profits from the Atlantic trade during the Napoleonic wars, and the countryside had also prospered. Violations of neutral American shipping, however, threatened to involve the nation in the European conflict. To keep the country out of war, the Jefferson administration in 1807 imposed the Embargo Act, which prohibited American ships from leaving U.S. ports. Prices in the countryside dropped by as much as 50 percent, and many people were driven to bankruptcy. During Madison's administration, Congress repealed the highly unpopular Embargo, but replaced it with the Non-Intercourse Act, which prohibited American merchants from trading with Britain or France until the two countries guaranteed American neutrality. Under these difficult circumstances few people wanted new houses, preferring to remodel older structures. Stearns took whatever jobs were offered to him and began farming his land. The farm provided security by meeting many household expenses; his carpentry and woodworking earned him credit at the local store and with his neighbors. For the rest of his life he combined carpentry and farming.[8]

Although it is probable that he did not consistently record the time that he worked for himself on his own farm, Stearns's accounts indicate he was more of a carpenter than a farmer. He was able to run a farm partly because local farmers sometimes worked off their debts to him by plowing, planting, hoeing, and harvesting. As his sons grew up they helped farm, but in the 1810s and 1820s while they were still young he occasionally

hired labor that freed him for woodworking. As a carpenter, Stearns worked in a medium—wood—not just at a craft. He could hew a frame for a house or shed, make a sleigh, putty windows, build a table, prepare a coffin, or assemble a fanning mill. Construction occurred in seasonal rhythms, but there was no off season. Winter—December through April—was the time for preparing millwork, for getting timbers from local woodlots, for making wooden objects, or for finish carpentry indoors. Late April to November was the prime building season, but the schedule depended upon the job. Stearns began building the Nevers house in January 1811, but he did not finish it until December 1813 because of disruptions caused by the War of 1812. The original agreement stipulated that Calvin, his brother Samuel, and James Barting would build the house for $600. By the time the job was over, Calvin had worked on the structure for 318 3/4 days and Samuel 102 2/3 days. James Barting apparently never followed through on his original agreement.[9]

The account and daybooks are not precise enough for us to learn much about the process of building the Nevers House, but in 1840 Stearns made a more complete record for the B. B. Murdock house, the last major building project he undertook for a client (Fig. 2). Murdock was an important merchant in Northfield and evidently wanted a stylish house in the Greek Revival mode. Although this structure was the first Stearns had built in that style, he framed the building in the usual manner: hewn sills, posts, girts, plates, and ridgepole; sawn studs, braces, and second-floor and attic joists; and peeled poles for first-floor joists and common rafters. Only the two-story columned portico required much calculating. Significantly, it was the only work that proceeded slowly as the crew figured out how to make the columns and install them.[10]

Stearns was assisted throughout the project by his son Charles and his son-in-law Harvey C. Field. They began building on April 14, when he noted, "Charles & I work on Murdocks Sills." The crew

Fig. 2. Benjamin B. Murdock house, 1840, Northfield, Massachusetts.

was busy framing the house until May 10, when the structure was raised. Next, they boarded and shingled the main roof and put on the subsiding. By the middle of June, they had set the window frames and put on the outside casings. The following week Calvin noted, "5 days of myself on fresse & Cornice &c." Charles assisted him while Harvey worked more on window frames. In July they turned to the ell, working on floors and clapboards, and taking several days off to complete haying back home. The exterior was far enough along and the weather was probably hot enough to encourage work on the interior at the end of July. Throughout August and the first week of September they worked inside, putting up partitions, casings, stairs, lath, and trim. As temperatures moderated, they moved back outside, finishing the roofing on the ell. Then they paused.

Late September and early October were a busy time in New England, and the crew had several interruptions. Charles had three days of militia duty and was out one day with a toothache. There

were also small projects on other sites that were still unfinished. Charles and Harvey both spent a day working at O. C. Evertts's place, and the whole crew took half a week shingling the Browns' roof. When finished, they headed back to Murdock's. While Calvin made the front door, sidelights, and trim at the beginning of October, Harvey took on the challenge of building the three two-story columns that supported the front portico. He had never built hollow columns before, and it took him a full month of steady work to figure out an approach and get them done. The crew raised the columns under the portico on November 7. Charles spent the next week hanging blinds; Harvey worked on the "Front Room"; and Calvin worked on doors, including the two large pocket doors that separated the front and back parlors. The interior finishing required six more weeks. During the first three weeks of December, Calvin built the front stairs that arced up to the second floor in a quarter-circle. Meanwhile, Charles finished hanging the many doors and blinds, and Harvey packed up his tools and went home. On December 26, Stearns recorded: "to five days of myself finishing off, to five days of C. H. Stearns & brought his tools home, Whole number of days I worked on B. B. Murdock house 206." By the next year Stearns was semiretired.

Judging from less complete building accounts for earlier dwellings and the evidence from surviving structures, the process Stearns followed at the Murdock house was fairly typical. Rural antebellum carpenters like Stearns were generalists. While they sometimes specialized in their tasks according to interests and skills, most master carpenters knew the full range of carpentry operations and were responsible for the overall design and construction of buildings. Even so, the accounts did not include the work of other contractors who were essential to the building process. Because Murdock would have employed a laborer to dig and stone the cellar, a mason to put up the chimneys, and a plasterer to finish the interior walls and ceilings, these men did not appear on Stearns's records. Nevertheless,

Stearns and his crew of carpenters were responsible for the general fit and finish of the building, and they relied on a division of labor to facilitate the work. Stearns himself was a particularly skillful finish carpenter; he put up the circular stairs, built the cornice and front door, and oversaw the details of final appearance. His assistants did some finish carpentry but were also responsible for much of the rough work: framing, boarding up the walls, clapboarding, roofing, hanging doors, and so on. These chores were hard physical work in the days when boards and shingles had to be hauled upstairs or onto roofs by hand; they were appropriate jobs for younger men.

There were also other types of specialization. Stearns's crew could have managed the fussy details of millwork at the site, but they apparently did most of it in the shop and brought it to the job. Larger decorative elements such as the columns, the front stairs, and the front doorway were made on site. Doors, windows, blinds, and probably many of the moldings came from the shop. The records for the Murdock job reveal relatively little about how Stearns prepared building elements, but other accounts indicate that his shop was a significant part of his business. There he made sash, doors, blinds, tools, and, occasionally, furniture. In larger communities someone might specialize in the millwork for buildings, but many rural carpenters did the work themselves. The comprehensive nature of Stearns's carpentry work should not imply lack of sophistication, but it did have the practical effect of limiting the choices customers had for finish work. To fabricate sash, doors, and blinds that worked properly, Stearns needed jigs and templates to achieve uniform size and fit. Once these templates were made, they were used repeatedly over many years. Although six-over-six windows were known in New England by the time Stearns was a journeyman, he favored twelve-over-twelve sash. Stearns's windows were usually a standard size with each sash holding a dozen five-by-seven-inch lights of glass. This style of window sash had been used in the region and throughout New England since the mid-eighteenth century, but Stearns continued to make it until the late 1830s, when he switched to a distinctive sash with six lights and simple chamfered muntins. Similarly, he used templates to make standard-size doors, generally four-panel doors for interiors and six-panel doors for exteriors. He continued to make this type of door until he retired.

Standardized conventions speeded construction, reduced unit costs, and fostered consistent quality. They also tended to act as a drag on stylistic change in local building tradition. Nonstandard building elements cost extra because of the time required to design and fabricate new templates. Few patrons seemed willing to pay for more fashionable windows or doors, since the Stearnses used only two types of standard window sash on the dwellings they constructed between 1811 and 1855. Only late in his building career did Calvin shift to more modern molding profiles and styles—a change that may have occurred because his sons had largely taken over the job of making sash and doors and seem to have favored the newer types.[11]

Just as Stearns attempted to reduce the risk of uncertainty in making doors and windows, he also developed house plans that he used over and over. This practice also helped modulate costs by saving time and promoted more consistent quality. In Northfield, the most popular model Stearns built for prominent local families was a two-story, center-passage house with an ell extending to the rear. At least five houses built by Stearns and his brother Samuel survive in Northfield with nearly identical dimensions. There were undoubtedly more, as Stearns recorded "writing up a plan and a bill of timber" for several people in the region who wished to build houses. The carpentry for this type of house cost $300, excluding materials, with special finish carpentry costing more. Aside from his own home, he built the earliest example of this kind of house in 1816 for Isaac Mattoon, one of Northfield's largest landowners, who added several options that drove up the price to $437.50 (Fig. 3). These options included a columned front porch,

Fig. 3. Isaac Mattoon house, 1816, Northfield, Massachusetts.

an elaborate exterior cornice, elegant mantels in the downstairs parlors, and a picket fence out front. Once the construction was finished, Stearns spent a week tearing down the old eighteenth-century house that stood on the lot.[12]

The plan of the Mattoon house was highly rationalized (Fig. 4). The front of the house was a symmetrical central-passage plan. The rear ell was one step lower than the front of the house and resembled a center-chimney plan turned at right angles to the front block of the structure. An entry separated the rooms in the ell from the south dooryard and drive. The kitchen was to the rear of the ell with the back stairs, a buttery, and pantry arrayed on the north side. Next to the kitchen was a dining room, the largest room in the house. With six doors opening off this space, the room was a mediating zone between the formality of the front parlors and the working space of the kitchen, a family sitting room as much as a center for eating and entertaining.[13]

The form of the Mattoon house reflected the larger cultural process by which New Englanders reshaped their landscape in the late eighteenth and early nineteenth centuries. The shifting of work spaces into ells or wings represented an important

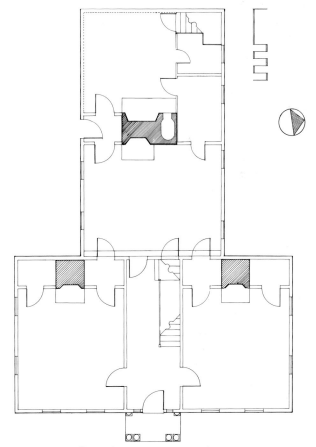

Fig. 4. First floor plan, Isaac Mattoon house.

conceptual restructuring of cultural practice and family space in which many activities such as laundry and food preparation were removed from the view of casual onlookers. Carpenters in Connecticut valley towns actively participated in this restructuring of the landscape between 1790 and 1830, basing their changes in part on the mansions of the valley's eighteenth-century elite. In Northfield, Stearns was building ells or refurbishing and expanding "back parts" even before he received major commissions like the Mattoon house. The fact that Isaac Mattoon had Stearns erect an elegant white picket fence in front of his new house, incorporate a service ell to the rear, and demolish the old home was a sign that families in Northfield were reshaping not merely their dwellings but their domestic landscape in new ways.[14]

Scholars such as Dell Upton and Henry Glassie have studied the general role of master builders in designing new architectural forms, but the Stearns accounts provide a glimpse into how the process worked in one town. Because carpenters like the Stearnses worked with standardized architectural elements and floor plans, their patrons had limited choices about what buildings would look like. These choices were always influenced by what they would cost and presumably by what the neighbors would think. Most of the families for whom the Stearns built homes made conservative choices about style, but when they saw innovations they liked, they could and did ask for them. In Northfield, the Stearnses presented their work to the local community through their own houses, which served as models for emulation.[15]

In general, the Stearnses built more innovative structures for themselves than for others. The house that Calvin started in 1805 fit the conservative traditions of the community but added features that were then uncommon. Like the later Mattoon house, his own house incorporated a kitchen, woodshed, and probably his shop into an ell, a form that would have seemed relatively new to most people in Northfield at that time (Figs. 5 and 6). The innovations in Stearns's floor plan are most appar-

Fig. 5. Calvin Stearns house, 1805, Northfield, Massachusetts.

ent when considered in context. Although a few examples are known to have existed from the early eighteenth century onward, houses with kitchen and service areas in the long ell that stretched out behind the front block were rare in the Connecticut valley prior to 1770. To most people in Northfield in 1805, Stearns's house would have seemed both familiar and modern. What they found strikingly new were combinations of details such as the federal era moldings, the fanlighted front door, and the delicate mantels in the two front parlors. Stearns would use many of his house's design features such as the hipped roof, the placement of chimneys and closets, and the details of door and window casings in his later work. As local people contemplated building a new house, they could look to Calvin's and visualize what their own would be like.[16]

A more innovative and in many ways more influential dwelling was the side-entry house that Calvin's brother Samuel built in 1820 (Fig. 7). He and Calvin began working on the frame late in 1819. From the south side, the house looked like one of many central-chimney New England houses, but the appearance of familiar form was deceiving. It was the street facade to the east that made the building so novel to local viewers. The front door and the entry behind it were located to the north

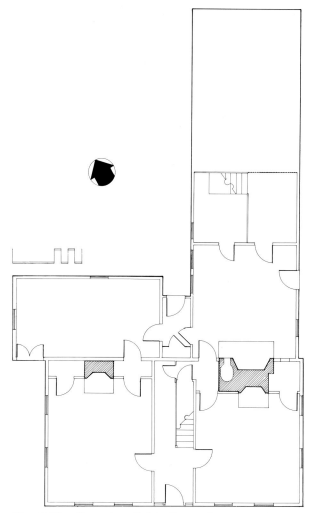

Fig. 6. First floor plan, Calvin Stearns house.

circle, attached only to the joists of the first and second floors and a small area of the north wall. Stearns worked on these stairs intermittently for several months in 1824. Evidently, it was the first curved staircase in Northfield, and it served as a spectacular demonstration of Calvin's expert craftsmanship and design abilities. We can only speculate on the gossip that this work must have caused, but the account books record that Stearns contracted for most of his major house-building commissions after Samuel's house was completed.[17]

The innovations in the basement were equally unprecedented in terms of Northfield's architecture. Like many urban townhouses, Samuel's house had a kitchen in the basement, a rare feature in the region's housing, and an innovation that no one outside the family chose to emulate. We can only speculate cautiously on the rationale behind this arrangement. Architectural pattern books of the 1820s and 1830s such as Asher Benjamin's sometimes included references to or plans for basement kitchens, but Calvin Stearns's copy of Asher Benjamin's *The American Builder's Companion* was the sixth edition printed in 1827, after Samuel Stearns's house was finished. Calvin and Samuel's inspiration for this form, then, was probably gleaned from experience or imitation of existing plans rather than from copying printed sources. In this case the material evidence suggests rather directly that the basement kitchen was a false start. Careful examination reveals that the kitchen hearth received limited rather than continuous use, that the bake oven was torn out and replaced with a boiler, and that the firebox was eventually bricked up and replaced by a stove. These modifications and wear patterns are consistent with or particular to the room's use as a secondary rather than the primary food-preparation area. In other houses in the region, set kettles were associated with shed spaces instead of kitchens; with nearly direct access to outside yards, the basement kitchen in the Samuel Stearns house, like the shed spaces of his neighbors, seems to have been used for the messier tasks

side of the front (east) elevation. Builders first constructed dwellings that were positioned with the gable end to the street in the federal rather than the Greek Revival style in the upper Connecticut valley, but in places like Northfield they were still exceptional in the 1810s. In a village where nearly all the houses on the main street ran parallel to the road, Samuel's dwelling was a powerful break with established patterns. The innovations in the dwelling show most clearly when looking at the plan (Fig. 8). In the front entry, Calvin built a freestanding staircase in the shape of a quarter-

Fig. 7. Samuel Stearns house, 1819–1824, Northfield, Massachusetts.

of preparing and processing large amounts of food or for laundry.[18]

Nineteen years after Samuel's house was completed, Calvin Stearns's son George built another house that prompted imitation. Trained by his father since he was fourteen, George Stearns had had a number of opportunities to travel to other parts of New England and to the Delaware valley, visiting family and teaching school. George's travels certainly expanded his vocabulary of architectural forms, but it is not always clear whether or how these trips influenced his later design work. Although he temporarily gave up carpentry for schoolteaching in the late 1830s, he had returned to Northfield by 1841 to take over the family carpentry business from his father. George began building his own house in 1843, clearly influenced by what his father had done in the B. B. Murdock house.[19]

From the beginning the George Stearns house departed significantly from the houses most people in the community were accustomed to. George Stearns designed the front portion of the dwelling as a cottage-scale temple with five fluted Doric columns supporting the second story (Fig. 9). The floor plan of the front part of the structure vaguely resembled the basic plan of an urban townhouse,

turned ninety degrees so that the main entrance faced the drive that ran past the south side of the building (Fig. 10). When the ell was completed in 1846, the house stretched over 120 feet from the columned porch to the rear wall of the shed. The plan is partially reconstructed based on the evidence that survives. The back porch on the south side is outlined with dashes. It appears in old photographs of the house. The present screened porch on the north side of the house and the small addition behind it are not shown, as they were added later, in the early twentieth century.[20]

Unlike other houses on Northfield's main street, there was no front doorway. Instead, guests entered from the drive by climbing an earthen terrace and moving past a columned porch into a commodious front hall. Visually and practically, the public entry to the house was more private than other houses in town, separating the public from the family inside and reflecting a more segmented use of space. Under the front portico, George placed four french doors on the elevation that was oriented to public view. A double parlor divided by sliding pocket doors extended across the entire front of the building. Behind the double parlor were the entry and stairs and a small sitting or

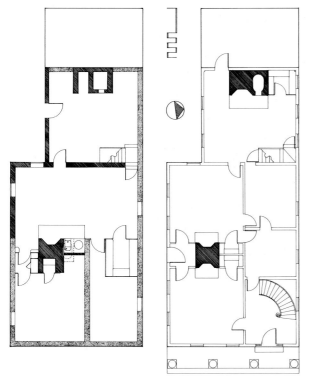

Fig. 8. Basement and first floor plans, Samuel Stearns house.

bedroom. Stearns placed the dining room on the first floor of the ell, adjacent to the front entry, and positioned the main kitchen, pantry, shed, and privy behind it.

All the working space in the house was located in the ell and the basement. Because the land sloped away from the front of the house, Stearns designed the ell's basement to have direct access to the south dooryard. This basement included a second kitchen with an outside set kettle and, behind the kitchen, his carpenter's shop, where his massive workbench still resides. The result was a stylish, hierarchically rationalized floor plan in which formal entertaining and polite social ritual were carefully segregated from the untidy chaos of ordinary living. There are other examples of this house form in New England, notably in Maine, but in 1843 this house was unique in the Northfield area and represented a new architectural challenge to

Stearns's neighbors, who had to accept it, modify its lessons, or reject it.[21]

Once they saw the possibilities, patrons who were planning to build houses responded to George's new design and the precedent established by the Murdock house. On January, 19, 1846, George Stearns met with Daniel Callender in Northfield to write out an agreement for a dwelling. Callender was known about town as a frugal man who spent his money with deliberation, and he wanted a building contract that spelled out the design and form of the new house. Stearns complied, writing down his copy of the "understanding" in the back of his account book. Callender's house was "to be 32 by 26 feet for [the] upright part after the fashion of B. B. Murdocks." Stearns would build the ell that extended out behind the front section of the house in "the same size and fashion of the George A. Stearns back part of house without cellar kitchen." The rest of the specifications elaborated by spelling out the few exceptions to the original models.

This was not the only example of copying from other houses in town. Next door to his own home, George built a house for Dr. Stratton in 1844, without the costly Doric columns that he had installed on his own dwelling. This model was more affordable, and many people asked George to recreate a version of this temple-style cottage for their new dwellings. Thomas Alexander specifically contracted with him to build a house 32 by 26 feet, with an ell that would be 17 by 30 feet, "To be finished off in as good style & after the fashion of George A. Stearns'. Excepting outside. That is to be finished like Dr. Strattons'." To keep down the cost of the building, Alexander agreed to provide the interior doors and the windows and other materials. Stearns was paid a total of $308 when the job was completed. Although nobody desired a basement kitchen, many patrons admired the other organizational principles designed into the ell of George's house and asked him to make copies. Daniel Callender's "understanding" is the only written reference to this type of request, but the evidence of copying survives in other buildings. Across

Fig. 9. George Stearns house, 1843–1846, North-field, Massachusetts.

the Connecticut River in the town of Gill, Stearns built a close copy of the front section of his house. At least two other examples of this house type were built away from the center of Northfield, suggesting that it was not always perceived as a village form.[22]

The Stearnses built other houses for family members that continued the tradition of innovative design. As carpenters, the Stearnses could try out ideas for themselves that were too expensive or too risky for their patrons. Charles Stearns, George's brother, built his house in 1857. Although in form his house followed the popular central-passage, single-pile houses designed by his father, Calvin, the framing techniques and the Gothic details reflected the evolution of local building practice and fashionable motifs. The frame was made of dimensioned lumber, for the traditions of braced framing were largely gone in local dwellings by midcentury. In addition, many style-conscious details signified the penetration of popular decorative motifs from design books, prescriptive literature, periodicals, and existing structures. A veranda

stretched across the entire front of the house. Above the front door were two arched windows and a gable at right angles to the main roof. Overlooking the drive to the south was a bay window with an ogee-shaped roof, and above it was another set of arched windows. The interior was finished with a mixture of Greek Revival and Gothic details, some made by the Stearnses and some, such as the front stair balustrade, purchased from suppliers. The overall effect was conservative yet modern, familiar but new. While clients did not rush to order copies of Charles's house, it was another example of the designs the family understood. Such innovations served to advertise the family's skills and to reflect the changing ways people in a rural town conducted social discourse.

To casual readers, the Stearns accounts fit the model of locally focused economic exchanges that many social historians have described and argued about. But the material evidence tells a somewhat different story because the family's design inspiration came from cultural exchanges that were much broader than community or region. Calvin

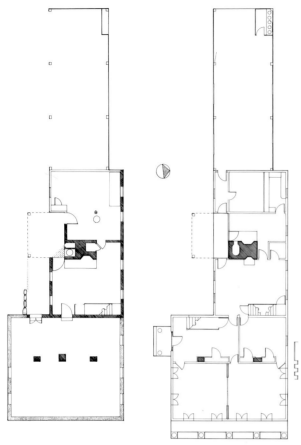

Fig. 10. Basement and first floor plans, George Stearns house.

Stearns's buildings demonstrate that he was clearly aware of change in an increasingly urbanized and industrialized culture; his accounts reflect the sophisticated business activities of someone who lived with the traditions of a small agricultural community and who prudently supplemented his carpentry income with farming. To a far greater degree, his sons separated themselves from their farm heritage to work as full-time builders, exchanging ideas within a much larger economic and design marketplace.[23]

The Stearns account books clearly indicate shifts in business attitudes between the first and second generations. Calvin Stearns farmed when carpentry business was slow. His farm and carpentry work was locally focused, and he seldom ventured far from home. These practices produced a certain amount of family security and a sense of roots in one community, and they were rational economic strategies considering that the local demands for his services were almost always uneven. This concern for home and community should not suggest a reactionary rejection of the outside world or an unwillingness to compete in the world of capitalism. Stearns might have continued tramping. Although he could have traveled to big commissions, the evidence suggests that he chose not to. Working a farm enabled him to raise a family without the disruption caused by long absences, and the responsibilities of a family and farm served to keep him closer to home. He took only a few jobs that were distant from Northfield in the years after he married, and he did not work at them for more than a few weeks at a time. For the most part he accepted these jobs when farm chores were light, when he was asked for help by a friend or his brother-in-law, and after his children were old enough to provide some help to their mother. Perhaps he simply had had his fill of tramping while working as a journeyman.[24]

By contrast, several of his sons, George among them, had little interest in following their father's strategy of combining farming and carpentry, preferring instead to make their livings by building. Dependent upon a steady flow of commissions, they had to range more widely into other towns. Most of the business listed in Calvin's daybooks came from Northfield and the adjacent town of Warwick. George's account book listed jobs in Orange and Gill, Massachusetts, Hinsdale, New Hampshire, and Brattleboro, Vermont, towns too far from family and home to permit convenient commuting. When he and his crew arrived on a site, they worked at the job steadily until it was finished. Then they moved on to the next building. In short, for rural carpenters like George Stearns who were working in the 1850s and trying to make a living solely from their trade, home was not the place where you returned in the evening after a day at a building site. Nor was it always a center of household production. Rather it could and sometimes did become a way station where the skilled worker stopped between jobs, where much of the time women dominated the day-to-day decisions of the household. Perhaps the expensive and elegant houses the carpenter brothers built for their families were partial compensation to their wives, serving as domestic bastions for the Stearns women who personally, psychologically, and socially had to adapt to their husbands' extended absences.[25]

The buildings and the written records of the Stearns family tell us much about architectural expectations in rural communities, about relationships between patrons and clients, and about the process of building and how it changed over time in the antebellum north. The Stearnses were successful, but countless other carpenters did not fare as well. They succeeded where others did not because of the quality of their workmanship and design, their sensitivity to local building needs, their willingness to innovate in ways that made sense to their patrons, and their reputation for hard work. During their building careers, they actively reshaped a middle- and upper-middle-class Northfield landscape. We can study that landscape and their lives only because they left us their biography through their accounts and their buildings.

GABRIELLE LANIER

SAMUEL WILSON'S WORKING WORLD
BUILDERS AND BUILDINGS IN
CHESTER COUNTY, PENNSYLVANIA,
1780–1827

Although American vernacular architecture has been analyzed in many ways, we still know surprisingly little about the historical building process. The aesthetic and economic aspects of construction have received considerable attention, but many questions about the ways builders designed and organized their own working lives remain unanswered. Thus when documents such as builders' accounts, building contracts, and mechanics' liens surface, they add a new dimension to our understanding of the social and temporal realities of craftsmanship. The account books of Samuel Wilson, a stonemason working in Sadsbury Township, in western Chester County, Pennsylvania, at the close of the eighteenth century, document the career of one builder who worked during a time of rapid change. They provide unusually thorough information about the way an individual builder operated within the larger contexts of his building and client communities. Wilson worked during a period characterized by a growing professional consciousness within the building trades. It was a time when significant shifts in the relationships among building craftsmen, their colleagues, and their clients were redefining work roles, modifying attitudes and expectations, and transforming the very nature of work itself.[1]

Three volumes of Wilson's accounts survive, covering the period 1780–1827. Like most farmers and tradesmen, Wilson posted debits and credits in a straightforward, abbreviated single-entry ledger system. Yet, although the accounts are fairly detailed, the story they relate is not seamless. They are not necessarily chronological; they often overlap one another and backtrack in time, making coherent interpretation difficult. Still, they provide rich and detailed information about Wilson's building activities over time. Because he often recorded dates and structural dimensions, building authorship can be firmly established. Similarly, economic patterns and seasonal rhythms that affected the building cycle begin to emerge. Together with the material record, information gleaned from tax lists, probate inventories, deeds, and the accounts themselves gives us the means to examine both the process and the products of building in Federal America.

For Wilson, building involved a variety of skills and a considerable commitment of time. He frequently collaborated with other builders for weeks on a construction project as large as a house, mill, or barn. Such complex undertakings involved quarrying and hauling stone to the site, excavating the foundation, laying the stone walls, pointing, and plastering. Smaller projects entailed simpler, less time-consuming repair work. His terse notations describe these jobs: "to arching the limekiln and

1 day at quaring Limestone"; "to Work a arched seller"; "to plastering the house betwixt the logs"; "to braking out a door and window"; "to walling a well 31 feet Deep at 1s per foot"; and "to setting a tombstone over [his] father and mother."[2] Wilson undertook such jobs alone or with assistants. He recorded these projects carefully in his accounts, often noting the hours or days spent at the site, the cost to the client, or the number of men present during construction. Payment for his labor was sometimes tendered in cash but, more frequently, bartered with goods or services such as milled grain, whiskey, weaving, livestock, or pasture for his horse.

The economic relationships between the builder and his clients are fairly explicit. Yet his accounts also implicitly define a more subtle constellation of intersecting relationships. For Samuel Wilson, the building process involved contractual relationships with his clients, working relationships with groups of fellow builders, and social, commercial, and familial relationships with members of his community. Although they are less clearly expressed, these implicit relationships ultimately defined Wilson's larger community, giving direction to his career and influencing the structures he built. Samuel Wilson's working community was broad and complex. It was characterized not by simple geographic limitations but rather by the extensive network of communication established among builders, clients, family members, and the surrounding agricultural population, and it was marked by the community of structures that gave form to Sadsbury's cultural landscape.

Because Wilson was one of only a small handful of local stonemasons, his skills were in demand during the building boom that engulfed post-Revolutionary Sadsbury. At the end of the nineteenth century, the township was a prosperous, grain-rich agricultural area with a small but growing population.[3] Located nearly two-thirds of the way between Philadelphia and the major inland market town of Lancaster, Pennsylvania, Sadsbury prospered from the regular commerce and cultural exchange between these two towns. Anglo, Scotch-Irish, and Germanic traditions melded to create the area's culture and built environment.

Like most of his fellow farmer-artisans, Wilson worked a regular seasonal cycle punctuated by intense periods of agricultural activity. The construction season started in early spring, when Wilson began anew the annual ritual of building or repairing deteriorated limekilns for another year of lime burning. April through June were the busiest months for building houses, barns, and outbuildings as well as accomplishing general repairs. The onset of summer altered the working cadence. Masonry work usually ceased abruptly in July when reaping, binding, mowing, and hauling grain took precedence. Agricultural and building activities overlapped in the fall, as major building projects resumed along with more seasonal construction tasks including setting stoves, repairing distilleries, and walling wells. Except for occasional repairs or a few short January days spent breaking flax, the winter months were usually quiet. Then, as today, broader construction rhythms followed the vagaries of the local economy. Thus, when drought or the Hessian fly wreaked havoc on a year's crops or when grain prices plummeted, building activity lagged; likewise, when times were good, building prospered.

Wilson, like some other successful builders of the nineteenth century, was working primarily for an elite.[4] It was the continued patronage of a small but influential group of wealthy landowners that fueled his business, assuring him an entrée into powerful social and kinship networks that could only aid his career. Distinguished by their privileged economic situation, these individuals were also conspicuous for their extensive property holdings as well as their uncommon houses. Symbolic of the power, status, and authority inherent in their economic and social positions, their dwellings and property dominated the area's landscape. Wilson built limekilns, mills, and farm buildings for these clients, but his most important contribution to their personal and symbolic estates was probably their houses. He built at least twenty-three houses between 1784 and 1808. He altered or enlarged many more. Usually much larger than the average house in the area, these dwellings were also characterized by complex plans and impressive elevations. And, of course, they were built of stone.

In Sadsbury, as in other parts of Chester County, stone was the preferred building material for dwellings by 1798. While log houses had once dominated the local landscape, the use of stone intensified dramatically around the end of the eighteenth century as builders responded to the demands that a growing population placed on the existing housing stock. The marked proclivity for stone as a walling material eventually embraced other agricultural buildings as well. Although availability and durability were certainly important factors in the final choice of building fabric, another set of cultural determinants may have been at work here. A survey of the 1798 direct tax shows that building materials were clearly tied to total property values, with the incidence of stone dwellings increasing as property values rose.[5] This prevailing preference could have only exerted a positive influence on a stonemason's career. To some extent, then, Wilson's client community may have been defined by the perceived cultural value of his chosen medium.[6]

Wilson's customers shared certain economic, geographic, and familial characteristics. Tax records reveal that most were a good deal wealthier than the rest of the Sadsbury population. This is hardly surprising in a township where nearly half of the inhabitants owned no land at all in 1799. Still, the bulk of Wilson's clients owned total estates well in excess of the average, and many ranked at or near the top of the population in terms of total property value as well as quantity and value of land. Often part of large and wealthy kinship networks, many of these individuals lived in close proximity to other family members and well-to-do landowners.[7]

Not surprisingly, most of these affluent individuals were taxed for secondary rental houses—dwellings that were listed as "tenements" on tax assessments—in addition to their other holdings. While only 10 percent of the taxable population was assessed for tenements, the overwhelming majority of Sadsbury's tenement owners were Wilson's clients. Historian Lucy Simler has identified tenancy in colonial Chester County as an economic strategy that could benefit tenants as well as landholders. For tenants, renting meant a chance at upward mobility. Similarly, maintaining a tenant was, for most landholders, like having money in the bank. Landholders who rented buildings and acreage to tenants encouraged appropriate stewardship of their land and simultaneously improved their economic status while maintaining their family's social position.[8]

John Truman was typical of Wilson's clients. A prosperous Quaker farmer—his taxable wealth placed him at the top of Sadsbury's propertied class—and a member of an established and prominent family, Truman was one of the stonemason's most frequent customers. Wilson built John Truman's new house in 1789, a house that has survived to the present with few alterations (Figs. 1 and 2). Nearly square in proportion, the house is a two-story, three-bay, double-pile building constructed of coursed rubble masonry walling. Wilson quarried local quartzite and schist for the Truman house and used solid stone lintels over the wall openings in this house as well as others he built. The first-floor plan consists of four rooms of nearly equal depth, with an enclosed central stair in the rear next to the kitchen. The second-floor plan echoes that of the first floor with the exception of a small fifth room over the entry. Interior embellishment is minimal. The three corner fireplaces on the first floor are built with segmental arched heads and recessed jambs; the fireplace and bake oven in the original kitchen have been concealed behind later doors. Exposed beaded ceiling joists and floorboards, raised panel doors, baseboards and chair rails, the cheeked fireplace jambs, and two drawers built under the two north windows constitute the extent of the first floor's ornamentation. The chest-

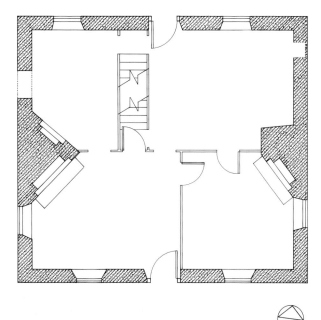

Fig. 1. John Truman house, Sadsbury Township, Chester County, Pa. First floor plan.

nut-framed common rafter roof lacks collars or wind braces, and evidence indicates that the house originally had a pitch reduction at the eaves.[9] Truman contracted with Wilson to build other structures on the property as well. Wilson built Truman's barn, his limekiln, his stone tenement, and his arched, sod-roofed springhouse.

Sometimes, instead of building a brand new house for his clients, Wilson altered an existing house, often effecting a dramatic transformation of the original structure. James Truman, John Truman's son, lived in a house measuring 30 by 25 feet that was described as "stone, old" on the 1798 tax rolls. In 1815, Wilson noted a major rebuilding of this structure that involved masonry work on the upper story. He probably lengthened the dwelling at that time to create the substantial main block.[10] Truman's "mansion house" survives today as a rental property (Figs. 3 and 4). Although little of the interior finish remains, the basement plan suggests that the structure was once a three-room plan, a type often associated with millers and other individuals involved in nonagricultural pursuits.[11]

Fig. 2. John Truman house, west and south facades.

James Truman was, in fact, a wealthy miller who maintained a profitable grist milling operation on the site and often paid for Wilson's services with grain from the mill. Truman's mill was itself re built at least twice by Wilson and his crew. The

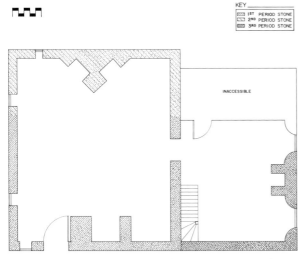

Fig. 3. James Truman house, cellar plan, showing relieving arches for original fireplaces in main block.

mill had been in operation since 1748 and was always an important local landmark (Fig. 5), although now very little of the original structure remains.[12] Most of the building's earliest fabric and mill equipment remain below grade. The mill shares construction features common to other Pennsylvania grist mills including a rectangular structure, an interior waterwheel and millrace, and grinding machinery located at one end of the building.[13]

Another house built for Wallace Boyd in 1794 represented Wilson's largest and costliest construction undertaking to date. A prosperous innkeeper and farmer, Boyd, like John and James Truman, was a regular client. He operated the house as a tavern for feeding and lodging travelers on the busy Lancaster turnpike. Boyd's house was a double pile, four-bay structure with a four-room plan. It stood two stories high with five chimneys and, at 35 by 32 feet, was Sadsbury's seventh largest dwelling in 1798.

How did houses like Boyd's and the Trumans' compare to the full range of dwellings in Sadsbury

Fig. 4. James Truman house, west and south facades.

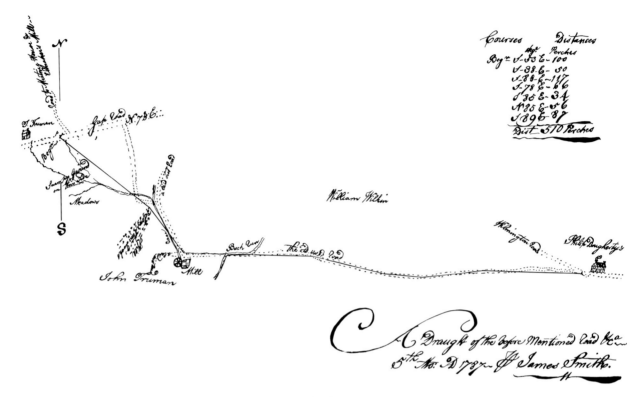

Fig. 5. Petition for a new road, showing Truman's mill as a landmark, 1787. Original Road Papers, 15:205ff. Chester County Archives, West Chester, Pa.

and neighboring townships? Data from the 1798 tax can help us answer that question. If there was a statistically typical house in Sadsbury in 1798, it was a two-story, owner-occupied stone structure devoid of additions, separate kitchens, tenant houses, or incidental outbuildings on the property, except possibly a springhouse. Compared to this average, Wilson's houses were larger, more extensively differentiated, and contained more windows. Not surprisingly, their tax valuations were a good deal higher.[14]

Most of the dwellings Wilson built served the obvious dual purposes of sheltering their occupants from the elements and providing bases of operations for the diverse agricultural activities of working farms. These multistoried stone houses, with their large dimensions, multiple windows, and differentiated interiors, also symbolically affirmed

the social and economic status of their inhabitants. The presence of such structures on the local landscape proclaimed the worldly successes of their owners while establishing Wilson's credibility and competence as a builder. Wilson's association with these clients in turn implied his own success and afforded him the upward mobility that ultimately defined his career.

The bulk of Sadsbury's architectural landscape was, then, controlled by a socioeconomic minority. At the close of the eighteenth century, a mere 20 percent of the taxpayers held more than 60 percent of the township's wealth, and more than 45 percent of the population owned no land at all. Despite the region's burgeoning population, most area building was commissioned by a fortunate few. A countryside controlled by such a privileged group was far from egalitarian.

Wilson's client community formed the nucleus of this minority, actively shaping the surrounding Pennsylvania landscape while simultaneously reinforcing the existing social order. We have seen that those clients can be characterized by their wealth, tangible capital investments, and extensive kinship networks. Can his community of builders be defined in a similar way? Did the craftsmen with whom he collaborated form a cohesive unit, or were they a loose and unrelated collection of individuals with nothing more in common than their occasional working relationships with one another?

The same documentary and artifactual evidence that defines Wilson's client community as a group with a distinct socioeconomic identity creates a different impression of Wilson's community of builders. The material record for this group is sparse, since few were wealthy enough to own their own land or dwellings. Additionally, since they owned so little, their names are listed less frequently on tax assessments. Those builders who do appear on the rolls rank at the bottom. A few show up one year and disappear the next, suggesting that they were itinerants who drifted from one construction job to another.[15] Wilson's accounts reflect the shifting composition of his community of builders; while he maintained consistent partnerships with some individuals over a period of time, he worked with others only once or twice. As a group, Sadbury's tradesmen may be characterized by their low economic status and their mobility, traits that placed them in marked contrast to Samuel Wilson, who benefited from a relative degree of prosperity and stability.

In terms of economic position, Samuel Wilson was an anomaly in his community. Like the majority of his regular clients, he was a property owner. Taxed as a landowner with forty-three acres between 1796 and 1802, Wilson also owned a combination stone and log dwelling, a stone springhouse, a log barn, and two horned cattle by the early nineteenth century. Few, if any, of his building colleagues could claim this degree of economic achievement. In 1799, Wilson's taxable property

of £360 placed him in the sixth decile in terms of total wealth held by individuals in Sadsbury township. Compared to his fellow builders, who usually ranked in the lowest deciles when they appeared on the tax lists at all, Wilson had attained an enviable economic position. He was one of the few construction tradesmen in Sadsbury who had managed to cross the threshold into the property-owning class.[16]

Just as Samuel Wilson's land, buildings, and cattle tied him to his client community, his status as an owner of rental property also linked him to the ranks of the well-to-do. Like many of his clients, Wilson was a landowner who rented property to a tenant. And, like some of his fellow builders, he was a tenant himself.[17]

It is significant that Wilson participated in the economic strategy of tenancy from two directions. Furthermore, he was the only individual in Sadsbury to do so. He rented his own property to a tenant from a tax rank directly below his own. At the same time, he lived as a tenant on a much larger and more highly valued land parcel owned by a wealthier individual. By living this way he encouraged appropriate stewardship of his own land and retained his landholding status while concurrently farming a larger and better parcel of land than he could afford. Thus, as both landlord and tenant, he could shrewdly maximize his economic return.

If Wilson's status as a property owner and landlord linked him with his community of well-to-do clients, his occupation and his position as a tenant on another man's land also tied him to his community of builders. Yet his economic rank placed him somewhere in between the two groups. Tax lists imply that Wilson may have used this intermediary economic position to his best advantage, for he increased his taxable property considerably over the years. His personal accounts suggest that he approached his occupational position within his community just as shrewdly.

As his building activity accelerated over the years, Wilson's work role gradually shifted. Over time, he became more of a contractor, or employer, and the division of labor grew more distinct as wage differentiation between workers became more explicit. While the building projects undertaken by Wilson and his fellow workers still represented the collective efforts of skilled individuals, it was Samuel Wilson who often directed this collaborative effort by monitoring the jobs the other builders performed, the time they worked, the time they lost on the job, and the wages they earned. He occasionally contracted individual workers out to other jobs independently as well, and ultimately collected payment from the client, usually distributing it to his builders.

In short, Wilson was increasingly separate from his building crew. Although he worked alongside his fellow builders on most projects, he also took charge of the building operation. He was actively involved in all aspects of the construction process and approached building as a highly structured business. In this respect he emerges from the documents as a professional middleman or undertaker, interfacing skillfully between his clients and the building community.

Economically and occupationally, Samuel Wilson was upwardly mobile. Linked by trade to his community of craftsmen, he was also connected to his more privileged and established client community by his middling economic position and his managerial role. His personal accounts tell the story of who he was and what he did; the dwellings he left behind hint at what he hoped to become.

The growing specialization that was occurring throughout the construction trades in the early nineteenth century is evident in the course of this stonemason's career. Samuel Wilson's emerging intermediary role in the building process reflects one aspect of the rapidly changing and increasingly complex nature of work in the Federal period.

MICHAEL J. CHIARAPPA

THE SOCIAL CONTEXT OF EIGHTEENTH-CENTURY WEST NEW JERSEY BRICK ARTISANRY

In the waning years of his life Joshua Evans recorded his beginnings as a young craftsman: "I must labour hard and by taking up my trowel I made out."[1] These words by Evans, an eighteenth-century West New Jersey Quaker, bricklayer, and yeoman farmer, entice us on many levels but also leave us with many questions, for in his diary he elaborates little on the essence or practice of his craft. How was Evans affected by the built environment he both constructed and observed as he moved around West New Jersey over the course of his life, from Mt. Holly to Evesham to Newton? As a member of the Society of Friends, he would have attended meeting in each of these locales. How did those buildings and the worship they sheltered affect his identity and work? Furthermore, how did Quaker meetinghouses and domestic dwellings work as cultural symbols and conduits for social action in Evans's life? All these issues are present by omission in Evans's diary.

In the Middle Atlantic region, the area known in the seventeenth and eighteenth centuries as "West New Jersey" arguably contained the most elaborate, community-derived brick building tradition in colonial or post-Revolutionary America. It is for this reason that Evans's words, as a brick mason, stir us. He, along with bricklayers and brickmakers who worked before and after him, was a participant in the florescence of an architectural tradition that was part of the visible, expressive structure of the area's social life. In past studies,

attention has centered primarily on the buildings themselves and on those who contracted for them. These studies have begun to refine our thoughts on the numbers of brick buildings erected in this region and how their construction was indicative of the posturing of those who were economically, socially, religiously, and politically influential. However, there has been a lack of attention to the artisans who actually constructed these buildings. This essay grew from a larger effort to reconstruct the social dimensions of brick artisanry in eighteenth-century West New Jersey.[2] Thus, this investigation into the social context of the mason's craft begins with the detailed examination of eighty-two bricklayers and brickmakers who worked in West New Jersey in the late seventeenth century and throughout the eighteenth century. While the study of all the occupational groups involved in the construction of the built environment in eighteenth-century West New Jersey is merited, bricklayers and brickmakers call for particular attention due to the extraordinary number of ornamented, pattern-brickwork houses built in the area during the colonial and post-Revolutionary periods, such as the 1754 Joseph Moore house (Fig. 1).[3]

Bricklayers and brickmakers were directly responsible for the construction of these pattern-brickwork houses, which represent one of West New Jersey's most powerful and meaningful artifacts. What was the social organization of this craft? How did artisan and artifact become focal points in the society? What was the craftsman's

Fig. 1. Joseph Moore house (1754), Evesham Township, Burlington County.

role in enacting these symbols and the values they represented? Was the brick artisan's social realm so wide-ranging that it was analogous to Richard Neve's observation of masonry in 1726 that "particulars render it too large to be comprehended under the general Head of *Bricklayer's work*"?[4] Brick artisans, carpenters, and joiners were responsible for building structures that expressed the hierarchical scheme of West New Jersey society, and it is necessary to explore how social factors related to their status and position in society. Close scrutiny of the lives of bricklayers and brickmakers, in particular, as well as of all who were a part of their entire occupational web in this time and place, will show the coherent scheme, design,

and meaning of these brick buildings.[5] It will further illuminate how eighteenth-century American communities may have established a craft hierarchy and allowed particular religious groups (in this case Quakers) to have a profound effect on the varied exercise of craft work.

The "social context" of brick artisans encompasses those societal factors that most closely influenced the planning, implementation, and realization of actual buildings. These factors include such elements as the family orientation of craft work, local and regional identity (as spatially framed by one's township and county residence, and occupationally framed by one's immediate and extended craft community), economic power (both where it was traditionally residing and where it was being newly transformed), craftsman-client relations, and, in light of the situation in West New Jersey in the eighteenth century, the powerful role Quakerism had in shaping the expressions and overall fabric of social life.[6] In seeking to construct a collective social portrait of the brick craft, I have examined a wide variety of documents reflecting religious institutional involvement (the minutes from Quaker monthly meetings), wealth levels (wills and probate inventories), political activity (local and provincial government records), the construction of artifacts (dwellings and meetinghouses), and spatial consciousness (geographical networks). These documents show that the clear majority of brick and patterned-brick architecture built in eighteenth-century West New Jersey was for Quaker clients, many of whom were "Weighty Friends." Of the brick artisans studied, 44 percent were clearly Quaker or Quaker-affiliated, with the phrase *Quaker-affiliated* indicating that the brick artisan was either a disowned Quaker or had a Quaker spouse.[7] The actual number may be even higher based on the number of artisans who shared surnames with some of the most deeply entrenched Quaker families in West New Jersey at this time.[8] The figures on religious affiliation among artisans are proportionate to the figures for the larger population and indicate the degree of social control the Quakers exerted in different West New Jersey locations throughout the 1700s.[9]

Any study that seeks to explain the social milieu of craftsman/client relations needs to reconcile a range of historical issues. Eighteenth-century West New Jersey was an agricultural society, with grain and cereal crops (primarily wheat and corn), livestock, and lumber (particularly cedar and pine) fueling the economy. These items were produced for export and primarily channeled through the feeder ports of Salem and Burlington on the Delaware River.[10] Agricultural staples were produced with the greatest economic profit on "plantations," owned in the majority of cases by "Weighty Friends." While there were cultural and economic similarities between Chesapeake and West New Jersey plantation life, the term *plantation* had its own meaning in West New Jersey, most likely deriving from English custom and Quaker doctrine, which extolled the virtue of "Plantation Work."[11] The prominent eighteenth-century Burlington County resident Charles Read wrote in his agricultural journal about the communication network

existing among these wealthy farmers and the cooperative efforts they exercised in keeping their farms economically powerful.[12] These farmers shared a variety of related interests that enabled them to control significant portions of land and exert substantial economic influence over their local economy.[13] Although consisting primarily of dispersed farmsteads, eighteenth-century West New Jersey was nonetheless characterized by profound economic, religious, and political linkages. The landed, controlling, native-born elites expressed these linkages in architecture. These successful farmers set themselves off, both individually and as a group, by making the focal point of their "home farm" or "home plantation" a conspicuously built brick house such as the 1788 Thomas Iredell house (Fig. 2). Advertised for sale in the *Pennsylvania Gazette,* the brick dwellings were described in terms such as "*A Very good Brick-House* . . . two Story high, with a good Kitchen adjoining, and Cellars under the Whole, all finished in the best Manner."[14]

Geographically, bricklaying and brickmaking in

Fig. 2. Thomas Iredell house (1788), Woolwich Township, Gloucester County.

West New Jersey were organized in a variety of ways. On a regional level they took place primarily in the inner coastal plain of southwest New Jersey, the area most vigorously settled in the eighteenth century, most agriculturally productive, and most easily accessed by its multitude of estuaries (Fig. 3).[15] English Quakers were the first Europeans to settle in West New Jersey in large numbers. The majority of these immigrants were from northern and western England.[16] The housing and landscape practices that came to characterize West New Jersey, Pennsylvania, and Delaware clearly are connected to these English source areas.[17] Brick building was thus being practiced within the larger context of Anglo-American settlement in the Dela-

ware valley. The building process was facilitated by Quaker networks and encapsulated in a corridor that essentially linked Bucks, Philadelphia, Chester, Delaware, and New Castle counties on the western side of the Delaware River with Burlington, Gloucester, Salem, and Cumberland counties to the east. The sampling of West New Jersey brick artisans used in this study reveals the significance of their movements and connections in the Philadelphia sphere. Brick masons were a clearly defined, identity-conscious group, and their trade, internal political workings, apprenticeship process, and demonstrated skills linked all the artisans in Philadelphia and the West New Jersey counties. In each area the work of resident brick artisans was character-

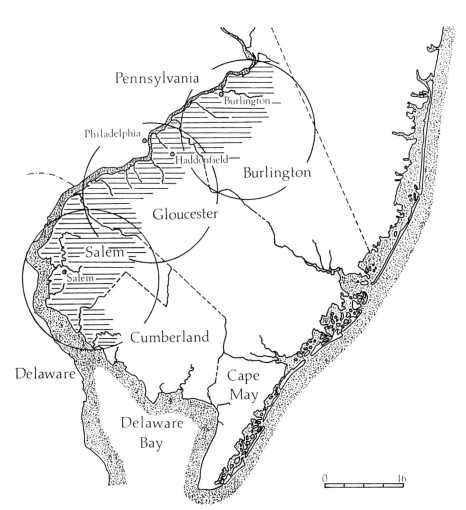

Fig. 3. Eighteenth-century West New Jersey Counties. The shaded portion represents area containing pattern brickwork architecture. The three circles define the primary scope/ network of eighteenth-century West New Jersey brick artisans. Dotted lines indicate county boundaries.

ized by slightly different formal and stylistic preferences. Overall, however, the entire region was united by a consistent brickwork practice.[18]

While the world of the brick artisans was deeply affected by the social rhythms and mercantile influence of Philadelphia, their immediate building practice and consciousness were framed within a local perspective. In this regard, these artisans proliferated in the areas contiguous to West New Jersey's two major towns, Salem and Burlington, as well as in the Newton Township/Haddonfield area. These towns, townships, or areas are best viewed as administrative reference points for economic, political, and religious life. There is no evidence that they exerted powerful social dominion over their respective outlying counties of Salem, Burlington, and Gloucester. Relevant to the high degree of Quaker affiliation among bricklayers, these counties were also the locations of the Gloucester-Salem and Burlington quarterly meetings. Thus, the majority of West New Jersey brick artisans worked out of a geographic frame that consisted of closely correlated sectarian and secular boundaries: Quaker local, monthly, and quarterly meeting association on the one hand, and township and county affiliation on the other. Most apparent are the territorial parallels that existed between quarterly meeting and county boundaries (Figs. 3 and 4). The available data on brick artisans show that they rarely moved far from their

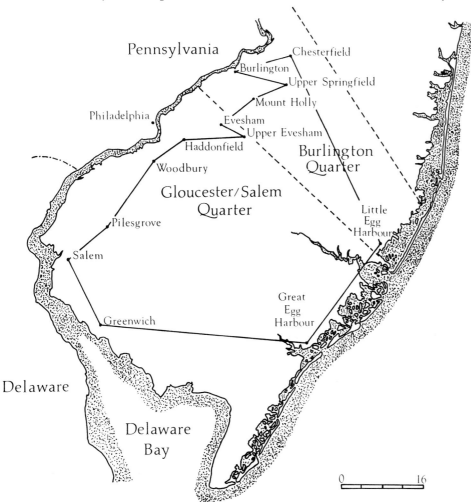

Fig. 4. Area encompassed by the Gloucester-Salem and Burlington Quarterly Meetings. Both of these quarterly meetings were under the Philadelphia Yearly Meeting. In 1794 the Gloucester-Salem Quarterly Meeting was divided into the Haddonfield and Salem Quarterly Meetings. Monthly Meetings indicated represent the more detailed craft networks that were facilitated by Quaker interaction.

place of birth or original settlement. Migration between counties did take place, but it was usually to closely adjacent areas. The notion that brick artisans worked within a defined radius of sixteen to eighteen miles, originating from their place of birth or initial settlement, is seen in the cases of Francis Collins, Joshua Evans, Jonah Scoggins, and the Fenimore family. The situation with these artisans strongly suggests that the geographic scope of the West New Jersey brick artisan was a function not only of the township and county of birth but also of the combined influence of extended family relations, monthly and quarterly meeting affiliations, and the practices of the local brick craft community and its contractual network.

Among the artisans examined, the first generation of bricklayers and brickmakers was clearly more geographically mobile than the subsequent generations. Generally, their movements occurred within a single county. The Quaker orientation of so many of these artisans may have played a role in this spatial scheme. The reverence Quakers gave to the nuclear family and its most immediate extensions, and the control they exercised in pursuit of spiritual attainment, influenced the demographic orientation of this craft.[19] This arrangement enabled the Quaker family to oversee the myriad aspects of the craftsman's life, and insure that they were consistent with their theological tenets. Friends viewed their young people as "Tender Plants," needing domestic environments displaying proper Quaker living and open to channels of spiritual revelation. This applied especially to Quaker apprentices who were in the midst of their difficult, transitional adolescent years. Striving to nurture the "Inner Light," Quakers faced many predicaments in transforming themselves from "Tender Plants" to mature spiritual embodiment, especially given the worldly temptations offered in the course of craft work. Joshua Evans said: "I often feel for Apprentice boys whose trade exposes them to ramble thro the Country as mine did."[20] Explicitly and implicitly recognizing the need for extended family support and oversight,

Quaker brick artisans of all ages did not wander too far. The migration patterns of brick artisans in West New Jersey conform in certain respects to Robert St. George's observation of local migration among seventeenth-century woodworking artisans in southeastern New England. St. George saw local migration and spatial control by artisans as part of a shift of power from towns to families. Towns, as organizational, social units were not a factor in eighteenth-century West New Jersey, and this region was definitely characterized by subregions of family control.[21] Similarly, in West New Jersey brick artisanry was marked by negotiation between static county orientation and movement as influenced by kinship and craft practices.

The juncture of family control and regional geography marked the exercise of brick artisanry in eighteenth-century West New Jersey in other ways as well. Brick craft dynasties were clearly in evidence at this time.[22] Noticeable in this regard are the three generations of Woodnutts who were bricklayers in Salem County, and the three generations of bricklaying Fenimores in Burlington County. In Gloucester County, successive generations of Clements, Kays, and Whitalls controlled brickmaking for the better part of the eighteenth century. Woodnutt family control and social position seem to have had the effect of making Mannington Township the center of bricklaying operations in Salem County, since a significant number of bricklayers made their residence there. While brickmaker identity was partially influenced by family tradition and control, artisans were also associated with water and land transportation routes. Thus, Thomas Kendall was known as the "bricklayer of Rancocas Creek."[23]

Landscape familiarity and family association certainly influenced brick artisans' decisions to stay in the same general area worked by their fathers and guardians. While established trade networks have always been an important asset, the community of brick artisans was affected by a broader range of intimate human relationships. For these artisans the European guild system provided the precedent of craftsmen forming communities along occupational lines. While colonial America did not duplicate this system, the highly sectarian nature of early American life offered a substitute. Not unlike the guild system, Quakerism framed much of the social action of the brick craft through its kinship strategies.[24] Out of the eighty-two artisans documented, eighteen of Quaker affiliation either married women with family ties to the craft, shared a father-son working relationship, or worked with a sibling in the brick trade. The career of bricklayer/carpenter Thomas Atkinson received its initial sanction through the Quaker community when it was announced:

> In pursuance of an agreement made with Wm. Atkinson at a Monthly Meeting of Friends at Burlington ye 11 month 1685, a. ye within named Francis Collings [Collins] do hereby further promise & engage to & so ye will inbound Tho. Atkinson to teach him ye Carpenters trade during his said apprenticeship so far as he is of a capacity to learn ye same & at ye expiration of sd. term to give sd. Thomas fifty acres of land.[25]

The nature of eighteenth-century architectural practice made for close occupational correspondence between the carpenter's and bricklayer's trades. Although the carpenter and the bricklayer were apparent partners in a common pursuit, an amendment to Atkinson's apprenticeship agreement hints at the social values that Quakers either brought with them or were beginning to construct around the masonry trade:

> In as much as things did not appear Clear between Francis Collings [Collins] & William Atkinson therefore Francis Collings [Collins] will pay 30 shillings to ye said William Atkinson & Instruct ye Ladd [William Atkinson's son, Thomas] in ye trade of a Carpenter *as well as a Brick Layer* [italics mine] . . . & to Insert it upon ye back Side of ye Indenture.[26]

Apprenticeship arrangements such as this one were commonly guided through official and unofficial Quaker channels. Quakers exercised social control through the coordination of apprentice-

ships. As a religious sect that came out of tumultuous seventeenth-century England, Quakers were especially sensitive to the issue of apprenticeship. They were aware of how "worldliness" affected youths, how rebellious they could be, and the threat they could pose to the sacred and secular order the Quakers were trying to establish in the Middle Atlantic area. George Fox reported on the benefits of strict oversight of apprenticeships: "Thus, being placed out with Friends, they may be trained up in the truth; and by this means in the wisdom of God, you may preserve Friends' children in the truth, and enable them to be strength and help to their families, and nurses, and preservers of their relations in their ancient days."[27] Quakerism's social umbrella, along with the brick artisans' network, facilitated the entry of Francis Collins's progeny into this craft. Four of his grandchildren retained connections with the trade—one who became a bricklayer, and three who married bricklayers—indicating how these interactive occupational and religious spheres shaped the traditions and practice of masonry in the area. West New Jersey Quakers such as John Edwards, William Sharp, and Jonah Scoggins found their way to the brick craft through adoption and guardianship. John Edwards was not only adopted by a bricklayer and trained as a mason, he also married Mary Ingram, the widow of Quaker brickmaker John Ingram.

Of all the social factors discussed, Quakerism is the most pervasive and revealing. Quakerism was a socially controlling and territorial force that purposely functioned in the brick-building process in eighteenth-century West New Jersey. In order to fully understand these artisans, and the artifacts they created, it is necessary to further analyze their specific location in, and the overall workings of, the Quaker social and economic web.[28] To begin to unravel this set of arrangements, we can start with the brick-building situation in one local Quaker environment, the area of southern Salem County that was approximately defined by the Alloways Creek watershed. In this area, from 1720 to 1734, "Weighty Friends" who associated locally with the

Fig. 5. John Maddox Denn house (1725), Lower Alloways Creek Township, Salem County.

Salem, Alloways Creek, and Cohansey (Greenwich) meetings, and regionally with the Salem Monthly Meeting, engaged in a cohesive brick-building scheme that centered on the highly decorated gable ends of their houses. Glazed brick headers were used to create overall decorative patterns, the preferred being the diamond diaper arrangement. Joseph Darkin (1720), Abel Nicholson (1722), John Denn (1725) (Fig. 5), John Remington (1728), James Evans (1728–1729) (Figs. 6 and 7),[29] and David Davis (1734) all preferred this aesthetic treatment, while fellow Friends Nathaniel Chambless (1730) (Fig. 8) and William Hancock (1734) decided on a different, yet similarly conceived, overall zigzag pattern. The spatial characteristics of these buildings were determined by the English antecedents of the first-generation elites, their newfound wealth and social position, and the dictates of modest Quaker expression. Ultimately, these houses were identical in form to those of the general community, being one and one-half or two stories, with gambrel or gable roofs and one-room or hall-and-parlor plans.

These dwellings were distinguished by the choice of building material. In this region Quakers were the principal patrons of brick architecture. These buildings were symbolic conceptualizations of Quaker sectarian participation in the political economy of eighteenth-century West New Jersey. Consistent with the Quakers' view of how these buildings functioned in the community's social structure, craft patronage was primarily restricted to those within their religious society.[30] The Alloways Creek clients previously mentioned kept Salem County Quaker bricklayers Richard Woodnutt and John Goodwin occupationally active. These artisans were vastly empowered by the contractual connections they received through their sectarian affiliation. However, to a large extent, their contractual privilege was contingent on proper social and religious standing in the sectarian community. In 1699 Richard Woodnutt was easily approved to do the brickwork for the new Salem Meetinghouse, but Robert Gillam, contracted to do the "woodwork," was investigated so "that friends hath no enmity with him as a friend to the truth."[31] For Quaker brick artisans the power of their craft hinged to a certain degree on how their community perceived their theological posture. It was this sort of standard that vested eighteenth-century West New Jersey brickwork with a distinctly Quaker cultural meaning. In being contracted "to put out the brickwork" these artisans engaged in, and oversaw, the craft process that resulted in the ordinary and decorative aspects of both Quaker brick dwelling houses and brick meetinghouses.

The role of Quaker brick artisans as builders of structures that were intended to delineate the contours of Quaker family power in a subregional context, and to mark the overall territorial scope of Quaker presence regionally, is revealed by the breadth of their social involvement. Not only did they associate with "Weighty Friends" as a function of craftsman/client relations, but some brick artisans were "Weighty Friends" themselves, with extensive political involvements. Francis Collins was a member of the Governor's Council and the Council of Proprietors, a land commissioner, twice a justice of the peace, and three times a member of the New Jersey Assembly.[32] Brickmakers Samuel Clement, Sr., and Samuel Clement, Jr., were both elected members of the New Jersey Assembly and held local township office a total twenty-nine times between them. Brick artisans Isaac Kay and Job Haines also held local office in Newton Township.[33] Both were selected "surveyors of the highways," and Kay also held the posts of "overseer of the poor" and "constable." All the activity of these Quaker brick artisans suggests they may have had exceptional social/political privilege and visibility based on their occupation or what it afforded them. Whether it was an individually achieved or socially prescribed process, many bricklayers and brickmakers appear to have occupied a social position that fully enabled them to understand, and have a personal class-reinforcing interest in, the public intent of their work.[34]

Generally, brick artisans in this region were prosperous. Comparing probate data from the West

Fig. 6. James Evans house (ca. 1728), north elevation. Lower Alloways Creek Township, Salem County. (Historic American Buildings Survey)

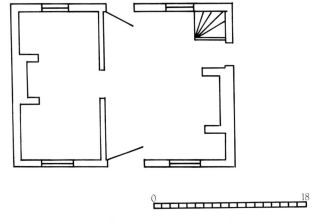

Fig. 7. James Evans house (ca. 1728), plan. Lower Alloways Creek Township, Salem County. (Historic American Buildings Survey)

Fig. 8. Nathaniel Chambless house (1730), Lower Alloways Creek Township, Salem County.

New Jersey region with data from the Pennsylvania-based studies of Gary Nash and Jack Michel, we find that these artisans were, at the least, an upper-middling group and, at the most, some of the wealthiest individuals in eighteenth-century West New Jersey.[35] The wealth of these bricklayers and brickmakers was reflected in their ownership of plantations that were "pleasantly situate"—agricultural settings similar to other landholdings in the area, but always containing the brick artisan's occupationally required "good Landing" and proper water orientation.[36] The economic posture of West New Jersey's brick artisans was further underscored by their own use of indentured servants.[37] Brickmaking by large landowners was often a trade or manufacture exercised as a means of economic diversification. The surplus capital of these individuals allowed them to construct permanent brick kilns, giving their plantations a more complex social and occupational identity. This was the case for prominent landowner and brickmaker George Eyre, whose 164-acre plantation was "com-

monly known by the Name of the Brickyards."[38]

Thus, in addition to their artisanry, many of these craftsmen were Quaker leaders, landholders of "gentleman" status, and local and state office-holders.[39] Their spheres of activity reveal brick-work not only as an ordinary component of community life, but as an icon of power for their clients and themselves. The range and degree of social interaction between these artisans and their clients point to the importance of brick as a building material and design strategy, as we can see when we corroborate studies of Quaker activity in other sectors of West New Jersey life with our findings concerning brick architecture. Thomas Purvis's work has shown the Quaker dominance and the oligarchic, hereditary, family nature of political activity in West New Jersey. Unlike Pennsylvania's Quakers, those in West New Jersey did not practice as marked a retreat from public service. Jean Soderlund has shown how slavery was less easily abandoned in West New Jersey, where Quakers apparently were less concerned by the worldliness and impairment of the "Inner Light" brought on by these institutions. On the eastern side of the Delaware River, Quakerism, as a social and economic force exercised by West New Jersey's native-born elites, clearly had a different impetus than in Pennsylvania. To this end, it ordained a particular craft group and building practice, brick artisanry, that itself was equally oligarchic, religiously specific, and hereditary, both internally and in its service to its clients.[40] By being mandated to execute architectural arrangements that embodied and expressed the unique, contextually specific dynamics Purvis has described, this artisan group took on (within the hierarchy of building occupations) the same power and oligarchic stance of the religious brethren they served. From this perspective, the extent of the brick artisans' role in shaping Quaker identity and hierarchy in architectural/landscape terms is compellingly revealed.

Quakerism provided a variety of circumstances that influenced bricklayer and brickmaker interaction in the Philadelphia area and the nearby West New Jersey counties.[41] The monthly, quarterly, and yearly meetings brought these artisans in contact with their craft brethren from other areas (see Fig. 4). Thus, the Quaker administrative system provided an active channel for the diffusion and exchange of house plans and decorative brickwork ideas. Quakers also engaged in general visitations that would have had the effect of making brick artisans more acutely aware of each other's work, thereby contributing to the coherence and consensus of brick design throughout West New Jersey.[42] Even non-Quakers were included in this web through their occasional work for Quaker clients.

Of all of the views we are afforded of the brick artisans of eighteenth-century West New Jersey, their activity in Quaker administrative proceedings in the monthly meeting process best illuminates their position in shaping Quaker identity through architecture. Their control was achieved through involvement in a high proportion of matters relating to the construction and management of Quaker land, meetinghouses, and meetinghouse outbuildings.[43] Through their participation in building matters at local and monthly meetings and the building contacts they obtained through the more extensive Quaker network, brick artisans were connected (among themselves and their potential clients) in a manner not shared by all building occupations. While their participation in Quaker building affairs shows how their religious affiliation contributed to their projection of themselves as artisans and Quakers, heavy involvement in Quaker administrative actions indicates how they were strategically located to propagate a larger Quaker identity through brick buildings.

The coordination of such administrative participation is further revealed upon close examination of the Salem Monthly Meeting Minutes. Over a period of thirty years, three brick artisans—Richard Woodnutt, John Mason, and John Goodwin—emerged as very active participants in the administration of Quaker matters. From the time of his first action assignment in 1704 until his death in 1727, Richard Woodnutt was involved in eighty-two actions, and John Mason was involved in sixty-five from his first assignment in 1707 until his death in 1726. John Goodwin was involved in thirty-three actions from his first in 1711 until his death in 1733. He was also often selected clerk of the Salem Monthly Meeting, giving him ample administrative exposure and influence.[44] *Action* indicates each time an individual was assigned to attend a quarterly meeting, investigate a fellow Quaker for "clearness" for marriage, attend marriage proceedings, draw up a certificate of removal, participate in review and organization of financial records, do building and grounds maintenance, or attend to the disciplining and warning of a wayward Friend. The very number of actions involving each of these artisans indicates they were not ordinary Quakers, and each most likely possessed his share of "weighty" status. In the case of Woodnutt and Mason, their consistent assignment to attend quarterly meetings gave them the opportunity to engage in frequent Quaker-associated travel that took them at least as far up the Delaware corridor as the Newton Township/Haddonfield area of Gloucester County. Travel strengthened Mason's and Woodnutt's geographic networks in both Salem and Gloucester counties. Travel also gave them a larger vision of the West New Jersey built environment, and the insight to see more fully how brick buildings worked in the organization of the landscape, and how their particular craft would continue to function in this building scheme.

The associational nature of these administrative involvements provided the connections that existed between these craftsmen and their clients. Of the thirty-two quarterly meetings Richard Woodnutt attended, twenty-three were with pattern-brick-work house owners. In John Mason's case, of the sixteen he attended, ten were with pattern-brick-work house owners. Joint observation and discussion during the course of their travels together provided the seedbed for a cohesively wrought architectural strategy. Not only were these brick artisans key players in how Quakerism exerted itself internally, but they also shared a constant working relationship with those who were to be

their most conspicuous patrons. Under the aegis of the Society of Friends, pattern-brick house owners and brick artisans traveled together, fraternized together, and administered together. The exercise of craft patronage made for the simultaneous wielding of social, economic, and political influence on the part of both client and artisan. Whether they were "Weighty Friends" themselves, or hopeful of the accumulative benefits provided in brick craft contractual privilege, these artisans negotiated the most powerful material expressions of the social order.

Brick artisans were part of an endeavor that was infused with dynastic feeling along both family and religious lines. Within the Society of Friends, and the brick craft itself, consolidation was achieved as fathers passed their trade on to their sons, families intermarried, parentless Quaker youths were adopted, and brick artisans passed time together. These brick artisans enacted Susan Forbes's notion of "Quaker tribalism" as they built a minority number of structures for a minority of power-wielding members of this religious group.[45] By

Fig. 9. Alloways Creek Friends Meetinghouse (1756, enlarged 1784), Lower Alloways Creek Township, Salem County. The formal and stylistic aspects of both portions closely resemble those of brick dwelling-house construction.

Fig. 10. Zaccheus Dunn house (1743), Pilesgrove Township, Salem County.

visually linking meetinghouses (Fig. 9) and dwelling houses (Fig. 10) through the choice of brick these artisans exercised unique control in shaping their clients', their religious group's, and their own identity. Brick artisans engaged the status quo of Quakerism and West New Jersey society in every brick structure, and marked out a favorable position for themselves as the process of class formation unfolded in this area. Intermarriage between artisan and client families shows the extent of human bonds associated with brick in this context as well as the force of social networks along artifact/craftsman/client lines. In this socially derived arrangement, brick artisans participated in, and were exposed to, the exercise of Quaker influence, economic power, and "tribal" authority. Through their own and their society's doing, brick artisanry provided these craftsmen with the opportunity to be "select men" in these regionally and locally circumscribed domains, architectural delineators of these realms, and artisans benefiting from the vast social extensions of Quaker sectarian power.

CATHERINE W. BISHIR

GOOD AND SUFFICIENT LANGUAGE FOR BUILDING

Most studies of the traditional building process use patterns seen in the buildings themselves as evidence of the thought processes of their makers. Although written evidence of the traditional design process is relatively slim, we can find aspects of it in specifications created by client and artisan to record their intentions about the house, courthouse, church, or barn they planned. Most of us have examined contracts and specifications to learn about the character of buildings themselves; we can also look at such documents as a genre whose patterns of expression suggest the thought processes behind them.[1]

We may begin by envisioning a building from traditional contract specifications. On February 14, 1774, in the little town of Windsor in northeastern North Carolina, carpenters Richard Gill and Benjamin Ward signed a Memorandum of Agreement with the client, Macon Whitfield, for 19 pounds 11 shillings.

To building him a fraimed house sixteen feet square, with a shed 8 feet wide on one side of it, the body of the house to be 10 feet pitch between joints, the shed 8 feet between joints in the Town of Windsor where the said Whitfield shall direct. One pannel door and 30 lights of sash, a pair of stairs, and the other doors to be batten doors, and all to be finished and completed the whole House in a workmanlike manner by the first day of May next. In witness whereof the parties to these presents have hereunto set their hands & seals this February 14, 1774.[2]

For most of us, there are important gaps between what this contract says and what we would have to know to build a building. This contract was signed, sealed, and witnessed. But would you sign it and expect to deliver on it? Most of us would not do so without knowing more than this document states about the intended structure. And of course that is the point. This document, like thousands used for traditional buildings in centuries past, was based on the essential assumption that both parties did know more than it stated.

Before exploring the significance of that assumption, let us attempt to fill in the gaps about the house planned in Windsor. It is not certain whether it still stands, but based on common precedent in the time and place, it is possible to make some educated guesses about its design, materials, and general character.

Although only the basics—the dimensions, the use of frame construction, and a few details about doors and windows—are defined, some of the other elements may be inferred from those in relation to common building techniques of the late eighteenth-century Upper South. The frame would have been made of mortised and tenoned timbers covered with weatherboards or clapboards. The reference to thirty lights of sash suggests two windows of fifteen panes each—probably six over nine or nine over six panes—though other arrangements are possible. The six-panel door was probably the front door, while the batten doors probably appeared on the side or rear, for paneled doors were considered more formal than doors made of boards. The sixteen-foot-square dimension suggests one main room, possibly a passage, and the mention of the stair indicates an upper chamber.

But there are other essential elements about which nothing at all is stated. There is no information, for example, about the roof. We may suppose from local usage that the roof was probably a gabled one of common rafters covered with wooden shingles. It might, however, have been a gambrel roof, for this form was also used for small houses of the late eighteenth-century coastal plain. For foundation and chimney, Whitfield probably hired a bricklayer separately, unless he relied on the carpenters to set the house on wooden blocks and erect a wooden chimney, a method that did appear in eastern North Carolina. For such matters as the location of the doors and windows, pitch of the roof, placement of the stair, details of the plan, and most of the finish and quality of the building, nothing is specified at all except that last phrase, "all to be finished and Compleated the whole House in a workmanlike manner."

Such a contract, with so much apparently left out, seems on the surface like a casual or inadequate approach to building. Perhaps these were simply provincial residents unfamiliar with composing more sophisticated specifications? Actually, such a document is neither a backwater oddity nor inadequate for the job at hand. This agreement for a little frame house presents an archetype of thousands of contracts and specifications executed for hundreds of years. Similar specifications appear frequently in English building practice from the medieval period onward and in America from earliest settlement through the nineteenth century. That two parties would create, sign, and consider legally binding such documents time after time, generation after generation, is one sure evidence of their sufficiency.

They were sufficient not in themselves but, as I suggested earlier, as part of a complex system at work. These documents, like any legally binding agreement, included as much as their makers believed necessary. Those things that went unstated, on the other hand, were those the participants in the contract saw no need to write down. It is into this seeming gap between what was said and what was left unsaid—which is no indication of things done and left undone—that we need to look.

Such brief specifications seem especially sparse in contrast to the long, fully detailed specifications we know from study of high-style and present-day architecture. There, explicitness is required to deal with the many possibilities of complex and diverse technologies; the desire to have the builder replicate closely an architect's design; and the very nature of the triangular relationship of architect, client, and builder. Traditional specifications, however, are part of a different dynamic—the traditional design process.

Several scholars have given us rich analyses of how the vernacular design process works. Henry Glassie's *Folk Housing in Middle Virginia,* Thomas Hubka's "Just Folks Designing," and several works by Dell Upton and John Vlach explain how vernacular designers manipulate concepts of form to create many variations within the narrow context of limited materials, technology, and social expectations.[3] Suffice it to say here that the traditional design process operates in communities where "tradition is the basis for action" and ways of doing things are shared, unstated assumptions. As Hubka observes, the traditional design process operates not through the intentionally original method of the architect, nor through some simple, naive folk spontaneity. Rather, the traditional designer operates within a complex mental system structured by tradition. The individuals who plan each building begin with an understood tradition and a set of rules that defines both a specific vocabulary of forms and techniques and an accepted syntax or structure for combining them. Change is accommodated as the traditional designer solves new design problems through old ways of problem-solving. Within this framework, many variations and new possibilities may develop to accommodate individual needs, new elements of technology or style, and other challenges.

Typically, too, the traditional design process involves the direct interaction of two parties: the client and the craftsman. In some cases, the client might deal with a single craftsman who undertakes the entire building project and subcontracts out those elements that he does not perform himself. This approach was especially prevalent in public building projects and became increasingly common in private projects during the nineteenth century. Frequently, however, in private projects, the client made separate agreements with the various craftsmen needed to complete his building—the carpenter, the bricklayer or stonemason, and perhaps others such as a joiner, a plasterer, a painter, or a glazier. In some cases, the client might agree to pay the workman by the day or piece. In others, the two parties signed a contract that involved a single or staged payment for the entire project or the work of a single trade on the project. It was in such agreements that they expressed their mutual expectations in written and more or less detailed terms.[4]

In each case, the client knew, assumed, or hoped that the artisan possessed basic skills that enabled him to apply lessons of experience and example to the job. Both parties assumed that they held, as members of the community, some shared definition of the type of building required, so they needed to define only the particulars. Indeed, often a private traditional building agreement was a verbal one; where much can be assumed both about the thing to be built and the reliability of client and artisan to meet a bargain, a verbal agreement is sufficient. In a traditional community, most interactions are face-to-face and verbal rather than written.[5] Although written agreements were normal for public buildings because of the bidding process and public financial responsibilities, private agreements were very often oral contracts. Berry David-

son, a nineteenth-century millwright in rural North Carolina proudly recalled, "Looking back over the years, I am safe in saying, I never found a man that asked me to sign a written contract, nor did I have an unsatisfactory settlement." The opposite side of the coin was expressed by a planter who recorded in his diary that Ruben, a mason he had hired, had "agreed to the bargain before Mr. Suter, [but] he seems to be a slippery fellow and I am determined to write out the contract & have it witnessed."[6]

Here we need to raise briefly the myth of the anonymous folk artisan. There is a popular image of the quaint but nameless artisan, wandering around the landscape, a sort of Lone Ranger type: "Who was that guy?" "I don't know. He wouldn't say—anonymous I guess. But look, he left a silver nail!" Ironically, the present anonymity of most traditional artisans stems from a lack of documentation, which springs in turn from their being so well known, so un-anonymous, in their community at the time. If a craftsman did not need to advertise his skills in newspapers to get work or need to sign written agreements with clients, he might leave little or no documentary record of a long and productive career. Ruben, unknown but apparently slippery, gained a written record to pin him down, whereas known craftsmen like Berry Davidson did not.

One approach to understanding the traditional design process, in which artisan and client participated, comes from a definition of linguistic codes provided by sociologist Basil Bernstein and used by Upton and others in analyzing building forms. This code also applies to building documents. Bernstein defines two kinds of codes at work in language and cultural behavior—elaborated codes and restricted codes. Many people use both types as the situation demands.[7]

In an elaborated code, there exist both a large range of forms and a low degree of predictability in both the vocabulary of particular forms and the syntax or grammar of putting forms together in a meaningful structure. In an elaborated code, one may choose from many alternatives in both vocabulary and syntax, which permits and encourages each individual to express himself in unique, original fashion. There are few givens and many possibilities. Hence using or understanding an elaborated code requires detailed and explicit explanations.

A restricted code, by contrast, assumes a high degree of predictability in vocabulary and syntax. Important givens define a narrow range of forms and structures for combining them. The restricted code is learned informally by repeated exposure to example, is understood by most members of the community, and promotes not so much individual originality as group solidarity. Expressions in a restricted code depend on a mutually assumed body of shared knowledge that "allows a few short words or phrases to stand for a whole complex of assumptions" and "removes the necessity of being explicit."[8]

We can see the distinction easily in foodways. In traditional cooking, members of a community share common definitions of traditional dishes—the givens and the possible variations—whether it is bouillabaisse in Marseilles, tamales in Mexico, or barbecue in eastern North Carolina. If preparation of a dish strays far from the norm, it simply is not bouillabaisse or barbecue; yet within that norm every cook has his own method, and members of the community may have strong preferences among subtly different variations. To explain what makes one version better than another, the traditional cook would not restate the obvious but would just note critical variations. Thus in explaining how to bake an especially good apple pie, a traditional American cook could assume many givens and simply say, "I use Winesaps, and a quarter brown sugar." That's a restricted code expression. On the other hand, haute cuisine, including, say, nouvelle cuisine, uses an elaborated code where formal training, spectacularly original creations, and much explicit and erudite discussion are expected.

❖ ❖ ❖

What are the elements of restricted code expression as seen in traditional building specifications? What are the patterns between what must be said and what is left unsaid? Such patterns are rooted in medieval English building and legal precedents and extend throughout building practice in America from early settlement through the nineteenth century. Although variations in specific elements reflect regional, stylistic, and technological variations with time and place, the consistency among building contracts is marked.

As is true in many types of legal documents such as deeds, wills, and other types of contracts, conventional phrases establish a basic framework. Characteristically, the contract states the parties involved, the date and place, and the financial arrangements. The building expected is usually defined in somewhat conventional fashion. First comes a description of essentials—the dimensions, basic materials, and perhaps the location of the building. Contract form and language take a structure familiar since medieval English building practice and probably earlier. An exemplary late-medieval English contract is one signed in Gloucester, England, in 1483, on June 20 "in the reign of King Edward the Fifth after the Conquest the First." The town stewards and carpenter David Sammesbury agreed that Davy was to "make an house by the Black Freris Gate in Gloucester conteyning in lengthe 47 fete in brede 15 feet, all the tymber sufficiant and of oke."[9] Across the Atlantic in New England two centuries later, housewright James Townsend contracted with John Williams to "fframe erect Set up and finish for him the sd Williams upon his Land in Boston in the place where his now dwelling standeth," a house 34 by 20 feet, built of oak with a stone cellar, a good brick chimney, and plastered walls.[10] In 1860 in the mountains of North Carolina, carpenter J. F. Gaddy agreed to build for farmer Thomas Lenoir a log house 16 by 20 feet "this spring in said Lenoir's field at a spot agreed upon."[11]

Then, in the body of the document, aspects of the building are further explained, by reference to community or trade standards, by reference to an existing model, by explicit description, or in more summary fashion. In some cases, a generally understood standard was invoked. Such was the case when Jobe Lane agreed to raise the frame of a house in Boston for Thomas Robinson in 1660. The contract noted, "The frame shall be Euery waye substanshall Acording to the Judgment of men."[12] In an 1828 contract for a courthouse and jail in Northampton County, North Carolina, the jail of twelve-inch-square heart pine logs was specified in detail, while an adjoining jailer's apartment was simply to be "built in the common way of good framed buildings."[13]

Reference to specific buildings as models is a common and age-old method for defining expectations.[14] A fifteenth-century Nottinghamshire house was to be "in all manner proporcion according as the new howse of John Taverner that William Roodes made."[15] So, too, in 1661 in Marlboro Massachusetts, a contract for a new minister's dwelling stated that the house was to be built "every way like to ye fframe yt John Ruddocke hath built for himselfe in the afforesd Towne of Marlborough."[16] In Anson County, North Carolina, in 1842, a meetinghouse was planned to have a pulpit to be "after the manner and form of the one in the Methodist church in Wadesboro, but entirely plain and of good hart plank."[17] Contractor Jacob W. Holt contracted in 1857 to build Eureka, an elaborate plantation house in Virginia, "in style and finish of work like Col. W. R. Baskervilles or not inferior."[18]

Some contracts drew upon more than one example for various components of the building. In Leominster, Massachusetts, Leonard Cozzens contracted in 1849 to build a frame, clapboarded house for Luther Osbourn. It was specified that "the pitch of the roof and the stile of the outside finish to be similar to the house next North of the Methodist meeting house built for their Parsons house." Inside, Osbourn wanted "the casings and Stile of the work to be Similar to that in the house of Mr. Bachellors, built by Mr. E. Robbins."[19] In Wil-

mington, North Carolina, builders John Coffin Wood and Robert Barclay Wood, brothers involved in brick building and natives of Nantucket, agreed in 1851 to build for Zebulon Latimer an opulent stuccoed masonry residence. They wrote thorough specifications for some components, but they defined the veranda as being "similar to Dr. Dixon's," the piazza as similar to Mr. Kidder's, and the "entire finish" of the interior to be "similar to that" in Dr. A. J. DeRosset's house.[20] Whether for the jettied frame of a seventeenth-century New England house or an Italianate house in a busy antebellum southern port, such references reveal traditional designers' adherence to the familiar, the existing, and the local as important sources for planning new buildings.

Some items in contracts are treated quite explicitly. Materials and their treatment are specified in a manner that reflects established local or regional knowledge. For frame buildings, contracts often specify the type of wood and the size of each element. The fifteenth-century Gloucester building was to be of oak, "the sills a foot square, the posts in height of 18 fete and a foot square, the walplates of thikness 9 and 10 inches." Bostonian John Williams required that James Townsend build his house frame of well-seasoned white oak and black oak. The 1860 North Carolina mountain house was to be of logs hewn 6 inches thick and the sills and the next round to be of chestnut. Luther Osbourn's 1849 house in Leominster, Massachusetts, was to have its roof boarded with hemlock boards and then covered with cedar shingles "to be laid not more than five inches to the weather." Jacob Brewner's contract for the simple framed meetinghouse in Anson County, North Carolina, was typical in its use of heart pine in a southern building and its precise specifications for sizes of components—heart pine bottom sills 12 inches square, 38 sleepers at least 6 inches across the face or top side, the cornerposts of good heart pine 10 inches square hollowed on the inside, door and window posts 4 by 6 inches, and so on. Often, contracts specified precisely the size of nails to be used, the finishing method and exposure of weatherboards, the pane size and number of panes of glass in the windows, the workmanship to be used in such components as window sills or doors, and, increasingly in the mid-nineteenth century, the brands of hardware and other merchandise.

At the same time, however, in many contracts, as in our first example in Windsor, many items are not mentioned at all, or they are required simply to be "sufficient," "necessary," "good," "neat," or, almost universal and still used today, "workmanlike." The house in Gloucester was to have "all manner windows, doors, stairs, beams, rafters," and so on to be "sufficiantly and able behoveful to the same worke." The materials for John Williams's Boston house were all to be "strong substantiall & workemanlike." The mountain log house was to have floors of "good plank," "a good stone chimney," and the whole to be "finished neatly and substantially in a good workmanlike manner." At the meetinghouse in Anson County, "The whole materials of said building [were] to be of a good and substantial kind . . . and all the workmanship to be executed in a good and faithful workmanlike manner." Such terms appeared regularly in all kinds of buildings.

The relationship between the explicit and the implicit was far from random. For those matters that gained detailed definition, the participants knew there were significantly different alternatives within their vocabulary of forms, materials, and workmanship. Furthermore, for the project under consideration, it mattered to the participants which of those alternatives was chosen, in terms of quality, durability, status, cost, and difficulty. The superior qualities of a certain type of wood—whether it was oak in New England or heart pine in the South—the sturdiness of a certain size of timber, the permanence or appearance of a certain way of finishing a weatherboard or lapping shingles were known quantities that differed significantly from other available alternatives. Conversely, if a preferred choice was not stated, it is likely that there was a single known standard that was considered

sufficient to the task or that any of several known alternatives would do. In some cases, the client and craftsman might have agreed to certain methods verbally. In others, both parties understood that the craftsman was to exercise his judgment within the established norms of his craft. Such was probably the case when Stevens Gray contracted with Gilbert Leigh in 1786 for 115 pounds to build "A house 28 by 18 the Bording to be pland with 6 windows 18 lights, 8 [windows] 15 [lights], 5 doors. The floors to be toung & Groved, the Windows & Door frames with out to be single archives [architraves] & within the lower rooms to be Double with [?] & Chair Boards round the rooms, a Box Cornice outside, a pair stairs, the above articles to be done in a good workmanlike manner what belongs to a carpenter & Joiner."[21]

When builders and clients adapted new elements into their buildings, they often relied on traditional terms and concepts. Unfamiliar elements were often described in some detail, as well as by reference to existing standards. In 1726, joiner Benjamin Porter promised to build a house for David Peabody of Essex County, Massachusetts; it was to have windows "of the bigness as they are generaly made now to housing newly built here abouts in the neighborhood."[22] When John Steele, a widely traveled planter and political figure, planned his new house in piedmont North Carolina in 1799, he included in his detailed specifications a clause that the "pitch of the roof to be rather flatter than the common run of the Buildings in or near Salisbury."[23]

In a few instances, as popular architectural books became increasingly numerous and influential in the nineteenth century, client and builder included reference to a published example in their agreement. In 1848 in Worcester, Massachusetts, builders Burton and Holmes agreed to erect for C. C. Chickering a house "to be a Cottage house with a basement to design III, plates 13 and 14 of Ranletts Architect." The contract then specified in detail the elements of the house from basement to roof, making frequent references to the building being "wrought according to the above design."[24] At Eureka in Virginia, builder Jacob W. Holt and his client Dr. Robert D. Baskerville likewise contracted to build a house "to be built by Design 31st plate 19th Volume 2nd Ranlets Architect"; then they specified a number of deviations from the model to accommodate the family's needs.

Often, however, novel elements were described in familiar terms by reference to existing models. In Salisbury, North Carolina, Andrew Murphy employed Michael Davis in 1853 to build for him a frame house that was to be "finished from foundation to the comb . . . in the best manner." For most elements, it was sufficient to specify "the neatest and most fashionable kind." For the unfamiliarly broad eaves of the hip roof, however, it was specified that "the eaves to project over at least two feet or more and to have bracketts and be finished off something like Robert Murphy's house."[25]

∗   ∗   ∗

Finally, we turn again to those broad terms, *necessary, sufficient, good,* and *workmanlike.* On the surface these appear meaningless, almost dismissals of matters of aesthetics, proportion, or workmanship. But, because we are dealing with a restricted code and its use of "short words or phrases to stand for a whole complex of assumptions," these terms are full of meaning. In legal practice today it is common to incorporate by reference. In a legal document a lawyer may state, "The provisions of such and such standards are hereby incorporated by reference and made a part of this agreement as if fully set out herein." Specifications for modern buildings often describe certain elements by reference to sections of a building code or a product manufacturer's published specifications. One can then refer to the cited volume for specifics.

This is what traditional specifications do in their loaded terms—*sufficient, necessary, good,* and *workmanlike.* In some building contracts, this assumption was itself made known: James Townsend's 1678/1679 contract with Bostonian John

Williams stated that Townsend was to "generally do all Carpentry and masons worke whatsoever necessary to the compleating and fnishing of sd Tenement or building to make it tenantable, although not herein perticularly expres't." More often, such assumptions went without saying. Like any restricted code, these documents incorporate by reference a whole set of community or trade knowledge and assumptions about what these qualities are. Their universal usage in legally signed agreements demonstrates that their meaning was considered enforceable by law.

Such contracts sometimes ended in suits that drew into court artisans and other witnesses to testify whether work met community and trade norms. As it turned out, John Williams insisted that housewright Townsend had not satisfied the terms of their contract for construction of a house. In January 1680, three men testified that they had inspected the house on Williams's behalf and found several elements improperly done—"Some of the Windows in the house open between the Window frames and the posts," and "The Partition in the Leanto is not done as it should bee by a workeman." Other elements of work they found lacking—"Two jetties not close[d] in the foreside: the one end and the foreside should have been boarded underneath the clapboards wch is not done" and "ffive gable ends to the house and not one of them fil'd," for example. Others defended the craftsman, such as William Dawes, mason, who testified that the work was "done workemanlike according to covenant," that the builder had done "rather more than he was obliged by covenant," and that "it is not usuall to Seel the jetties when the Roomes are not Seeled." Deponent Cornelius White likewise explained that "it is not usuall to fill gable ends where a house jetts." For these participants in the building process as for many others, their understanding of traditional and "usual" norms was the basis of action and judgment.[26]

And so, we can recall our first brief contract for a sixteen-foot-square house in Windsor, to be "finished and completed the whole house in a workmanlike manner"—and from it we can sense not inadequacy or simplicity, but adequacy and complexity. We may not know exactly what kind of building Macon Whitfield and carpenters Gill and Ward intended, but we know they knew—and they knew so well they didn't have to write it down. We can see such a document as a genre within a traditional society's intricate, controlling web of expectations and assumptions. In such a context, such specifications were indeed good and sufficient language for building.

Appendix

Three examples of specifications for simple wooden buildings planned in the first half of the nineteenth century in North Carolina illustrate a range of levels of specificity depending on needs and circumstances.

1. A private agreement between owner and artisan, where timing and business arrangements are the principal concerns and the buildings are assumed to be part of established local tradition. Granville County Miscellaneous Land Records, North Carolina State Archives, Raleigh.

Memorandum of an Agreement made and entered into this 9th day of April A D 1845 Between Thomas H. Raney of the first part and Russell Kingsbury of the second part both of the county of Granville & State of North Carolina. Witnesseth that the said Thomas H. Raney agrees with the said R. Kingsbury to do the following carpenters work [inserted: in Oxford], one house thirty six by Eighteen, eighteen feet pitch, with an impediment at one end with thirteen, fifteen light windows, two outside doors, and four inside doors, with a stare case, Wash Board & Chair Board [inserted: Chimney pieces and all other things necessary to complete the woodwork of said building in plain stile]. Also a kitchen of the following description, Eighteen by Twenty, ten feet Pitch, one floor, one door, and two small windows. Also a Smoke House, Twelve feet square, and twelve feet Pitch, a floor & one door. The said Thomas H. Raney agrees to furnish all the wood materials of

good & suitable quality and build the above described Houses, in a workman likes manner, for the sum of three Hundred and fifty dollars. And the said Russell Kingsbury on his part agrees to furnish all nails Hinges and all other articles necessary except the wood portion of said buildings as they may be called for by the said Raney and when the said Raney has completed the aforesaid buildings agreeable to the above agreement the said R Kingsbury binds himself and his heirs &c. to pay to the said Raney the above sum of three hundred and fifty dollars. The said Thomas H. Raney binds himself to have said buildings so advanced by the 15th of Sept. next that the masons may do their portion of the work, such as Building chimneys &c, the said Raney is to board himself and hands while doing the work. The parties hereto bind themselves each to the other in the sum of Two Hundred and fifty dollars to stand to perform the foregoing contract and agreement. Witness our hands and seals this day & date above. Thomas H. Raney. Russell Kingsbury. Witness L. A. Paschall.

2. Specifications for a public building, a schoolhouse, to go to contractors by bids, defining requisite elements of quality within a widespread, economical log-building tradition. John L. Clifton Papers, Manuscript Department, Perkins Library, Duke University, Durham, North Carolina.

School House No. 4. The dimensions as follows 18 ft by 24. The logs squared & butted, the sills sleepers plates & joists hewed a good shingle roof, the rafters sheeted with rough edge plank the logs to be hewed inside & out set upon 8 good lightwood blocks a plank floor dressed & laid. The House to be 10 feet high in the body from the sleepers to the joists a good in frame doubbed stickd dirt chimney. For the roof of the House to cover the gable ends to be weatherboarded with square edge plank. Two doors & shutters & hinges four windows & shutters & hinges & hooks 7 staples with six panes of glass & sashes inch. Say a good & complete log house all the materials to be good & new The cracks to be ceild with dressed plank inside of the house.
NB. If the builder or contractor of sd House finishes the same by the first of December next so the commissioners will receive the same, then they are to have the subscription or such a part as will satisfy the

contract for the building of sd House. The commissioner to superintend the work &c.
[Signed] Henry Stevens, Henry J. Darden, J. L. Clifton for Benjm Hargrove, commissioiners. Bid off by Thomas Chestnutt for the sum of Fifty dollars. Abraham Chestnutt, (X) Thomas Chestnutt. Witness, J. W. Clifton.

3. Specifications, 1816, for a courthouse to be built in Jackson, Northampton County. A detailed description for a public building let to a bidder, for a neatly finished building within a frame construction tradition. Northampton County Miscellaneous Records: County Building Records, North Carolina State Archives, Raleigh.

The above plan represents a House forty feet square 14 feet pitch, the wings to be 16 feet Square & 8 feet pitch. The main building to be set three feet from the ground on brick underpining, 18 Inches Thick to be laid with good lime Mortar. The Wings to be 9 Ins. lower than the main building on underpining. The Timbers of the main building to be of the following sises (viz) The sills to be 16 by 12 Inches with a girder of the same sise each way of the House. The cornerposts 12 by 15 Ins; guttered. The Braces 12 by 4 Ins; one directly across the middle of the House, the other two diagonally across the House. The Rafters 6 by 4 Ins. The Roof to be a square Roof with a ridge pole and two supporters, the Joists to be braced in order to support them. The Timber of the Wings to be of the following sises (Viz) The Sills 8 by 12 Ins; the Sleepers 8 by 4 Ins. The Joists to be 6 by 4 Ins; the rafters 4 by 3 Ins; the Posts & Braces 6 by 4 Ins; the corner posts 12 by 8 Ins; Guttered. The Studs 4 by 3 Ins; The inside of the whole building to be Ceiled all that is exposed to view. The Collar beams to be about half way the rafters. The roofs of the Wings to be square Roofs; the Roof of the whole building to be sheated with square jointed Plank. The Timbers that are exposed to View are to be Plained & beaded if required. The Floors are to be laid of plank 2 Ins Thick & 9 Ins. wide, laid with 20 [crossed out] 30 d Nails, Sheating Ceiling to be ¾ Ins. thick to be nailed on

with 10 d nails. The Featheredge Plank to be 9 Ins wide of the usual thickness to raise 6 Inches and nailed on with 20 d Nails. The Shingles to be 18 Ins. long and ¾ Ins thick to raise 6 Ins. & to be nailed on with 4 d Nails. The top of the whole building is to be painted of Slate Colour & the body white, all in a workmanlike manner. The Doore to the Court House to be a Folding Doore 7 feet wide; the Doores to the Wings to be of a usual Height and Width. There is to be one Chimney in each Wing to be laid of good Brick & lime Mortar. There is to be 14 eighteen lights Windows, glass to be 8 by 10 Ins, to put in the House agreeable to the annexed plan. The Lawyer's bar to run across 14 feet from the back of the House, with an entrance in the Centre; the Jury rooms to be taken off as in the annexed plan, say begining at the Lawyer's bar & describing the figure as laid down or annexed. The seats of the Courts to be four feet from the Floor banistered round. The Clerks Table to be fixed at one end of the Lawyer's Bar; the Floor back of the Lawyers bar to be laid of good tile, the balance of Plank as before described, all the Timber to be of good hart Pine of which this Building and every part thereof is Composed. The inside of the buildng to be painted brown as high as 8 feet & the balance White. The work of every description &c &c is to be done in a workmanlike manner. To each door of said Building there shall be one 9 inch plate Brass knob Lock.

Based on these specifications and attached plan, builder William Grant took the contract on May 15, 1816, for $2,899. As work proceeded, the commissioners reported after its completion in 1818, "some alterations in the plan of the courthouse was suggsted by the commissioners, such as haveing the roof under a Square, the Ceiling plane instead of being Circular, the floor of plank entirely instead of a part being tile, all of which alterations the commissioners beg leave to say in their opinion would thought would be for the best & that the said William Grant ought to be allowed one hundred dollars in addition to the sum he contracted at to build the Court House."

HOWARD DAVIS

EXPLICIT RULES, IMPLICIT RULES, AND FORMAL VARIATION IN VERNACULAR BUILDING

In a particular place, much of the vernacular building of the past may be marked by a balance between two formal properties. On one hand, there is typological repetition from building to building, with different building characteristics—including plan, roof shape, arrangement and design of openings, materials, and details—treated in similar ways, resulting in recognizable building types and subtypes. Since choices may be available within each of these characteristics—different plan types, different materials, different details—a good deal of building variety may arise just as a result of different combinations of the possibilities. Much recent scholarship in vernacular architecture is concerned with identifying types and subtypes and determining their relationship to geography, history, and cultural migrations.

On the other hand, there may also be variation within the type or subtype itself, to help the type achieve a built reality. These variations take the form of specific, local adjustments and may sometimes be explained in terms of contextual or programmatic contingencies, not accounted for in the definition of the type itself. The land slopes one way or the other, the site has an odd shape, the client wants this room bigger or that one facing the yard. The formal symmetry of a particular nineteenth-century house type on the Greek island of Sifnos, characterized by a main room with two minor rooms symmetrically placed to either side of

its minor axis, takes on a slightly different form with each house (Fig. 1). Adjacent London row houses, built by different builders before the era of large-scale speculation, similar in their linear room arrangements, take on slightly different dimensions and relationships to the street in each case, and sometimes slight differences may also arise out of functional considerations (Fig. 2).

The existence of this balance between unity (the repetition of formal type) and variety (small differences among similar buildings) is a well-known phenomenon and has been noted by such authors as the art historian Ernst Gombrich and the architect/builder Christopher Alexander.[1] The question of how, from a procedural point of view, this balance arises, is a difficult one—the distinction made above between variety arising out of combinatorial choice and variety arising out of specific adjustments within the type or subtype may prompt some objection. In *Folk Housing in Middle Virginia,* for example, Henry Glassie implies that all variation can be explained by what he calls the "rules of subtypification," or the "small clutch of formal variations on the basic types." According to Glassie, the knowledge of the builder is typological, and his job includes the "selection and organization of geometric entities [types and subtypes]; the entities are moved through transformations until they become complex shapes."[2]

However, the distinction between formal type and actual building is a real one. The building is

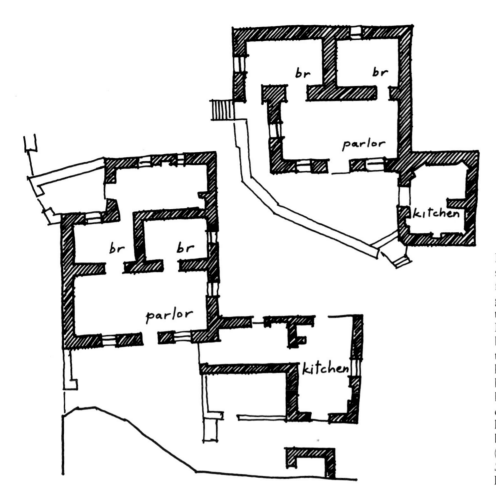

Fig. 1. These two houses show both typological differences as well as site-generated variation within typological similarities. Note the sitting room between the kitchen and the parlor in one of the houses and not the other, but also the differences in bedroom dimensions, exact courtyard shape, and parlor window arrangement between the two houses. (After Anastasia Tzakou, *Sifnos* [Athens: Melissa Publishing, 1984], 34, 35)

not just a complex arrangement of subtypes, but an arrangement of subtypes that is precisely fitted to its context—so precisely that infinitesimal variations, far too many for each to be understood as a separate type in the mind of the builder, are possible. How else can we explain the real differences among Greek village houses or early London row houses, except by seeing the builder's skill as one that naturally allows for this kind of precision? In addition to his knowledge of formal types and subtypes, the builder has considerable skill to shape the building to local conditions. This combination of restraint to type and skill in making type fit precisely is the procedural counterpart of the unity in variety of form.

This essay has three parts investigating the procedural origins of the balance between unity and variety. The first part describes a particular rule that helped lead to this unity in variety in some urban situations. The second describes the general nature of building rules that can lead to this balance. And the last suggests future work, to help test these ideas in different circumstances of building history.

❖   ❖   ❖

In 1882, a case that originated in Plymouth (*Dicker v. Popham*) came before one of the English appellate courts. The plaintiff owned a house in an alley that was occupied by an umbrella repairer.

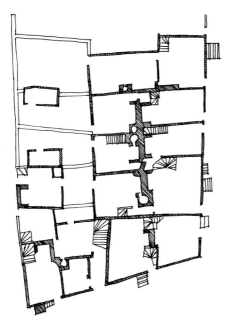

Fig. 2. These row houses show characteristics similar to the Greek village houses in an urban context. (After Clothworkers' Company Plan Book, 41, from John Schofield, ed., *The London Surveys of Ralph Treswell* [London: London Topographical Society, 1987], fig. 5)

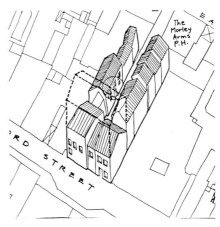

Fig. 3. Drawing showing the physical situation of *Dicker v. Popham,* Plymouth, 1882. In this case, and in the ones that follow, the proposed building is shown outlined with dotted lines, and the affected window is circled. The drawing was done using information presented in the law report, superimposed on a large-scale urban map. Only about a dozen cases, out of 160 studied, could be reconstructed in this way: most law reports of ancient lights cases did not include enough information to locate the affected properties on urban maps of the period. This particular case, in which the plaintiff (the owner of the building with the circled window) was able to prevent construction of the building shown in dotted outline at the end of the alley, seems to indicate that the ancient lights doctrine might have been a factor in determining, over time, the scale of local urban districts.

The defendant was proposing to build a house at the end of the alley, 57 feet high, which would block the light to the plaintiff's house (Fig. 3). The plaintiff sought and obtained "a perpetual injunction to restrain the erection of such building so as to obstruct her access of light," and this opinion was sustained on appeal.[3]

The basis for the plaintiff's claim was an old doctrine of English common law, known as the doctrine of ancient lights.[4] Simply, the doctrine states that a window that has had light coming into it for a certain amount of time is entitled to continue the enjoyment of that light. This right exists even if the window is directly on the property line with a neighbor, and even if it restrains the ability of the neighbor to build. In certain cases, then, this doctrine allowed for the same thing that modern zoning regulations allow for—light and air. But it did it in a very different way, through judgment rather than proscription, through local adjustment

rather than universal rules. As we shall see, the simple specification that the light to windows that have been in place for a long time has to be protected allows for specific responses to local conditions, and the consequent development of building variety.

The doctrine apparently represents the legal recognition of customary practice. The conditions in England in which such customary practice might have arisen and then become formalized seem clear. One of the first recorded cases is in the early seventeenth century, when the textile industry was growing, but still highly decentralized and operating out of peoples' houses. These houses were sometimes modified with special windows that

Fig. 4. Houses in Spitalfields, London, showing top floors with weavers' windows added, probably in the early eighteenth century. Such windows, designed and placed to admit good natural light, were characteristic in both urban and rural situations.

admitted the good light needed for such operations as sorting wool and particularly weaving (Fig. 4). Of course England does not have perpetual sunshine, and one can easily imagine that, in such a place, a mutually shared need for good light might have been translated into a mutual respect for windows. As towns grew larger, traditional rights were insisted upon, and that insistence eventually formed the backbone for the law.

The doctrine first appeared in English national law reports at the end of the reign of James I, in the

first part of the seventeenth century.[5] Reports appeared all through the eighteenth century and were most plentiful after the middle of the nineteenth, following the Prescription Act of 1832, an act of Parliament dealing with rights acquired through use or enjoyment, which set at twenty years the amount of time that a window would have to be in place to be considered ancient.

Most of the cases studied—160 in all—date to the nineteenth century, which allowed for correlation of the law reports with detailed urban maps and the reconstruction of the actual physical situation for several cases. Some of the reconstructed cases are illustrated here and demonstrate important features of the doctrine: first, those features that defined the doctrine itself, and the nature of cases to which it applied; and second, those that helped determine how much blockage of light actually constituted an actionable interference.

The nature of the cases to which the doctrine applied is shown in both *Senior v. Pawson* and *Higgins v. Betts.*[6] Each involved a proposed building across a public street from a window that would be affected, and in both cases the plaintiff was able to stop the proposed obstruction (Figs. 5 and 6).

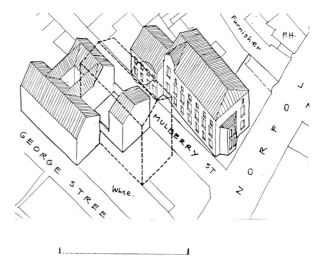

Fig. 5. Drawing showing the physical situation of *Senior v. Pawson*, Sheffield, 1866. This case illustrates that a street in between the proposed construction and the affected window would not take away the right to light.

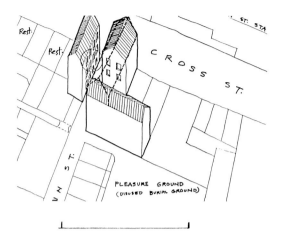

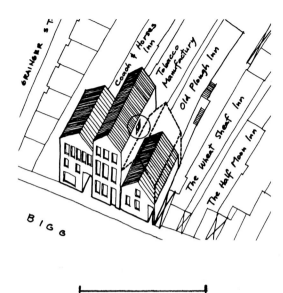

Fig. 6. Drawing illustrating the case of *Higgins v. Betts,* London, 1905. In this case the defendant argued that by cutting off the corner of his existing building at the corner of Benjamin and Cow Cross streets, enough new light would enter Benjamin Street to compensate for the loss of light caused by the new construction. The judge did not agree, and judgment was for the plaintiff.

Fig. 7. Drawing illustrating *Dickinson v. Harbottle,* New-castle-upon-Tyne, 1873.

The doctrine was not universally applicable. It did not apply to views,[7] or to sunlight (only to daylight),[8] or to light to yards or public streets, or to windows that had been in place less than a certain number of years. It did apply to greenhouses and skylights;[9] to buildings that had been rebuilt with new windows substantially the same as the old;[10] and to properties that shared a boundary as well as those that were separated from each other by a street or yard. This specific range of application accrued to the doctrine through the building up of precedent over the years, case by case.

In the same way, the two cases of *Dickinson v. Harbottle* and *Robson v. Whittingham* illustrate that the amount of light blockage required to be actionable could be known precisely, and that evidence had to be convincing (Fig. 7).[11] In *Dickinson,* it turned out that the sloping roof next to the plaintiff's window was not blocking too much light; in *Robson,* the only evidence presented by the plaintiff's tenant was a statement that because of the new building across the street, he had to light the gas lamp earlier in the afternoon than before. In both of these cases, the defendant prevailed.

In fact, case law reveals a precise honing of the standard for loss of light. This began as far back as 1752, when it was ruled that the blockage of light had to be so great as to constitute a nuisance; it included an important decision at the turn of this century that "there must be a substantial privation of light, enough to render the occupation of the house uncomfortable *according to the ordinary notions of mankind*"; and as recently as 1967, a court accepted the idea that standards for daylight were increasing, that the "ordinary notions of mankind" were changing.[12]

The fact that the law required reference to the "ordinary notions of mankind" indicates not a vague or poorly constructed law, but instead that the law recognized that an implicit rather than an explicit rule could form the basis for judgment. The absence of a numerically defined standard meant that the law needed to be immediately responsive to human desires, and that it might be directly understood, and commonly shared as such.

Along the way, to help make judgments, different tests were used to measure light in individual cases, including mathematical rules; the idea of a "grumble line" in a room, being that line behind which you "grumble if you are a reasonable man, and turn on the light";[13] as well as visits to the affected room by experts or even the judge, who might be seated in a chair reading the *Times,* so that he could see for himself the effect of panels held up in the position of the proposed building. While such tests seem archaic today, it is important that in all cases, even ones where explicit numerical rules were referred to, it was in the end human judgment and not any explicit rule that had the final say.

The doctrine was carried over to this country following the American Revolution, and many similar cases can be found in early American law reports. But what was seen as a need for rapid development of American towns eventually won out over neighborly respect. In the first part of the nineteenth century, economic expansion of the young country seemed important, and in 1838, the New York State Court of Appeals threw out the doctrine partly on economic grounds.[14] The court apparently felt that the doctrine represented an unreasonable constraint on the development of urban land, since it meant that land which might be otherwise developed would have to be left free to maintain access of light to neighbors' windows. The court wrote, "[The doctrine] cannot be sustained in the growing towns and cities of this country without working the most mischievous consequences."[15] At least twenty-six states eventually followed suit, although American cases involving ancient-lights disputes occurred well into the twentieth century.

In the decades following 1838, conditions in large American cities eventually made zoning seem necessary, and the first comprehensive zoning ordinance in the country was instituted in New York City in 1916. Even though zoning represented the same sort of economic restraint on development as the ancient-lights doctrine—it too had the effect of restricting the amount of development that could take place on any given lot—there was no chance for anything like the old common-law decision-making. Based on uniformly applied explicit rules, zoning seemed fair and administratively easy. It was attractive partly because it eliminated discretionary judgment from the decision-making process. It helped set the course of American urban growth in this century, and it is only in the last ten years or so that its content—if not its basic premise—has begun to be seriously challenged.

At this point, the ancient-lights doctrine is not well known in the United States, but it is of interest to the study of vernacular architecture because it may exhibit the precise mechanism through which a social custom becomes a part of building practice. It has several characteristics that, I conjecture, are inherent in some rule systems of vernacular building.

First, the doctrine is implicitly as well as explicitly understood and is as close a statement of its own intent as possible—"Don't block the light to old windows." Because it is stated in terms of a commonly understood intent, it is itself widely understandable. In fact, the application of the law apparently extended to some rather destitute situations, including one where the judge remarked, "It was no defence for the defendants to say that the building injured was only a miserable cottage; the lights of a cottage were as much entitled to the protection of the law as those of a mansion."[16] When a social habit dating from sometime before the start of the seventeenth century first began to take on the force of law, the law may have been only an expression of what was going on anyway, implicitly: people acting according to custom and what they saw as common sense. By comparison, modern zoning is also widely applicable, but its rules are more removed from their intent. A clause in a zoning ordinance that requires a building to be set back five or ten feet from a property line makes no reference to the reason for this. The gap between intention and rule seems especially evident in situations where, for example, building separations are required even when there are no windows, and no prospect for windows.

Second, the standard of performance within the doctrine is also implicitly understood, so that one can make a fairly precise intuitive judgment about whether or not too much light is being blocked or would be blocked with a proposed building. The operative phrase in the law, "comfort according to the ordinary notions of mankind," was supported by various numerical standards, but they were only guidelines, allowing the enforcement of the basic implicit rule without changing at all the common-sense nature of the rule. They only served to help make it more precise. For example, one guideline stated that sky should be visible above a line drawn at an angle of 45° to the horizontal, in a vertical plane perpendicular to the window. This only gave guidance to the implicit judgment—and again, this is different from modern zoning, in which the desired performance standard, for example the quantity of light in a room, is not mentioned in an ordinance that sets out building separations.

Finally, as a statement of intent, the doctrine does not specify formal solutions. Any solution within the available types that satisfy the intent is possible. Each situation, a building with its own place in the city, begins in a unique way, and applying the rule increases variety even more. This can be seen in the buildings of an architect such as Delissa Joseph, who worked in the 1920s. Joseph was not pleased with the doctrine of ancient lights. In the cause of abolishing height restrictions in London, he complained bitterly that for forty years he had been forced to practice "in the continuous glare of ancient lights," causing him to make buildings that were not only less profitable but also "lopsided."[17] But in those of his buildings that still survive in London, we see that the solutions he came up with to maintain light to neighbors' windows act precisely to make buildings more unique within an overall local order. For example, in designing the building at 109 Kingsway and his apartment building in Knightsbridge, Joseph shaped the buildings very precisely to preserve the light to buildings across the street. He did this differently in each case, creating unique buildings, but the law's intent of respecting ancient lights was also achieved in each case (Figs. 8 and 9).

Fig. 8. Office building designed by Delissa Joseph at 109 Kingsway, London, as it appeared in August 1985. The building was kept extremely low at the street in order to protect the light to the windows across the street, to the left.

Fig. 9. Apartment building designed by Delissa Joseph in Knightsbridge, London. In this case, Joseph chose to keep a large chunk of the building to only four stories. The effect of this, in addition to maintaining adequate light to the buildings across the street to the left, was to form, with those buildings, a symmetrical composition around the street, along with a well-proportioned building in itself. (Photograph by Jim Havlat, March 1986)

At this point, given the relatively small number of recorded cases, it is possible only to speculate about the effect the doctrine may have had on the fine-grained form of towns in England. It was obviously only one of a number of influences, which also included the persistence of particular shapes of urban lots, the development of certain plan types, and the use of particular construction techniques. The cases illustrated here—the Delissa Joseph buildings as well as the reconstructions from law reports—do suggest that the doctrine's effects were extremely local and particular. The doctrine resulted in building adjustments that had a relatively small impact on the city as a whole (except in the case of central London, whose scale may have been kept down largely as a result of the doctrine) but a noticeable effect on the way in which local variety was generated. This suggests—but of course does not prove—a connection between the nature of the implicit rule and the subtle variety of the resultant environment.

*   *   *

Is it possible to generalize about the nature of rules that lead to "unity in variety"? With the ancient-lights doctrine, we have seen that there may be a seamless connection between the intention of the rule and the simple expression of the rule in terms of this intention, and then a smooth connection between the rule itself and explicit ways of pinning it down without changing its intent.

Two hypotheses are suggested: First, the fact that the rule is implicitly understood in terms of its intention gives some degree of freedom to shape a building individually, thus allowing for a variety among different buildings that are shaped under the impact of this rule. The freedom arises because the statement of the rule solely in intentional rather than prescriptive terms means that different ways of achieving the intention are acceptable. Second, the application of the implicit rule is extremely fine-tuned, case by case, and based on reality, allowing for a precise result. An explicit rule is easy to administer, but the administration of an implicit rule is more dependent on sensitive human judgment. The freedom inherent in the implicit rule is not unbridled and arbitrary. In order for such freedom to exist—for the person making the building decision to be able to use his own best judgment of how to best meet the intention of the law—his own judgment, as well as that of others who may be responsible for seeing to it that the intention of the law is met, must be quite precisely tuned. The freedom that the implicit rule gives to decision-making is reined in by the precision of judgment, looking at the real situation. In the case of the ancient-lights doctrine, the implicit standard of sufficient light "according to the ordinary notions of mankind" is given considerable precision through case law and the accumulation of experience in looking at actual situations.

Both of these hypotheses are central to the creation of the "unity in variety" that is typical of much of vernacular architecture. The simply stated, implicit, and intentional rule allows buildings to take on whatever shape they need to within the constraints of their type. Accompanying the implicit rule is a sensitive process involving human judgment that gives precision to this detailed shaping and variety.

This last concept is only suggested by the case study of the ancient-lights doctrine. If true, it would represent an important modification of the purely typological explanation of vernacular building form. It suggests that the knowledge of the builder includes more than formal types and subtypes, and that his work has to do not only with choosing appropriate types, but also with bringing about their material realization in a real context. Constrained by the availability of a fixed number of formal types and subtypes, but faced with the context of an oddly sloping piece of land, or an irregularly shaped site, or the need to preserve light to a neighbor's window, or available roof timbers of a certain length, the vernacular builder must call on precise discretionary judgment in order to transform those chosen types into a real building. Such discretionary judgment, it is conjectured, is brought about through a framework of implicit rules that may allow for a good deal of local precision.

From a procedural point of view, "unity in variety" represents a balance between application of a formal type and specific, contextual adjustment. The unity that is characteristic of much of vernacular architecture comes about because the builder's basic choices are finite and limited; he is working in a cultural system that at any moment helps to define what is available through the specification of types and subtypes. This is the point made by Glassie in *Folk Housing in Middle Virginia,* which forms the basis of much current re-

search. But the variety that is characteristic of much of vernacular architecture at the same time has its origin not only in the multitude of combinatorial choices that are accepted within the available typological system but also in the rule systems of decision-making and craft that allow some degree of discretion to the builder as to how a particular typological arrangement will be realized. In turn, the discretion is itself limited, and the building form given precision, by experienced judgment applied to the particular situation.

❊   ❊   ❊

The ancient-lights doctrine supports the previous observations but does not provide enough evidence by itself to test them completely. The doctrine only applied in English law, and even then only to buildings that were in a position to block neighbors' windows. The building process as a whole, however, in England or in any other country, includes a number of different rule systems that guide the work of the builder and affect most buildings. These rule systems include culturally shared building types and subtypes, understandings about appropriate materials, craft techniques, understandings about relative roles of clients and builders, as well as public laws that promote health, safety, or urban aesthetics. These rule systems are present in one form or another in any society in which buildings are being made. Together these rule systems provide the procedural framework within which buildings are built, by setting out both the available types (the cultural understanding of what is to be built) and the means to realize the types in material form (building itself).

Within this framework, one may look for rule systems, more generally applicable to the building process than the ancient-lights doctrine, to help test the conjecture that explicit rules and implicit rules may have complementary roles to play in the production of buildings. The building contract, for example, is an indicator of the human relationships in the building process, of the nature of trust inherent in those relationships, and of the kind of information transmitted among the different participants. One can look at contracts in terms of this same balance between explicit information in the contract and implicit information outside it—and this means that contracts cannot be looked at alone, but have to be looked at in terms both of what is stated and what is not. Contracts have changed over history, and one way of characterizing that broad change is that more and more explicit information has come to be included in the contract, and less and less implicit information has been left out. This suggests some questions that may shed light on the human processes that lie behind vernacular building.

For example, do decisions that leave the specific shaping of the building to individual circumstances depend on a contractual relationship in which information is implicitly understood rather than explicitly stated? In a considerable number of early building contracts the explicit specification of the building consists of perhaps a page or so of written text, sometimes accompanied by one or two simple drawings containing a few key dimensions (Fig. 10).[18] In today's terms, these contracts would not provide enough information for the builder to make all necessary decisions—too much is left out of the specification, and the drawings are too rough and incomplete. But it obviously was the builder's responsibility to determine the exact form of the building—and indeed to *build* it—and it was commonly understood that his own knowledge and skills would supplement the information provided in the contract, to allow him to do this.

Following the conjectures outlined earlier, two aspects of the contribution that the builder was expected to make may be reflected in the form and content of the contract. On one hand, the detailed knowledge of types and subtypes on the part of the builder, and their acceptance by the client, may be assumed by the brevity of the contract, and the fact that just a few words in the contract may have to yield a good deal of complexity and detail in the finished building. In this sense, we might look at

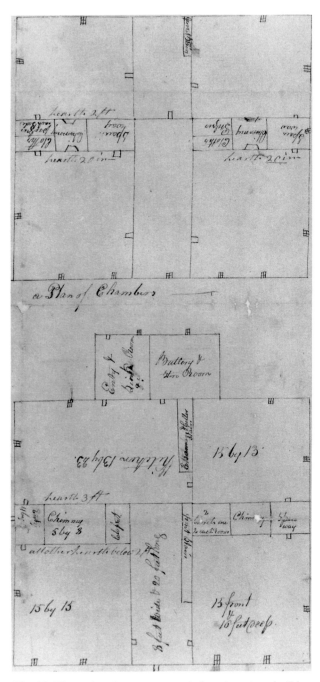

Fig. 10. These drawings accompanied an American building contract drawn up in October 1799. The rest of the contract consisted of three pages of text, with no other drawings. (Henry Francis du Pont Winterthur Museum, Joseph Downs Manuscript Collection, no. 68 × 51)

the specification of the building in the contract as no more than a catalyst—or a statement of mutually shared intention—to spur the builder to elaborate, through actual construction, a whole set of socially understood types and subtypes in particular combinations. Since the types and subtypes are commonly understood, they do not have to be specified in the contract; what *is* specified in the contract is enough to allow the builder to proceed.

On the other hand, the form of the contract (and the form of the human relationship that it embodies) may allow the builder a certain amount of discretionary judgment in carrying it out, enough to allow him to make immediate responses to contextual or programmatic demands. Imagine the built results for any one of the following hypothetical situations in the same place at a particular time: (1) two identical contracts, same client, same builder, two different sites of similar dimensions; (2) two identical contracts, same client, different builders; (3) two identical contracts, same builder, different clients. It is of course impossible to carry out this hypothetical experiment, but it is also difficult to imagine that the two buildings would be identical, even if the typological choices made were the same. No two buildings are exactly alike (except those produced on an assembly line or as a result of another form of mass production), and the differences between them arise because the builder has freedom, within the basic type definitions, to make choices and adjustments.

We also surmise that this freedom, given the builder by rough plans or general verbal descriptions, must have been balanced with rules that helped give precision to his decisions about the construction of the building. With contracts that relied on implicit information, these rules were largely inherent in the craft itself.

These ideas clearly need a good deal of historical testing. There is much room for work on the contractual relationships among clients and builders, especially as they relate to the design and form of buildings. As a document that provided building instructions of one kind or another, the contract may tell us quite a bit about how building decisions were made, and how the character of those specific decisions affected buildings.

In the most general terms, the question of how the vernacular world was produced, over time, is one that may be considerably broader than the identification of types, even as those types relate to social and cultural frameworks. The building process involves transforming types (which are mental constructs) into buildings (which are real things, of stone and brick and wood). This transformation—the construction of the building—usually involves some degree of adjustment, even if it is extremely subtle. But the results, in the vernacular world, are differences from building to building that overlay variety onto a framework of typological continuity.

If it is indeed the case that this kind of adjustment depended on rules that were implicitly stated, then we may see the difference between explicit and implicit rules as not only involving the character of information but also resulting in differences in the characters of buildings themselves.

REBECCA SAMPLE BERNSTEIN AND CAROLYN TORMA

EXPLORING THE ROLE OF WOMEN IN THE CREATION OF VERNACULAR ARCHITECTURE

The role of women in the design, construction, and use of vernacular architecture is little understood. While a growing body of literature is helping to define the topic and the approach, few researchers have asked women themselves appropriate questions concerning their involvement in architecture and its creation.

The process of conducting oral interviews for a survey of historic sites in South Dakota led to a recognition of the nature of the information missing in previous studies. One of the first insights came from eighty-seven-year-old Flora Doran, whose ranch in the dry southwest corner of Custer County was surveyed in the summer of 1988. For forty years, Mrs. Doran has lived on her own in the original homestead "shack" with a small early ad-

dition. Although she has a nephew who comes a couple of times a week, she is in charge and the sole worker of her modest cattle operation. In terms of design, she is much more interested in and pleased with her outbuildings than with her home (Figs. 3 and 4). She says, "I like the way my barn and corrals are arranged since it's getting difficult for me to throw the bales of hay very far."[1] Mrs. Doran's interest in outbuildings is noteworthy, since women's influence on buildings other than the home traditionally has been seen as peripheral.

The second insight came from Lillian Rantapaa, a retired schoolteacher and American-born Finnish-American. In describing the rural Lawrence County community in which she grew up, Rantapaa noted that "not every member of the com-

Fig. 1. Single women standing before the claim shanty of one of the women. Single women made up 12 to 30 percent of the homesteading population in the Great Plains in the 1868–1920 era. (South Dakota State Historical Society)

64

Fig. 2. A woman, her two children, and two dogs pose by the front door of their sod claim house in South Dakota. Modest, small, one-room dwellings were typical of the claim houses on the Plains. Many families captured the adventure of homesteading in photographs such as this. (South Dakota State Historical Society)

Fig. 3. In an interview conducted in 1988, rancher Flora Doran's architectural concerns focused on her corrals and animal shelters. (Rebecca Sample Bernstein, South Dakota Historical Preservation Center)

munity was a skilled Finnish craftsman" and that several log buildings had collapsed due to the ineptitude of their construction. In her humorous account of these disasters, Rantapaa went on to explain in technical detail the appropriate way to build a log and sod roof.[2]

Flora Doran's lack of interest in a pretty home and her knowledgeable reflection on her ranch buildings, as well as Lillian Rantapaa's command of log building, suggested a question: If women understood how to build and what constituted a useful building, did they also actively participate in designing and constructing buildings? This essay explores that topic.

In her article entitled "Women in the American

Fig. 4. Living alone in rural Custer County, Flora Doran has only marginal interest in the appearance in her house, which she refers to as a "shack." (Rebecca Sample Bernstein, South Dakota Historical Preservation Center)

Vernacular Landscape," Sally McMurry identified two main issues in the study of women and architecture: how were women active participants in shaping the landscape, and how did the landscape affect women? This study is concerned primarily with the first of these questions. In addition to the major inquiries, McMurry formulated a series of more discrete questions. Five of these are pertinent to this study and will serve as the framework for discussion: (1) How much control did women historically exercise over design and arrangement? (2) Were men's and women's senses of appropriate design different? (3) Over what aspects of design (or architecture generally) did women have the most control? (4) How did marital status affect women's roles in architecture? (5) What influence did social class have on architecture and its creation?[3] To this we add a factor highly significant for the region examined in this study: What effect did ethnicity have on women's roles?

The region encompassed in this essay is the mid-continent of America—the prairie and plains states from Indiana to Colorado. Settled by white pioneers from the mid 1800s through 1920, the region has a recorded history that is relatively recent. A rich body of source material was left by pioneer women and their daughters in their letters, journals, diaries, biographies, reminiscences, and interviews. Indeed, the Midwest and western United States may be one of the few places where this wealth of firsthand accounts can be found in enough quantity to allow for a meaningful study of women's own views on the creation of historic architecture.

Although the literature on women's history relative to architecture is substantial, when one turns to primary source material, a major stumbling block is encountered. Women seldom recorded the process of constructing or even using their particular space—the home. Evidence of women's avoidance of the discussion of design and construction details is found in the dairy of Emily French, who lived in Denver in the 1890s. This is all the more surprising because French kept a diary for many years and

recorded her desire to have a home of her own as well as the immense effort she spent to satisfy this desire. Incurring debt and sacrificing relationships and even health, French built her home in the new suburbs of Denver. Although she mentions the process of purchasing her property, and going herself to buy the materials for the house, no sense of the physical appearance of the house is discernible. In the introduction to the published journal, Janet Lacompte describes the house as a four-room, story-and-a-half frame structure, but Emily French never indicates the measurements, proportions, style, or plan.[4]

This lack of detail is remarkable since she expended so much time and energy on the project. Why did she not elaborate on the physical character of the house? Was she so familiar with the house that she saw no need to verbalize her knowledge? Did she not care as much for the details of plan and proportion as for the completion of the structure? Or, was there for Emily French, an otherwise independent, nontraditional woman, some taboo regarding expressing her thoughts on the spatial arrangement, style, and window placement in her house? One explanation may come from Elizabeth Hampsten, who analyzed a number of women's journals and letters in *Read This Only to Yourself: The Private Writings of Midwestern Women, 1880–1910*. Particularly helpful is her observation that women described themselves in relation to other people rather than to specific locations on a map. Indeed, "women's letters tend to be filled with information about other people—illnesses, letters received, occasional visits, gossip and news—but except for mentioning the weather, they say very little about physical surroundings."[5]

This problem of reticent observers was also encountered in the writings of South Dakota women who homesteaded in the 1862–1920 era. A remarkable collection of autobiographies and biographies of women was collected in the 1940s and 1950s by the South Dakota Federation of Women's Clubs.[6] Of the 193 biographies included in the published version of these accounts, only 18 make any reference to women's participation in the building and designing process. Many women, however, described their pioneer or claim home.

Added to the problems encountered in documentary research are the special problems inherent in fieldwork. For example, the amount of information available on the participation of women in the creation of architecture may depend on which family member is interviewed. Clearly, if the interviewer has access to the women who create, such as Flora Doran, the information will be rich. In another case, at the Stearns Ranch in Custer County, information on the mother's contribution to the house was accessible through one son, but not the other. The older brother, William, was not home at the time the house was built, and therefore did not know that his mother had requested a south-facing bay window for plants and built-in cabinets in the kitchen.[7]

The response to McMurry's first question—how much control did women historically exercise over design and arrangement?—is twofold. The first answer comes from the descriptions provided by the Daughters of Dakota. The majority of the houses described in these accounts were constructed by husbands, brothers, fathers, or hired workmen. Often a house was built before the woman arrived on the homestead.

Yet Emily French was not entirely alone, for evidence remains of how other women independently designed and built their structures. David Murphy describes a Polish immigrant woman in Sherman County, Nebraska: the "Roschynialski house was built in 1882 by Mary Zwfka Roschynialski, wife of Joseph who was detained building wood-framed Catholic churches in the community at the time. After mixing the clay and straw together in a pit near the site, she laid up a layer a day until the walls were complete."[8]

Cora D. Babcock's reminiscences of 1880 to 1885 in frontier Dakota Territory indicate that Babcock "filed a claim near Bridgewater, constructed a sod shanty on it and raised a successful crop of flax that paid all the expenses of her claim."[9] In

another example, homesteader Grace Fairchild moved to rural Stanley County, South Dakota, in 1902 with her husband and two children. Fairchild assumed the role of family "architect" when she discovered that her husband was not up to the demands of the job. Eventually divorced, Fairchild took over one job after another, including designing and supervising the construction of home improvements and outbuildings. Her responsibilities also encompassed raising the cash to purchase the needed building supplies and hire a mason.[10] A third example is cited by historian Glenda Riley. Matilda Pietzke Paul of Iowa in writing about her childhood "described how her widowed mother constructed the family's long-planned new home by using bricks that had been prepared by her recently deceased husband; she hired bricklayers, but put her older sons to work as carpenters and laborers."[11]

The common element running through all these examples is the absence of the husband through death, incompetence, injury, or another job. These women stepped into a breach and did what evidence suggests was traditionally a man's job. Yet their knowledge of design and construction, especially Mary Roschynialski's, was large enough to accomplish the task with little difficulty.

Closely related to the issue of control is McMurry's question of whether men's and women's senses of appropriate design were different. A few women objected to, commented upon, or complained about their husband's or other men's architecture. One was Mrs. Harriet Ward, who was interviewed about her life as a rancher in rural Custer County, South Dakota. Mrs. Ward took great pride in her home and home site (Fig. 5). A native of Alabama, Ward had graduated from a home-economics program and had a high school degree. After working for wealthy families in Syracuse, New York, she received a marriage proposal from Mr. Ward of Custer, South Dakota. She accepted. When she arrived as a new wife in 1933, Ward was living in a homestead shack—she refused to stay unless he built her a proper home. The resulting two-story

Fig. 5. Although the house is unoccupied today, evidence remains of Harriet Ward's garden and landscaping around her rural Custer County, South Dakota, house. Even the fence and gate used to keep the cows out of the garden remain standing. (Rebecca Sample Bernstein, South Dakota Historical Preservation Center)

house had wood floors, built-in wood cabinets, fancy windows, and a modern kitchen. Mrs. Ward also planted flowering bushes, laid a rock garden, and placed rock paths within the yard fence. She would have done without the fence, but she needed to protect her garden/domestic space from her husband's cattle.[12]

The ever-energetic Grace Fairchild provided another example. Fairchild simply dismissed her husband's building attempts as inept. She recounted, in somewhat loving detail, how she and her children redesigned the house, rebuilt the barn, and designed and constructed new outbuildings.[13] Still another homesteader, Anna Langhorne Waltz, joined her husband in the small town of Burke, South Dakota, in 1911 to discover that he had had a small frame house constructed for them. Waltz said of the small two-room house that there "was no provision for anything like a kitchen because my husband had taken his meals out at different places, so until we could fix up some arrangements for cooking, we ate at a place called a hotel." Later, Waltz settled on their claim with their first child, while her husband worked as a minister in Deadwood. Once again, her husband designed and, this

time, built the "soddie" for his family. However, in this second attempt he was more successful, and Waltz measures her husband's love for her in the great care he took to assure her comfort and convenience in the house and on the claim.[14]

Annette Atkins, a historian of rural Minnesota women, has observed that in order to understand the significance and definition of gender roles, one must understand the dynamic of the family.[15] While the place a women holds within the family relates to her marital status, it is not limited to that. A woman can affect familial control or dynamics without the absence of the man. For example, neighbors' stories reveal that Harriet Ward had a strong personality; although not the major breadwinner, perhaps she was the controlling force in the family. Such dynamics may be subtle; it is important to view architectural influence in terms of personality and family dynamics and not simply gender.

Before these three examples are dismissed as highly unusual, McMurray's third question and some striking statistics must be considered. The question—over what aspects of design did women have the most control—is difficult to answer from this evidence. Nonetheless, the question informs this entire essay, for there appears to be no one area or aspect of architecture to which women were limited. Indeed, the idea of limitations is challenged by the statistics on who homesteaded and for how long. A statistic to be considered is that between 12 and 30 percent of all homesteaders making claims in the prairies and plains were single women. As significant is the evidence from a Colorado study showing that they had every intention of fulfilling their obligation as homesteaders; while only 37 percent of all men made final claims on their land, 42.4 percent of women filed final proof.[16] The situation of the homesteaders in the late nineteenth and early twentieth centuries was a highly unusual one. Women not only made up a significant portion of the population, but many also possessed an unusually high degree of financial and social independence as well as courage and a taste for adventure. Many of the women claimants were schoolteachers who lived on their claims in the summer and taught in the winter at another location.

One such schoolteacher was Martha Stoecker Norby, who left a memoir of her homesteading experiences. She related how she and her brother made claims in Stanley County, South Dakota. "At the end of two years brother George decided to give up his claim, but I went out the spring of 1906 to live all by myself. Rev. Vogt had a man take out lumber for the group and build our shacks, which were to be 9 × 12, but the builder evidently wasn't too good at measuring so they were 8 × 10. The lumber, hauling, and building cost me $12.50. I still have the bill."[17] Martha Stoecker Norby's account reveals how McMurry's fourth question—how did marital status affect women's roles in architecture?—relates to the first two. In many cases, when men were absent, women controlled the design and sometimes the building of architecture. Yet many women homesteaded independently of men, and not all chose to be involved in the design and construction of buildings. In the absence of men, not all women automatically assumed the role of primary designer, supervisor, and/or builder.

The role women played economically in financing the erection of homestead buildings is also significant. McMurry does not consider this issue in her article, yet who owned the property and who supplied the capital for building relates directly to the issue of how much control women held over architecture. Problems concerning the financing of her home were central in Emily French's diary entries regarding the erection of her house. She enumerated trips to obtain lumber and other materials, and sometimes detailed costs. She also mentioned borrowing money. When the family moved in, the house was not yet complete and extra money was raised for boards, some bricks, and paint. Flora Doran made all her own financial decisions. She preferred to spend her income on repairing her ranch buildings rather than on personal comforts. Her neighbors resorted to paying

for a telephone in order to keep a watchful "eye" over their elderly neighbor.

Many pioneer women worked to help support the family economy. Some worked outside the home; others provided services from the home for cash payment. Several women recounted how they used this cash to help finance building projects. Bessie Bagby Lumley taught school in Sully County between 1896 and 1902 earning $28 to $35 per month. Eventually she saved enough money to purchase the old hotel at Okobojo and move it to her father's land. The two-story building was converted to a house, and the entire undertaking cost Lumley $250.[18] Lucia Peretti, a native of Italy, moved to the gold-mining town of Lead, South Dakota, with her husband in the 1880s. While her husband, Batiste, was off mining in other communities, Mrs. Peretti, "with Batiste's approval grubstaked a prospector on the edge of town to the extent of about $900, a little here, a little there." Later Batiste and Lucia Peretti moved into the house the grubstaker had built. After her husband's death, the enterprising Mrs. Peretti "built the first house on Sunnyside in Lead, with the help of friends and though one other house that she built and owned was abandoned and 'went down the cut' as Lead people say, that first house still is a Lead landmark."[19]

This raises a question about the bias of the data examined for this study. First, although the Daughters of Dakota collection was open to all women, a larger proportion of American-born women recorded their pioneer experiences. Second, we may assume that the women who did write biographies may have had a higher social standing in the community, as evidenced by their association with the Women's Clubs. Third, many of the women who wrote accounts, both in the Daughters collection and in other publications, were educated. Historian Mary Hargreaves questions many of these same sources: the "fact that all these women were well educated raises further questions concerning the value of their reports as source documents typical of homestead experience."[20] Indeed, McMurry's question of what influence did social class have on architecture and its creation may be impossible to answer with the present data, because the data represent only a small segment of the social structure.

When we turn to the final question of the effect of ethnicity on women's roles, we discover a striking pattern. Immigrant women's biographies and reminiscences recount a slightly different process of building than do American-born women's. Immigrant men and women worked together to erect buildings. All the more striking is the fact that only the biographies of immigrant women indicate that this pattern of cooperative building occurred.

In a biography of Kate Jilnek Bouzek, her daughter says, "Women and men would help each other in building their soddy farms. They not only had soddy houses, they built barns and covered the roofs with long thatched bundles that made the roof rain proof." Kate Bouzek emigrated from Bohemia to Hyde County, Dakota Territory, in 1882.[21] Norwegian-born Margaret Hjelmeland Knutson homesteaded with her children in the Mitchell area of Dakota Territory. Without a husband to assist her, Mrs. Knutson called upon the aid of a neighbor. "Mr. Jacobson broke the first ten acres for oats and a half for garden. All the garden sod was cut into 2 foot strips and Mrs. Knutson carried every foot of it to sod the sides and ends to the shanty."[22]

Anna Marie Byers Mausbach was born in Germany in 1847 and came to Dakota Territory in 1871. While Anna Byers had done "all kinds of farm work," her husband was a blacksmith and novice homesteader. "In the spring (of 1872) they built their sod house on their claim walking 7 miles each morning, carrying their child and lunch and laying sod all day and walking 7 miles back at night; but at last it was completed and they moved in."[23] In 1884 Mari Elizabeth Shindler of Pisele, Bohemia, and her husband, Michael Reha of Budapest, settled in Dakota Territory. Their daughter described their building efforts. "Father and mother built a 2 room adobe house, which was very warm, the walls being two feet thick."[24]

Is ethnicity enough to explain why the pattern of building was remarkably different between immigrant and nonimmigrant settlers? Hargreaves provides another explanation. Her studies revealed that a large number of homesteaders were inexperienced farmers and ranchers. She notes, "Over a quarter of the tenants listed in the North Dakota *Census* of 1920 lacked previous farm experience. The lure of speculative profits to be gleaned from the last of the dwindling public domain attracted an unusually large number of settlers whose hands were uncalloused."[25] In contrast, as Anna Mausbach's biography reveals, the European immigrants who settled on the plains and prairies were largely rural people with ample farm experience. Therefore, the split witnessed in these biographies may simply be between women who no longer had any need to be involved with building in urban areas and immigrant women for whom building was a natural part of their working lives.

Evidence from immigrant women and their daughters suggests another important issue not touched upon by McMurry. The first comes from an interview with Eva Larson of Frederick, South Dakota. Mrs. Larson was born into a Finnish immigrant family and married a Norwegian. Although Larson and her husband built on his land and built American buildings, they also erected a Finnish sauna in the 1930s. When questioned as to how the structure was built, Mrs. Larson said her husband and his brother erected the sauna. As neither had any experience with sauna building, Mrs. Larson was questioned further. She replied that she instructed the men and supervised their building.[26] This indication that ethnic women were the bearers of architectural tradition is reinforced by the observable patterns of building in the Danish community in rural Yankton and Clay counties. The Trinity Church community was settled by immigrant Danes starting in 1869. Several of the Danes built large, two-story "pair" or "parstuga" houses that had a traditional Danish or Scandinavian floor plan. Other Danish immigrant buildings on the farms included large horse and dairy barns. Not all the parstuga houses and large horse and cow barns were built on Danish farms. At first, it was assumed that the non-Danes simply copied their neighbors. Later it was discovered that the mistresses of these farms were Danish. One oral interview indicated that a Danish wife insisted that her Norwegian husband build a parstuga house.[27]

To conclude, what then was women's role in architecture? The answer is complex, for evidence indicates that women designed, built, redesigned, and reacted to architecture. In addition, their response was not uniform. This contradicts the most recent historical interpretations of scholars such as Glenda Riley, who in *The Female Frontier* argues, "Such factors as social class and ethnicity, race, religion, education and marital status did not substantially alter the gender roles and the expectations of women on the prairie and plains."[28] In respect to architecture, a review of much of the same primary source material indicates that Riley is quite wrong. In fact, the variables she cites are crucial to an understanding of the architectural process.

Riley is not alone in her assumptions. Although much excellent history on women in the midcontinent is being written, too often architecture and other telling details are ignored. Many historians assume that all pioneering women's experiences were the same. For example, Joanna L. Stratton's *Pioneer Women: Voices from the Kansas Frontier* overlooks this data. In her chapter "Homes of Puncheon, Homes of Sod," Stratton assumes that a strict division of labor existed. She claims, "While the men set to work building the house, the women gathered to brew hot coffee and bake special breads or cakes for the occasion."[29] Yet, despite her assumption that women were not involved in designing and building, she extensively quotes women's knowledgeable observations on buildings. Therefore, a researcher seeking information on architecture should not settle for the published accounts, but should rereview the original data.

How can the researcher overcome this bias of either ignoring women's contributions or viewing all women's experiences as the same? First, techniques of research need to be expanded. Although not a new method for research, oral history is, nonetheless, an underused technique for studying architectural history. An example of how rich a source oral history can be when used rigorously and thoroughly is Charles Martin's *Hollybush: Folk Building and Social Change in an Appalachian Community*. Martin's work explores how a community is defined through its physical features and how those features, in turn, have meaning for the community and its individual members. Although Martin does not address the subject of gender, he provides more evidence for the participation of women in the creation and use of architecture. Martin says, "One informant recalled details by centering on images of her father, who died when she was only thirteen: 'I helped my father put up those shelves,' and 'That room had a stone foundation because I remember handing him those flat stones.'" Later, Martin explores the interior decoration of houses and states that it was "by and large the province of women."[30] However, because Martin was not seeking to understand cultural gender models, his work does not explore the community in any great depth in terms of divisions—divisions created by age, social status, family dynamics, or gender.

Vernacular architecture and gender studies demand new techniques and approaches to research and surveys. The changes must affect all aspects of research and not be limited to thematic studies of women and historic resources. An appropriate place to begin is with a more comprehensive approach to the issue of "how a building gets built." An excellent model for this approach is Peter N. Moogk's *Building a House in New France*, which examines everything from the source of design ideas and financing to who performed which tasks in the actual erection of the structure. Perhaps out of surprise, Moogk comments several times on the participation of women, which appears to have been quite rare. However, in early records, he found evidence of one woman acting as a building contractor, one women directing the work on the family house in the absence of her husband, and one widow having to defend her dead husband's craftsmanship in court.[31]

McMurry has set researchers on the appropriate path to the discovery or recovery of women's history relative to vernacular architecture. In this study of the midcontinent, we found several additional variables or issues to be considered. These include: What economic control did women have not only over architecture, but over their lives? How did the dynamics within the family affect roles and consequently participation in the architectural process? And will additional studies show that European immigrant women played a significantly different role than American-born women in the construction of buildings and in transference of architectural ideas?[32] The subject of women and the creation of vernacular architecture is a rich one, worthy of much more study.

II. Buildings and Regions

Jay Edwards

The Evolution of a Vernacular Tradition

In most cases there were no blueprints for it. We idealized it, you know? You see it through your imaginary eye. I always said if I have the thing in my brain I don't need a blueprint. You're only wasting time because when I have a blueprint I have to go and show the fellow.
—*Interview with Linzale Brandt, master designer–builder, seventy years of age. San Andrés Island, Colombia, August 1970*

American vernacular landscapes are seldom simple. Even when established by settlers from a single common provenience, buildings are rebuilt in new forms, new traditions are introduced and blended with older, established ones, and entire types disappear, leaving only subtle influences in their descendants. In an economically and ethnically dynamic historic environment, diffusion, innovation, reinterpretation, and loss combine to cloud our understanding of the past. Even under ideal conditions, years of study are required to describe the cultural processes that produced a single tradition of vernacular architecture; in some cases even this may be insufficient. Yet, on occasion, one is fortunate enough to happen upon a case study that clarifies our understanding of processes that have defied previous interpretation. Such a study is provided by the vernacular architecture of the tiny and remote West Indian archipelago of San Andrés, Colombia.

Information upon which this paper is based was gathered in field studies on San Andrés Island in 1966–1967, 1968, 1970, 1974, and 1979. A survey of 140 houses was conducted. Measured plans were taken of 63 houses felt to be representative of the local tradition. Extensive interviews were conducted with the most experienced vernacular build-

ers, including one seventy years of age. Interviews were also conducted with numerous home owners on San Andrés and its neighboring islands.

San Andrés Island is located approximately 120 miles east of the Mosquito Coast of Nicaragua. Together with its sister island, Old Providence, fifty miles to the north, it has been a site for settlement by English-speaking planters and their slaves since 1629, though not continuously. In the seventeenth century, English and Spanish forces wrestled the archipelago from one another repeatedly, driving all members of the "enemy" population from its shores. The island was also abandoned for years at a time in the seventeenth and early eighteenth centuries. The last phase of settlement dates from the middle of the eighteenth century when cotton planters from Jamaica, the Cayman Islands, and other English-speaking areas of the western Caribbean resettled the archipelago after its abandonment by conquering Spanish forces.[1] They imported slaves from the Guinea Coast of Africa. Words from Kwa-group languages are still common in the local Creole English dialect.[2] There was no permanent aboriginal population on the island prior to European settlement.

Today, the population of San Andrés Island is composed of both English-speaking West Indians and Spanish-speaking Colombian continentals. In 1970, approximately six thousand "native" West Indians resided on the island, representing an amalgam of African and European Americans. The vast majority of the Spanish-speaking "Colombians" are relative newcomers, emigrating from the South American continent after San Andrés was declared a free port in 1953. The continentals now outnumber the natives, residing mostly in the urban community of Northend, with small numbers scattered throughout the island.

The vernacular architecture of San Andrés Island is unique in three important respects. First, the origin of the native West Indian tradition can be dated to 1853. Because the beginnings of this tradition are comparatively recent, a number of the buildings of the earliest phases of development survive. Second, due to a fortunate configuration of social and economic circumstances, the San Andrés vernacular tradition evolved rapidly through the stages of development common to the more complex North American vernacular traditions. Early processes of development and change are clearly revealed on San Andrés. Third, on San Andrés there have been no widespread devastating catastrophes such as fires, earthquakes, or hurricanes to expunge disproportionate numbers of any individual historically significant form.[3] Since destruction has been, for the most part, piecemeal and random, an adequate sampling of every major historical period and architectural form survives.

Some data on the history of San Andrés exist. The economic and architectural situation of the island at the end of the eighteenth century was described in the report of a Spanish traveler: "The number of inhabitants . . . reaches a total, including all classes, ages and sexes, of 373 persons, who live without forming a village, each family on a farm of its own. . . . The adornment and bareness of their houses, the poor character of their clothing and the lack of luxury for their women, all indicate that they possess no more than is necessary for existence."[4]

Historic documents reveal that the population of the island consisted of small planters who lived under conditions of near poverty. They resided for the most part in small, thatched-roof houses little better in size or quality than those of their slaves (Fig. 1). The events disrupting this idyll of remote and tranquil subsistence included violent slave revolts in the first half of the nineteenth century. Two nearly successful revolts were harshly suppressed. There is evidence of continuing animosity between the field slaves and the planters thereafter.

While slave emancipation in Colombia was proclaimed in 1850, it was not until 1853 that a local American missionary, Philip Beekman Livingston, organized the emancipation in San Andrés, pressuring the planters to free their slaves. Nearly to a man, the former field slaves refused to work for meager wages on the lands of the planters. Within a few years the cotton plantations had been ruined for lack of labor and many of the planters had given up and left the island. Their lands were sold or distributed to the former slaves.[5] The transformation of the island's population into a black English Creole–speaking Protestant society was nearly total.

At this point a remarkable story begins. It was succinctly described in an informational dispatch to the U.S. State Department from Philip Beekman Livingston, dated December 31, 1873.[6] Several passages are worth quoting. Livingston's description

Fig. 1. Thatched hut with attached fireside (corrugated iron covering) and rear kitchen shed. Much cooking is done in the open. San Andrés Island, 1966.

of life in 1850, when the island population was around 1,275, begins: "Cotton . . . coconut oil and tortoise shell . . . were exchanged for cloathing and other necessaries by the slave holders, who were themselves comparatively poor, living mostly in houses thatched with grass and wattled with sticks." Livingston describes how around that time several of the planters had begun to plant coconuts as a second source of income. As soon as slave emancipation was completed, the slaves cleared their newly won lands and also undertook the cultivation of coconuts. By 1856 the island was covered with coconut farms, and Yankee captains made San Andrés a regular port of call, buying the product with American "red gold" coins. The price of coconuts rose steadily over the next eight years, climbing from eight dollars per thousand to more than twenty-five dollars per thousand: "The controllers of the commerce of the island are principally those who used to be slaves or their posterity; their homes are now shingled, boarded round and painted, much nicer and more expensive than their owners houses were. Money is plentiful."

In 1873 coconuts were bringing about ninety thousand dollars annually into an economy in which one American gold double-eagle went a very long way. A comfortable wooden cottage could be built for a few hundred dollars (Figs. 2, 3). The total population was approximately twenty-four hundred people.[7] In a mere twenty years this little island had witnessed a social and economic revolution of unparalleled vigor, accompanied by an architectural revolution of equal magnitude. By 1900, the tiny "room and hall" cottages of San Andrés had flowered into multistory timber framed plantation houses, surrounded by galleries and capped with fancy dormers (see Figs. 4, 8–9, 11–12, 15, 17).

It is clear from Livingston's personal observations that even before 1873 many natives of San Andrés could afford for the first time to construct "proper" wooden houses for themselves. At first, a modest frame cottage of two (occasionally three) rooms was adopted (Figs. 3–4). No kitchen was included, for

Fig. 2. Type b2 core cottage with MF1 rear kitchen shed expansion, San Andrés Island.

Fig. 3. ML1 cottage with windows in the gables. Note extended kitchen shed.

Fig. 4. Type f1 four-room cottage with MF1 and MLB1-S expansions, San Andrés Island.

cooking was done at a detached fireside (see Fig. 1). Food was carried into the hall to be eaten.

After the local forests had been cut down and replaced with coconut groves, fustic cedar, pine, and hardwoods were imported from the Mosquito Coast of Nicaragua for construction materials.[8] Each house was elevated one or more feet above the ground on stout cedar or ironwood posts, or on stones (later cement pillars; see Figs. 4, 9, 13).

A single basic conception of house form was widely adopted by the designer-builders of San Andrés Island.[9] From the very earliest years there appears to have been a strong tendency toward geometric standardization. Both West Africans from the Guinea Coast and British Europeans shared a preference for a two-room rectangular cottage with its door on the long side.[10]

On San Andrés, the dominant geometrical aesthetic was one of a cottage with outside dimensions approximating 5:7, or $N:N\sqrt{2}$. These proportions can best be explained as derived from the rotation of the diagonal of a square. This method would not be employed wherever standardized measuring scales were in use. Rather sticks or string were the original tools of measurement. Such a method has been previously described by myself, J. M. Jenkins, and Arthur J. Lawton. A somewhat related method was hypothesized by Henry Glassie for Virginia.[11]

The long-term dominance of the geometrical aesthetic that originated from this method may be seen in the consistency of the proportions of houses surveyed on San Andrés (Fig. 5) and on neighboring islands. The aesthetic survives in the proportions of hundreds of standing structures, long after more sophisticated methods of layout had been adopted by builders.

I will now describe the pattern of evolution of the San Andrés house from its simple beginnings around 1860 to its condition in 1970. Certain definitions are required. What I shall refer to as a *base module* is the simplest unit that conforms to the definitions of the tradition and that can stand alone. The base module for San Andrés was a two-room, hall-and-parlor-plan cottage of modest proportions

(Figs. 2, 3). It was generally covered with a gabled roof, hip roofs being unusual even today. Its outer proportions conformed to the favored 5:7 standard.

After 1870, successful farmers could afford to build increasingly larger houses (Fig. 4). Builders adopted two quite distinct approaches to the problem of expansion. The first was to simply enlarge the modular cottage while retaining the favored 5:7 relationship between its side and front walls. This approach, called *internal modular expansion*, resulted in larger houses that appeared much like the smaller houses because they shared the same external proportions. The designer-builder could fit additional rooms into the interior of a new and larger house without changing the outward appearance. This method appears to have been important to the early phases of development. Interestingly, houses were not expanded through the addition of extra

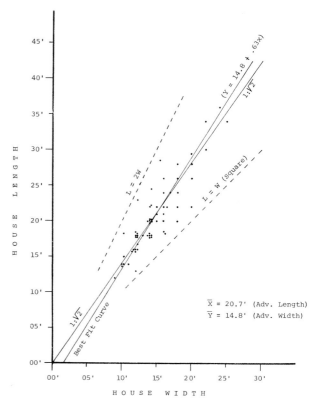

Fig. 5. Dimensions of core cottage modules, San Andrés Island, Ca. 1870–1970. N = 63.

modules, as they were in Barbados (Fig. 6). Though both islands employed similar basic modular cottage forms, there was a radical difference in the pattern of elaboration and expansion between the two areas.[12]

Internal modular expansion resulted in increasingly elaborate *plan types* (Fig. 7). Evolutionary expansion occurred in a step-by-step fashion; thus, each plan type represents a stage of expansion in an overall lineage. On San Andrés, two different lineages of internal expansion were adopted. Each began with the basic asymmetrical "room-and-hall" plan I classify as Type b (Figs. 2, 7 Type b1). The first stage of enlargement began with the segmentation of the original hall into a front hall and a smaller rear dining room (Fig. 7 Types d1, d4; Figs. 4, 15). As the core cottage continued to expand, the original bedroom was similarly bifurcated, creating a four-square base module (Fig. 7 Types f1 and g3; Figs. 8, 9). Eventually, houses with six or more rooms within a rectangular core evolved (Fig. 7 Type j1; Figs. 10, 11).

Smaller plans also evolved out of Type b. Smaller two-room houses (Fig. 7 Types b-1, b-2), and a single-room plan (Type a1), represent a kind of devolutionary lineage. Type b- consisted of a room-and-hall module in which the bedroom was too narrow to permit a bed to be placed across the short

Fig. 6. Chattle house expansion by the addition of modular units, Bridgetown, Barbados, 1975.

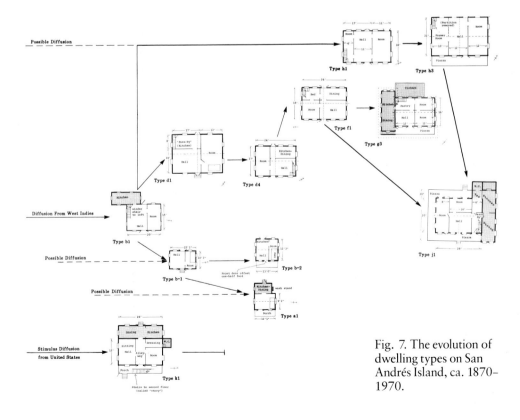

Fig. 7. The evolution of dwelling types on San Andrés Island, ca. 1870–1970.

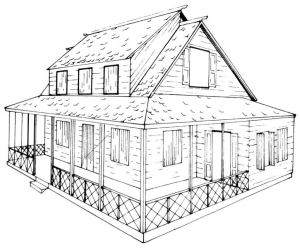

Fig. 8. MF2 packsaddle roof cottage showing access to kitchen shed via side piazza.

dimension, thus limiting the room to a single bed. The smaller cottages were carefully designed to mimic the larger ones while remaining within the limitations of smaller than acceptable budgets. Single-room houses were often divided by a fabric partition into two asymmetrical spaces.

A different approach to internal modular expansion was to begin with a Type b plan and add an extra bedroom on the opposite side of the hall from the "room," creating a plan with three full-depth rooms *en suite* (Fig. 7 Types h1, h3). These plans were popular in the last decades of the nineteenth century and the first decades of the twentieth, but they went out of style thereafter.[13] Another plan type was also experimented with. This was a symmetrical (or near symmetrical) central-hall plan in-

Fig. 9. A raised shed roof house, MF2 Plan Type g3, with an MLB1-S loft expansion and an MB2 "Bottom House."

Fig. 10. Type J1 house with an MF2 encircling piazza and an MLB2-S shed roof expansion, Sound Bay, San Andrés, 1970.

Fig. 11. Large, two-and-one-half-story MF1/MB1 house with front galleries and an MLA1-H, "hip-and-gable" garret, of the type invented by Linzale Brandt.

troduced with a two-story I house around the turn of the twentieth century (Fig. 7 Type k1). While the idea of a "two storage" house caught on, the "alleyway" or "passageway" plan did not. After a decade or so, two-story I houses were being built with Type b, room-and-hall plans (Fig. 12). The local vernacular tradition had expunged a foreign element derived from North American neoclassical high-style architecture.

The facade geometry and fenestration patterns of these houses are complex. By looking at the base module as it grew through various stages and plans, it was possible to establish four facade classes on the basis of two geometric principles—symmetry and axiality. A symmetrical facade was balanced upon a center line; an asymmetrical facade had one opening (usually the door) adjusted from six to eighteen inches to the right or left of the center line. The purpose of such a curious deformation was to permit a central partition to be placed at the center line, where the central door might otherwise have been if the rules of facade symmetry had prevailed. The door was adjusted slightly to one side (Fig. 7 Types d4, b-2). This was probably originally done to permit a bedroom to be expanded at the expense of the hall, thus allowing two beds to be placed within it.

The second principle was that of axiality. An axial facade had a door in the middle of the facade, balanced by equal numbers of windows (or doors and windows) on either side. A nonaxial facade had an even number of openings, with none on the midline of the facade. Any combination of the four geometric possibilities was acceptable:

Facade Class	Axiality	Symmetry
1	yes	yes
2	yes	no
3	no	yes
4	no	no

A base module type is composed of one plan type and one facade class. For example, Type b3 is an asymmetrical two-room plan coupled with a nonaxial symmetrical facade in which two or four openings are evenly spaced.

The nineteenth-century vernacular designer-builder soon discovered that internal expansion of the core cottage had limitations. For example, tightly enclosed rectangular cottage modules were rather poorly adapted for the hot, humid tropics. More important, a rectangular cottage was hard to expand once it had been constructed—it was a closed geometric unit, rather than an open, incorporating form. Yet the very essence of vernacular architecture is expansion, particularly under conditions of rapid economic development.

An entirely different approach to cottage expansion was undertaken—*external modular expansion.* This pattern seems to have begun with the addition of a full-length veranda across the front of a modular cottage (Fig. 4), or with a shed room across its rear (Fig. 2). Prior to 1900 it became common practice to extend a rear shed about five feet beyond the side wall of the house. This allowed for the installation of a cooking stove in the extended section, always placed in a downwind position (west or south; Fig. 3). Cooking could proceed without the heat and odors of a cooking fire filling the house. This innovation may be dated to ap-

Fig. 12. Type d3 cottage with MLC1 full second story with piazza. An increasingly popular house type in San Andrés.

proximately 1880, when cast-iron, wood, and later kerosene cooking stoves were introduced. Even though they were temperamental and rather cumbersome, they rendered the external fireside, with all of its disadvantages, superfluous.

The process of external expansion may be described in terms of *levels of modular expansion.* Modular levels are basically independent of the internal plan types. A rectangular core cottage without external additions may be classified as an *MF0 cottage module* (a basic, core cottage module [M], unexpanded [0], on the first floor [F]). Without external additions, a module is classified as a "zero-expanded" cottage, regardless of how simple or complex its internal floor plan. An MF0 module might have one room or six.

A cottage with any combination of a full-length front veranda and a full-width rear shed is designated as an MF1 cottage (Figs. 2–4).[14] Whether one or two extensions are added to the exterior of a cottage is not the critical factor in the determination of modular level. Rather, it is the relationship between the added components of one level and those of the next. Expansion elements of each successive modular level are dependent upon the prior existence of those of an inferior level. Thus, an *MF2 cottage module,* characterized by at least one side piazza (Fig. 8), is dependent on the prior existence of a front piazza (Fig. 4). Side piazzas do not occur on San Andrés cottages unless front piazzas are also present. Of course, both may be added simultaneously in any specific building.

Environmental and siting conditions must be considered. If only one side piazza is added, it is placed in the downwind position so that a connection with the extended portion of the kitchen shed is established. A door is placed in this position to permit the housewife to "back" (carry) groceries directly into the kitchen without passing through the hall (Fig. 8). Once side piazzas have been added to the base module, they can be enclosed and turned into extra bedrooms (Figs. 9, 13). Thus, an MF2b1 cottage could be turned into a four-room-wide house without changing the base module plan type

Fig. 13. Raised type e4 cottage with MF2 side piazza, enclosed, and an MLB1-S shed-roof dormer; North End, San Andrés Island, 1970.

(b1). Whether the side piazzas are enclosed or remain open is immaterial to the designation of the modular level. The enclosure of side piazzas leads directly to a third level of expansion. Certain enclosed-piazza MF2 cottages were expanded once again through the addition of an outside encircling gallery placed around the bedrooms and perhaps across the rear of the building as well. This resulted in an MF3 cottage (Fig. 7 Type J1; Fig. 10).

As the modular cottage was being completely encircled in piazzas and sheds, a different direction of external modular expansion was also being adopted—*loft expansion.* A major problem in tropical vernacular architecture was how to make the loft more livable. The intense solar radiation experienced at between 12 and 13 degrees north latitude meant that living under the eaves during the day was not comfortable. Yet the loft with its steeply pitched roof was potentially usable space that could not be ignored in houses where every square inch was needed.

Designers experimented with a variety of strategies for expanding the loft. Three different bases for expansion may be described: Type MLA0 was an unexpanded "low-loft" cottage. The rafters rested directly on the same wall plates that supported the ceiling joists (Figs. 2, 14A). Type MLB0 was a "double wall-plate" cottage in which parapet walls extended the height of the front and back walls

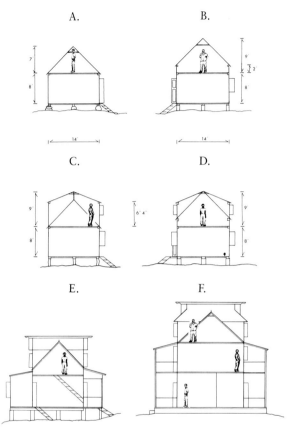

Fig. 14. The relations between loft types and roof types, as seen in section views. A. low-loft MLA0 cottage; B. double-wall-plate (parapeted) cottage, MLB0; C. pack-saddle expansion, MLA1-P; D. shed-roof cottage, MLB1-S; E. MLB1-G "garret" expansion; F. MLA1-H "hip-and-gable" expansion.

above the wall plates (Figs. 4, 14B). Such walls added a foot or more to the height of the loft—sufficient to permit a person to stand and walk under the collar beams that stiffened the rafters. Both strategies are common to Euro-American vernacular traditions. An MLC0 house was a full two-story house (Fig. 12).

Hip roofs were unpopular, not only because of the added expense of fitting members, but also because they were less easily ventilated. In order to cool the loft to make it usable for sleeping, small windows or louvers were placed in the end gables (Fig. 4). Even though these were sometimes ex-

panded into doors (Fig. 15), they remained inadequate—cross-ventilation was required. At first, small gabled dormers were added to the front and rear roof surfaces creating an MLA1-D or MLB1-D (first modular loft expansion-dormer form), but these were still insufficient. Shortly after 1900, a particularly successful designer-builder proposed large, two-window "garret" dormers that capped the entire roof (MLA1-G, or MLB1-G, or garret form).[15] A number of houses were constructed with garrets, but they never became very popular (Fig. 14E). Even taller "hip-and-gable garrets" (MLA1-H or MLB1-H) were constructed on a few houses (Figs. 11, 14F).

About the same time, a New England–style shed dormer was added to some MLB0 "double wall-plate cottages" (those with a parapet wall; see Figs. 4, 13, 14D, 15). This innovation is designated MLB1-S (B class [double wall plate], modular loft expansion level 1, shed-roof form). The "shed-roof dormer" spanned almost the entire roof, leaving only a narrow "wing roof" on each side to indicate the original pitch. The shed-roof dormer was an instant success and was adopted on increasing numbers of cottages in the late nineteenth and early

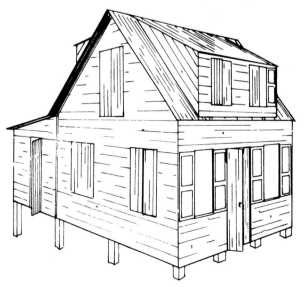

Fig. 15. A New England shed-roof dormer, MLB1-S, added to a type d1 cottage.

twentieth centuries. Three or more shuttered windows could be fitted along the front and rear of an average-size shed-roof dormer, providing abundant cross-ventilation for the loft (Fig. 9).

A similar form of dormer was then designed to accommodate the MLA0 low-loft cottages (those without parapet walls). A cap called a "packsaddle dormer" (MLA1-P) was placed across the entire top of the cottage (Figs. 8, 14C). All forms of dormer (ML) expansion are, of course, independent of all forms of first-floor modular expansion (MF).

One final innovation was necessary to complete the evolution of the form of the San Andrés cottage. The packsaddle and shed-roof dormers were extended forward (and backward) to provide an elevated second-floor front (and rear) porch over the first-floor piazza. The floor of the loft was extended out to the front piazza and rear shed plates, and one or more windows on the face of the dormer were converted into doors (again enhancing loft ventilation).[16] The wing roofs of the shed and packsaddle expansions were integrated with the roofs of the piazza and the rear shed (Fig. 10). Thus, the owner of the house had an elevated porch on the front and rear of his house, whence he could survey all he possessed.

Full, two-story houses became popular in the early decades of the twentieth century. The MLC0, two-story type, was typically built with a full-width second-story piazza, creating an MLC1 (Fig. 12).

Fig. 16. Two-story I house with encircling MF2/MLB2 piazzas. Note stairway location on side piazzas.

An MF2+ML1C could be expanded into an MLC2 house with an encircling gallery on both the first and second floors (Fig. 16). In this case, the stairway to the second floor was often placed outside, on the side piazza.

Another method of vertical expansion has become increasingly popular in the mid-twentieth century. Since all houses of this tradition are raised on piers, it is a simple undertaking to construct tall posts and to mount the entire house eight feet above the ground (Figs. 9, 13). Later, walls may be erected between the posts, creating an enclosed basement, or "bottom house" (Fig. 17). These spaces are used for commercial purposes in town, or for work or added domestic space in rural areas and for rental property. MB0 ground floors are expanded toward the front in order to support the typical wooden first-floor gallery (MB1). If the house has an encircling gallery, an MB2 ground floor is required (Fig. 17). Thus, three-story houses are made possible by application of these various methods of vertical expansion. Even modest-size houses are expanded in this manner.

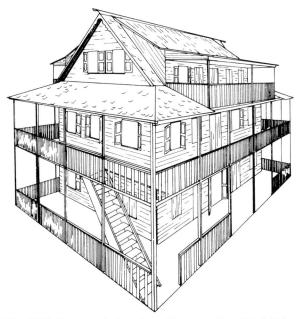

Fig. 17. Fully expanded shed-roof house with MF2, MB2, and ML2-S expansions. Note typical stairway location (stairway to second floor may be located on front piazza).

Fig. 18. "Ungrammatical" house, San Andrés Island.

On San Andrés, the process of evolutionary expansion is continually being experimented with and modified. Many innovations have been tried, but not widely adopted—for example, the enclosure of ML2B second-story piazzas (Fig. 18) and the addition of external stairways to the gabled ends of MF0-MF1 cottages. Such stairs are situated so that they rise to a "flying" door set in the gabled end of the loft—an ingenious connection. Access to the loft of the San Andrés house is traditionally via a winder stair placed inside a rear corner of the core module (Fig. 7 Types b1, d1, d4, f1). Such stairs, however, are so narrow that they prohibit the lifting of double-width beds into the loft—hence the common curiosity of second-story doors that seem to lead nowhere.

Conclusion

In formal terms, *cultural tradition* refers to a set of cultural forms that are united through the operation of a set of fundamental defining rules. These rules account for shared similarities as well as basic variations—a discipline of freedoms and constraints. A sample of related house forms may be viewed as being united through the operation of a grammar that defines the components and sets out the operations employed by designer-builders as they begin the process of composition—the laying out of pleasing forms.

A single cultural tradition may subsume a surprisingly high level of form diversity. Any single realization of a tradition—such as an individual house—may not appear precisely like any other. On the basis of superficial examination, the nature of the relationships between participating members of a cultural tradition may be covert. They may be constructed of different materials, using different techniques, and exhibiting different styles. They may display enormous differences in size. Nevertheless, apparently dissimilar forms may be shown to be united if their internal patterns of organization share definitive common relationships. Such relations are part of the implicit knowledge of a cultural tradition shared by its informed bearers. They may be revealed (or, more properly, reconstructed) through point-by-point comparisons and quantitative analysis of a large number of related forms. The architectonic dynamic expressed in the relationships among the various components of the San Andrés tradition resulted from a piecemeal evolutionary process. Though established as part of a unique historical and evolutionary sequence, and though modified by conditions of climate and siting, the components function synchronically as part of a totally integrated grammatical system—a living cultural tradition. Competence in the system requires a simultaneous knowledge of all of these rules as well as others, beyond the scope of this essay.

Employing a method such as the one suggested here, any cottage of this tradition can be economically described by a simple listing of the modular levels of its various floors, together with a plan and facade type.[17] Despite individual innovations and unique modifications, all houses of the San Andrés tradition share much in common. All are based around an approximately 5:7 MF0 core module derived from an archetypical geometric image. It

matters not that this image results from a long-obsolete method of layout. Although the MF0 cottage core may be the product of a primitive and ancient technology, its geometric legacy remains part of a vital aesthetic expressed in every participating house.

Once established, the core module was modified—expanded and contracted—according to new principles. The basic, underlying contrast between internal and external modular expansion, and the complex relations between them, characterize not only the vernacular of the southwest Caribbean Sea but also the vernacular architecture of the southeastern United States. There is a close link, for example, between the traditional solutions to expansion adopted by the vernacular builders of San Andrés and those of the North Carolina Tidewater and of Creole Louisiana. The analysis of the evolution of such solutions in different locations may, one day, lead us to a more fruitful and penetrating understanding of the nature of Creole and other American vernacular traditions.[18]

CHRIS WILSON

PITCHED ROOFS OVER FLAT
THE EMERGENCE OF A NEW BUILDING
TRADITION IN HISPANIC NEW MEXICO

Spanish settlement in New Mexico was confined to a small area along the upper Rio Grande, roughly from Albuquerque north to Taos, for nearly two centuries following the first settlement in 1598. Beginning about 1790, a variety of factors triggered a major expansion of this core area. A 1786 peace treaty with the Comanches lessened the threat of attacks by nomadic Indians. The availability of smallpox vaccine after 1805 led to an increase in population beyond what the Rio Grande settlements could support. The opening of the Santa Fe Trail in 1821 and the presence of the U.S. military after 1846 provided cash markets for local products and increased the level of protection from Indian attacks.[1]

The expansion ended about 1880 as Hispanic settlers pushed up against other expanding groups: Anglo-Americans (mainly from the Midwest and Upland South) to the north in Colorado, Anglo-Texans in eastern New Mexico, Chihuahuans in southern New Mexico, Navajos to the west, and Mormons to the northwest. In less than one hundred years, from 1790 to 1880, the area of Hispanic settlement grew tenfold and the population sevenfold, from approximately twelve to eighty thousand. More than half of the territorial expansion occurred in the final three decades, from 1850 to 1880.[2]

The Spanish pioneers who moved outward in all directions from the Rio Grande area carried a shared architectural tradition. The buildings that they constructed, which remain standing by the thousands in New Mexico and southern Colorado, share a basic plan and a common set of materials and construction techniques. A number of local variations of this tradition developed, however, in response to differing climatic conditions, locally available materials, and proximity to the railroad and to neighboring cultures. Mountains that isolate one valley from another encouraged this local variation. Perhaps the most distinctive local style developed in the six villages of the Tierra Amarilla area.

There, as elsewhere in Hispanic New Mexico, houses have single-file plans, corrugated metal roofs, walls of adobe, and horizontal logs or vertical logs (*jacal*). In Tierra Amarilla, however, the roof is often raised on a tall parapet wall to create a second-story space used for bedrooms as well as for storage. These story-and-a-half houses frequently have dormers, gable balconies, and porches lining two and sometimes three sides of the building. These porch and roof features were introduced into the region by Anglo-Americans and integrated by Hispanic builders into their previously flat-roofed building tradition. By the early 1880s, a localized, hybrid architecture had taken shape, one that predominated in the valley through World War II and continues to influence building even today. This distinctive local architecture offers a vivid demonstration of historian Eric C. Wolf's adage that "populations construct their cultures in interaction with one another, and not in isolation."[3] Individual builders found typical as well as idiosyncratic ways to combine Anglo-American innovations with the regional Hispanic building tradition, itself the product of earlier interchange between Spanish colonists and native Americans.

The New Mexican Hispanic building tradition is modular; the basic building unit is the single room.[4] A family generally began by building a single, self-sufficient room, usually rectangular in shape with a single door on one of the long sides. Research on Hispanic houses elsewhere in New Mexico suggests that in the mid-nineteenth century, even in large houses, a single room often served as the focus of all household activities: sleeping, cooking, eating, bathing, and entertaining.[5] As the growth of the family required, and as resources allowed, additional rooms were added.

Each new room was essentially like the first, a separate module with its own exterior door. Changes in materials from one room to the next are clearly visible in some deteriorating Tierra Amarilla houses. In better-maintained houses, plaster conceals the underlying material, whether adobe or log or a combination of the two. This change of materials from one room to the next is one sign of the additive, modular tradition. Another is the frequent occurrence of steps between rooms, a result of rooms being built directly on the ground and following the slope of the building site.

While each room typically had a door to the outside, there were not always interior connecting doors. Movement from room to room often occurred, instead, outside the house. The narrow porches frequently added after 1880 sheltered this exterior circulation. Interior doors between rooms were added in some houses as late as the 1950s.

Many one- and two-room houses still stand in the Tierra Amarilla villages, although none are occupied. Most houses consist of three or four rooms arranged in a single file. If more rooms were added, a corner was usually turned to form an L-shaped or U-shaped house. The presence of more than five rooms (and doors) frequently indicates a row of two or more connected houses that were originally occupied by related families. Underlying this additive process was the Spanish ideal of the courtyard house of fifteen or so rooms arranged in a square or rectangle to form an enclosed patio. Some full-courtyard houses were built in the Hispanic homeland along the upper Rio Grande, but no Tierra Amarilla houses achieved this form, in part because the development of second-story living space redirected later additions upward.

The first sawmills were established in New Mexico shortly after the American occupation of 1846, and milled lumber and wooden roofing shingles became widely available with the arrival of the railroad in 1880. The availability of these materials, coupled with the influx of Anglo-American carpenters, led to the incorporation of the pitched gable roof into the Hispanic builders' repertory. The vast majority of Hispanic houses, particularly north of Albuquerque, now have pitched roofs, either from original construction or through the remodeling of earlier flat-roofed houses. The storage attics that these roofs create, like the rooms below, are conceived as discrete units with their own exterior, gable-end doors reached by ladders. The attics of many Tierra Amarilla houses are used in this manner only for storage and the drying of food.

With the coming of the first sawmills, carpenters began fabricating simple Greek Revival details for door, windows, and porches. After the arrival of the railroad, lumberyards began supplying New Mexican builders with stock wooden details successively in Italianate, Queen Anne, and Classical modes. The availability of lumber also allowed log construction to be superseded by a variety of horizontal and vertical plank construction forms. Plank construction was typically finished with wooden lath and earthen plaster both inside and out.

These, then, were the norms of the New Mexican Hispanic building tradition during the late nineteenth and early twentieth centuries: adobe or log construction, single-file plans with multiple exterior doors, steeply pitched roofs over storage attics, and a sprinkling of modest, contemporary wood detailing.[6] A good example of these characteristics is the Rascon house, which stood in Los Ojos until it was demolished about 1985. It began in the late nineteenth century as a *fuerte*—a one-room, flat-roofed, hewn-log house. A three-room addition built early this century consisted of hori-

Fig. 1. Valdez house, Los Ojos, begun about 1865.

zontal planks covered with lath and earthen plaster, the form of construction that superseded log construction locally about 1900. The addition was leveled on a partial stone foundation, but its floor stood seven inches lower than that of the original cabin. The pitched roof, with two dormers on the front side, was added at the same time as the three-room addition, along with the interior stairs and a partition dividing the original cabin into two rooms. Multiroom additions and the partitioning of existing large rooms often indicate the development of specialized rooms—a kitchen, a parlor, bedrooms, or storage.

The Valdez house (Figs. 1 and 2) is a more elaborate example of the local type. The continuous slope of the roof over the porch disguises the story-and-a-half construction. Like the Rascon house, this house was also built in stages. The original flat-roofed, one-room house was constructed about 1865. The two rooms added twenty years later stand fourteen inches higher than the original portion, necessitating steps between rooms and on the porch. This addition of about 1885 also created second-story bedrooms and storage under a unifying gable roof. The stock Queen Anne porch posts, brackets, and ridge crest finials (since removed)

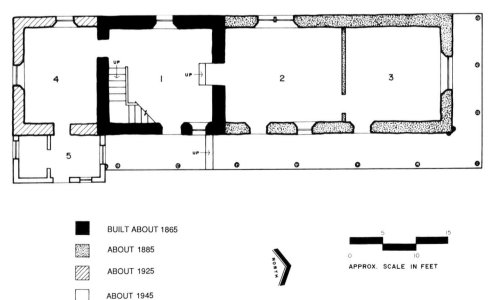

BUILT ABOUT 1865

ABOUT 1885

ABOUT 1925

ABOUT 1945

NORTH

APPROX. SCALE IN FEET

Fig. 2. Valdez house, plan. (Drawing by Jim Caufield and Mary Caufield)

added a fashionable touch. In this century, the new shed-roofed kitchen and finally a small bathroom were added. Although the narrow porch serves as an exterior corridor, the primary circulation on the ground floor is inside, from room to room.

The first pitched roofs in the area were built at Camp Plummer (later called Fort Lowell), which was active from 1865 to 1869.[7] A historic bird's-eye view and a plan of the camp show the officers' quarters consisting of four separate units each composed of sixteen-foot-square modules (Fig. 3). The five-room commander's quarters (second from the right) had a centered door flanked by symmetrically placed windows. The front entrance opened onto a fourteen-foot-wide room, which served as a corridor to the rooms on either side. In the three-room junior officers' quarters, the front door opened onto a similar public room, which probably served as a living room and led to a bedroom to the side and to what may have been a kitchen at the rear.

Five Tierra Amarilla houses combine features from the commander's quarters and the smaller junior officers' quarters to form a distinctive local house type. One example, situated close to the fort site, is commonly referred to as the Officer's house. The Sanchez house (Figs. 4 and 5), two miles to the north, was built about 1880 of adobe, using a five-room T-shaped plan. Its distinctive facade symmetry, with a window on either side of a tight window/door/window group, which characterizes this local Officer's house type, is adapted from the commander's unit.

In terms of circulation, the Officer's house plan translates the popular Anglo-American center-passage house plan into the sixteen-foot-square modules of the log fort and of the local Hispanic tradition. The front door opens into a living room, which doubles as a passageway to the dining room and kitchen at the rear and to bedrooms on either side. The stairs in the kitchen lead to second-floor bedrooms and storage. This floor plan can be viewed as the L-shaped junior officers' quarters with another room added to the side of the entry room, in the manner of the commander's quarters, and with an extra room placed to the rear, perhaps reflecting the Hispanic linear tradition. (A bathroom and closets were added within the last ten years.) Camp Plummer and the subsequent Officer's house type introduced pitched roofs, facade symmetry, and the separation of public and private space into individual rooms. Military post construction had a similar impact on local architecture throughout the Southwest.[8]

The arrival of the railroad in 1880 greatly affected both the economy and the architecture of Tierra Amarilla. While no builders or carpenters are listed on the 1870 census enumeration sheets, fourteen carpenters, three masons, and a bricklayer appear on those from 1880, twelve with Hispanic surnames and six with non-Hispanic names. A handful of local houses adopted Anglo-American house plans outright. One of these was a two-story, two-room-deep, hipped-roof type with a centered entrance and centered halls on both floors. The origin of this symmetrical double-pile

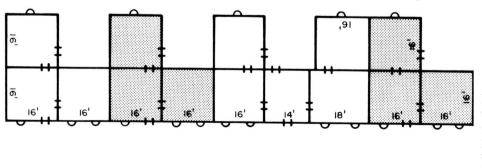

Fig. 3. Officers' Quarters, Camp Plummer, 1867. (Redrawn from historic plan [see note 7] with shading added to every other unit by Jim Caufield and Mary Caufield)

DOORS   WINDOWS

plan can be traced back through the Greek Revival to the Georgian house of the English Colonial period.[9] Indeed, most examples of this type in the Tierra Amarilla area have Greek Revival detailing. Six of these center-passage houses were built during the 1880s for wealthy Hispanic livestock own-

Fig. 4. Sanchez-March house, north of Los Ojos, built about 1885.

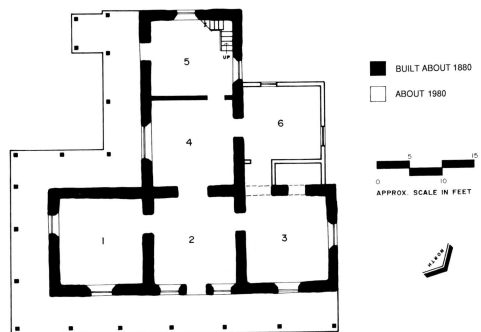

BUILT ABOUT 1880

ABOUT 1980

APPROX. SCALE IN FEET

Fig. 5. Sanchez-March house, plan. (Drawing by Jim Caufield and Mary Caufield)

ers and merchants. The Jose R. Martinez house (Figs. 6 and 7) in Tierra Amarilla is a good example of the local interpretation of the type. Interestingly, a subsequent addition to this structure follows the Hispanic linear tradition.

Another Anglo-American house plan adapted locally was the one-story, double-pile, hipped cottage. The best example of this type, the Lopez house in Los Ojos, has symmetrically placed windows, doors, and rooms, like the two-story mansions (Fig. 8). But its centered hall extends only halfway into the house: at the front of the house, the hall is flanked on either side by a pair of rooms, but this hall opens directly into the middle of the three rooms at the back. These two house types introduced the hipped roof and center halls and reinforced other design elements already suggested by the Officer's house type.

Most Hispanic builders, however, chose to adopt one or two new elements—the hipped or gabled roof, facade symmetry, or a full second story—while retaining the local tradition of linear accretion. The builder of the two-room-wide, two-room-deep Frank Esquibel house in Tierra Amarilla, for instance, continued the tradition of an exterior door for each room, but arranged the two front doors symmetrically. This builder also combined a hipped roof with the story-and-a-half form normally used only with linear houses.

Another approach to the combination of a second story with the Hispanic linear tradition was taken by the builder of the L-shaped Lente house in Los Ojos. In a sense, this house is a traditional, six-room, U-shaped house, split in half and stacked in two stories. By wrapping the two-story porch around the house, the builder maintained access to each room's exterior door. Although this is an efficient solution, only three local houses combine a full two-story porch with a linear plan, and the four-square Esquibel house is unlike any other remaining local house.

The more typical two-story houses in the area use the story-and-a-half form with gable or wall dormers. A similar story-and-a-half form with ga-

Fig. 6. Jose R. Martinez house, Tierra Amarilla, begun about 1885.

ble and wall dormers was common to Gothic Revival houses built across the country from the 1840s to the 1880s.[10] Relatively few examples of this form are found in New Mexico, however, and none remain in Chama, the closest Anglo-American community. Drawings of Gothic Revival cottages did appear in house pattern books that may have been seen by local builders.

Only two other concentrations of story-and-a-half houses exist in the Hispanic core of northern New Mexico and southern Colorado: one in Wagon Mound, New Mexico, and the other in the San Luis valley of Colorado. The houses in both of these areas lack the gable balconies and elaborate porches of Tierra Amarilla. While Wagon Mound is over one hundred miles to the east, on the far side of two mountain ranges, contact between La Tierra Amarilla and the San Luis valley, fifty miles to the northeast, has been common since the 1860s.[11] The story-and-a-half form appears to have been introduced to the San Luis valley through an enclave of Mormon villages—Richfield, Sanford, and Manassa—established starting in 1878.[12]

By the early 1880s, a number of symmetrical story-and-a-half houses had been constructed in these new Mormon communities of the San Luis

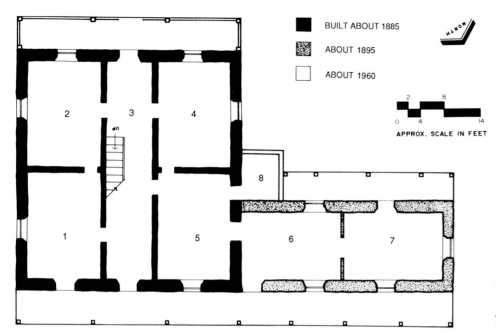

BUILT ABOUT 1885

ABOUT 1895

ABOUT 1960

APPROX. SCALE IN FEET

Fig. 7. Jose R. Martinez house, plan. (Drawing by Jim Caufield and Mary Caufield)

Valley, houses similar to those of the Sanpete valley around Manti, Utah, from which many of the settlers had come. These houses employ both hall-and-parlor and center-passage plans and, on the exterior, a centered gable dormer with a door that opens onto a balcony over the entrance porch. These gable dormers are also often flanked by wall dormers.[13] The Vigil-Chavez house in San Pedro, Colorado, began as a flat-roofed, linear, three-room house but was later expanded under the influence of the Mormon houses. The builder reconciled the Hispanic requirement for an exterior door to each room with the Mormon-introduced facade symmetry by providing a door to the front off the middle room and a pair of symmetrically placed doors to the rear off the side rooms.

There is some historic documentation suggesting direct contact between La Tierra Amarilla and the Mormon communities. However, Mormon architectural ideas may well have been passed through the intermediate Hispanic villages of the San Luis valley.[14] Tierra Amarilla builders adopted the story-and-a-half form and either wall or gable dormers, but not both dormer types in any one house.

In contrast to the symmetrical facades of the Mormon houses, the dormers and multiple doors of Tierra Amarilla houses are located informally, in relation to interior spaces rather than for exterior formality. In addition to architectural features, Mormon hay derricks were also adopted in the Tierra Amarilla area.[15] Hispanic-Mormon contact seems apparent from these material culture features and logical given the proximity of the two

Fig. 8. Lopez house, ca. 1895, Los Ojos.

groups. Indeed, cultural influence moved the opposite direction: Mormons learned to make adobes, which they called Spanish bricks, from Hispanics. And, in the San Luis valley, Hispanic villagers provided food and shelter to help sustain the Mormons through their first winter.[16]

The balconies of Tierra Amarilla houses are located on gable ends, unlike the facade balconies of Mormon houses or the balconies of the local two-story, center-hall houses. The gable-end balconies continue the traditional linear axis of expansion. These balconies extend the long, narrow porches, which connect the multiple exterior doors, around the corner and up to the attic door. It is an easy progression from a ladder reaching a gable door to permanent exterior stairs, and from that to the extension of the gabled roof over the stairway, and finally to a full balcony.

The Fernando Martinez house in Los Brazos (Figs. 9 and 10) is one of the largest, most elaborate examples of the distinctive Tierra Amarilla house type and of the gradual growth of a house along with a family. According to family tradition, the original three-room, flat-roofed, adobe house was built in 1868. Fernando married Soledad in 1876; as children began to arrive in the 1880s, the house was expanded by a fourth room on the ground floor and a pitched roof that created three additional rooms (above rooms 1–3). The family grew to eight children, and in 1910 Fernando built a large building, thirty feet to the south, which housed a grocery on the ground floor and a three-room residence above. In 1912, the family built the large wing on the north of the original house for the oldest son, Pedro. Another son, Jose Espiridion, first inherited the store, which later passed to Fernando, Jr. After Fernando's death in 1914, Soledad remained with the younger children in rooms 1 and 2 of the original house and those directly above. Two of the sons formed two-room households with a kitchen/parlor on the ground floor and a bedroom above: Jose del Carmen in room 3 and the one above, and Onecimo in room 4 and above. A pantry and the first bathroom were added to the rear (room 8 and part of 9) about 1925.

By the mid-1940s, the house was compartmentalized into three households with separate owners, and the doors were blocked between rooms 2 and 3 and between 4 and 5. Over a number of years, Medardo Sanchez and his wife, Clorinda, a granddaughter of Fernando, Sr., purchased the separate sections from relatives, and in 1986 they converted the house into a bed-and-breakfast inn. The second floor was divided into seven bedrooms, two baths, and a sitting room.

Bathrooms and kitchens containing modern utilities, which have been added to local houses since about 1925, are generally shed roofed and about evenly divided between those added on axis with the other rooms, in the traditional linear fash-

Fig. 9. Fernando Martinez house, Los Brazos, begun about 1868.

ion, and those added to the rear of the building. The most significant factor in determining where these additions were positioned appears to have been the relationship of the house to the property line. The rear additions also may reflect the acceptance of two-room-deep floor plans, those plans introduced through the one- and two-story, double-pile Anglo-American houses. There is also a distant precedent for two-room-deep linear plans in the Hispanic tradition seen in Santa Fe, most notably in the Palace of the Governors, and the more urban areas of Mexico.[17] This does not prove that local builders knew of these precedents, however, since the compositional logic of the Hispanic tradition allowed for two-room-deep plans so long as each room had an exterior door, whether front- or rear-facing.

The pattern of linear additions seen in the houses also shaped outbuildings and barns. The basic, modular unit for service buildings is the rectangular log crib, generally with a door and sometimes a window in one long side. Additional units (sometimes with a different log-notching style) were added in linear fashion but one room's width away

from the first section. The span between the units was then bridged by log cross-beams, and the rear wall was completed with *jacal* or vertical wood planks. These barns were originally flat-roofed and piled high in the fall with hay. Most barns were given pitched roofs, and many of these employed plank walls to raise the gable roof, as with the half-story wall of local houses. A dormer door or a simple break in this plank wall allowed access to the hayloft. Shed-roofed rooms sometimes were added at the ends of these barns, and a variety of small sheds and outbuildings complemented the typical barnyard.

In the Spanish tradition, residences and outbuildings were often arranged into a single rectangular courtyard unit known as a *casa corral*.[18] The residence generally stood at the front along the street, with the farm buildings to the rear and, if necessary, an adobe wall completing the enclosed compound. A few larger examples, in older communities such as Santa Fe and Taos, had a full residential courtyard with a second, attached corral courtyard to the rear.

This tradition underlies the placing of many Ti-

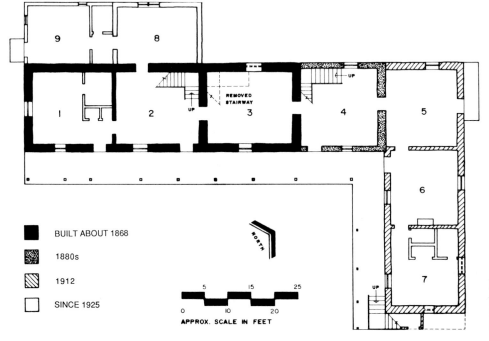

BUILT ABOUT 1868

1880s

1912

SINCE 1925

APPROX. SCALE IN FEET

Fig. 10. Fernando Martinez house, plan. (Drawing by Jim Caufield and Mary Caufield)

erra Amarilla buildings, such as the house and barn complex built by Gumercindo Salazar (Fig. 11) in La Puente during the 1890s. The house (1 on the plan) was destroyed by a fire in the early 1980s. It stood at the front of the complex, but with a porch facing the street and a fenced front yard in the Anglo-American style. The large barn (6), hog pens (5), a chicken coop (4), a portion of the neighbor's *jacal* and horizontal log outbuilding (10), and a six-foot-high plank fence completed the corral compound. One of the barn's log cribs stored tools and farm implements; the other, which is earthen plastered, probably was used to store grain. The middle section of the barn formed a stable for Salazar's team of horses, and the hayloft ran above all three sections. In addition to the workhorses, hogs, and chickens, sheep were occasionally kept in the compound at shearing time. A three-foot-tall wire fence separated the corral from a women's work space along the rear of the house. There, in easy proximity, were the well (2) located in the kitchen; the *horno* (9), an outdoor adobe oven used for baking bread and drying food; a log room with an exca-

vated storage cellar (3); and a garden plot (11).

A few traditional houses were built after World War II, but the static population created no great demand for new construction. In recent years, many young couples have preferred to purchase a mobile home, which brings with it convenient financing and a full set of modern conveniences. Many mobile homes stand beside ancestral houses gradually disintegrating in the elements. Federal funding for housing, while it was still available, was directed into a HUD tract development of standard houses rather than being used to recondition existing houses or to subsidize local vernacular construction.

But the local building tradition does continue in a handful of owner-built homes. One house, for instance, is under construction by Gumercindo Salazar of La Puente, a junior-high school computer and math teacher, sheep rancher, and founding member of a local economic development cooperative. He began to build anew after the house erected by his grandfather (and previously discussed) was destroyed by fire early in the 1980s.

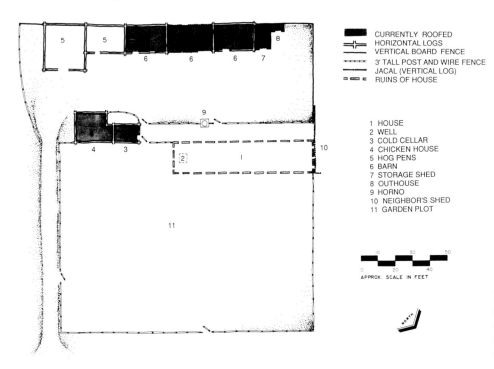

CURRENTLY ROOFED
HORIZONTAL LOGS
VERTICAL BOARD FENCE
3' TALL POST AND WIRE FENCE
JACAL (VERTICAL LOG)
RUINS OF HOUSE

1 HOUSE
2 WELL
3 COLD CELLAR
4 CHICKEN HOUSE
5 HOG PENS
6 BARN
7 STORAGE SHED
8 OUTHOUSE
9 HORNO
10 NEIGHBOR'S SHED
11 GARDEN PLOT

APPROX. SCALE IN FEET

NORTH

Fig. 11. Gumercindo Salazar house-barn-corral complex, plan, La Puente. (Drawing by Jim Caufield and Mary Caufield)

The new house is of wood frame construction, with a layer of insulation inside and, outside, a layer of adobes, many of which were salvaged from his grandfather's house. The ground floor is a basic two-bedroom ranch-style plan with an over-size kitchen and living room, ample enough to accommodate large family gatherings. The upper level, though, has the traditional half-story design, with wall dormers and a gable-end door.

* * *

There was substantial innovation in the architecture of Tierra Amarilla, especially during the last three decades of the nineteenth century. In most cases, changes were brought about through contact with Fort Lowell, the railroad town of Chama, itinerant carpenters, and, most likely, Mormon influences transmitted through the Hispanic villages of southern Colorado's San Luis valley. Although it is tempting to read such innovation as evidence of general cultural change, even as a direct measure of the degree of acculturation, archaeologists and cultural anthropologists have cautioned that it is difficult, if not impossible, to infer beliefs, values, and identity from physical artifacts alone.[19] It has often been asserted that isolated, relatively homogeneous populations such as the settlers of Tierra Amarilla have less need for overt demonstrations of ethnic identity than urban populations in daily contact with other cultural groups. If this is so, then there may have been little need or inclination to employ architecture as a symbol of cultural identity in Tierra Amarilla.

The amount of highly visible ornament and the number of formal architectural innovations derived from Anglo-American sources do demonstrate a negative proposition—that architecture was not employed as a symbol of Hispanic identity (as it would be elsewhere in the state this century with the advent of the Spanish Pueblo Revival style). However, the opposite, positive proposition—that these changes in Tierra Amarilla architecture indicate a desire for assimilation—can not be stated with equal certainty. The adoption of the

pitched roof may have been primarily functional: the pitched roof better protects a house from moisture than a flat earthen roof. Likewise, the elevation of the roof an extra two or three feet above the flat roof doubled the usable interior space derived from the purchase of relatively expensive roofing materials. However, these roofing changes and fashionable ornamental vocabularies, especially when combined with a new house type such as the two-story, center-passage plan, may also have expressed a desire to be modern and progressive.

That the tradition of incremental accretion and linear plans remained widespread, even if combined with roofing and ornamental innovations, reveals a conservatism in the spatial design aesthetic and, by implication, in social use patterns within households. While the average farmer/stockmen continued significant aspects of the Hispanic building tradition such as the linear plan, wealthy merchants and large sheep owners tended to be those who first and most completely adopted architectural innovations such as the double-pile plan. The wealthy were primarily Hispanic, although they also included two Hispanic women who married an Irishmen and a French Canadian. The economic position of the wealthy derived from family capital or access to outside capital with which to stock a store or to let out sheep to others on *partido*—a form of livestock sharecropping.[20] The wealthy also maintained personal and business ties with the economic elite outside the immediate area, especially in Santa Fe; they also had the ability and inclination to either send their children away to boarding school or hire a family tutor. While the wealthy of Tierra Amarilla continued to share food preferences, language, and religion with their neighbors, their houses, social connections, and education set them apart. Architecture may well have functioned as a sign of economic class: not merely as an indication of the wealth to build a fashionable new house, but also a sign of identification with an emerging social class and a progressive entrepreneurial spirit linked to the rise of mercantile capitalism in the West.[21]

CHARLES BERGENGREN

THE CYCLE OF TRANSFORMATIONS IN SCHAEFFERSTOWN, PENNSYLVANIA, HOUSES

The area of Schaefferstown, Pennsylvania, in the southeast corner of the Lebanon valley, was first settled by Palatine immigrants in the early 1730s and bears the unmistakable imprint of their German architectural heritage.[1] An unusual number of Germanic house types can be found in the area; in fact, some of these buildings first inspired the definition of their types.[2] Most if not all of these buildings, however, were altered during the late eighteenth or early nineteenth centuries according to the needs and values of succeeding generations. To a large degree, these transformations followed patterns familiar in other parts of the country—a movement from social openness to closure and from an irregular fenestration to one of increasing symmetry and formality.[3] The story of architectural use and re-use did not stop there, however. Significant waves of remodelings occurred as well in the second half of the twentieth century. Although seemingly unconnected, these periods of architectural revision may in fact be seen as part of a larger cycle of transformation in which the changes wrought by previous generations were in many cases undone and the social openness of the early German period was recapitulated in a new form. This essay follows this cycle through several generations of architectural changes, using statistics derived from an intensive study of a single small town and ending with a consideration of that town's most recent renovations.[4]

Schaefferstown is a town of some five thousand people located at the foot of the iron-bearing "Furnace Hills," on the southern edge of the Lebanon valley, in Lebanon County, Pennsylvania. The area was settled with scattered farms in the early eighteenth century, with a few buildings just to the north belonging to a well-traveled group of Palatine Germans, who had spent time in England and then New York before arriving in the Schaefferstown area around 1723. The town itself was laid out sometime between 1740 and 1758 using a Philadelphia-type central square and grid plan—clearly baroque in spirit—by Alexander Schaeffer, from the Odenwald hills outside Heidelberg. Within approximately one mile of the Market Square (a zone that includes much of the surrounding farmland), thirty-nine houses remain that can be safely dated to the eighteenth century. Of these, fully thirty (or 76 percent) were of the well-known German *flurkuchenhaus,* or "open kitchen" type (sometimes also called the "continental German" type).[5] This house type is well represented in Schaefferstown by the story-and-a-half log house built for locksmith Philip Brecht about 1760 (Fig. 1). The floor plan consists of three rooms: a long and narrow hearth room or kitchen to one side of a chimney stack, with a squarish *stube,* or parlor, in front of a narrow *kammer,* or bedroom, behind it on the other side of the stack. Although one-, two-, and four-room variants also occur, the diagnostic feature unifying this type is that the front

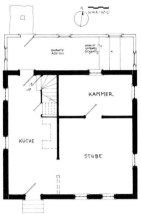

Fig. 1. The Philip Brecht house, circa 1760, west elevation and first-floor plan.

door enters directly into the multipurpose cooking and dwelling room, the one where the hearth was located.[6] A glance at this spatial configuration tells us that whoever passed through the front door of such a house entered directly into the main social space of the dwelling; there were no barriers between visitors and the work, mess, play, and comfort areas of the house. Contemporary pictorial evidence suggests that the obligatory hospitality of the era was encouraged by the habit of leaving the front door invitingly ajar and, during the day at least, expecting even strangers to enter without knocking.[7]

A second important eighteenth-century house type in Schaefferstown is the *kreuzehaus,* or "cross-plan" house, of which three examples remain (or 8 percent). The *kreuzehaus* consists of four rooms of different sizes clustered with the pairs of larger and smaller rooms diagonally opposite. Though there are variations, this house type is generally characterized by a partition in front of the hearth that closes off the hearth or kitchen from the front door, creating a small entry room (Fig. 2). Though this house type was rare in eighteenth-century Schaefferstown, it has antecedents in Germany, with at least three examples of separate houses (and twenty-one more variants as parts of housebarns) to be found in the folios of the Verband Deutsche Architekten.[8] The American *kreuzehausen* became common, however, in the nineteenth

century, with thirty-seven of them (or 40 percent of the nineteenth-century houses) to be found in Shaefferstown alone.

An additional four eighteenth-century houses in Schaefferstown (10.5 percent) are variants of the *durchgangigen* house type. This word literally translates as "through-hallway," but it is significant that there are really two subtypes of these eighteenth-century center-passage plans. The most numerous (with three local examples) is an asymmetrical plan (Fig. 3) having deep roots in the peasant architecture of Germany (four examples of this type are in the Verband's folios, with ten more as parts of housebarns).[9] This traditional version of the *durchgangigen* house features a long narrow passage with an enclosed rear-facing stairway. Such a stair can be seen from the rear door, to which it opens directly, but is virtually invisible from the front entrance.

A final house form in Schaefferstown during the

Fig. 2. Lynn Wenger's house, first-floor plan, typical of the eighteenth-century *kreuzehaus* type.

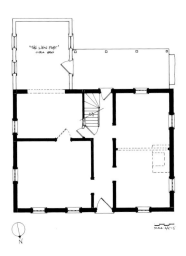

Fig. 3. Lyle Krall's house, north facade and first-floor plan, a late eighteenth-century *durchgangigen* type.

eighteenth century was the full Baroque, or center-passage, house: grand and imposing as befitting the Age of Absolutism on the Continent. It is important to remember that though this house type is usually given the name of an English king, it represents the triumph of Renaissance ideals of harmony and proportion as they were commonly manifested in northern Europe—Germany, Holland, Scandinavia, and England—during the period of the Baroque. These houses have the symmetry of windows and of rooms, and especially the broad imposing passage and the elegant forward-facing stairway, that make the kind of social and class statement often associated with the "Georgian" style (Fig. 4).

Given their age, it is not surprising that most (thirty-two, or a full 82 percent) of Schaeffers-town's eighteenth-century houses have undergone major alterations.[10] Documenting and dating the changes, however, reveals two significant periods of rebuilding. During the first period of transformation, in the late eighteenth and early nineteenth centuries, two trends can be detected: an early acceptance of stoves for heating and an increase in the number of rooms in the house. The rooms, it should be noted, also became smaller and the activities associated with them more specifically focused. The second period of remodeling occurred in the late twentieth century, and curiously in-

volved a return to the original social configurations of the initial settlement period.

Although only one example of the Baroque formality of the full Georgian house type remains from eighteenth-century Schaefferstown, the presence of this new and conspicuously elite form among wealthy (and mostly English) Pennsylvanians did have its impact. New construction in the nineteenth century reflects both superficial exterior modifications—a nod to visible fashion—and more fundamental changes in the interior plan, denoting a shift toward a more closed social behavior. Fifteen percent of Schaefferstown's early nineteenth-century houses were variations on the Georgian plan, with its full central passage. These

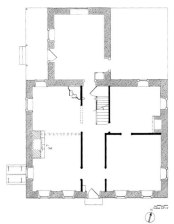

Fig. 4. Bill and Deborah Tice's house, first-floor plan, the eighteenth-century Georgian type.

passages were of the kind useful only for increasing privacy in the house—making it possible for the inhabitants to pass between rooms without "intruding" upon people occupying the other rooms—and especially for making an outward show of that privacy. In a house with such a passage it was also possible to make visitors wait to be received into the sociable areas of the house. Houses with such wide center passages were built as late as 1890 in Schaefferstown.

Older forms, too, continued to be built in the nineteenth century but now showed signs of the increasing trend toward internal privacy. Thirty-two percent of the town's nineteenth-century houses were of the open, direct-entry *flurkuchenhaus* type. A quarter of these had balanced four-bay facades with two doors, thus achieving a symmetrical Georgianized appearance on the outside while preserving the older German plan on the interior.[11] However, 41 percent of the town's nineteenth-century houses were of the *kreuzehaus* type, a type that had been utilized only rarely in the eighteenth century. These houses were built with increasing symmetry, both internal and external. The *kreuzehaus* became extremely popular in the nineteenth century; when outfitted with the externally "Georgianizing" symmetry of two front

Fig. 5. John Robert's house, the "Pennsylvania Farmhouse" type.

doors (as well over half of them are), it is often referred to as the "Pennsylvania Farmhouse" type (Fig. 5). It is important to note that in terms of interior spacial/social arrangements, the *kreuzehaus*/Pennsylvania Farmhouse type represents a compromise between the openness of the *flurkuchenhaus* and the closure of the Baroque/Georgian house, for while the kitchen is indeed closed off from the front door, the resulting room is not merely a corridor between rooms but can be used as a social space—a second parlor or living room—on its own. In this way the Pennsylvania Germans were in fact more progressive than those in other colonies (such as New England) who often kept an entirely traditional floor plan inside their modernized—Georgianized—exteriors.[12]

In the face of the changes in architectural thinking that occurred during the nineteenth century, Shaefferstown's eighteenth-century houses were frequently brought up-to-date. Many early houses—82 percent—underwent significant alterations, and six examples (15 percent) exist in which the open *flurkuchen* plan was converted to the closed *kreuzehaus* or Pennsylvania Farmhouse type, as early as the late eighteenth or early nineteenth century. Though such a change could be accomplished by simply inserting a single partition on the front side of the hearth, the entire first floor of the original house could also be gutted and the interior rebuilt, a seeming extravagance in view of the relatively modest shift in placement of some of the walls. The increase in the number of rooms may well be related to a heightened need for privacy in the early nineteenth century, when these changes were made. It is also surely related to the greater conceptual partitioning of functions such as work and pleasure, eating and cleaning, sleeping and socializing, that was a characteristic effect of the Enlightenment on American houses generally.

Doors also gravitated to more symmetrical positions on facades, and windows were sometimes shifted to more evenly spaced positions as well, even in the amply thick walls of fieldstone masonry. In short, in Schaefferstown as elsewhere, the organic irregularities of earlier house types were discarded for a more formal, "rational" exterior appearance and a more formal, compartmentalized interior.

The single most common change made to early houses in Shaefferstown during the first wave of transformations was the removal (in 77 percent of the houses surveyed) of the original fireboxes and chimneys (Fig. 6). Such alterations indicate a major change in the method of heating houses—from fireplaces to stoves—and possibly of cooking and food preparation as well. While it is difficult to know just when such changes were made (in one case the chimney was removed in sections), the architectural evidence does suggest that when remodeling did begin, the chimney was the first thing to go. In at least one house the chimney was removed before the end of the eighteenth century; another house, clearly of late eighteenth-century construction, apparently never had fireboxes at all. The examples of alterations to accommodate freestanding iron stoves in Schaefferstown are significantly earlier than similar changes in other areas such as New England and may be related to both the well-established German tradition of heating with attached five-plate stoves[13] and the prominence of iron foundries producing these stoves as early as 1758 in the "Furnace Hills" just south of town. Indeed it would have been hard to remain unaware of the Elizabeth Furnace in particular, what with its immediate proximity and the flamboyance of its ironmaster, the self-styled baron Heinrich Wilhelm von Steigel.[14]

Perhaps most telling, in five instances (13 percent of the total) when the center chimney was removed, it was replaced by a partition forming a center passage. In some cases, the stair, however elaborate, remained facing the rear door; in others it faces the front but is tucked out of sight, like the enclosed stairs of old. In the Sheetz house (see fig. 11) the windows and doors were realigned to allow a symmetrical plan, and a broad hallway was installed, displaying the forward-facing staircases so typical of the prestigious Baroque-Georgian ideal.

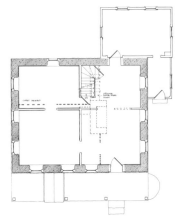

Fig. 6. Leon Kline's house, first-floor plan, showing the location of the original fireplace and stone steps to the basement, with the relocated walls and steps superimposed thereon.

*   *   *

If a house can undergo a major alteration to suit the changing needs of one generation, there is no reason it cannot happen again. The form of a house keeps changing to match the life-style of its owners; that which was put in in the nineteenth century can readily be taken out (or moved, or reoriented) in the twentieth. Houses, thus, are not immutable, and it is that, if anything, which makes them records of ongoing history.

In the last twenty years there has been a renewed wave of modernizations and remodelings in Schaefferstown houses. Much of this recent work has, like that of previous periods, been concerned with the stylistic looks of the houses, the cosmetic veneer (whether inside or out). Common to these changes have been the updating of trim or renewing of tired walls with a skin of manufactured (smoother, cleaner, and often vinyl) siding for exteriors or paneling for interiors.

Other changes are more substantial, involving functional rearrangements in the way a house is used, and thus alterations to the spaces in which people live. The two most visible trends in recent years are a return to larger rooms and the finding of new uses for the space that was the central passage.

In the case of the central passage, the primary function of this space as a social statement and possibly as a barrier to entry into the more private zones of the house never did sit well with the Pennsylvania German farmers. Such an explanation of the fancy woodwork in them or the imposing vistas from the door simply (and rightly) elicits befuddlement today: "Why would they want to do that, who would they be showing off to?" A farm community of any kind requires more than occasional cooperation among its members, and particularly with the Pennsylvania German plain sects—Amish, Mennonites, Brethren—the cooperative ideal is made a religious virtue. In an egalitarian ethos, ostentatious behavior is dimly regarded indeed.[15]

In Schaefferstown, the central passage has met with a number of different fates, none of them nice. In the northern sections of the United States passages are generally not so commodious as those in southern houses, so adaptive reuse of the space as a parlor or bedroom does not seem to be feasible. In some cases the elegantly finished space is simply left unused or used only as a passage. In several instances, the restoration ethos of the current owners (often commuting sons and daughters of local farmers, or retired professional people from outside town) allows them to set an antique side table or two in the passage, thus approximat-ing with this display of heritage the original function of social distinction that the space connotes.[16] But mostly the passages are obliterated: either the partition wall is removed altogether and the passage reabsorbed into a surrounding room, or the hall is cut up into unrecognizable closets and cubbyholes. In the Alice Bomberger house, built in 1884, Leroy Shaak has opened his passage up into the living room (Fig. 7). But Dr. Zimmerman, in his early nineteenth-century Georgian plan house, has cleverly turned the bannister and newel of his stairway (formerly in a broad passageway) to face into the living room instead and has cut the rest of the passage into closets and patient examination rooms. In my favorite example of center-hall "abuse," it is locally related that Niles Laser, a former owner of Abrahm Zimmerman's house, butchered a pig in that passage, hardly an activity in keeping with the showy cutout balusters visible on the stairs. Abrahm Zimmerman has also cut away part of the wall to incorporate the "front" door (which leads to the cornfields, actually) into the living room, and boxed off the rest of the passage for a bathroom (Fig. 8).

In fact, installing a bathroom in a section of the hall has been the most logical solution for many Schaefferstown residents: the resulting rooms are about the right size, and they are also just off a convenient traffic route (the stairs). No less than

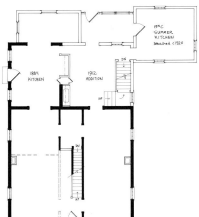

Fig. 7. The Alice Bomberger house, 1884 (Leroy Shaak's), first-floor plan, a nineteenth-century Georgian type with central-passage wall removed, and view of enlarged living room, looking toward the front door.

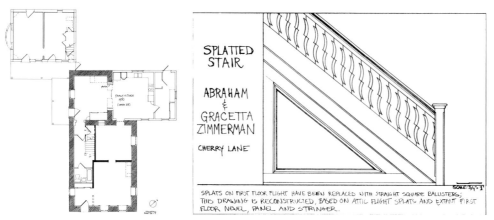

SPLATTED
STAIR

ABRAHAM
&
GRACETTA
ZIMMERMAN

CHERRY LANE

SCALE: 3/4"= 1'

SPLATS ON FIRST FLOOR FLIGHT HAVE BEEN REPLACED WITH STRAIGHT SQUARE BALUSTERS;
THIS DRAWING IS RECONSTRUCTED, BASED ON ATTIC FLIGHT SPLATS AND EXTANT FIRST
FLOOR NEWEL, PANEL AND STRINGER.

Fig. 8. Abrahm Zimmerman's house, first-floor plan and the splatted stair, scene of a hog butchering by Niles Laser.

six households in Schaefferstown have opted for this solution; an equal number have made closets in this space, and some have done both. In one instance, a very fancy piece of Rococo hardware, a center door pull, intended for a very courtly two-handed (and thus bowing) entrance into a room, is now used to hang up a son's bath towel.

The second major trend in contemporary renovations has been to increase the size of the rooms. Within this work a pattern of motivation may be found: although some gentlemen farmers and professional types are restoring their houses to their idea of a past aesthetic, more of the local farmers, many from "plain" backgrounds such as Amish, Mennonite, or Brethren, are making modern renovations (Formica and all) that nevertheless return the social and spatial configurations of their houses to the openness familiar to their ancestors. Though the results are similar (enlarged rooms), the values embodied are almost opposite: a romantic evocation of the past expressing status on one hand, and a practical expansion of home that expresses a continuity of family and community values on the other.

A nineteenth-century precursor to these spatial changes and enlargements is the David Zug house, built for a miller on Old Mill Road in 1850. It is a bankhouse, with a full-length porch across the front on the main level. The plan features one open room all across the front of the house inside the porch (despite the two doors entering into it). Behind this expansive room a stair, enclosed between two smaller rooms, rises to a landing in the center (Fig. 9).

The Zug house is unique within the study area, and I have heard of only one other like it, a house built by a first-generation immigrant to Wisconsin.[17] It was undoubtably avant-garde for its day, imitating perhaps the large double parlors found in urban houses such as Philadelphia's Willig house, in the upscale nineteenth-century development of the 900 block of Spruce Street.[18] However, many other houses in Shaefferstown have (by 1989) had a partition removed to create this effect, most within present memory. Sometimes it is the partition along the center hall that is removed, or in the case of a Pennsylvania farmhouse, two rooms front to back can melt into one. Often, the very partition that had Georgianized the house in one century—for instance the one that bisected the kitchen of Lyle Krall's *durchgangigen* house—is jettisoned to create the spacious, gracious feel of today (see Fig. 3).

In nine cases this renovation has resulted in a large living room, much like those common in the standard suburban ranch house of the 1960s. But even more significantly, in seven cases it is the original open kitchen that has been reconstituted, al-

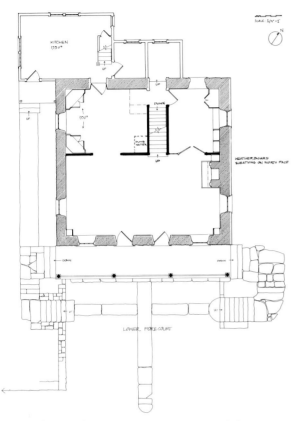

Fig. 9. The David S. Zug house, 1850, ground-floor plan.

very early house, rebuilt the enormous hearth and central chimney stack, and even more painstakingly handcrafted the appropriate hewn moldings to re-create his original *flurkuchen* plan. The space this rarely used fireplace consumes is eloquent testimony to its importance as a statement of pride in the antiquity and true magnificence of the house. Though farm families often also take enormous pride and care in their houses, such a huge feature as an original hearth cannot be suffered if it serves only (or even primarily) for display; the one still extant at the Johanes Phillippi house, for instance, has had a desk built into it, taking advantage of not only the space but also the radiant heat from the modern furnace flue routed up through it.

An additional contrast between the professional family's restoration ethos and the Amish and Mennonite farm family's adaptive (or traditional) pattern of reuse is in the choice of location for new kitchen additions. The professional families often put such a modern feature discretely (and more privately) to the rear. For example, Dr. Zimmerman's kitchen is now in the circa 1900 addition on the original rear of the house, and his breezy "Florida room," where all the informal living of the house seems to take place, is an ell adjacent to this kitchen, and thus set well back from the front.

The farming households, for their part, have generally built an entirely new kitchen in the last ten years or so, to suit the large family gatherings on which their culture thrives, and they have generally put it on the functional, if not the formal, front of the house. During my fieldwork, I was swept into one of the giant meals/gatherings, for which these huge rooms are designed, on an ordinary Sunday afternoon. There were over fifty people present, including great-grandchildren. But whether these kitchens are newly built or literally carved out of other parts of the house—in one case a large section of the rear masonry wall was removed and an I-beam installed to carry the upper floor—they are put at the front of the traffic flow, usually in the corner closest to both the outside road and the barns, from which visitors (who in-

beit sometimes in a slightly different position. In six of these examples the current configuration represents the second (or third) transformation that the house has undergone. In only one case are these new *flurkuchen* or open kitchen spaces the result of conscious restoration: rather, occurring chiefly in Amish and Mennonite farming households, they are the clear result of a continuity of life-style and the social functioning of the rooms.

The kitchen additions of professional families contrast with those of farm families. The professional families have tended to restore their houses to the original pattern for aesthetic reasons, while the farm families remodel to suit their needs, without reference to notions of "authenticity." Thus, Ken Eckert, a field manager at IBM, carefully removed the nineteenth-century accretions to his

Fig. 10. The Landis Place, circa 1750, reconstruction of dwelling periods I–III and view of the new kitchen, from the door.

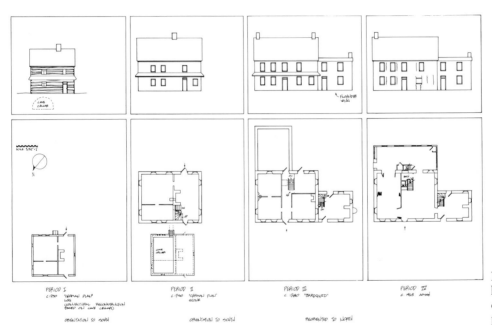

Fig. 11. The Peter Sheetz house, circa 1750, developmental sequence, periods I–VI.

variably arrive by vehicle and park by the barns) and family (working in the barns) would approach. Thus these new spaces restore the activities, and particularly the hospitality, of the open kitchen found in the early *flurkuchenhausen*.

If the room is simply appended to the old house, the new doors to these kitchens become the only ones ever used. Thus, the Mennonite farmer Dan-

iel Hoover completely blocked up his center passage (itself already from the second period of construction) with a closet and bath, and further blocked the former front door with cartons and boxes. In addition, he not only removed one of the Georgian partitions—making a nice large living room—but also added a commodious wing with its own kitchen entrance onto the east gable (Fig.

10). And rather than a fixed work "island," the Hoover's new kitchen has a dining table at the center, easy to move and regroup with other temporary tables for the really big gatherings. An upholstered chair is just visible in the foreground of the photograph, and a sofa and another easy chair sit along the wall of the old house (out of view to the right), making other combinations of activities (sociable and light work) possible and comfortable.[19]

Whereas the Mennonite families within the study zone seem to have preferred to add large side wings for their kitchens, in the one Amish household that fell within the study area, the old Sheetz place, the family kitchen was re-created almost exactly where it had been to begin with. This large stone house was grand enough in 1797 to have provoked a disinherited daughter, Elizabeth, and her husband, John Hauer, to contract murder for want of it.[20] The house has been through at least three stages of construction and remodeling, all subsequent to the building of an early log house of which all that remains is a "cave" cellar under the front yard (Fig. 11). The present house began life as a *flurkuchenhaus,* but then (with its orientation reversed) was Baroqued or Georgianized; that is, the chimney was removed and the center hall put through. To accommodate the large meetings of the contemporary Amish community (each family hosts a Sunday worship in turn), nearly every one of the Georgian partitions have now been removed. Some were replaced by folding walls, which pre-

served the spatial dimensions of the parlor and master bedroom but allowed those areas to be used for very large gatherings. As for the central hallway, a bath was tucked under the stair landing and a closet to the front of that, but the rest of it was removed altogether. Thus the original front door to the *flurkuchen* kitchen (now at the rear) was reunited with the newer front door to the hallway, making again a large open room with doors to the front and the back. With the central fireplace long gone, and the smaller gable fireplace gone too, the resulting room is bigger than any that preceded it. But with the front door altogether removed for the summer (as is the Amish habit), and the gas stove cookers looking into the yard along the front wall, this room re-creates the spatial, functional, and social aspects of the traditional *flurkuchen* plan more completely than any other in town.

Clearly, the reconstitution of the open kitchen in this Amish household was not a result of a restoration ethos but rather proceeded from a continuity of values within these communities over the centuries. The privatistic (or fashionable) needs of the late eighteenth or early nineteenth centuries, when these houses were first transformed to Georgian or *kreuzehaus* plans, no longer (and probably never did) sit well in the households of strongly communal groups; the enormous family gatherings of the Mennonites and the religious gatherings of the Amish have caused the reinstitution of the *flurkuchen* floor plans of the forefathers.

WILLIAM CHAPMAN

SLAVE VILLAGES IN THE DANISH WEST INDIES
CHANGES OF THE LATE EIGHTEENTH
AND EARLY NINETEENTH CENTURIES

Slave villages in the Danish West Indies (now the U.S. Virgin Islands) underwent a dramatic transformation in the last decade of the eighteenth century and the first two decades of the nineteenth. The main change was from relatively impermanent wattle-and-daub structures to more durable masonry buildings. Another change was the introduction of multi-room tenements, with as many as three or four residential units, usually of two rooms each, replacing the earlier, single-unit cottages. All of these changes were informed, in turn, by what appears to be a direct borrowing of European architectural ideas, including greater formality, a reliance on classicizing motifs, as well as a more consistent use of European-derived framing and masonry techniques.

This shift in the characteristics of plantation slave villages has been documented on other Caribbean islands as well. Jerome S. Handler and Frederick W. Lange, for example, suggest a comparable change in Barbados slave housing during the same period, and a similar sequence of development took place in Jamaica and on other sugar-planting islands.[1] Generally, such changes have been interpreted as part of an almost isolated evolutionary process, one shared from island to island, but with little sense of interrelationship.[2] While the influence of European design traditions is widely recognized as overriding and contribut-

ing ultimately to the synthesis represented in West Indian vernacular building traditions,[3] the specific sources for such influences, at least in the case of slave villages, have been largely neglected. This study, then, is an attempt to look more closely at available architectural sources, especially literary sources, and also to examine the wider social and economic context for the changes in slave housing design during the late eighteenth and early nineteenth centuries—changes that ultimately would have an impact on West Indian vernacular architecture during the latter part of the nineteenth century and on into the twentieth century as well.

The Danish islands were only three of many West Indian islands dominated by plantation-based and slave-dependent sugar production during the eighteenth and early nineteenth centuries. The Danes themselves were relative latecomers to the Caribbean, having acquired St. Thomas, an important trading center, in the 1670s and claimed St. John, despite protests from the British on adjacent islands, in 1718.[4] St. Croix, the most important sugar-producing island held by the Danes during the eighteenth century, was acquired by purchase from the French Crown only in 1733. All three Danish-held islands were dominated by sugar production; and plantations operated on all the islands, though with diminishing importance on St. Thomas and St. John by the middle part of the eighteenth century. During the latter part of the century, St. Croix dominated the economic and cultural life of the Danish islands and also played a significant role in international affairs, with strong ties to Great Britain, Holland, and the American colonies. Most of the examples used in this study are taken from St. Croix. However, it should be emphasized that comparable changes also occurred among slave housing on other islands.

Culturally, the Danish West Indies were not strictly Danish. The Danish West India and Guinea Company, which regulated the islands until 1754, when the Danish Crown assumed authority, emphasized rapid development and had an unusually open immigration policy in order to attain that goal. Many of the planters were Dutch and English, with English and Irish planters probably dominating by the late eighteenth century. Dutch merchants, as well as a significant number of French Huguenots and Sephardic Jews, the latter coming to the islands by way of Brazil, dominated much of the commercial life of the islands. African slaves, numerically the greatest single population group, were from a number of places in West Africa, the majority imported through the Danish-held Gold Coast in what is now Ghana. While government business was mostly conducted in Danish, Dutch and Dutch Creole were widely spoken, Dutch Creole mainly by the slave population. By the middle of the eighteenth century, however, most Europeans relied on English; newspapers were typically printed in English from 1750s on, and English was the language of trade. The British planters maintained strong cultural ties with other British islands (as well as the American colonies) throughout the eighteenth and early nineteenth centuries; in addition, the Danish islands were possessed by Great Britain from 1801 to 1802 and from 1807 to 1815, further reinforcing cultural connections and directly affecting architectural ideas.

English and other planters had started sugar estates on St. Thomas, St. John, and St. Croix by the 1750s. St. Croix, with its rich and relatively flat lands, dominated Danish West Indian sugar pro-

duction and offered the greatest opportunities for agricultural development. Following some experimentation with cotton, nearly all plantations had shifted to sugar production by the 1760s.[5] In all there were over three hundred plantations listed by 1754. Most consisted of individual 150-acre plots, though many of these would later become combined holdings. The slave population, upon which development and production were dependent, grew from approximately nine thousand in the 1750s to twenty-two thousand in the 1790s. By 1803, the 181 operating plantations had a slave population of 35,235, most living in agricultural villages attached to estates. The population of white planters and administrators grew from around two thousand to a little over three thousand during the same period.[6]

Early slave housing on all the islands consisted almost universally of wattle-and-daub cottages, roofed with grass or sugarcane leaves (Fig. 1). Contemporary illustrations of slave housing indicate that much of it conformed to types found on other Caribbean islands as well. Illustrations from F. C. Von Meley's 1779 map of the Crown-held

Fig. 1. Traditional Virgin Islands housing, ca. 1890. Such housing, common into the twentieth century, probably preserved many features of earlier wattle-and-daub slave residences on the sugar estates. (Charles Taylor, *An Island of the Sea and a Few Words on St. Croix* [St. Thomas: For the Author, 1895], opp. 20).

section of St. Croix show plantation villages of approximately thirty separate houses, arranged neatly in rows, with adjacent garden plots.[7] The Danish visitor J. L. Carstens reported finding similar "cane-covered huts," usually with single doors opening into buildings set slightly below grade. He described such buildings as "lying in a group on a plantation . . . [where] they present a whole large village." He found a similar settlement of regularly placed "clay huts" (presumably wattle-and-daub construction) outside Charlotte Amalie, St. Thomas's main town, where both slaves and the island's small free colored population were housed.[8] The military surveyor P. L. Oxholm's detailed cartographic records of the late eighteenth century show a similar pattern for plantation housing, with some villages in large St. Croix estates having as many as seventy to eighty units.[9]

The most detailed description of these estates is found in a two-volume compendium of 1777 by the German Moravian traveler C. G. A. Oldendorp. Oldendorp, who visited the islands and Moravian missions there in 1767–1769, explained that "alongside the plantation buildings, the negro huts stand close together, resembling a little village" (Figs. 2 and 3). A typical sugar estate, he continued, had as many as fifty to sixty houses, all arranged in rows. Those on "the English plantations" were especially "neat and trim."[10] The houses themselves were two-room dwellings, again, as Carstens had explained, set slightly into the ground.

From Oldendorp's descriptions it is clear each house provided a sitting or work room and a smaller sleeping chamber, with each unit providing housing for a single family or several single laborers. The buildings were constructed with four corner stakes driven into the ground. These were forked on the ends to receive "horizontal boards," on which rested pole rafters "which came together in a crest" to form the roof. Further vertical stakes were driven between the posts and "branches . . . woven among these." The whole was plastered with mud and cow dung and covered with a fur-

Fig. 2. View of New Herrnhut, a Moravian-owned plantation in St. Thomas. New Herrnhut was apparently typical of the villages described in Oldendorp. (From *C. G. A. Oldendorps Geschichte der Mission der Evanglischen Brueder auf den Caraibischen Inseln S. Thomas, S. Croix und S. Jan* [Barby: C.F. Laur, (1770)], courtesy the Royal Library, Copenhagen)

ther coat of lime plaster. Floors were unfinished earth, and roofs were covered usually with sugar-cane leaves. There were in most cases several small windows and a single door. "The Negroes," Oldendorp concluded, "seek neither beauty nor comfort in their living quarters. Instead they are satisfied if their basic needs are taken care of in their accommodations."[11]

The origins of the type of house described by Oldendorp are largely open to speculation. Pole-in-ground construction is associated with a number of cultural traditions. Perhaps significantly, it is, according to Jay Edwards, Jean-Pierre Sainton, and others, particularly common among indigenous building traditions, many of which may have been sustained in plantation contexts by Europeans and Africans who inherited those traditions in the New World.[12] The hall-parlor house type described by Oldendorp also is common to European and African traditions and probably cannot be ascribed to any single cultural group, though its use was clearly sustained and encouraged by Europeans, who ultimately, as in other slave-based economies, determined what was to be built. Masonry-reinforced pole-in-ground construction has

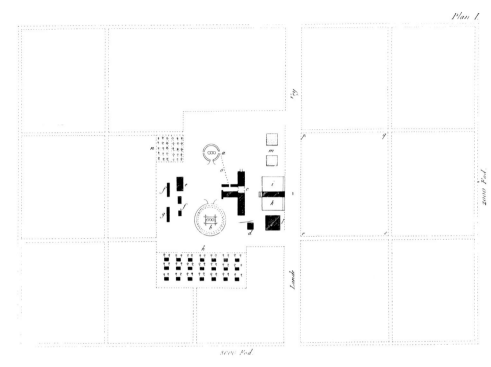

Fig. 3. An idealized version of an eighteenth-century sugar estate, including an extensive slave village. The letters indicate: (a) wind-mill, (b) horse mill, (c) sugar factory, (d) well, (e) planter's or manager's house, (f) servant houses, stables, (g) sick house (for slaves), (h) slave village, (i) cattle pen, (k) mule stable, (l) bagasse (crushed cane) shed, (m) middens (refuse), (n) kitchen gardens, (o) columns supporting the cane juice gutter to the mill, (p–s) agricultural plots. (From P. L. Oxholm, *De Danske Vestindiske Öers Tilstand* [Copenhagen, 1797], courtesy the Royal Library, Copenhagen)

been documented for both plantation houses and utilitarian buildings in the Danish West Indies, mainly on St. Thomas and St. John, from an early period.[13] Whether this practice was widely applied to slave housing is unclear. Most slave housing of the middle part of the eighteenth century appears not to have relied on masonry either for footings or for the reinforcement of vertical posts, and the standard building type described by Oldendorp appears to have been generally accepted.

Significantly, the architecture of the planter class during the same period differed markedly in design and overall character. This would conform to patterns on other islands and to practices observed in other intensive plantation economies, such as in the coastal United States. Most plantation houses, as well as town houses, were constructed of wood (usually sided with cedar shingles), sitting on masonry ground floors or basements.[14] Basements were generally used for storage; upper floors, consisting of central salons with bedrooms and offices, were devoted to domestic life. There were

occasional two-story masonry structures, especially on St. Croix, but these were unusual. Oldendorp explained that "wooden structures are cooler . . . [and] not as easily disjointed and loosened by the usual earthquakes, as the stone ones." Strikingly, wood buildings were also thought to withstand hurricanes better than masonry ones, in obvious contrast to present thinking. Masonry construction was consigned to utilitarian structures, as Oldendorp explained: "Buildings constructed entirely of stone are used for the storage of goods."[15] The shift to stone for slave housing a few years after Oldendorp's visit provides, therefore, a telling insight into the planters' attitudes toward their slaves.

In terms of style or design, the planters' residences, as well as houses for overseers, town houses, and administrative buildings, borrowed both from European vernacular traditions and, most importantly, from the neoclassical canon of the 1600s and 1700s. These more high-style buildings were relatively symmetrical, usually with emphasized central pavilions and supporting wings. Neoclassical embellishments included raised keystones and quoins for masonry elements. Wood quoins and molded entablatures were also widely used. Interior details, including arched screens marking transitions from salons to galleries, were commonly employed, as were classically derived plaster and wood moldings. As on other islands, as well as on North American plantations, slave housing and the planters' buildings coexisted as separate design traditions with little if any mutual borrowing.[16]

While specific dates for the change to masonry construction for slave housing are often difficult to confirm, archaeological evidence and judicious reference to property inventories provide fairly clear evidence that the major shift occurred late in the century, probably after 1790.[17] The earliest of the masonry houses in the Danish Islands appear to be little more than masonry versions of wattle-and-daub structures. Remaining examples at Estate Slob, in the middle of St. Croix's rich central valley and once a part of a village of at least sixty such houses, provide rare insights into eighteenth-century construction techniques. The examples at Slob are two-room units, with exterior dimensions of approximately 16 × 26 (Fig. 4). Walls are of rubble masonry, with cut stone (locally available limestone) and coral blocks used to reinforce corners and window openings. Walls are sixteen to eighteen inches thick, with splayed window and door openings. Roofs are hipped, following both

high-style conventions and the general outline of earlier wattle-and-daub cottages. Until the introduction of sheet-metal roofing in the mid-nineteenth century, most such houses would have been roofed with cane leaves or grass.[18]

In part, the new masonry buildings appear to have been a logical extension of existing housing, though apparently built at a slightly larger scale. Illustrations and descriptions from as early as the 1730s of town buildings, as opposed to plantation properties, suggest that similar two-room masonry units were used by both Europeans and African slaves in urban areas from an early period.[19] The use of masonry for urban building was also encouraged (though not stipulated at this period) in local building codes and later accepted as a matter of self-interest in fire-prone urban areas.[20] The two-room plans, again, have both European and African precedent and cannot be ascribed to any particular cultural preference. However, the use of masonry was clearly a European tradition and conforms to techniques used for manor houses and secondary buildings. Slave dwellings similar to those at Estate Slob were built at several other St. Croix estates during the same period. Sprat Hall, for example, located near the second St. Croix town of Frederiksted, was originally Dutch-owned but purchased by the British planter William Rogiers (Rogers) in 1759 and by a Dr. George Gordon in 1775. By the late eighteenth century it had a masonry village. Gordon housed a slave population of 111, as of 1790, in approximately thirty

Fig. 4. Estate Slob 1982, the much altered great-house and five remaining residential units in 1982.

units spread along the hill below the earlier great-house, again in a pattern comparable to that at Slob.[21]

While most of the earliest masonry units were two-room cottages, an alternative tradition is suggested by the impressive fifteen-unit (approximately thirty-room) terrace or row house at Estate Hogansburg, also in the central valley of St. Croix. Hogansburg was owned by the Danish planter Adam Sobotker (Soeboetker) in the 1750s but had descended to his offspring by the 1790s, when the terrace appears to have been built. Measuring 17 × 240 feet overall, the slave housing unit incorporated what amounted to the whole village within a single masonry shelter lining the main estate road leading to the greathouse.[22] Hogansburg's terrace is unusual for this period but suggests a precedent for the terrace housing that became more common later on St. Croix sugar estates. Its architectural pedigree, however, is probably far different from most later row houses on the islands. There is much to suggest that Hogansburg's terrace derives from European terrace housing, common to England and Holland (as well as Denmark) from the late seventeenth century. Examples such as the well-known brick terrace at Tattersall in Lincolnshire especially seem to be of the same general "family."[23]

As with smaller masonry units, there was local precedence for terrace housing as well. Early illustrations and descriptions, including P. L. Oxholm's detailed surveys of the 1770s and 1780s, and some still-existing examples in St. Thomas and St. Croix, suggest that multiunit masonry rows were coming into use in urban settings during the late eighteenth century. These were used to house both household servants and slaves leased out as day laborers by in-town owners.[24] In contrast to later estate row houses, the earliest terraces are relatively wide, usually seventeen to eighteen feet, and are lower in elevation, often extending no more than eight feet above grade. All have irregularly placed windows and doors, unlike later, more uniformly configured estate row houses.

It is clear that a new and separately derived architecture appeared rather suddenly upon the scene, either concurrently with the masonry units at Estate Slob and Hogansburg or, more likely, at a slightly later date. This new architectural tradition can be dated between 1795 or 1800 and 1810, but the newer building types were also constructed into the 1820s and possibly as late as the early 1830s. So widespread was the new slave housing that nearly all of St. Croix's approximately 180 active sugar estates witnessed some degree of slave village rebuilding along new lines.

The new estate housing followed two general patterns: two-unit (four-room) masonry cottages, arranged often along the access road to the estate; and row houses with four or more units (eight or more rooms), arranged as separate residential quarters, usually placed well away from the estate guest house and often adjacent to the extensive sugar-processing complex. Whether reinforcing the formal character of the estate or sited for more utilitarian reasons, the villages were placed on the least usable land, often steep or rocky sites unsuitable for intensive sugarcane production. Almost always they were sited west, or "downwind," of the principal estate residence, a fact long recognized for St. Croix's slave villages in particular.[25]

Good examples of two-unit villages exist at Estate Grand Princess, near Christiansted, where ten two-unit cottages were built by Councilor Heinrich von Schimmelman, probably in the late 1790s; at Estate Diamond Ruby, in the center of the island, where a comparable series of paired, two-room cottages was constructed around the same period; and at Estate Prosperity, in the west end of St. Croix, where an eight-house (sixteen-unit) village was constructed around 1800–1810.[26] All of the newer, two-unit cottages are distinguished from earlier masonry buildings, such as those at Estate Slob, by elevated floors (usually marked by a projecting basement or water table), regularly placed doors and windows, occasional raised window and door surrounds, and, especially, narrower dimensions, usually fifteen feet with internal measurements of about twelve feet.

Variations on the two-unit cottage type, in some ways intermediary between the two principal types suggested, included villages with three-unit and in some cases four-unit cottages (six to eight rooms), also arranged as rows, often (but not always) visually complementing the greathouse. Such villages were built at Estate Enfield Green, again in the west end of St. Croix, at Estate Lower Love, in the central valley, and at nearby Estate Castle Burke. Each followed a similar pattern of uniform rows, with individual structures measuring approximately 15 × 40 feet, with occasional three-unit houses measuring between 52 and 60 feet in length. Again the floors of still-existing examples are about eighteen inches above grade and are nearly always wood; door and window openings are regularly placed, with occasional raised keystones or architraves. Roofs are either hipped or, more commonly, have raised masonry gables, in marked contrast to earlier masonry slave houses, which were uniformly hipped.

A final variation, often associated with larger estates, consisted of separate slave compounds, arranged not in rows along estate approaches, or even in adjacent areas, but in separate walled enclosures. Each usually contained from three to as many as twenty or more multiple-unit terraces. The best St. Croix examples are at Estate Clifton Hill, near the center of the island; Castle Coakley, near Christiansted; and Estate The Williams, located along the coast near Frederiksted. Clifton Hill's village consists of what appear to be five separate, four-unit row houses, located in a compound west of the original greathouse. The complex appears to have been built between 1808 and 1816, when the estate underwent a series of capital improvements overseen by owner Peter Markoe (Marcoe). The slave population numbered 119 in 1816, suggesting that the present complex housed a major portion of the population.[27]

Castle Coakley included a twenty-one-building complex around 1800–1810. Each of the buildings was divided into four two-room units, with each building measuring approximately 14 × 58 feet.

The row houses were uniformly placed along a hillside southwest of the greathouse, close to the sugar factory and other utilitarian estate buildings (Fig. 5). Remnants of a bell tower and perimeter walls are still visible on the north side.[28]

Estate The Williams was first developed in the 1750s and acquired by Augustus Boyd "of London" by 1766. The improved slave houses were probably built after 1794 and possibly as late as 1812, when the property changed hands.[29] The Williams's units are among the longest and most compactly sited on St. Croix. In all there are nine remaining row houses, measuring from about 60 feet to as many as 97 feet in length, with average widths of about 15 feet (Fig. 6). As with Castle Coakley, The Williams's village was enclosed by a wall, into which the outer walls of some of the buildings are incorporated. Unusually, the village occupied a flat and potentially agriculturally productive site, prone to flooding, west of the greathouse near the sugar-processing complex.

All of the larger slave compounds shared features with the two- and three-unit row houses. Floors were raised and nearly always of wood; doors and windows were evenly placed; roofs were usually constructed with raised masonry gables. Exteriors and interiors were finished with lime plaster and often included raised door and window surrounds and projecting basements or water tables. Internal partitions, as with two- and three-unit cottages, were wood, rising to the plate level to allow for internal ventilation.

The newer complexes dramatically changed the landscape of the Danish islands.[30] All of the newer complexes possessed a number of common details, especially a uniformity in dimensions, a comparable rhythm of windows and doors, similar projecting bases, and an increasingly reliance on raised masonry gables. While no complete eighteenth-century roof framing remains, fragments and continuing patterns suggest a similar use of framing techniques, most noticeable in the reliance on collar beams and corner braces. All appear, in short, to share a common pedigree and character.

Fig. 5. Aerial view of Estate Castle Coakley, a still occupied former slave village near the middle of St. Croix. Note the nearby factory complex and animal pens to the left and the windmill and greathouse above the village, at the top of the photograph. (Betty Ausherman, 1983)

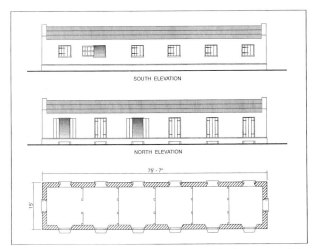

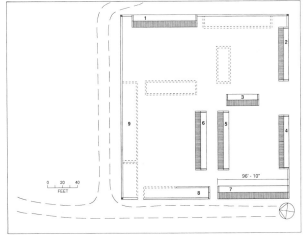

Fig. 6. Estate The Williams, a compound of nine remaining row houses on the western shore of St. Croix, built ca. 1810–1815. Overview and plan and elevation of one row-house unit. (Brian Davis, Cartographic Services, University of Georgia)

Where did this newer building form come from? The dramatic changes in the character and quality of slave houses in St. Croix become understandable only in the wider context of agricultural and industrial practices during this period. Particularly in Great Britain, the late eighteenth century had been a time of wide-reaching reappraisals, especially in the area of farming practices and farm organization.[31] British landowners began a dramatic series of farm improvements during the eighteenth century, ranging from experimentation with new crops and rotational practices to redesigning of farm buildings and, most significantly for this study, improvements to estate workers' housing. What is now known as the enclosure movement was causing the dislocation of many rural villages, whose inhabitants, in turn, required new housing. What were viewed as model housing units were constructed at a number of Britain landed estates. Lord Harcourt, for example, built a much publicized pair of terraces at Nuneham Courtenay in 1766, replacing an earlier village.[32]

Landowner initiatives were reinforced by a growing body of architectural literature. Following a tradition extending back to Serlio's designs for cottages of the 1540s,[33] British architects designed new experimental houses and published treatises on appropriate designs for agricultural and industrial housing. Nathaniel Kent's *Hints to Gentlemen of Landed Property* of 1775 was the first such book to offer plans for cottages, but similar pattern books were issued by John Miller in 1789 and by John Plaw in 1790. The progressive farming chronicle *The Annals of Agriculture* also published drawings for agricultural housing, as well as reviewing recent examples, commenting on materials and design and generally endorsing newer, more hygienic and comfortable residences for agricultural workers.[34]

Without doubt the most important manual, and the most significant in terms of West Indian construction, was John Wood's *A Series of Plans for Cottages or Habitations of the Labourer either in Husbandry or the Mechanic Arts,* first published in 1781, reprinted in 1792, and reissued in "A New Edition" in 1806. Wood, who with his father was responsible for the design of much of the English resort town of Bath, was clearly committed to the cause of improved housing. "No architect," he commented, "had, as yet, thought it worth his while to offer the publick any well constructed plans for cottages."[35]

After examining existing housing, which he found to be "wet and damp . . . or in low dreary spots," and, significantly, interviewing cottage residents, Wood arrived at seven basic principles for improved construction: (1) buildings should be "dry and healthy," elevated at least fifteen to eighteen inches above the ground and with walls at least eight feet high; (2) they should be "warm, cheerful and comfortable" with walls at least sixteen inches thick and sufficient windows to provide light; (3) they should be "convenient," with separate rooms for parents and children; (4) internal dimensions should not exceed twelve feet in width, and roofs should be built with collar beams to allow for greater headroom; (5) residential units should be built in pairs or in other combinations for economical reasons; (6) housing should always be built of masonry, with lime mortar and plaster; and (7) a space be set aside for a garden. Roofs, he continued, could be thatched, tiled, or covered with slate; timber was thought to be too susceptible to fire. Plans were provided for two-, three-, and four-unit cottages, usually with hall-parlor layouts reflective of long-standing traditions and the cottagers' own preferences (Fig. 7).

Wood's and other treatises had an important impact on the English-speaking agricultural world. Numerous Wood-inspired cottages and rows were built in Britain, and it is not surprising that Wood's treaties would have had a concomitant impact on estate planning in the colonies, as already evident in the parallels suggested by St. Croix examples. West Indian planters, both in the Danish West Indies and elsewhere, were especially receptive to progressive agricultural ideas. Sugar planting was a capital-intensive and complex industry, involving both agriculture and production.[36] West Indian planters kept abreast of the newest agricultural developments, shared an openness to new procedures, and increasingly experimented with new sugar varieties. In the eighteenth century, a greater number of windmills were introduced, and as early as 1817 on St. Croix the use of imported steam engines to power crushing mills had become common.[37] Sugar production, it should be emphasized, was, in the eyes of contemporaries, a "progressive" industry, despite the seemingly paradoxical reliance on slavery.

West Indian planters had a strong vested interest

in adopting progressive farming measures, including improved housing. Slavery itself was under attack in the 1780s and 1790s. An act to end the slave trade was passed by the Danish government in 1792, and other countries, especially Britain, were ultimately to adopt comparable measures.[38] The late eighteenth-century planters worried that the population necessary to sustain agricultural growth would not be available without the continued infusion of new slaves from Africa. Population figures for St. Croix, for example, during the period between 1780 and 1804 suggest that there was a negative population growth among slaves of 1.1 percent.[39] Obviously, West Indian planters were going to have to improve living conditions in order to maintain the agricultural labor force necessary for continuing production. The connection between adequate housing (and health) and propagation was widely recognized, and this equation was not lost on West Indian planters.

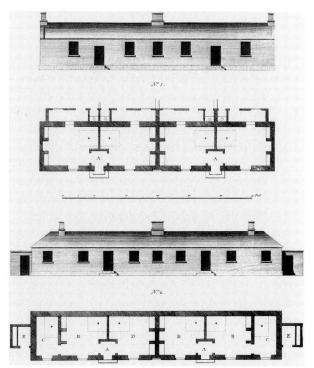

Fig. 7. Plate 3 from John Wood's *A Series of Plans for Cottages or Habitations of the Labourer* (London, 1806).

The attitudes of West Indian planters toward slavery were complicated during this period, just as were those of planters in the slave-owning colonies of North America.[40] Partially in reaction to philanthropic attacks on slavery, West Indian planters increasingly assumed a posture of self-justification. Numerous tracts, as well as reports of West Indian legislative committees, attested to more enlightened treatment of African slaves. A report on "The Condition, Treatment, Rights and Privileges of the Negro Population" on the British-held island of Dominica, printed in 1823, explained, "The state of slavery . . . is soothed and ameliorated by the kindness and humanity of the West Indian Proprietor." Improved housing was an expression of perceived largesse, therefore, as well as a logical outcome of prevalent utilitarianism. A slave "secure in the possession of a comfortable house," the same report continued, could "never know the misery of seeing his family and children thrown from the shelter of his roof, by the cruelty of a creditor or the hardships of the times."[41]

Finally, the very fact of the wealth produced by sugar contributed to the improvements in slave housing. The years between 1750 and 1780 had been the main period of growth in sugar profits. In St. Croix, annual production had grown from approximately three thousand hogsheads (a hogshead was equal to fifteen hundred Danish pounds) in 1755 to twenty thousand in 1766.[42] In 1773 over 18 million pounds of sugar were produced in the Danish islands, most of it on St. Croix. Nearly 45 percent of all land on St. Croix was devoted to sugar production by the late 1770s; and though total acreage in cane would begin to decrease toward the beginning of the nineteenth century, overall production rates and prospects for future profits continued until the 1820s.[43]

As a result, funds, mainly in the form of bank and, increasingly in the nineteenth century, government loans were readily available for recapitalization of estates. Also, while sugar production was labor intensive, there were considerable periods of "downtime" for estate laborers, freeing up fieldhands for such projects as the construction of masonry perimeter walls and, especially, masonry animal pens and housing. The periods of 1801–1807 and 1812–1817 were especially boon periods for sugar profits.[44] Not surprisingly, these were the years during which much newer slave village construction occurred.

While the overall context of slave housing is relatively clear, then, the specific architectural influences are more difficult to ascertain. Unfortunately, there are no estate inventories identifying by title books that may have been in the possession of the planters.[45] Considerable circumstantial evidence, however, suggests that Danish West Indian planters would have been aware of current architectural literature. Most planters were well traveled and closely tied to international affairs. Interaction among islands, as well as with port cities such as Philadelphia, was widespread during the late eighteenth and early nineteenth centuries, with many planters traveling to the coastal United States and Europe for both business and pleasure. Planters did read extensively and closely followed journals, news, and fashions.

Architectural fashions were a part of this awareness. Plantation greathouses and various institutional and religious buildings all had an increasingly high-style character by the early nineteenth century. Much of this was pattern-book architecture, with obvious debts to editions of Palladio and Serlio. Classicizing elements, especially projecting quoins, molded entablatures, and freestanding and engaged columns became more common in the nineteenth century, introduced by European-trained craftsmen as well as by architecturally trained building inspectors and surveyors.[46]

The best documentary evidence of planter interest in architecture and the application of architectural ideas to the problem of improved slave housing is found in a short manual titled *Practical Rules for the Management and Medical Treatment of Negro Slaves in the Sugar Colonies,* published in London in 1803 and attributed to a Dr. Collins. Collins was apparently a planter from St. Kitts (St.

Christopher), a Leeward island in close communication with the Danish West Indies. Like other West Indian planters, Collins was concerned with the threatened end of the slave trade and its repercussions for the slave population. "Though the entire abolition of the slave-trade should not take place," he commented, "yet the restrictions already imposed upon it, and which we have reason to suspect will be aggravated by subsequent statutes, from session to session, will tend, in time, either to operate its virtual extinction, or so greatly to enhance the price of negroes, as to leave them within reach only of the opulent." Collins's main recommendation, as a planter with "20 years" experience, was to provide better food, clothing, and housing, which, in turn, would improve the health and reproductive rate of slaves. Such "an expenditure," he suggested, "when judiciously applied, is not a waste, but the investment of a capital with a view of producing a return."[47]

Collins's manual offers specific recommendations for slave housing, and these are strikingly parallel to those set out by Wood for laborers more generally. "Nothing contributes more to the disordering [poor health] of Negroes," he offered, "than bad lodgings."[48] In all, improved housing, according to Collins, offered three things: "the preservation of the health of the negroes"; "their protection from tempest"; and "their security from fire." Collins emphasized that houses should be properly elevated, at least six to eight inches above grade, should ideally be constructed of stone, and should be evenly spaced, at least thirty feet from one another. Most tellingly, he suggested units containing at least two double-roomed residences as the most economical, with the ideal being three units in a single row. Recommended internal dimensions were 12 × 66 feet. This, of course, suggests a striking parallel to both Wood's designs of the same period and to many St. Croix examples.

The new model slave-house ideal exerted a tremendous impact on the design and redevelopment of St. Croix slave villages down to the early part of the nineteenth century. In 1831, for example,

Benjamin De Forest extensively recapitalized his estate, Middle Works, by building an impressive sugar works, stables and animal pens, and a large slave village, lining the hillside, just north of the earlier wattle-and-daub village. This village still exists (Fig. 8), consisting of twenty-one separate row houses, each with five to six bay divisions and three to four units per row. All were built of masonry, with standing gables and other details strikingly similar to the designs offered by Wood and Collins.[49]

DeForest's development, while impressive, was in many ways indicative of changing attitudes to slave housing, especially in the years just prior to emancipation in 1848. Efforts throughout the intervening years centered on estate village improvements. In 1840 an ordinance was passed by the colonial government specifying precise building dimensions and minimal distances between buildings. This law dictated, finally, what many planters already recognized as their own self-interest.

The years from 1790 to the early 1830s were an important period in plantation growth and slave-housing construction in the Danish West Indies. Much of this expansion was underwritten by the great wealth made, or at least promised, by sugar production and motivated by planters' recognition of the need to provide for a population that could no longer be replenished through the once-thriving slave trade. Danish West Indian planters, many of them English or at least English-speaking, saw themselves as part of a new move toward enlightened farm management and the scientific application of new ideas. The general improvement of slave housing was a product of this reassessment and, at least in the Danish Islands, was directly influenced by the architectural literature that reflected and promoted the new approach to agricultural advancement. Planters on St. Croix, as well as on other islands, constructed slave-housing complexes that borrowed many of their details from books, including those published in Great Britain by housing-improvement advocates such as

Fig. 8. The newer slave village of Estate Middle Works, built ca. 1830 and occupied until the 1970s. This photograph was taken in 1983.

John Wood. The resulting buildings were, in a sense, high-style versions of what were essentially vernacular structures, informed both by vernacular preferences in plan and layout and by the joint impulses of utilitarianism and neoclassicism that so characterized this period of both European and West Indian history.

The infusion suggested by Wood's treatise and other mostly English design books would continue to resonate in West Indian architecture well into the twentieth century. Agricultural housing, when it was revived for reorganized estates in the late nineteenth century, continued to repeat the row-house patterns of the early part of the century; though the new "barracks," as they came to be known in the Danish islands, were nearly always constructed of wood rather than masonry. The same was true of urban housing, which proliferated in the post-emancipation years (Fig. 9). Greater availability of timber and other wood products, such as shingles, was probably a major reason for this change of materials, but it is tempting to suggest that perhaps the planters' earlier preferences for wood construction had resurfaced, in a sense, in their new expectations for former slaves. The improved slave housing of the late eighteenth and early nineteenth centuries thus contributed to the late nineteenth-century vernacular of the Danish West Indies. Based on relatively formal architectural precedents, the newer housing types almost completely replaced earlier slave housing and, in turn, contributed to what might be consid-

Fig. 9. Wood frame row house, Frederiksted, St. Croix, in 1982 (now demolished). Such buildings are typical of mostly rental properties built after Emancipation throughout the West Indies and preserve many of the characteristics of slave row houses of an earlier era.

ered the vernacular traditions of the islands. Thus, the architectural literature of the eighteenth and early nineteenth centuries offers another potential source for early African-American housing throughout the British-oriented colonies and former colonies—one that is clearly worth further investigation in both the North American and the Caribbean contexts.

GREGG D. KIMBALL

AFRICAN-VIRGINIANS AND THE VERNACULAR BUILDING TRADITION IN RICHMOND CITY, 1790–1860

Recent scholarship has emphasized the often vague physical and psychological boundaries between Virginia's white and black populations in the colonial period. Mechal Sobel in particular has focused on the interrelationships among blacks and whites in eighteenth-century Virginia and has shown that blacks and whites shared many aspects of the world of work, including the building trades, in which the practices of training and apprenticeship linked white and black craftsmen.[1]

The growth of urban areas in Virginia after the Revolution did not change the colonial tradition of interracial work patterns. The construction of domestic structures in nineteenth-century Richmond was done by whites, free blacks, and slaves in close association, using vernacular forms that have been delineated by Henry Glassie and other students of Virginia's vernacular tradition. A large body of evidence shows both apprenticeships and work relationships among slaves, free blacks, and whites in Richmond. This evidence supports the conclusions of Catherine Bishir, regarding builders in antebellum North Carolina, that "building was accomplished by a mix of black and white artisans and laborers working together in a variety of roles and relationships."[2]

As Richmond developed, however, the role of urban black artisans became more circumscribed.

Fearing competition, native white and immigrant artisans began to protest against slave and free black workmen. The practice of hiring poorly supervised slaves out to the city led to general fears of slave insurrection and disorder, exacerbated by memories of Gabriel Prosser's failed plot in 1800 and Nat Turner's rebellion in 1831. Increased use of slaves as laborers and factory hands emphasized a growing association of blacks with unskilled "nigger work," which was not lost on the white laboring population. Free blacks came under increased legal control and suspicion as they mingled with the growing slave population. These conditions caused tensions between slaves and free blacks and a growing economic and social disparity in the free black and slave community.

The activities of free blacks and slaves in the building trades in the antebellum South have been well documented, if not generally recognized.[3] Richmond was a particularly fertile ground for blacks in these professions due to the rapid and constant development of the city from 1790 to 1860 and the widespread practice of hiring slave artisans from masters to work in the city. Despite the wariness of urban whites toward free blacks and slaves, the black population in Richmond never declined as in other Southern cities.[4]

Large numbers of free blacks and slaves were employed in construction trades as carpenters,

121

plasterers, and bricklayers throughout Richmond's history. The earliest known city census for Richmond, done in 1782, listed four white carpenters. Two of these men owned seven and six tithable slaves (above the age of twelve), respectively, high totals for the sparsely populated town. White carpenter John Hawkins also owned nine slaves under the age of twelve, who may also have been employed as child labor in rough carpentry. Henry Anderson, Richmond's only mason, owned five tithable slaves. Also, two hired slave carpenters were specifically mentioned: James, a slave belonging to Mr. Armistead, and Richard, a carpenter belonging to Edward Harris of James City County.[5]

Slaves employed in the building trades were often hired out to the towns, as were other skilled slaves, and eventually many settled in the cities after the Revolution. The problem of control implicit in slave hiring was reflected in an 1806 Richmond ordinance that changed the organization of the night watch and appointed a "master of police . . . charged with the responsibility of prohibiting slaves from hiring their own time and going at large in the city."[6]

Advertisements for runaways in the *Richmond Enquirer* during the 1820s listed numerous slave craftsmen from other Virginia counties. Masters placed these advertisements in anticipation that their slaves might come to Richmond. Ned, "35 or 40 years of age, a carpenter by trade," ran away from his master's home in Mecklenburg County. Ned had been raised near Winchester, Virginia, and was thought to have been "carried to Richmond by a Negro waggoner from the neighborhood and may stay in the neighborhood of the city some time."[7] Richmond craftsmen also sought the return of slave property. Martin Drewry, a Richmond carpenter, offered a $100 reward for Lewis, a slave carpenter. Lewis bore distinguishing marks related to his profession, including "a knot or scar on one of his feet, occasioned by the cut of an adze," as well as "other similar scars, occasioned from the use of edged tools."[8]

Not only were slaves employed as builders by their white masters and hirers, but some whites apprenticed free blacks in the building trades. George Winston, a Quaker and builder, appears to have apprenticed free blacks almost exclusively. Winston took on several free black orphans and apprenticed as many as thirteen free blacks from 1805 to 1819. The census of 1820 listed twenty-one male free blacks ranging in age from fourteen to twenty-five living with Winston.[9]

In a typical case, the Overseers of the Poor, through the Henrico County courts, placed with "George Winston, House joiner, Daniel, a free black orphan boy to learn the trade art or mystery of a House joiner which the said George now useth and with him as an apprentice to continue and serve from the date hereof until the full end and term of nine years nine months and seven days." The indenture specified good behavior on the part of Daniel and bound Winston to provide "the Apprentice sufficient meal, drink washing and lodging and other necessaries" as well as "twelve dollars for freedom dues."[10] The black artisans trained in Richmond's early days benefited from men like Winston, who taught occupational skills and probably literacy. Winston was a trustee of the Gravely Hill School, a Quaker institution for the education of blacks. While most white builders did not apprentice as many blacks as Winston, they nevertheless made use of black as well as white labor. William Saunders, a Richmond bricklayer, apprenticed two white men, a free black, and a slave between 1812 and 1817.[11]

The 1852 city directory, the only Richmond directory before the Civil War to include a listing of free blacks, shows both the large number and the wide use of free black builders. Out of a list of approximately 150 male free blacks with occupations other than laborer, 16 were carpenters, 6 bricklayers or brickmakers, and 5 plasterers. Moreover, the directory only represented about a fifth of the total free black population. The employment of free black builders by Richmonders was obviously frequent enough to make it expedient to include them in the city directory.[12]

The close association of white and black builders in Richmond facilitated the melding and passing on of common building traditions. The so-called trowel trades, bricklaying and plastering, had a long history of association. This was often due to the frequent employment of blacks as hod carriers and tenders in the most physically demanding aspects of masonry construction. Claudia Dale Goldin reported the case of a Richmond bricklayer and brickmaker in the 1860 census who owned about eighty slaves. In the same census Henry Exall, a Richmond architect, was listed with over forty slaves.[13] By working closely on construction sites blacks often "picked up" their skills through observation and experience, rather than learning them through a formal apprenticeship.[14] Free blacks continued to hold on to their position in the trowel trades even as the general level of skill among free blacks declined in the 1850s. Fifty percent of all plasterers and 17 percent of all bricklayers in Richmond were free blacks in 1860.[15]

Some free blacks did serve formal apprenticeships. In 1850 white plasterer John H. Hillyard and builder Henry J. Goddin both wrote testimonials for Ebenezer Roper, a free black plasterer. Hillyard wrote that Roper "faithfully served his time with me [and] while as an apprentice to me I could trust him to do my best work whether I was present or no" and that Roper was "one of the best plasterers I know of in this place." Goddin, a partner in the building firm of Goddin & Morris, also testified to Roper's skills, mentioning that he had often employed him. Hillyard also testified before the Richmond Hustings Court to Roper's status as a freeborn citizen, as recorded on Roper's "free papers," a document free blacks were required by law to carry as proof they were free.[16]

Such close relationships between black and white workmen were becoming less prevalent by the 1850s. The controversy over free versus slave labor began to emerge in Richmond and other southern cities as more immigrants came to populate the cities and compete with slave and free black labor.[17] Some Richmond mechanics sought to remove slaves from the mechanical professions, declaring, "We do not aim to conflict with the interests of slave owners, but to elevate ourselves as a class from the degrading positions which competition with those who are not citizens of the commonwealth entails upon us."[18]

Entry into the craft professions was traditionally limited through control over apprenticeship. Early unions established strict rules about working with nonunion or unskilled workers and established minimum prices for wages. The earliest Richmond craft unions published constitutions and bylaws regulating prices and conduct. In 1850 the Association of Journeymen Stone-Cutters of the City of Richmond declared, "Each and every Journeyman working piece work, shall be governed by the Richmond Bill of Prices; and each day workman shall work for no less than $1 50 per day." Workmen were forbidden from working with nonunion members, and scabs were to be penalized by a fine of $20. The fear of slave competition was noted in a regulation that "no member of this Association shall work in any shop or yard with a Negro Stone-Cutter, until taken into consideration by this Association."[19]

Opposition to slave workmen was a main feature of white working-class agitation in the 1840s and 1850s. As John O'Brien has noted, white workmen "feared that employers would depress wages, break strikes, circumvent apprenticeship programs, and whip them into line if they had access to slave artisans." O'Brien's work reveals the emerging class conflict between employers and workers over slave labor in the 1847 Tredegar Iron Works strike and during antebellum strikes of the Typographical Union and the Journeymen Stone-Cutters.[20] Some slaveholders worried that putting slaves on a footing with white mechanics might give them false ideas about their station in life and destroy the growing racial stratification of labor. Some scholars have argued that the percentage of skilled workmen in the slave population of southern cities declined in the late antebellum period with the influx of Irish and German workmen and the increased reliance on slaves as industrial workers, and this may well have happened, although the concept of skill in the industrial workplace needs to be more accurately defined. There is no doubt that free blacks were pushed out of, or prevented from entering, some trades, and that a lower percentage of them were artisans and tradesmen than was true for foreign-born or native white male workers by 1860; in fact, slaves even ranked below the Irish.[21] One of the few exceptions to this trend was in the trowel trades, as noted above.

Due to the limited opportunities for free blacks and slaves in the 1850s, men and women who had previously established themselves in small businesses and trades and had become property-holders rose to leadership positions in their community. In 1847 a group of Richmond free blacks, "feeling," as they expressed it, "a deep interest in the welfare of our race," organized the Union Burial Ground Society. The trustees of the society were given a half-acre of land in Henrico County, bought for the society by Peter and Maria S. Roper, a free black husband and wife who had lived in Richmond since the early 1800s. The society was formally established and a constitution adopted on January 23, 1848.[22] The original list of members and trustees included many names from families of distinction in Richmond's black community, such as Roper, Anderson, and Harris.

Distinctions of color were not important among the organizers. Of the thirteen original members that could be reliably located in the 1850 census, eight were listed as black, including two of the trustees, while five were mulatto. Overall, the ratio closely mirrored Richmond's black population as a whole. Although the society was organized by "Free Persons of Color," a section of the cemetery was set aside for the "burial of strangers," and an examination of the cemetery site revealed that the society's founders allowed slaves to own lots and be buried there. Membership in the society was limited to those who could pay the ten-dollar subscription. Of the fourteen original members whose

occupation could be determined from the 1852 city directory and 1850 census, seven were in the building trades, two were blacksmiths, one was a shoemaker, two were laborers, one was a porter, and the only female member was a washerwoman.[23]

The leadership of other black organizations was similarly constituted. Of the thirty First African Baptist Church deacons listed in 1842, thirteen were also enumerated on the 1850 census, and of this number seven were listed as black and six as mulatto. Both slaves and free blacks served as deacons, although free blacks predominated.[24] O'Brien concludes that the deacons of First African Baptist Church were "usually tradesmen and property owners."[25] The common thread that identified these people as black leaders was skill. They included blacksmiths, carpenters, shoemakers, and bricklayers in numbers far in excess of the general population. Craftsmen and artisans were also quite often property owners and ran shops throughout Richmond's commercial and industrial districts.[26]

As the limited wealth of the black community became concentrated among a leadership of artisans and small businessmen, many used their property and skills in practical ways to assist the community. Like Peter and Maria Roper, other blacks contributed property and money to support black institutions. Richard C. Hobson, a barber, purchased his freedom in 1841 and that of his wife and children in 1850. In 1862, Hobson and John Adams, a free black plasterer, served as trustees of Ebenezer Baptist Church and purchased the church property from Robert Ryland, the white minister of First African Baptist Church.[27] Skilled blacks became natural leaders because of their educational advantages and the skills they could contribute, particularly in the building trades. This leadership role also continued after the Civil War. Of the thirty-three blacks who served on the city council and board of aldermen of Richmond from 1871 to 1898, nine were in the building professions, most having been born before 1850.[28]

Richmond's domestic architecture reflects the development of craft traditions involving both black and white builders, as outlined above. Early building reflected a common Virginia tradition of vernacular forms, particularly the translation of the rural cabin and outbuilding into urban forms. Later building shows the transition to the urban side-hall plan and an increased stratification in the style and location of black housing. As racial and class tensions grew in the 1850s, skilled blacks increasingly used architecture to distinguish themselves from the unskilled. Free blacks with economic means increasingly lived in better areas of Richmond in better houses.

Richmond's domestic architecture just after the Revolution was not significantly different from the folk housing that dominated the surrounding countryside. Samuel Mordecai noted in 1860, "Many non-descript specimens of architecture existed, and some still exist in our city. It is only of late years that edifices to which the term architecture can be applied, have been erected." Benjamin Latrobe expressed a similar view in a draft of a letter when he "wrote of the 'unfortunate though cherished mixture of Gothic with refined manners' current in the immature city of Richmond."[29] Latrobe's sketch of a one-story wooden house owned by a Major Watt with its lean-to addition illustrated the artist's idea of "Gothic."

A number of early one-room structures of modest dimensions can be documented in Richmond. The insurance policies of a group of houses owned by Daniel Vandewall, and lived in mostly by free blacks, are typical. One structure is described as "a wooden dwelling house 16 feet by 16 feet one story high—underpinned with brick," with "a wooden shed of 12 feet by 16 feet one story high." The rough elevation on the policy shows chimneys on both the lean-to shed and building (Fig. 1), and photographs indicate the chimneys were constructed of brick.[30] Of the nine policies Vandewall took out in 1818 on properties around the north end of Second and Third streets, four were for wooden one-story buildings of 16 × 16 feet and four were for brick one-story buildings of 18 × 18 feet. The other house was made of brick, measuring 18 × 12. All the houses had wooden roofs. Among the residents of the houses were Patsy Carter "a wooman [sic] of color" and "Bridget Anderson (A negro Woman)."[31] Later residents and purchasers of Vandewall's properties included Mingo Jackson, Lucy Mingo, and Eliza Jackson, all free blacks.[32] The dimensions of these structures are typical of similar buildings found frequently in rural Virginia in the eighteenth century.[33]

The gambrel-roof cottages that show up often in early insurance policies and "give more idea than any other houses left in Richmond of how the city must have looked in the years just after the Revolution" were generally one-room, one-story structures.[34] One of the earliest of these cottages, at 400 Duval Street, was built by or for a free black, Abraham Skipwith, around 1793–1797 (Fig. 2). The one-room house was common to both white and black Richmonders of the artisan and laboring classes from 1790 to 1820.

The double-unit slave quarter was expanded upward in the urban environment (Fig. 3).[35] The double- or triple-unit, two-story brick outbuilding was typical of urban Richmond and influenced the domestic architecture of many Richmond blacks and whites. These structures served as kitchens,

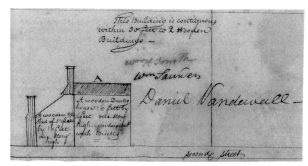

Fig. 1. The one-room cottage or cabin was typical in the antebellum urban environment, displaying common features such as the lean-to addition. Drawing from insurance policy for Daniel Vandewall's property on Second Street, occupied by Nancy Judah, 17 June 1818. (Volume 55, policy number 1157, Mutual Assurance Society Collection, Virginia State Library and Archives, Richmond)

Fig. 2. The gambrel-roofed cottage was a common housing form for both blacks and whites in early Richmond. Roper cottage, 400 West Duval Street, owned by free black Abraham Skipwith, built 1793–1797. Later rebuilt at Sabot, Goochland County. (Palmer Gray Collection, Valentine Museum, Richmond, Virginia)

Fig. 3. The urban outbuilding served multiple functions, including housing for slaves. The double- or triple-unit design was carried over from rural structures, but urban outbuildings were usually two stories and brick by the 1840s. Outbuilding of the Samuel Hardgrove house, 2300 East Grace Street, built ca. 1849. (Photograph by Travis McDonald, 1988)

laundries, servants' quarters, or combinations of the above. Many examples can still be seen in Richmond, and insurance records and photographic evidence indicate it was a common vernacular form.[36] The typical Richmond back building was two stories high, one room deep, and several rooms wide, with two or three separate rooms having entrances. Access to the second floor was usually through an exterior stair built into a full-length, second-floor porch. Urban outbuildings were usually two stories and constructed of brick. These adaptations were important in the urban setting. As in other cities, the need to conserve land on urban lots, the integration of slave housing and work space, and the threat of fire probably all led to the two-story brick design.

The house of William Griffin, a free black carpenter, indicated the use of the double-unit design in other domestic contexts. Griffin may well have been the same "Billy Griffin" who was apprenticed to master builder George Winston in 1819. Griffin's house, constructed circa 1842, was located on McCance Street in the Shockoe valley, where many free blacks and slaves made their homes (Fig. 4). Although its general stylistic lines, particularly its roof, dormers, and end chimneys, made it look like a house of the hall-and-parlor design, the two doors on both the first floor and the basement level indicated a double-unit design. This interior arrangement is confirmed by the observation of Mary Wingfield Scott that "small as it is, the two halves have, oddly enough, belonged to two different owners ever since 1850."[37] The same outbuilding types were used in the houses of whites. Edward McSorley built a house on Venable Street, not far from Griffin's house, in 1845. Once described as a "one story double cottage," this building had a central chimney and two entrances.[38]

The side-passage variations on the Georgian plan common to the Delaware valley and "also the predominant, traditional town house type . . . in cities such as Washington D.C. and Richmond, Virginia" were used extensively, usually in the substantial houses of whites.[39] Houses built in the

Fig. 4. The house of William Griffin, a free black carpenter, on McCance Street, built 1842, shows the influence of the double-unit design on domestic architecture. (Mary Wingfield Scott Collection, Valentine Museum, Richmond, Virginia)

1840s and 1850s by or for free blacks often reduced this plan to a depth of one room and a height of two stories. One might view these structures as "the working man's town house," scaled-down examples of structures found in better neighborhoods (Fig. 5). Built primarily after 1840, these houses reveal the increasing sophistication of the free black community.[40]

As the racial division of work and economics increased in the 1850s, a growing social division among blacks, particularly between skilled free blacks and slaves, began to be manifest. Skilled free blacks began moving away from industrial areas where slaves predominated, forming new churches, burial societies, and social associations. This growing division was reflected in the city's demographics and the architectural choices in Richmond's neighborhoods. Skilled, property-holding free blacks (and urban whites as well) built modest side-hall-plan houses. Industrial slaves and free black laborers continued to live in low-lying areas such as the Shockoe valley, Fulton Bottom, and Penitentiary Bottom, as well as in the alley networks within elite white neighborhoods. The pattern is clearly seen in the development around Ebenezer, or Third African, Baptist Church.

Ebenezer Baptist Church was founded primarily by free blacks who were settling in an area in northwest Richmond away from the confusion and stench of the industrial Shockoe valley in the 1840s and 1850s. The new church members came from First African and Second African Baptist, both located near industrial areas and with overwhelmingly slave memberships. The church was built in 1858 and quickly changed its name from Third African to Ebenezer Baptist Church.[41] Several houses in the vicinity of Ebenezer reflect the status of their owners. John Adams, who had been successful as a plasterer and contractor, had a house at 227 West Leigh Street that he built in 1846, directly across the street from where the church was built (Fig. 6). Adams was "the owner of thirteen houses and lots, the largest number of separate pieces of property held by a free Negro in the entire state."[42] In the late 1850s two free black seamstresses, Catherine Harris and Sophia Hill, built side-by-side houses just east of Adams at 221–223 West Leigh on land they purchased from another free black woman (Fig. 7). These dwellings embodied variations of the urban side-hall plan.[43]

Some free blacks were successful enough to buy even more substantial brick dwellings earlier occupied by whites and chose to live in predominately white neighborhoods. Barber George P. Gray purchased a property at 827 North Second Street in 1851, a central-hall, brick, Georgian-style house as fine as any dwelling in the neighborhood. Another barber, John E. Ferguson, referred to one of his properties in his will as "my Mansion house." Benjamin W. Judah, a shoemaker, lived in a house at Fourth and Leigh streets, a middle-class area

Fig. 5. A common housing form for both whites and blacks was the side-passage plan, two stories high and one or two rooms deep. Many free blacks built houses of this type. Houses of James Sabb (or Saab) and John Jones, free blacks, 512 and 514 West Leigh Street, built 1841–1842. (Mary Wingfield Scott Collection)

Fig. 6. House of John Adams, 227 West Leigh Street, built 1846–1847. (Mary Wingfield Scott Collection)

Fig. 7. Houses of Sophia Hill and Catherine Harris, free black seamstresses, 221–223 West Leigh Street, built 1856. (Mary Wingfield Scott Collection)

populated mostly by whites. Judah owned "more real estate than any other man of this trade in the state," and "his six or more houses and lots had a valuation of $4,300."[44]

The urban outbuildings of Richmond, and the domestic architecture related to them, reflected the lives of industrial slaves and free black laborers. Double- and triple-unit structures with separate entrances were a way to deal with a severe lack of housing and the boarding of industrial slaves and free blacks. The design of tenements and workers' housing in the late antebellum period and into the late nineteenth century reflected the influence of both rural and urban outbuildings.[45]

A common solution to limited space in domestic architecture was to use basements as living areas. A rare black household inventory reflects the use of all available space and the prevalence of slaves boarding out in Richmond. Free black Amanda Cousins's inventory in 1860 included two rooms, a basement, and a kitchen. Cousins took care of her deceased cousin's two children. The two rooms and basement all contained bedsteads and mattresses, with the basement containing two beds.[46] The amount of bedding suggests more occupancy than the three free members of Cousins's household. Indeed, slave boarders often lived with free black workers or relatives. For instance, the will of Anna Thacker provided for the sale of her house in the Shockoe valley and its contents, the proceeds to be given to her slave husband Frank, whom she owned, presumably to buy his freedom. The available wills of free blacks confirm the connections between free blacks and slaves and suggest that the census was an inadequate measure of the size of a typical black household.[47] Skilled free blacks were able to escape to better housing and healthier neighborhoods, but even they might take in relatives or laborers associated with them.

Antebellum black builders and property owners in Richmond drew on well-established vernacular traditions that had been developed by blacks and whites together. The careers of William Griffin and John Adams reflected the changes in that tradition and the social and economic structure of the black community during the antebellum period. Griffin was born around 1800 and trained as a carpenter in the early National period. His house reflected the aesthetic of the small vernacular houses that defined early Richmond and the rural areas of Virginia. Located in the Shockoe valley, Griffin was close to mills and factories, and his neighbors were the slaves who labored in Richmond's industries. John Adams was born after the Southhampton County rebellion, which was a watershed in the history of free blacks in Virginia. A plasterer, contractor, and major landowner, Adams became part of a shrinking elite of free black craftsmen and businessmen who provided leadership in the black community. That leadership was expressed through a substantial house in the vicinity of other houses occupied by free blacks and whites, as well as through his contributions to church affairs. Adams passed on both his skill and his leadership to his son John, a plasterer who served on the Richmond city council after Reconstruction and who took his place in the growth of the emerging "Black Bourgeoisie."

MARGARET M. MULROONEY

A LEGACY OF COAL
THE COAL COMPANY TOWNS
OF SOUTHWESTERN PENNSYLVANIA

In the past, little attention has been given to the role of bituminous coal towns in determining the physical and social character of a geographic region. Noted geographer Raymond Murphy was one of the first to recognize the significance of such communities, and in 1954 he made a plea for the increased study of American mining settlements, stating, "The investigation of mining regions reveals the interplay of the mining process with other elements of the local setting, including the people who work in the mines, the houses they live in, the transportation pattern, the other industries that are present, and the other items that go to make up the unique character of the region."[1] This interplay is particularly evident in southwestern Pennsylvania, where development of the region's vast bituminous coal seams led to eventual establishment of coal-company towns as the dominant form of settlement between 1880 and 1930.[2] Dependent upon natural geography and geology for their existence, these communities shaped not only the physical landscape but also the cultural identity of the region.

Pennsylvania's bituminous coal seams are part of the Appalachian region, which extends from the northeastern corner of the state through eastern Ohio, West Virginia, western Maryland, western Virginia, eastern Kentucky, and central Tennessee to central Alabama. This region has historically been considered to have the most important de-

posits of coal in the United States. Of these states, Pennsylvania was consistently ranked as the leading producer of both bituminous and anthracite coal between 1880 and 1930. The Appalachian region produced 92 percent of the total amount of coal mined in the United States in 1925. Pennsylvania, alone, contributed about one-third, or 34.5 percent.[3]

Coinciding with the dramatic expansion of the coal industry in the late nineteenth century, rural southwestern Pennsylvania witnessed the opening of hundreds of coal mines. The success of these mines, however, depended upon the maintenance of a large and loyal work force. For the most part, coal operators attempted to attract and retain labor by building inexpensive dwellings near the work site. Yet while coal operators realized the necessity of providing houses, they did not build them for altruistic reasons. The purpose of miners' housing was to increase productivity and profits by attracting labor, reducing job turnover, and establishing control over the labor supply.[4] This strategy worked best when houses were owned as well as built by the company. Discontented miners were less likely to cause trouble when faced with the threat of eviction. Although commended in the early stages of the industry as a practical and economical means of obtaining a labor supply for remote mines, coal towns came increasingly under fire after 1900 for what were seen as inherently exploitative methods of labor management and substandard living conditions.

Designed and constructed, for the most part, by mine engineers rather than architects, Pennsylvania's coal towns share a number of distinguishing characteristics. First, and most important, these towns were usually financed, built, owned, maintained, and operated by only one company. Companies provided houses, schools, churches, medical facilities, and a store where miners bought food, clothing, and supplies. In small towns, the store also housed the post office, once it had been established, and meeting rooms for various social functions. Larger communities had separate social halls and often boasted a hotel or movie theater as well. Streets were wide, with shallow setbacks; most were unpaved, although cinders and waste from the nearby slag heaps, called "red dog" or "boney," were used to keep the dust down.

A second distinguishing feature of these towns is that the dominant dwelling throughout the period was a two-story house, either detached or semi-detached (Fig. 1). Families generally preferred detached or semi-detached structures over row houses or tenements, and although such houses were more expensive to build, coal-company housing took this form because coal operators consciously wanted to attract married men. Contemporary articles indicate that employers believed men with families to be far less transient than their single counterparts. In fact, a federal survey of bituminous coal towns in 1917 revealed that more than 95 percent of all miners occupying company houses were married.[5] Companies did hire bachelors, but they were usually required to live in boardinghouses. And when the boardinghouses were full, families took single men in as boarders to supplement their meager incomes.

A third characteristic of Pennsylvania's coal towns was economy of construction. Several factors influenced the amount of a coal operator's housing investment, including the number of houses to be built, the projected life of the mine community, and the amount of available capital. For many years, mine engineers were not able to conclusively predict the life span of the mine. Consequently, coal towns were considered temporary settlements to be abandoned when the mine was worked out. Operators deliberately limited the amount of their initial investment in order to minimize their losses when the mine closed.

Fourth, the physical layout of Pennsylvania coal towns was remarkably consistent. Settlements were built in close proximity to the mine site to maximize the ease, speed, and economy of the operation and to minimize the amount of land to be developed (Fig. 2). One source recommended that the work site be no more than a fifteen-minute walk from town, or thirty minutes by "dependable transportation."[6] Laid out in a grid or linear plan,

Fig. 1. Semi-detached miners' houses built by the Washington Coal and Coke Company at Star Junction, Fayette County, Pennsylvania, circa 1895. (Photograph by Jet Lowe for HAER, 1988)

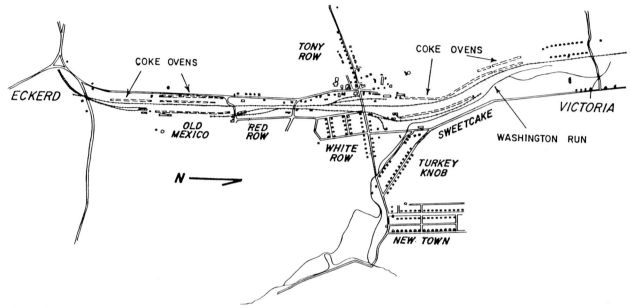

Fig. 2. Star Junction, Pennsylvania, circa 1920. (From a 1930 map entitled "Surface Tracts of the U.S. Steel Corporation at Washington Works"; courtesy Tony Grazziano, U.S. Steel Mining Office, Washington, Pennsylvania)

and usually conforming to the site's natural topography, streets had an average width of forty-five feet. Fifteen-foot alleys and large backyards served as firebreaks between houses. Lots were often generous in rural coal towns but varied according to house size, availability of land, and the benevolence of the operator.[7] Average lots were between fifty and sixty feet wide and one hundred feet deep to allow room for individual gardens, chicken coops, and perhaps a cow. Built in tight, straight rows at the extreme front of these lots, miners' dwellings presented an image of monotony and uniformity (Fig. 3).

A distinct hierarchy of housing types is a fifth coal-town trait, with marked differences between the residences for management and labor within most communities. The typical Pennsylvania miners' house was a plain, two-story, semi-detached, balloon-frame dwelling with an average of four to six rooms per unit (Figs. 4 and 5). Detached houses were also common and still generally followed the two-story, four-to-six-room arrangement. In either case, clapboards, weatherboards, or boards-

and-battens were typical forms of exterior cladding and provided the only barrier to wind and cold; interior surfaces were given one rough coat of lath and plaster. Few houses had running water and fewer had indoor toilets even as late as World War II. Instead, water was supplied by a small number of outdoor pumps scattered throughout the settlement. Privies were shared, too, with the most common structure being a combined outhouse/coal bin designed for two families. Most company houses did have electricity, however, since each mine had its own generators. Heat was provided by a coal stove in the kitchen. A system of flues and grates sometimes circulated warm air to other rooms, but because they were uninsulated, miners' houses were almost always cold and drafty.

Management houses were larger and better built, although still arranged in neat, identical groups. Often they were situated near the mine so that an official would always be on hand in an emergency. In some cases, the location of management housing was determined by proximity to the

Fig. 3. Company houses at Eureka #40, built in 1905 by the Berwind-White Coal Mining Company at Scalp Level, Cambria County, Pennsylvania. (Photograph by Jet Lowe for HAER, 1988)

Fig. 4. Construction drawing by the Berwind-White Coal Mining Company (1897) showing front elevation and section of semi-detached miners' houses built in Windber, Somerset County, Pennsylvania. (Courtesy the Berwind Corporation, Windber)

company store or other public buildings. But in some cases conditions were such that no location was necessarily better than another. This was especially true in coke towns, where noxious fumes and sooty air emanating from the coke ovens polluted all sites equally (Fig. 6). Regardless of their

location, management houses often had larger kitchens and parlors, more bedrooms, and a full, indoor bath. Other amenities may have included finished interiors, steam heat, exterior ornament, closets, and cellars. The mine superintendent's house possessed all of these features and was the largest and most ornamented dwelling, as befit his status in the community. Such differences resulted in a hierarchy of architecture that was rigidly defined and maintained from community to community. Yet, while the architecture of coal towns suggests a clear division between management and labor along occupational lines, it does not necessarily reflect the subtle distinctions that existed within each group, nor the peculiar occupational hierarchy of the coal industry.

Evidence suggests that houses in coal towns were segregated not only by occupation but also by ethnic group. In 1911, the U.S. Immigration Commission conducted a detailed investigation into the living and working conditions of immigrants in the bituminous coal industry. The commission noted that, on the whole, "American whites occupy a

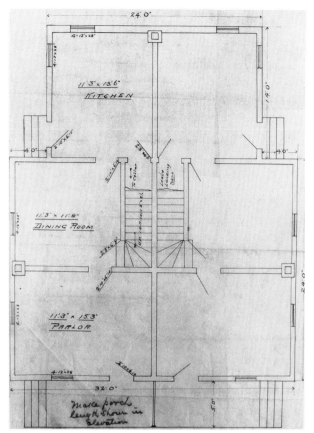

Fig. 5. Construction drawing by the Berwind-White Coal Mining Company (1897) showing the first floor of semi-detached miners' houses built in Windber, Somerset County, Pennsylvania. (Courtesy the Berwind Corporation, Windber)

Fig. 6. Partial view of Star Junction, Pennsylvania, showing proximity of housing to ash dump, railroad, and coke ovens circa 1900. (Courtesy Betty Palonder, Perryopolis, Pennsylvania)

somewhat better and commodious house as compared with the foreign-born, and that the foreign-born, with the exception of Mexicans, are practically living in the same general style of company house."[8] The commission also noted that foreigners were better housed than blacks, and blacks were better housed than Mexicans. Such was the case in Colver, Pennsylvania, where Italians, Hungarians, Slovaks, and other Eastern Europeans lived in four-room houses to the south of the main street, while Americans, Germans, Irish, and Scots lived in six-room houses to the north.

In addition, the nativity of an individual helped determine his occupational status. As architect Leslie Allen indicated in his book *Industrial Housing*

Problems in 1917, there were two distinct classes of workers:

> First, the unskilled workmen, mostly foreigners or negroes, uneducated, unused to American houses and American standards of living, earning a low wage and second, the skilled men, mechanics, machinists, etc., earning a higher wage, mostly Americans, living according to American standards, demanding more and willing to pay more for the comforts that the foreigner does not consider essential.[9]

Amenities not considered essential for foreigners included closets, cellars, screens, and bathtubs.

Despite the influence of such factors, the physical appearance of miners' housing was primarily the result of economics and only partly of prejudice. Above all, a coal town was to be run as a business, not as a charitable institution. Even in model communities, basic comforts were often sacrificed so that houses could be built as cheaply as possible (Fig. 7). Such policies were ostensibly designed to benefit labor as well as management. Industrial housing authorities justified their spare designs by explaining that even if extras like cellars, bathtubs, and closets were provided, the unskilled miners would be unable to afford them. Leslie Allen summarized the feelings of many when he stated:

> Many of the workingmen whose homes we wish to build have come from countries where four walls and a roof are considered sufficient shelter from the elements to make a home. . . . We do want to house the

Fig. 7. Reflecting one of the most inexpensive forms of construction, these semi-detached, vertical-plank miners' houses were built by the Berwind-White Coal Mining Company at Eureka #35, outside Windber, Pennsylvania, in 1900, as part of a "model" mining community. (Photograph by Jet Lowe for HAER, 1988)

lowest-paid man in a sanitary and hygienic home, but it is not necessary that this home be furnished with all the conveniences and appurtenances that are considered necessary in the American home.[10]

Judging by the documents they left and the houses they built, bituminous coal operators in Pennsylvania clearly concurred with Allen and his colleagues. For example, even as late as 1922, less than 3 percent of all miners' dwellings nationwide had bathtubs or showers.[11]

These conditions applied to coal towns throughout the United States, suggesting that coal towns encompassed an ideology for labor management that transcended architecture and planning. In fact, the interrelation between ethnicity, job status, occupational mobility, and housing can be seen as a cyclical progression. Each component of the progression determined and reinforced its neighbors in such a way as to establish an unbroken chain. Thus, the ethnic group to which a miner belonged determined the status of the job he held; this, in turn, determined his earning power. Companies then used earning power to compute the amount of rent an employee could afford, generally one-fourth of his monthly wages. Each company then used that figure to calculate how much it would spend on construction so that, ultimately, the amenities provided were a direct result of how much the employee earned. And to bring the cycle to a close, companies based the exclusion or provision of certain amenities on the ethnicity of their workers. But unlike other cause-and-effect rela-

tionships, this progression was not proportional; that is, an employee might alter the status of his occupation, and hence his earning power, but he could never change his ethnic origins and so remained somewhat limited in terms of housing. This aspect of coal-town life did not change until after World War II, when mine workers were finally able to purchase their own houses.

Housing segregation within coal towns by ethnicity and occupational status is indicative of the tremendous power wielded by the coal operator in his position as landlord. Simply put, "a housed labor supply is a controlled labor supply," for by holding the lease on an employee's house, an employer secured a total control not possible in a normal management-labor relationship.[12] In addition, employers used special police forces like the Coal and Iron Police to enforce company policies. From the long waiting list for houses, company officials could pick only the most skilled and most loyal employees for housing privileges. Similarly, on the pretext of reserving the best houses for the best qualified, company officials often practiced extreme racism and favoritism. Furthermore, blacklisting enabled most companies to deliberately exclude union sympathizers and organizers from their towns. In fact, some firms went so far as to insert exclusion clauses into leases that banned all persons the company considered objectionable from company property. Company property, of course, included not only the mine, tipple, and breaker, but the roads, houses, church, school, and store as well. But the most effective weapon employers used was the threat of eviction.

As early as 1865, coal operators in Tioga County, Pennsylvania, pressured their state representatives into legalizing a ten-day eviction clause.[13] Under this law, an employer could evict an employee from company housing if he failed to uphold his part of the labor contract for any reason whatsoever. Such practices continued well into the twentieth century. During the nationwide coal strike of 1922, for example, several thousand miners and their families were systematically evicted from company houses and forced to spend the winter months in tents.[14]

In response to this strike, the federal government established the U.S. Coal Commission, the first official body ever formed to study the American coal industry. The commission's findings revealed that in addition to long hours, low wages, and substandard housing, coal-town residents were being denied basic civil liberties. Outside observers concluded that coal towns prevented development of the sense of independence and self-reliance that was so closely associated with the American dream and called company towns "a great anomaly in the midst of a free country."[15] Gradually, labor reformers realized that labor unrest was not entirely due to lack of adequate pay; it was also the result of poor living conditions and the physical and psychological effect of these conditions on workers' families.

The dissatisfaction of American mine workers with their living and working conditions in the late nineteenth and early twentieth centuries manifested itself primarily through transiency and strikes. Finding it increasingly more difficult to retain labor, coal companies slowly began to heed the advice of outside reformers, who advocated improved housing as the best method for solving the problem. But while housing reforms represented an important step in the right direction, they were useless by themselves. By their very nature, the housing policies of a coal company were intricately linked with labor relations. Housing reforms thus ultimately failed to placate mine employees by failing to address the deeper problems of the company-town system.

Predictably, living conditions in Pennsylvania's bituminous coal towns did not noticeably change until the companies departed in the 1950s. Faced with increasing competition from cheaper fuels, the American coal industry went into a sharp decline after World War II. For some firms, this meant a complete reorganization of corporate holdings, including the closure or sale of mines and housing. Many miners and their families moved away in search of better jobs, but those that remained eagerly bought their company houses when the surface land and its improvements went on the market. Sometimes the miners purchased and moved to houses elsewhere in town, while in other cases houses were sold to outsiders. As a result, Poles were soon living next to Scots, Italians next to Americans, and foremen next to miners. And for the first time in their lives, these miners and their families could begin to enjoy all of the privileges and responsibilities associated with owning property. Understandably, their first step was to make alterations intended to both modernize and individualize their homes.

The first thing most miners did was add indoor bathrooms and updated heating systems. Windows were changed, doors moved, porches replaced, and asbestos shingles or siding added. Old privies became sheds, sheds became garages, and additions were formed from porches and lean-tos. The retired miners proudly point out such changes and draw attention to how nice the houses are now (Fig. 8). Since the coal dust and smoke are gone, coal-town residents have beautified their yards with shrubs, flowers, and various yard ornaments. Yet, despite these cosmetic changes, the repetition of forms and regularity of placement continue to mark these communities as coal-company towns. Reflecting a unique ideology of their own, these coal towns provide an excellent opportunity to study the neglected physical and social legacy of the coal industry in southwestern Pennsylvania.

Fig. 8. When built in 1912, these miners' dwellings at Colver, Pennsylvania, were clad with clapboards, but the company covered them in asbestos shingles in the 1930s to reduce maintenance costs. Sold in 1954, the houses now reflect the needs and tastes of multiple owners.

ANNMARIE ADAMS

CHARTERVILLE AND THE LANDSCAPE OF SOCIAL REFORM

Concern about the desperate living conditions of industrial workers in Britain peaked in the 1830s and 1840s with a severe economic depression and unprecedented housing shortages.[1] Politicians, authors, and architects, among others, used legislation, fiction, and buildings to illustrate viable alternatives to industrial capitalism. Their method was to compile evidence on social evils and then to suggest reform through an often radical reordering of the human and physical landscape. Embedded within this Victorian social manifesto were numerous plans for utopian communities that offered a critique of existing conditions while at the same time proposing alternatives in comprehensible terms. The town of Charterville, located in Oxfordshire, England, was one such community, the product of Feargus O'Connor's Chartist Land Plan of 1842. The relict landscape of Charterville remains today as an important reminder of the difficulty of reconciling political intentions with the design of the cultural landscape.

Charterville was established in 1848 as the third of five Chartist settlements.[2] It consisted of a school and seventy-eight small stone cottages constructed on individual lots of four acres or less along a major road from Minster Lovell to Brize Norton.[3] The basic objective of the Chartist Land Plan was to give working-class people access to land on which they could live and grow their own food. Because political power was still tied to landown-

ership, it also enabled them to vote. The plan was intended to reduce unemployment in the overcrowded cities and at the same time offer a viable alternative to industrial capitalism.

Charterville and the other four Chartist estates were made possible through the establishment of the National Land Company. As described in a handbill of 1847 (Fig. 1), the plan was for subscribers, mostly factory workers from industrial centers, to pay weekly dues toward the purchase of land being obtained by Feargus O'Connor, the charismatic Irish leader of the movement. As the handbill promised, the benefits, distributed by lottery, included "good land," a "comfortable house," and a sum of money. A pile of manure was also supplied at the gate to each property; individual leases were for life.[4]

But Chartism entailed much more than the Land Plan. As historian Dorothy Thompson has illustrated, it suggested an entire alternative culture. Between 1838 and 1848 working people from all over Britain joined forces to end the exploitation of wage laborers by industrialists and to extend voting rights to England's nonlandowning working class. It was one of the largest mass movements in modern history, with more followers than many of the groups that overthrew other European governments in 1848.[5] The People's Charter of 1838, from which the movement drew its name, established the official Chartist program. The group sought universal male suffrage, the aboli-

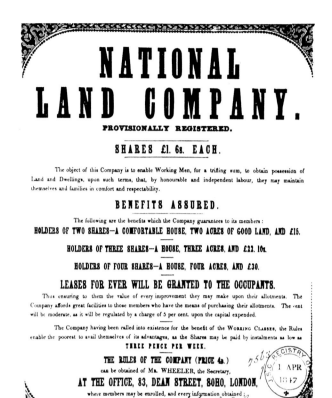

Fig. 1. Handbill issued by the National Land Company in 1847. (Courtesy *Oxoniensia* and Kate Tiller)

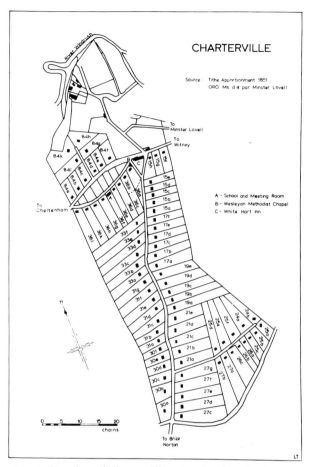

Fig. 2. Site plan of Charterville as it existed in 1851. (Courtesy *Oxoniensia* and Kate Tiller)

tion of property qualifications for members of Parliament, the payment of members, equal electoral districts, and annual parliaments. At the heart of Chartism lay the belief that access to political power provided the only chance to reform industrial society.

Although the political platform of Chartism appears radical, the architectural manifestations of the Land Plan at Charterville were surprisingly conservative, reflecting an idyllic image of rural life and glorifying the individual. Productive labor occupied a central place in the plan of the Chartist cottage, but the site planning and exterior design of the buildings recalled times when workers enjoyed little power. The architecture of Charterville reveals conservative aspects of Chartism that illustrate, perhaps more clearly than other documents,

the inevitable failure of the movement.

O'Connor purchased three hundred acres of land near Witney in June 1847 at a cost of more than ten thousand pounds sterling.[6] The choice of site was unfortunate; there was no rail connection or nearby market, and the soil was poor. In addition, the land was on high terrain, making water difficult to obtain. Three wells supplied the entire estate. As historian Kate Tiller has said, "Just as the Chartists believed in access to the land as a God-given right, so their water-supply appropriately came direct[ly] from heaven."[7]

The plan of Charterville (Fig. 2) was laid out by O'Connor and company director Christopher

Doyle.[8] They located most of the cottages along the main road from Minster Lovell to Brize Norton; similar lots were defined on two minor, perpendicular streets. The school and eighteen houses were located on Upper Crescent, in the north, while Bushey Ground on the south was a cul-de-sac. Charterville was immediately popular despite the problems of isolation, limited land, and poor farming conditions. Workers inhabited the cottages within fourteen months.[9]

In the design of Charterville, O'Connor postulated a return to a completely agrarian society. He intended tenants to raise their own food and provided no facilities for trade or communal labor. O'Connor warned in his book, *A Practical Work on the Management of Small Farms,* of the "ignorant landlords . . . induced by as ignorant writers to adopt the large farm system." He insisted that two hundred acres farmed by one man would never be as productive as fifty men working on plots of four acres each because of the distances involved in carrying manure and drawing produce.[10] There was much debate over whether four acres could support a family, particularly as many of the inhabitants had no previous farming experience.[11]

A diagram of a Charterville cottage published by O'Connor in 1847 shows a three-room house with a row of service spaces in the rear (Fig. 3). A courtyard behind the main block of the house was surrounded by outbuildings for animals and storage. The plan presented clear functional zoning: three main living spaces faced the street, less polite domestic labor took place behind this zone, and the back of the building housed large-scale agricultural labor. In the front, the large, central kitchen stepped out from the main block of the house. The flanking rooms, intended as bedroom and sitting room, were accorded secondary positions but were equal relative to the kitchen. Paneled doors separated these three interconnected rooms, each with its own fireplace. Entry to the house was directly into the kitchen without a vestibule space or porch.[12] Like Henry Glassie's kitchens of Ballymenone, the kitchens of Charterville were public

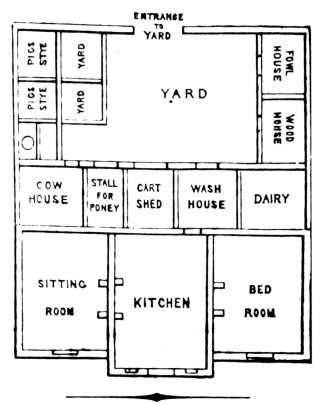

Fig. 3. O'Connor's plan for a cottage, published in *Northern Star,* February 13, 1847. (Courtesy Leeds University Library)

places—"vulnerable, open, and occupied."[13]

The prominent position of the kitchen in the cottage plan was consistent with the Chartist emphasis on self-sufficient productive labor. In *What May Be Done with Three Acres of Land,* O'Connor had promised a weekly yield of 14 pounds of bacon, 1.5 stones of flour, 4.5 stones of potatoes, 20 duck eggs, 2 pounds of honey, and a further income of 44 pounds sterling "after a consumption and the best of good living."[14] He believed that this could be achieved with 157 days' labor. The large Chartist kitchen became the space where tenants processed the fruits of the land and presumably realized the joys of family life and labor.

The builder of the Chartist cottage supplied the kitchen with a store-cupboard, range, and dresser, intending the space for more than cooking and eating.[15] Larger than the sitting room, the Chartist kitchen probably acted as the primary space for family interaction and for entertaining visitors. Access to other parts of the household came only through the kitchen, and thus the space served as a central circulation area mediating between private and public spaces, much like the central passage in other house forms.

In these ways the plan of the Chartist kitchen was in keeping with the backward-looking political and social agendas of the Land Plan.[16] The Chartists equated power with access to the land; they guaranteed happy family life through self-sufficiency and attempted to transfer the control of time from the factory to the home. The kitchen's prominent position, relative size, and accessibility to the yard and the land celebrated these values in architectural terms.

However, this aspect of the cottages was unintelligible from the exterior; the elevation of the Chartist cottage obscured the message of the plan and in the process revealed one of the central contradictions of O'Connor's politics. In plan the stepping out of the central kitchen had served several purposes. It made the kitchen larger than the adjacent rooms and thus marked the prominence of the space in the life of the settlement. As the center of activity in the house, closely connected to public space, the kitchen recalled the hall of medieval houses and was therefore consistent with the nostalgic ideology of the Land Plan. When considered in elevation, however, the Chartist kitchen, roofed by a projecting gable, translated into a classical temple front. The smoothly rendered quoins emphasized the jut, and a small roof ventilator decorated the pediment. The Chartist cottage, from the street, was a tiny Palladian villa (Fig. 4).

The potential of architectural features such as these to express, rather than to deny, the functions within a farmhouse had been highly developed and publicized by John Claudius Loudon by this time. In his *Encyclopaedia of Cottage, Farm and Villa Architecture* of 1833, Loudon had presented the designs for many rural houses employing classical language, but in his houses the style was used as a way of expressing the plan on the exterior. As George Hersey has explained, Loudon saw the house as a kind of "informational appliance," and he matched specific meanings to elements of buildings, suggesting that windows, doors, chimneys, and porches acted as "signifiers," communicating messages about a building's interior layout.[17] In the *Encyclopaedia* he illustrated houses in which portions were shifted forward to express the locations of major rooms, while the position of the porch, he claimed, revealed the place of the hall. In Loudon's terms the Chartist cottage was unfit and dishonest, using style as a costume.

To begin with, the front elevation of the Chartist cottage refers to a specific classical plan type at odds with the layout of the rooms. The three-part division of the facade and symmetrical placement of the windows are those of a Georgian central-hall house with flanking living spaces. The absence of a mediating porch or vestibule adds to the expectation that the space marked by the projecting gable is a hall or passageway. The central chimney rising from the kitchen further confuses the reading of the space; it just barely peaks over the

Fig. 4. The Chartist Cottage, from the street, seemed to be a miniature Palladian villa.

ridge of the main roof and is no more prominent than the end chimneys. Loudon would have insisted that the kitchen chimney be more robust, more decorated, and much taller than the less important end chimneys; he also would have differentiated the sitting room windows from those of the bedroom. Different room functions required different signifiers in elevation; conversely, irregular openings should represent irregularities in floor plan. Such expression, for Loudon, was the function of a building's elevation.

Apart from this "dishonest" use of classical elements in the elevation as a way of disguising the working life glorified in the plan, the classicism at Charterville also connected the cottage to a tradition that, at first glance, might seem in direct opposition to the larger sphere of Victorian social reform (Fig. 5). During the eighteenth century, the classicism of Italian Renaissance architect Andrea Palladio had been embraced by English architects in their designs for large country estates as a way of marking man's domination of the landscape; it was a mode associated exclusively with the Whig aristocracy and was popularized by conservative, well-educated architects and patrons, notably William Kent and Lord Burlington. Palladianism stood for a book-learned awareness of current fashion, and architects readily adopted it for the design of ostentatious country villas. Although neoclassicism has, at times, been appropriated to express the relatively independent status of gentlemen-farmers, this form of classicism was more often used for the houses of those who directed laborers than for the houses of the workers themselves.[18]

Palladianism was inconsistent with the larger objectives of social reform in its glorification of the individual, its domination of the landscape, and its clear reliance on historic precedent. The style succinctly expressed, however, the conservative aspects of O'Connor's Land Plan. Its adoption in the Chartist cottage was intended to assert the landowning status and consequent political power of the tenants by association with the great country estates. Without challenging the existing rule of landownership, O'Connor's Land Plan simply provided a way for working people to support the status quo. Modest Palladian villas on individual lots were the architectural expression of this conservatism.

The site plan of Charterville was an even more potent material statement of this conservative ideology. Inefficient in both labor and materials, the dispersed arrangement of the estate, the generous setback of the cottages from the street, and the clear marking of territory by fences and gates glorified the individual tenant rather than the cohesion of the movement as a whole and pointed to the contradictions in O'Connor's position on private property. Because the vote was still tied to the land, O'Connor saw the occupation of individual lots as critical to the intentions of Chartism. This was a divisive issue within the movement.[19] Marx and

Fig. 5. Marble Hill House, built in 1724–1729 for Henrietta Howard, mistress of George II, is a superb example of the Palladian style. (David Brady)

Engels, whom O'Connor met in 1845, believed that the private holding of land prevented major changes in society. O'Connor's commitment to private property, rather than land nationalization, was criticized as "encouraging selfish, narrow views amongst the lucky holders of Land Company plots, benefiting a few but not really getting to the heart of the problem."[20]

Although Chartism was a mass rebellion and its Land Plan was based on common ownership, its architecture indicates the extent to which the plan served only individuals. In Charterville there was no church, no market, no town hall, no palace of labor; there were only individual houses. The architecture of the Chartist cottages was not at odds with the ideology of the Land Plan. It revealed the inherently reactionary posture of the vision.

The presentation of Charterville in the press underlined the complex message of its architecture. One view of the settlement published at the time in the popular press deviated from reality in several important ways, revealing how the architecture of the largest radical movement in Britain might have been expected to look from a reform point of view (Fig. 6). To begin with, the focus of the drawing on the school and the houses of Upper Crescent is deceptive. In the drawing the school

seems to be the architectural focus of the settlement; individual lots are not differentiated. In essence, the artist depicted a communal settlement where tenants might share large buildings and expanses of land. In addition, the cottages in the drawing are much more attenuated than those actually built; that is, they are Gothic rather than Palladian. The roof pitch is too steep, openings are too vertical, and the quoins have been omitted in most of the cottages. The artist even dared to decorate the windows of one cottage with pointed arches rather than the classical frames actually used in Charterville. All traces of classicism, even the telltale central chimney, were omitted. The drawing was a fiction, but one that by its omissions reveals much truth.

In fact, the artist saw Charterville as a manorial village, as part of the system of land division that had formed the core of the medieval English landscape. Like the Chartist cottages, the main blocks of manorial houses had been set parallel to the street without a mediating porch or entryway. The manorial village was an appropriate model for Charterville in that it had been an agrarian, self-sufficient system. The architecture had an equalizing effect; each family had the same house. But in the manorial system the towering presence of the

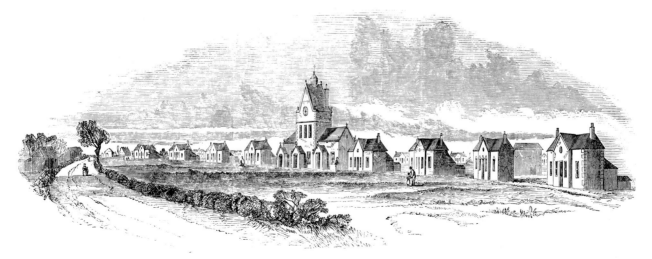

Fig. 6. Drawing of Charterville published in *Illustrated London News* 17 (October 12, 1850): 296. (Courtesy of the Illustrated London News Picture Library)

manor house and/or church was a constant architectural reminder of the serfs' limited power in the landscape. The land in the manorial system also played a fundamentally different role than in the politics of Chartism. Small holdings were forfeited in exchange for military protection from the lord. The land provided food and work but absolutely no political power. Like the Palladian references, the resemblance of the site plan to the manorial system recalled an oppressive period for workers. It served to dilute the more radical aspects of the vision and marked the divergence of the conservative and radical roots of Chartism.

Charterville lasted only three years as a Chartist land settlement. When O'Connor attempted to obtain rents from the tenants to alleviate the financial troubles of the company, the tenants refused to pay, insisting that they already owned their land. The classical architecture of their houses, as we have seen, supported their claim. The financial and legal basis of the Land Plan, however, were found unsound by a Parliamentary Select Committee. In 1851 the cottage properties at Charterville were sold.

The changes made to the buildings in their resuscitation as free-market commodities are telling. The plan was changed drastically. A plan of a cottage as used in the 1970s (Fig. 7) shows how the central room, the former Chartist kitchen, became a sitting room—a place of show and tell rather than the center of family production.[21] The kitchen, as we might expect, was reduced in size and moved to the rear of the house. Next to it, in place of the former washhouse, was a formal dining room.

In contrast, the elevations were changed minimally (Fig. 8). The symmetrically placed windows now truthfully expressed the functions within, as both side rooms became bedrooms. Small entry vestibules were added to the fronts of many houses, protecting the private realm within. Several owners added stucco or other surface materials in order to assert their individualism. The projected temple front, the sign of gentility and

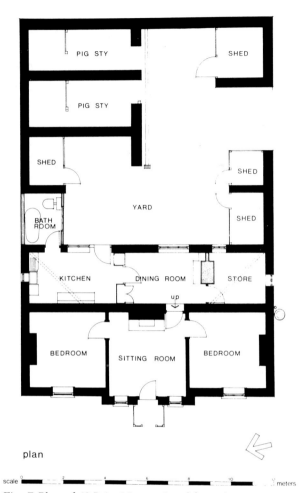

plan

Fig. 7. Plan of 69 Brize Norton Road from the 1970s. (Oxfordshire Museums Service, courtesy Oxfordshire Architectural and Historical Society)

status, remained intact. The meaning of classicism survived the failure of Chartism unscathed.

The Chartist cottages now sell for 150,000 pounds, the land is not farmed, and new, larger houses awkwardly occupy the narrow spaces between the original plots. The relatively reactionary elevations of the building now truthfully express the equally conservative plan. Charterville is no longer an ambiguous landscape; it speaks clearly of the values against which the Chartists rebelled. The message, however, has come full circle. In O'Connor's time occupation of the landscape was the measure of political power; ownership of a plot

Fig. 8. A Chartist cottage today. Many owners have added entries to their houses, emphasizing their classical forms.

of land ensured a vote. Today every citizen of Great Britain over the age of eighteen can exercise a vote, and it is now the land itself that is inaccessible to working-class people. Even the present-day archi-tecture of Charterville underlines the notion that power and freedom under industrial capitalism entail more than the extension of the franchise.

MARK REINBERGER

GRAEME PARK AND THE THREE-CELL PLAN
A LOST TYPE IN COLONIAL ARCHITECTURE

Graeme Park, an early eighteenth-century country house located seventeen miles north of Philadelphia in Horsham, Montgomery County, Pennsylvania, has long seemed an anomaly to historians. Although it received early attention as the only surviving home of a colonial Pennsylvania governor, its plan, evolution, and even original purpose have remained in doubt. The chief difficulty lies in its form. In the Delaware valley, the colonial country house tradition has been defined by strictly symmetrical, center-hall, double-pile houses such as Stenton, Hope Lodge, and Cliveden. Because Graeme Park was the country house of a governor, historians have expected it to conform to this tradition. However, its plan, with three very dissimilar rooms and a contracted stair hall (Fig. 1), and its asymmetrical, if controlled, elevations (Fig. 2) place it outside the bounds of any recognizable type in the region. Further complications have arisen from questions about Graeme Park's chronology and the discordancy between its unclassical exteriors and its high Georgian interiors, some of the finest in the Delaware valley (Fig. 3). All of these questions demand explanation and recommend the house as a fruitful topic for further investigation.

The unclassical nature of Graeme Park's exterior form and plan has given rise to disparate theories of its origin. Specifically noting its uncanonical form, several historians have proposed that it was built as a malthouse and only later converted to a country house. However, archaeology and

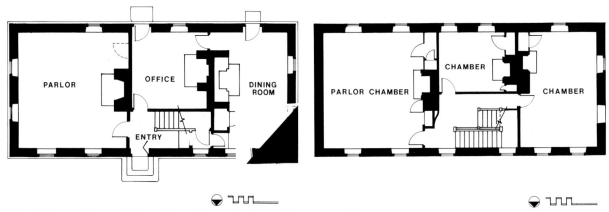

Fig. 1. First- and second-floor plans, Graeme Park, Horsham, Pennsylvania. (From Martin Jay Rosenblum, R.A., and Associates, "Graeme Park Historic Structures Report," Philadelphia, PA, 1987)

Fig. 2. North (front) elevation, Graeme Park, ca. 1870. (Photograph by E. L. Henry, courtesy York State Museum, Albany, Henry Collection, 40.17.854)

Fig. 3. West elevation of parlor, Graeme Park, photographed ca. 1920 by Frank Cousins. (Courtesy Essex Institute, Salem, Massachusetts)

documentary sources allow us now to identify a former structure in front of the mansion as the original brewhouse.[1] Another line of thinking hypothesizes that Graeme Park's origins lay in Swedish planning traditions, specifically the Swedish *parstuga* form. However, a review of Swedish sources reveals only the most rudimentary similarities between the *parstuga* and Graeme Park.[2] Further, misunderstood chronology has skewed

other discussions of the house, at times resulting in errors about colonial stylistic evolution.

This essay reexamines Graeme Park, focusing on the house's original, three-cell plan. Beginning with the site's documentary history and a close reading of the house's physical form, we can elucidate the original plan and some aspects of how it functioned in the colonial period.[3] This understanding of Graeme Park will then allow us to identify English sources for the plan and locate similar early houses in the Delaware valley and elsewhere in the colonies.

In 1719 Governor William Keith obtained title to almost two thousand acres in Horsham. By 1722 he had established a plantation on the site and convinced the Governor's Council to lay out a road to it. Keith, a somewhat impoverished aristocrat who always lived well beyond his means, had been appointed governor of Pennsylvania in 1717. At first he enjoyed great success as governor, but for both political and personal reasons he eventually lost the support of the Penns and was deposed as governor in 1726.[4]

About his Horsham plantation, Keith first stated that he intended to erect a small distillery and brewery, to provide a market for local grain farmers hard hit by an economic depression. His first comment on the scheme, dating from early 1722, mentioned that he had "yet no view to a Dwelling house or anything thats ornamental."[5] However, he must soon have changed his mind and begun the mansion, for after he was deposed as governor in 1726, he was quickly forced into bankruptcy, strongly implying that what he built at Horsham was done by that date. He fled to England in 1728 to escape his creditors and never returned to America. An advertisement offering the property for sale and a survey map of 1737 indicate that both the malthouse and the mansion, as well as a frame barn, had been built by Keith.[6]

Although structural evidence indicates that Graeme Park's shell, framing, and chimneys are original, it is doubtful how much of the interior had been finished during Keith's ownership. A

1726 inventory of Keith's Horsham estate lists a veritable profusion of furniture, plate, linens, and other utensils, but items are listed by type, rather than by room, as if the material was packed away in storage after having been shipped from Keith's main residence in Philadelphia. Indeed, the amount of furniture listed would not have fit into Graeme Park even if the house had been fully completed. Moreover, paint analysis of the house indicates that only a few rooms were painted at this early period. The second owner, Thomas Graeme, at first advertised the property for rent, stressing the availability of the malthouse, which he thought might be used for other industrial purposes. The advertisement also mentions a "large stone house and a good barn all in order for a tenant to enter upon," surely an understatement if the mansion had been completed in its present form.[7] As late as 1755 Graeme noted that he had greatly improved the park but had not yet significantly improved the house, an indication that the fine high Georgian parlor and parlor chamber at least were not yet finished.[8]

Thomas Graeme, the son-in-law of Lady Keith and a physician who also held several public posts in the colony, owned Graeme Park from 1737 until his death in 1772. While at first he intended only to rent the property, he changed his mind during a prolonged illness in 1747 and announced his intention of retiring from practice and moving to Graeme Park.[9] He embarked on a series of major improvement projects on the property. He converted part of the estate into some semblance of a polite retreat (complete with allées, gardens, and a deer park), although he continued to farm much of it. He altered and redecorated those rooms in the house that had been finished by Keith and finished those areas previously left in a rough state. Although he never retired full-time to Graeme Park, he and his family spent every summer there from about 1750 until his death.[10]

Inventories and advertisements from the period immediately after Graeme's death indicate that the mansion then had the room configuration it still possesses (Fig. 1).[11] The garret held the stair hall and four rooms—two small spaces to the west that served for storage and two heated rooms that served as chambers. On the second floor were three well-appointed bedchambers as well as the stair hall. On the first floor, the east end was occupied by the large parlor. The other three spaces were named in a letter by Mrs. Graeme from 1764: the family called the small stair hall the "entry"; the middle room was the "office," where Dr. Graeme read and presumably also supervised the running of the estate; the western space was called the "dining room."[12]

In front of the mansion was a formal garden bounded by a stone wall and Keith's watercourse (Fig. 4). Behind the house stood a detached kitchen and servants' quarters, now somewhat inaccurately reconstructed. The Graemes converted the malthouse into a secondary dwelling, called the "longhouse" in Graeme family letters, which accommodated a second family that summered with the Graemes. In an unknown location was a milkhouse with an ornamental grove nearby, suggest-

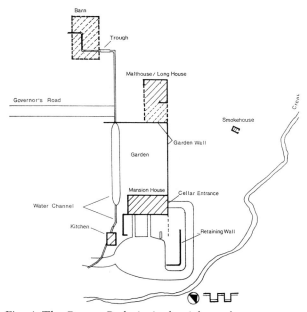

Fig. 4. The Graeme Park site in the eighteenth century. (From Rosenblum and Associates, "Graeme Park Historic Structures Report")

ing the character of the picturesque retreat sought by the Graemes.[13]

This documentary evidence provides a background for a careful analysis of the physical fabric of Graeme Park, an analysis indicating that the house as altered by Graeme differed in plan from Keith's original structure. We must peel away Graeme's changes in order to reconstruct the plan of Keith's house.

The house seems to have been laid out with a fairly clear and simple geometric formula (Fig. 5). The internal dimensions are 22 × 53 feet. Geometrically the plan resolves into a square parlor whose diagonal equals the length of the rest of the house, which was then subdivided into two equal pieces to form what were originally the hall and kitchen cells.

Physical evidence for early alterations allows a reconstruction to be made of Keith's original floor plans, beginning at the garret. This consisted originally of only three spaces, divided at the lines of the chimney blocks. The longitudinal partitions and the present trim were added as part of Graeme's high Georgian refurbishing. The present stair too was inserted, its header being grafted onto the joists in a manner uncharacteristic of the house's original framing. Originally the only stair to the garret was a tight winder in the corner of the west room. Evidence for this stair includes a header in

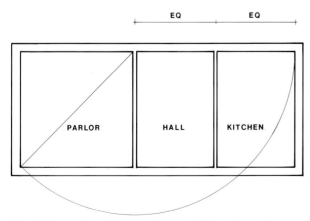

Fig. 5. Proportional layout diagram of first-floor plan, Graeme Park. (Brooke Vincent)

the floor framing and scars from winding treads. The stair to the roof hatch was originally open. The longitudinal partition now dividing the west garret chambers was inserted against the original stairway.

The second floor also shows significant changes. Originally the winder service stairs continued down to the first floor, landing on the second floor at an unheated passage space divided from the dining room by a partition. When Graeme had this partition removed to create a larger chamber, he closed the north window on the west wall to make space for the bed, whose location at this spot is shown by the remains of the bellpull drop.[14]

The second-floor framing for the stair in the center section of the house also shows extensive reworking. The present stair header was inserted into the original framing to create a double-width opening for the scissor stair that now exists. However, remains of an earlier header still survive, indicating that a major stair (with only a single-width opening in the floor structure) existed, or at least was intended, from the start of construction. The detailing of the present stair indicates a probable date of 1740–1760: its closed stringer is an older form, but its balusters stylistically match other Delaware valley examples of the period 1750–1760.[15] Graeme's insertion of a new stair probably also determined the present alignment of the partition dividing the stair hall from the office chamber. The narrower original main stair would have allowed the center chamber to be larger and to have a symmetrical fireplace wall.

As indicated above, the original first floor had a three-room plan (Fig. 6). Graeme's dining room was originally the house's kitchen. Within its present small fireplace lies the original cooking hearth, complete with its iron trammel rod. The room evidently became a dining room after Graeme erected the detached kitchen. The winder service stair was removed and a passage to the entry was inserted. With the installation of paneling and wallpaper, the status of this space was thus raised, as the service space was relegated to the outside. In

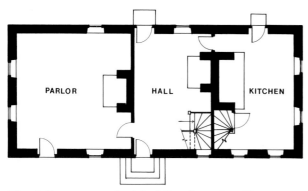

Fig. 6. Reconstructed original first-floor plan, Graeme Park. (From Rosenblum and Associates, "Graeme Park Historic Structures Report")

another significant change, Graeme divided the entry/stair passage from the rest of the middle room, creating his "office" and eliminating what would have been the living hall for the original house.[16] He also closed the original exterior door from the parlor to the front grounds before adding the present paneling. Consequently, the stair hall became a strict controller of space within the house and the only access for the most formal and highly decorated room.

Thus Keith's original plan offered three rooms in a line: a parlor, a hall with the main stair, and a kitchen with a service stair to the garret. All three rooms had exterior entrances—the parlor to the front, the kitchen to the rear, and the hall to both the front and the rear, suggesting a cross passage separating the hall and parlor. All three rooms were heated, and the interior chimney stacks each contained four fireplaces. Finally, there was a cellar under only the parlor.

Parallels in surviving American colonial architecture to the original plan of Graeme Park are difficult to find.[17] Indeed, the three-cell plan has received little attention in studies of American vernacular housing, and few sources have noted it as a distinct type. Rather, among multiroom houses, the general pattern of development has pictured the hall-and-parlor type giving way over the course

of the eighteenth century to the center-hall type in either a single- or a double-pile form. The situation is very different on the other side of the Atlantic, where the three-cell type has long been recognized as one of the most important of the postmedieval house forms.

A review of English rural vernacular housing reveals many examples comparable to Graeme Park in basic plan features, even if Graeme Park differs in some significant details from its English parallels. Certainly, at the simplest level of analysis, the three-cell plan was extremely common in England for rural houses of the yeomanry and lower aristocracy in the seventeenth century. Many English houses could be cited that have Graeme Park's string of spaces—kitchen, hall, and parlor.[18]

Such houses are often divided into two groups: those with a through passage and those without. Houses of the second, generally later form (called an "undivided house" form) usually have a lobby entrance against an internal chimney stack.[19] Graeme Park does not fit neatly into either category but has affinities with both. On the one hand, the opposing front and back doors in its original hall imply a through passage, and in this way its plan suggests West Country English examples. Usually the passage separated the kitchen and service areas from the hall and parlor, but examples are known in which the passage occurs on the parlor side of the hall.

On the other hand, Graeme Park shares characteristics with the undivided house type, not only because there is no true through passage but also because its plan is largely predicated on the importance given to its enormous parlor. The increased importance of the parlor was one of the chief motivations for the development of the undivided plan. Related to this is another feature of Graeme Park's original plan, the separate entrance for the parlor, a feature that increased in frequency throughout England from the mid-seventeenth through the early eighteenth century.[20]

With such a long-lasting and widespread tradition for three-cell houses in England, it is surprising that the type has so few occurrences in American colonial architecture.[21] Although the type survives only as a rarity, archaeological and documentary evidence suggests that it may once have been fairly common. It should be noted that this comparative analysis has aimed at the identification of single-pile structures built at one time and having three cells functioning as parlor, hall, and kitchen. Such plans could also come about through accretion, though these are beyond the scope of this investigation and indeed form a separate category. The economic ability to construct a three-room house all at once distinguished what was probably a select group of early colonial families.

In his book *In Small Things Forgotten* James Deetz pointed out the danger of relying only on extant examples for our knowledge of early colonial architecture. Noting the apparent homogeneity of surviving hall-parlor New England houses, he discussed several three-room "longhouses" found by archaeology in Plymouth Colony sites. For example, the Standish and Alden sites had houses with plan proportions not dissimilar to Graeme Park, with, in the case of the Alden site, a cellar under one room.[22] Another interesting parallel is provided by the eighteenth-century plan of the Bray Rossiter house in Guilford, Connecticut, which is very similar to many West Country English houses. It had a kitchen, through passage, hall, and parlor.[23]

The Tidewater record is similar. In Virginia and Maryland, archaeology has discovered several single-pile, three-room dwellings, although the lack of known detail prevents close comparison with Graeme Park. The parallels are suggestive, however, because many of these examples seem to have been homes of the early colonial elite, a group to which William Keith belonged.

At Middle Plantation in Anne Arundel County, Maryland, a three-room house measuring 20 × 42 feet has been discovered. Similarly, a three-room dwelling was discovered at Mathews Manor in Warwick County, Virginia.[24] In what seems an especially intriguing parallel to Graeme Park, probing at the Thomas Swan house site in Surry County, Virginia, revealed a three-room house measuring 23 × 60 feet with a cellar under the room at one end.[25]

The archaeological record at Greenspring, James City County, is clearer.[26] The house's main block was 25 × 97 feet and was divided into three extremely large rooms, all heated, two by an internal chimney and one by an end chimney. A plan of the 1790s showing the aboveground basement suggests that there may have been other, nonstructural divisions, such as a stair passage between the kitchen/service wing and the rest of the house.

A search in the Delaware valley for examples comparable to Graeme Park has discovered evidence that the early Pennsylvania colony had a number of these single-pile, three-cell houses. All examples discovered so far were built in the late seventeenth and early eighteenth centuries by wealthy colonists who were recent emigrants from Great Britain. Given the extremely low survival rate of Pennsylvania's first-generation houses (even those at the top of the social ladder), it is likely that many more once existed. Thus Keith would have been building within a recognized local context.

A surviving building similar in plan to Graeme Park is the Wrights Ferry Mansion in Columbia, Pennsylvania, built in 1738 by a family originally from Lancashire, England (Fig. 7). John Wright (1667–1749) and his daughter Suzanna (1697–1784) came to Chester, Pennsylvania, in 1714, and moved in 1726 to what was then the western frontier of the colony. Besides being a Quaker minister (the move to the west was partially motivated by a desire to proselytize and stabilize the frontier), John Wright was a merchant, a justice of the peace, and a member of the colonial assembly. In what would become Lancaster County, the family farmed, ran a gristmill, and operated the first ferry across the Susquehanna River.[27]

Wright's Ferry Mansion was all built at one time, and its elevations exhibit the same controlled asymmetry as Graeme Park's. In plan, the major dif-

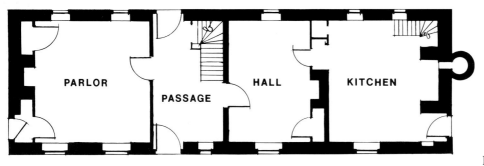

Fig. 7. Plan, Wright's Ferry Mansion, Columbia, Pennsylvania. (After plan in Wright's Ferry Mansion archives)

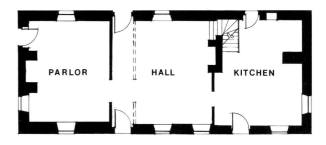

Fig. 8. Plan, Shoomac Park, Philadelphia County, Pennsylvania. (After Historic American Buildings Survey, PA-1067)

ference from Graeme Park is the presence of a fully divided stair passage separating the parlor and hall, instead of Graeme Park's only implied cross passage. At the west end is the same large, perfectly square parlor; in the center the smaller hall; and at the east end a large kitchen. Like Graeme Park, the parlor and kitchen have separate exterior doors in addition to those in the passage. Two end chimneys and an interior one heat the three major spaces. The interior dimensions of the house are 18 × 61, very close in size to Graeme Park but slightly longer due to the passage. Also like the original state of Graeme Park, the kitchen had a separate service stair that rose all the way to the roof.

Even closer to Graeme Park was the original form of Shoomac Park, near Philadelphia, probably built by the Robeson family about 1700 and now demolished (Fig. 8). Andrew Robeson, Sr., and Jr. (his nephew) came to America in 1676, settling first in West Jersey. Originally from Scotland, they came to the colonies from Ireland, having been lately in London. The elder bought the Shoomac Park property and moved to Philadelphia County in 1690, and his nephew followed in 1702. Both were active in the governments of West Jersey and Pennsylvania. Their estate at Shoomac encompassed approximately fifteen hundred acres and was most noted for a gristmill, one of the earliest in the colony.[28]

Although the house at Shoomac Park was later extended in width, the original single-pile plan could be read in the cellar. The original exterior dimensions were 23 × 55 feet, almost exactly those of Graeme Park. The house had three nearly equal-size rooms: a kitchen (indicated by a large relieving arch in the cellar), a hall, and a parlor. The hall had an internal chimney, and the parlor and kitchen possessed end chimneys. The entrance was either directly into the hall (as at Graeme Park) or into a through passage between the hall and the parlor. Due to massive later rebuilding, further details cannot be discerned.[29]

Similar to Shoomac Park is the extant Thomas Cowperthwaite house near Moorestown, New Jersey (Figs. 9–10). Traditionally dated 1742, it may

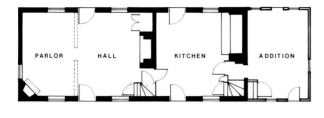

PARLOR   HALL   KITCHEN   ADDITION

Fig. 9. Plan, Cowperthwaite house, Moorestown, New Jersey. (Brooke Vincent, after Historic American Buildings Survey, NJ-471)

Fig. 10. Northeast elevation, Cowperthwaite house. (Brooke Vincent, after Historic American Buildings Survey, NJ-471)

have been built before 1732, when John Cowperthwaite willed the property to his son, Thomas, with a house on it. John, the pioneer settler in the Delaware valley, bought the property in 1702. Both John and Thomas Cowperthwaite were prosperous yeomen and were active in the community and the local Quaker Meeting.[30]

The plan of the Cowperthwaite house is very similar to that of Shoomac Park, except that the parlor has a corner fireplace, a feature seen often in New Jersey. The house is very much intact, containing a majority of its eighteenth-century woodwork. The kitchen contains a large cooking fireplace and winder service stair. The hall stair has

been altered, but the original winder form is recorded in Historic American Buildings Survey drawings. The partition between the hall and the parlor no longer survives on the first floor, but its original alignment can clearly be seen, and its corresponding dividing wall in the brick-floored cellar still exists. The room proportions of the parlor and kitchen reverse those of Graeme Park, as the Cowperthwaite kitchen forms a square, the diagonal of which roughly equals the length of the hall and the parlor. The overall interior dimensions of the plan are approximately 18 × 48 feet.

The exterior of the house was quite finely treated. Two and a half stories, of brick, and with a continuous plaster coved cornice, the original front (northeast elevation) was laid in flemish bond and originally had a pent roof. Its fenestration had the same studied asymmetry as Graeme Park's front.

Available evidence indicates that all the builders of these early Delaware valley houses were persons of substance, owning large tracts of land and other sources of income such as mills, furnaces, and ferries. They were also members of the colonies' first generation, having been born and raised in Great Britain. All were active in the colonial government or community affairs. William Keith, the builder of Graeme Park, also fits this pattern and, indeed, as governor of the colony would have known them all personally, with the possible exception of John and Thomas Cowperthwaite of New Jersey.

In subsequent generations this class would completely forsake the single-pile, three-cell house for a different model: the double-pile, center-hall plan, a form most influentially embodied in Pennsylvania by Stenton, built at nearly the same time as Graeme Park, in the 1720s. This pattern of change can perhaps best be seen in the Growden family of Bucks County, Pennsylvania. The first generation of Growdens erected before 1696 a three-cell house, noted in that year as a "very noble and fine house pleasantly situated." Joseph Growden, who came from England in 1683, erected this house on a five-thousand-acre plantation in Bucks County, which he had received from William Penn. Growden was a major figure in the early colony, representing first Philadelphia and then Bucks County in the assembly and serving as speaker of the assembly from 1690 to 1693. Growden also invested in mills, ferries, bridges, and other land in Pennsylvania and Delaware.[31]

Joseph Growden's inventory of 1730 indicates that the first floor of his house had a well-furnished parlor, a hall used primarily for dining, and what was called a "room adjoining the hall," which was used as a bedchamber and for spinning. By this date the house had a detached kitchen. Thus it would seem to conform to the three-cell scheme, a common form in the Growden's native Cornwall. When in about 1740 a later generation of Growdens built Trevose as the new family mansion, they erected the double-pile, center-hall structure that survives today.[32]

The two generations of Growden houses represent a general change that occurred in the Delaware valley as the new Georgian fashion, propelled by the increasing wealth of the colonies, came to dominate its architecture.[33] This and subsequent periods of rebuilding effaced the record of the colony's earliest architecture. However, enough survives to conclude that in Pennsylvania, and elsewhere in the colonies, the single-pile, three-cell house (a form with a strong English pedigree) was much favored among the earliest generation of wealthier colonists. Graeme Park's importance, therefore, lies not only in its traditionally revered high Georgian interiors but also in its plan, a surviving example of a now rare type, a knowledge of which can deepen our understanding of early colonial architecture and of its connections with the vernacular architecture of England.

Laura A. W. Phillips

Grand Illusions

Decorative Interior Painting in North Carolina

Bold streaks of pink, yellow, blue, green, and gray . . . what appeared through the dirty window screens of the abandoned Flinchum house to be an example of 1960s psychedelic painting turned out to be much, much more. Indeed, it is the occasional discoveries of such treasures as the Flinchum house parlor that supply the thrill to architectural survey work.

The Flinchum house, located near the town of Pilot Mountain in rural Surry County, North Carolina, was a mid-nineteenth-century one-story frame dwelling with simple Greek Revival detailing. Around the turn of the century it was enlarged to a full two stories, becoming a vernacular I-house typical of the region with a symmetrical three-bay facade, a gable roof, gable-end brick chimneys, and a one-story rear ell (Fig. 1). While the Flinchum house was a representative building type of its time and place, it in no way suggested the surprise that lay within.[1]

The painted parlor of the Flinchum house is a flamboyant example of decorative painting from the second half of the nineteenth century (Fig. 2). The vibrant pastel walls are "blocked" like ashlar, the yellow blocks containing marble "veining." Crowning the walls is a delicately painted vine-and-flower border. The painting scheme of the flush-boarded walls is complemented by the boldly painted ceiling, composed of a central medallion with a green and yellow geometric center bordered by concentric bands of the freehand vine-and-flower border and a broad band of deep azure

blue—the whole set against a dark brown ground. The rest of the Flinchum house was apparently

Fig. 1. Flinchum house, Surry County, a typical I-house of the piedmont region.

Fig. 2. Flinchum house parlor, flamboyantly painted with marble-blocked walls and a vine-and-flower cornice border.

155

devoid of decorative painting.[2] Thus, the concentration of color and decorative design in the parlor served to accentuate its role as the most prestigious room in the hierarchy of domestic spaces.

The realization that such a fully developed, if somewhat eccentric, painting scheme could be found in an unassuming farmhouse like the Flinchum house served as a catalyst for the study of decorative interior painting in North Carolina. During the past twenty years, numerous examples of decorative painting have been identified in the course of recording thousands of buildings through North Carolina's historic survey program.[3] Nevertheless, the state's decorative painting as a whole has received little attention and has remained little understood and rarely appreciated.

Most published works treating some aspect of decorative interior painting focus on examples dating from before 1850 and located in New England or other areas of the Northeast. By comparison, little has been published concerning decorative interior painting elsewhere, creating a significant gap in our overall understanding. This essay seeks to lay the groundwork for pursuing a systematic, comprehensive analysis of North Carolina's decorative interior painting—with the primary focus on examples found in nineteenth-century domestic architecture—in order to interpret its role in the state's architectural history. In particular, the study is aimed at determining the nature of decorative painting in North Carolina—its quantity and quality; its range of types, styles, periods, and geographic distribution; its role in the vernacular architectural traditions of the state; who the painters and owners were and what effects they were trying to achieve; and the relationship between North Carolina's decorative interior painting and that found elsewhere in America, particularly in the South.[4]

The early stages of this long-term study have provided insight into some of these questions. Thus far three hundred properties with decorative painting have been recorded, and more than one hundred additional examples have been identified

for future recording.[5] Nearly one-half of the recorded properties display more than one type of decorative painting—wood-grained, marbled, stone-blocked, smoked, stenciled, polychromed, scenic, trompe l'oeil, or other painted decoration. Although the survey is not complete—and may eventually include more than five hundred examples—it nevertheless provides a strong representative sampling of North Carolina's decorative interior painting.

Examples from the late eighteenth century through the early twentieth century have been recorded, with nineteenth-century domestic examples most heavily represented. The surviving examples, like the buildings themselves, probably represent only a fraction of what once existed. Decorative painting has been identified in sixty-six of the state's one hundred counties, ranging from the coastal plain through the piedmont to the isolated mountains. The heaviest concentration has been found in the counties of the north-central piedmont, particularly those near the Virginia border.[6] A variety of period styles has been recorded, including Federal, Greek Revival, late Victorian, and Works Progress Administration regionalism. In execution the decorations range from the highly sophisticated and primly academic to unschooled and sometimes bizarrely energetic examples of folk art.

At present, knowledge of the painters themselves is relatively limited, other than that they varied significantly in training and in manner of operation. Many remain anonymous itinerants who flourished in North Carolina as elsewhere in America during the nineteenth century. The essential mobility of itinerants made their names less memorable than were those of the "homegrown" artists and craftsmen, thereby making the task of identification more difficult. Even when a painter's name is associated with a particular painting example, as is the case with the Flinchum house, often little else is known. According to Flinchum family tradition, the painter of that exuberant parlor was a man named McKnight: "We're pretty sure of his name, but don't know anything about where he was from. Back in those days painters would be in the neighborhood searching for work and we understand he was one of those people, did the work, and was on his way."[7]

Advertisements in local newspapers suggest the frequency with which some painters moved from town to town and sometimes mention training in Philadelphia, New York, or elsewhere.[8] In addition to itinerants, other painters—like the Harris family of Wilkes County and Martin Luther Hutcherson of northeast Stokes County, were resident artisans who practiced their trade in their surrounding neighborhoods.[9] Still others were highly trained artists, like Edward Zoeller, a Bavarian-born fresco painter who executed sophisticated painting in Edgecombe County for years.[10]

The clientele was as varied as the painters themselves. As might be expected, some were wealthy landowners and entrepreneurs who occupied large and architecturally impressive houses. At the same time, a surprising number could be described best as "middle class" and lived in relatively simple vernacular dwellings such as the Flinchum house. In short, decorative painting was commissioned both by those who could afford fancy wallpapers and other decorative devices as well as by those who could acquire the services of a traveling painter in exchange for room and board and perhaps a little money.

Of the wide variety of decorative interior painting types found in North Carolina, by far the most common was wood graining, which remained popular well into the twentieth century. Different types of wood were imitated, with mahogany, bird's-eye maple, tiger maple, and oak being among the favorite choices. Examples range from the realistic and precisely executed to the brashly stylized.

Within the genre of a particular period and style of graining and a particular type of wood imitated, a wide interpretative range can be seen easily. A case in point is the Federal-style graining found repeatedly in the North Carolina piedmont during the 1820s and 1830s. The style consists of mahog-

any graining with panels detailed with yellow ocher outlines and quarter-round (or in rare cases three-quarter-round) cutout corners to give the illusion of raised panels. While the doors of the William Carter house in Surry County exhibit a refined version of the style that is fairly realistic in depiction, the Edwards-Franklin house, also in Surry County, possesses doors with a bolder, more fluid interpretation that is much more abstract in feeling (Fig. 3).[11] Wood graining was used primarily for doors and secondarily for wainscots, mantels, and other architectural elements where wood would naturally have been used. Where wood graining occurred, it was likely to be found throughout the house.

Fig. 3. Edwards-Franklin house, Surry County, chamber door with stylized version of typical Federal period graining.

Following closely behind wood graining in popularity was the imitation of various types of stone, categorized generally as marbling. Marbling was frequently used in conjunction with graining in a more comprehensive, well-integrated approach to interior painted decoration. A variety of types of marble were imitated, as well as other stones like granite and Virginia greenstone. As with wood graining, examples range from the highly realistic to the stylized. Marbling was used primarily for mantels, baseboards, and stair risers, and secondarily for wainscots, door casings, and other trim.

A related painting type, stone blocking, was simply an ambitious subcategory of marbling. While stone blocking constitutes one of the most dramatic forms of decorative painting found in North Carolina, it is also one of the rarest surviving forms. Only thirteen examples have been identified; of these, two have been painted over or replastered and several are currently in ruinous or near-ruinous condition. Most examples are painted on plastered walls and thus have deteriorated more rapidly than have the few western piedmont examples painted on flush-board sheathing.

The technique of stone blocking involved the use of painted lines to break marbling into neatly arranged blocks that covered entire walls. Usually the blocks were rectangular in imitation of ashlar, but they were not always so. At the Thorne-Rue house in Halifax County, the blocks are diamond-shaped, defined by precisely painted white lines, and joined at the corners by painted "bosses." The blocks include a variety of marble types in soft shades of gray, ocher, blue, and green. Despite the fact that the decorative painting at the Thorne-Rue house is among the most sophisticated in the state, the house itself is a modest one-story frame cottage with a hipped roof and simple classical detailing, dating from the third quarter of the nineteenth century.

Judging from surviving examples, stone blocking in North Carolina usually imitated marble. An exception, however, is found at the mid-nineteenth-century James A. Johnson house in Harnett County. The center passage of this one-story frame cottage is dramatized by the use of ashlar-blocked walls in imitation of dark gray granite. The granite blocks are interspersed occasionally with blocks of white and ocher marble.

Stone blocking was related to the use of ashlar-patterned wallpapers popular in America from the late eighteenth century through the mid-nineteenth century. The formality of stone blocking as a decorative treatment dictated its use for hallways, parlors, and dining rooms where its effect could be best appreciated. While most examples are rather academic in approach, a few, like the Flinchum house parlor, represent freewheeling folk expressions of this painting form.

Stone blocking is one of the most sophisticated types of historical decorative painting in North Carolina, yet it can be found in small, or at least modest, dwellings such as the Thorne-Rue house, the Johnson house, and the Flinchum house as well as in larger, more architecturally ambitious houses. Stone blocking thus reflects one of the characteristic features of North Carolina's decorative painting as a whole—that ornamental painting as a form of interior decoration was not confined to the dwellings of the wealthy.

A variation on the marbling theme was the smoked ceiling, created by waving a lighted torch, a pine knot, or a kerosene lamp across wet paint so that the smoke created a marbled effect on the paint surface. Although smoked painting was a simple form whose effect was relatively easy to achieve, only eight examples have been recorded in North Carolina. Of those, six are located in the contiguous western piedmont counties of Stokes, Surry, Yadkin, and Wilkes. The example in Wilkes County was painted by one of the Harrises, a family of black painters who lived in the county for several generations.[12] Other examples in the area may also have been painted by this family or at least influenced by their work. Although the distribution of surviving examples is somewhat localized, smoked painting does not appear to have been an indigenous form of decorative painting.

Indeed, examples are also known in Georgia and Texas.[13]

Stenciling, an art form practiced during several historic periods, gained some popularity in North Carolina during the late nineteenth century. Stenciling was typically used as a ceiling or cornice decoration, but examples are also found around doors and windows, on a wainscot, and even on stair risers. While only twenty examples of stenciling have been recorded in North Carolina, some of these are among the finest examples of decorative painting in the state. Representative are such highly sophisticated work as that found in the Second Empire Redmond-Shackleford house in Tarboro (attributed to Edward Zoeller) and the somewhat less polished, though artistically stunning, parlor ceiling of the vernacular Gothic Revival Rucker-Eaves house in Rutherfordton (attributed locally to an Italian itinerant).

While any number of painters could use identical stencils, they often combined stencils with freehand elements to achieve designs that bore their particular artistic signatures. The ceiling of the Rucker-Eaves house illustrates this point (Fig. 4). The ceiling painting follows a parterre organization with a series of central circular bands and four paths leading from the outermost circle to the four edges of the ceiling. Within this plan are a multitude of details, including a variety of stenciled elements combined with a freehand vine border, a compass rose, and paneling. The ceiling painting of the Rucker-Eaves house is visually outstanding in and of itself, but is also intriguing in its relationship with the Edwards-Maxwell house in Alleghany County and with an unnamed house in rural Chatham County, as well as with the Damascus Methodist Church in Lumpkin, Georgia, and the Calhoun-Perry house in Chireno, Texas. All share a combination of stenciled and freehand elements that suggests some link in authorship.[14]

One of the most visually fascinating forms of decorative interior painting in North Carolina is trompe l'oeil. Unlike much of North Carolina's decorative painting which involved imitating a particular building material on existing architectural elements, trompe l'oeil painting created illusionary architectural elements where none existed. Recorded examples include imitation door panels, window, wainscots, wall niches and panels, cornices, ceiling medallions, and ceiling and stair panels. Like other types of decorative painting in the state, examples of trompe l'oeil work range from the highly sophisticated, such as the dramatic stair paneling at Coolmore in Edgecombe County, to simple folk art, such as the batten door at the James F. Slate house in Stokes County, which is painted to resemble a two-panel door.

Although scenic painting does not appear to have been prevalent in North Carolina, it offered a diversion from the more popular forms of decorative painting in the state. Of the twenty-four examples thus far recorded, more than one-third are post-office murals painted primarily during the 1930s under the auspices of the Works Progress Administration. Other examples include scenes painted on mantel friezes. The most exciting examples, however, are the window views painted at the Reich-Strupe-Butner house in Forsyth County. Here, marble-blocked walls in the parlor are painted with trompe l'oeil windows with deep "stone" reveals. Through these "windows" are romantic landscape views—one with a gristmill and mill pond, and the other with a farm scene complete

Fig. 4. Rucker-Eaves house, Rutherford County, parlor ceiling with stenciled and freehand painting.

with a herd of cows and mountains in the distance.

Another type of decorative painting in North Carolina can be described best as polychromed, with the decorative effect achieved primarily through the use of color. In some cases, certain architectural features were delineated with color, while in several houses in Vance, Warren, and Edgecombe counties delicate plaster decoration was enhanced through the use of color.

Some of the most visually exciting examples of decorative interior painting in North Carolina defy categorization by type. Such is true of the extensive painting at Waterloo, the home of the Grady family in Duplin County. Though it resembles stencil work, the delicate painting arranged in a series of borders was instead created with a brush and fingerprints (Fig. 5). The results look much like embroidery; in fact, Grady family tradition attributes the work to the talents of house owner Eliza Anne Grady Simmons (1801–1855).[15]

Another form of painting that defies categorization is perhaps characterized best by its element of surprise. Found primarily on doors and wainscoting in Gates, Edgecombe, and Alamance counties, this painting is used as if it were wood graining, yet its visual effects bear no resemblance to any type of wood found in nature (Fig. 6). Indeed, the highly stylized images resemble Mardi Gras confetti and serpentine, exotic designs of possibly African influence such as leopard-like spots and large feather plumes.

Although nearly half of the recorded properties exhibit more than one type of decorative painting, most of these display a combination of wood graining and marbling. Surviving properties retaining several types of painting are rare and constitute some of the most impressive examples of decorative interior painting in the state. One such property, mentioned previously, is the Reich-Strupe-Butner house in Forsyth County. This late eighteenth-century two-story frame dwelling of vernacular Germanic design retains one room— the parlor—with a wealth of decorative painting. The effect of the painting is powerful in juxtaposi-

Fig. 5. Waterloo, Duplin County, fingerprint painting suggestive of embroidery. (North Carolina Division of Archives and History)

tion to the simplicity of the rest of the house. The parlor painting is comprehensive in scope. Below a chair rail the dado is painted solid brown, while above the chair rail the plastered walls are marble-blocked with a high degree of realism. A trompe l'oeil dentil molding crowns the walls, and above that the brown plastered ceiling features a large central medallion that is a combination of stenciling and freehand painting. The most fascinating aspect of the extensive painted decoration, however, is the trompe l'oeil niche above the mantel with its still life of flowers and fruit and the two trompe l'oeil windows along the front wall with their landscape scenes (Fig. 7). Family tradition claims that this remarkable work was executed by

Fig. 6. Costen-Rountree house, Gates County, door with abstract painting. (Tom Butchko)

Fig. 7. Reich-Strupe-Butner house, Forsyth County, painted parlor with marble-blocked walls, trompe l'oeil dentil cornice, and trompe l'oeil window with romantic landscape scene. (North Carolina Division of Archives and History)

painter Naaman Reich, who owned and occupied the house during the third quarter of the nineteenth century.[16]

In Franklin County, the Archibald Taylor house, which dates from the 1850s, is a large and elaborate Italianate dwelling, the work of Warrenton builder Jacob Holt.[17] Though decorative painting is found in several rooms, it is concentrated in the front stair hall to immediately impress anyone entering the house. Here the plastered walls are mar-

ble-blocked in a bold combination of blue, ocher, and white. On the plastered soffit beneath the stair, evidence remains of a trompe l'oeil framed portrait. The blue ceiling contains a collection of trompe l'oeil devices, including a bracketed cornice, panels, and colorful medallions and other "plaster" ornamentation (Fig. 8). In addition to the richness of the hall walls and ceiling, the Archibald Taylor house contains black marbled baseboards, wood graining, and flowered panels and other painted detailing on window aprons. De-

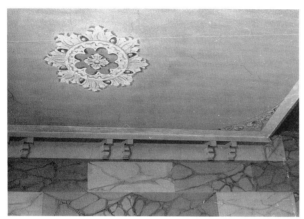

Fig. 8. Archibald Taylor house, Franklin County, elaborately painted stair hall with marble-blocked walls and trompe l'oeil bracketed cornice, ceiling panel, and ceiling medallion. (North Carolina Division of Archives and History)

Fig. 9. Munday house, Catawba County, parlor wall detail with trompe l'oeil paneling and cornice. (North Carolina Division of Archives and History)

Fig. 10. Munday house, nineteenth-century vernacular dwelling of log and frame construction. (North Carolina Division of Archives and History)

spite the original grandness of the house, it stands abandoned, with much of the painted plaster in ruinous condition.

One of the most striking collections of decorative painting in North Carolina is found at the Munday house in Catawba County. The majority of the painting is concentrated in the parlor, though other rooms complement that effort with more modest displays of painting. The comprehensive treatment of the Munday house parlor—which appears to date from the late nineteenth century—includes a marbled baseboard, walls fully covered with trompe l'oeil paneling, a trompe l'oeil dentiled and roped cornice, a wood-grained Greek Revival mantel, and a fancy polychromed and stenciled ceiling. Other rooms contain stenciled cornices, simple wall paneling, and stenciling around the border of the ceiling. The painting at the Munday house implies an architecturally impressive dwelling. The fact that the house is, instead, a simple vernacular structure of log-and-frame construction is a forceful reminder that grand illusions were not confined to the finest houses in North Carolina (Figs. 9 and 10).

The importance of North Carolina's decorative interior painting is not that it exists, but that so much of it survives and in so many forms. Spanning a cross section of time periods, geographic regions, economics, and cultural influences, this rich and diverse collection provides an excellent opportunity for detailed study of an art form integrally related to the architecture in which it occurs.

MARK L. BRACK

DOMESTIC ARCHITECTURE IN HISPANIC CALIFORNIA
THE MONTEREY STYLE RECONSIDERED

The study of domestic architecture in Hispanic California has been dominated by interpretations that attribute changes in the territory's houses to imported architectural ideas from non-Hispanic sources. Americans began immigrating to the Spanish territory in 1816, and most modern histories credit the design of the largest domestic buildings erected in California during the 1830s and 1840s to their influence. These so-called Monterey style buildings, which are characterized by their second-story balconies or porches, are popularly viewed as a hybrid of American and Hispanic design ideas (Fig. 1).[1] Yet the acknowledgment of the Hispanic contribution to these buildings rarely extends further than the adobe bricks used in the construction of their walls. The most prominent account of the Monterey style houses, Harold Kirker's *California's Architectural Frontier*, contends that "everything" about the Monterey style "testifies to its New England origin."[2]

Extensive field and archival research in California and central Mexico, however, suggests that Monterey style buildings actually display more continuity with Hispanic traditions than has been previously allowed. A detailed analysis of the origins of the principal features of the Monterey style

Fig. 1. Blue Wing Inn, Sonoma, California, ca. 1849. This building was constructed on one of the main streets leading to Sonoma's central plaza. The patronage of this structure has been traditionally ascribed to James Cooper and Thomas Spriggs, immigrants from the United Kingdom who operated a hostelry in the building, which was originally called The Sonoma House.

houses reveals that the designs continued to reflect prominent Hispanic building ideas and practices even as they incorporated new adaptions and innovations introduced by the Americans. Although California's Monterey style buildings were indeed erected after the immigration of Yankee merchants and carpenters to the territory, social and economic changes within the Hispanic community itself are far more likely to have been the stimuli for the creation of these buildings.

In order to understand the significant issues of cultural confrontation, continuity, and change illustrated by the buildings of this period, it is first necessary to isolate the distinctive contributions of the American and Hispanic building traditions of early and mid-nineteenth-century California.[3] This is not always easy to do, for Americans and Hispanics shared a number of similar design ideas whose vernacular manifestations are difficult to separate.

Written accounts and drawings of California towns before the significant influx of Americans confirm the existence of a number of recognizably Hispanic design features. Sun-dried adobe bricks, also a common building material in Mexico and Spain, were used to create walls two to three feet thick. Houses were one story in height and usually limited to one or two rooms.[4] These small buildings reflected the limited economic development of the territory during the first decades of settlement, and they are virtually indistinguishable from houses found throughout Mexico and Latin America today.

Roofs, particularly in Southern California, were flat and covered in adobe and/or natural asphalt. Lithographs and drawings of Los Angeles in the 1850s confirm the continuing popularity of flat roofs, more than a decade after the American conquest.[5] Although the Hispanic buildings shown in these views have almost entirely disappeared, the image they created of a small Mexican pueblo is replicated by innumerable villages throughout Mexico. Pitched and shed roofs running parallel to the main facade were also common in Hispanic California. These were often covered with a thatch of sticks and grasses or wood shakes. The stereo-

typical curved Mexican tiles were being used on some houses as early as 1829.[6]

Another observable Hispanic feature of the early California houses was their occasional lack of internal connections between rooms (Fig. 2).[7] Instead of the common American pattern of internal hallways and communicating rooms, these buildings sometimes featured noncommunicating rooms whose doors opened only to the exterior. Individual rooms, in fact, were often served by both a front and a rear door. The lack of internal connections, coupled with a multiplicity of external ones, may have been a way of achieving a

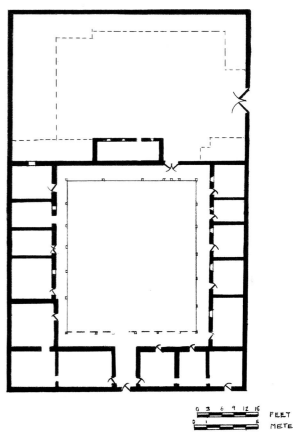

Fig. 2. The Coutts adobe, also known as La Casa del Rancho Guajome, near Mission San Luis Rey, San Diego County, California, ca. 1851. This rural ranch house was erected for Ysidora Bandini and Cave Coutts, her Anglo-American husband. (Drawing by Edward B. Byrne, after Historic American Buildings Survey)

degree of privacy in a household that could include hired workers and unrelated dependents as well as several generations of family members and their spouses.[8]

Typical of vernacular houses in Mexico and Hispanic California is an asymmetry of fenestration and door placement. Doors and windows are irregularly placed on a facade according to the needs (or size) of the interior room. The presence of so many exterior doorways distinguishes Hispanic designs from American ones, which tend to have single, often symmetrically balanced front doors.

The prevalence of large households in nineteenth-century Hispanic America required that most rooms function simultaneously as work spaces, entertain-

ment spaces, and bedrooms. Only the largest houses had separate *salas* (parlors), chapels, and kitchens. Indeed, many vital aspects of Hispanic family life took place on the outside of the house, under porches or detached *jacales* (simple, open-sided shelters of wood and brush) where cooking, playing, working, and socializing mixed. The multiplicity of exterior doors reflects this close relationship between interior spaces and utility spaces outside the building. In contrast to the nineteenth-century American conception of domestic space, the area surrounding the adobe house was part of the building itself, serving as an open-air room. This active use of the out-of-doors is further evident in the prevalence of exterior stairways, which provided the only circulation between the floors of multistory linear houses.

A distinctly Hispanic element of design is the linear or single-file arrangement of rooms. Although there are obvious exceptions to this generalization, a significant proportion of vernacular houses in Latin America exhibit a single-file arrangement of living spaces in the form of an *L*, a *U*, or even a quadrangle in the case of larger houses whose rooms encircled a central courtyard or patio (Fig. 2).[9] These shapes often give evidence of the incremental development of a particular building, but more important, they demonstrate that the Hispanic house of California followed a culturally determined pattern of growth that accentuated the role of outdoor living areas as domestic space. Even houses that were not extended to enclose patios often had a private courtyard behind the house created by means of a wall or walls. Courtyards are also common features of domestic architecture in Spain, and their origins can be traced back through the Moors to the Romans and even earlier cultures of the ancient Near East (Fig. 3).

The most striking architectural features evident in the early illustrations of California were the porches (*portales* or *corredores* in Spanish) that almost invariably extended the length of the main facade (see Fig. 1). Porches, colonnades, and arcades are ubiquitous features of Mexican civil,

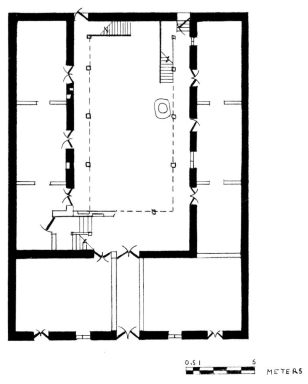

Fig. 3. Urban courtyard-plan house, San Sebastián de la Gomera, Canary Islands, Spain, undated. The courtyard is encircled by a wooden two-story balcony. Buildings with such plans and details are the oldest surviving houses on the island of Gomera. (Drawing by Edward B. Byrne after Luis Feduchi, *Itinerarios de arquitectura popular española* [Barcelona: Editorial Blume, 1973–1978], 4:434)

Fig. 4. Building in Pátzcuaro, Michoacán, Mexico, dating from the mid-nineteenth century. This structure is located on a road connecting Pátzcuaro with nearby villages.

ecclesiastical, and domestic design (Fig. 4). In fact, such features were viewed as valuable communal amenities. The Laws of the Indies (1573), which dictated the planning of Spanish towns in the Western Hemisphere, required that arcades or colonnades be erected along a settlement's main square and principal adjoining streets.[10] These porches or colonnades were at times multistoried, creating upper-level loggias. Balconies (*balcones*) that cantilevered over the sidewalk on decoratively carved wooden beams were also used. The sheltering streetscapes created by these buildings are characteristic of Spanish colonial developments throughout the Americas. Early printed views and photographs of Sonoma, Monterey, and Los Angeles clearly demonstrate that these California towns exhibited the same enduring Hispanic tradition.[11]

Although the Hispanic origins of California's early domestic landscape are undeniable, a number of specific features may be traced to American sources. Most surviving California adobe houses feature at least some American-influenced millwork. Six-over-six-pane, double-hung sash windows, typical of the second quarter of the nineteenth century, were used to replace the characteristic Hispanic casement windows.[12] Baseboards, plank floors, chair rails, cornices, wood shingle roofs, doors, and door frames also display profiles and patterns typical of the American architecture of this period. Exactly when these materials were applied to adobe houses is difficult to determine, as the malleability of adobe easily facilitates alterations. Yet their presence is not unexpected, since many American immigrants worked as carpenters in Hispanic California, and it is believed that they operated the territory's first mechanized sawmills. Here again, however, the picture is complicated by the persistence of indigenous traditions. American motifs frequently appeared beside other details, such as french doors, common to Mexican architecture of the period.

Interior fireplaces may have also been an American introduction. Several accounts state that all cooking in Hispanic California took place outside.[13] However, given the tradition in New Mexico and Mexico of interior cooking or heating facilities, particularly small corner hearths and built-in braziers, the complete absence of such items in California would seem peculiar. Nevertheless, the formal mantels found in many surviving adobe houses must be viewed as American introductions.

The scoring of the plaster on adobe houses to simulate ashlar masonry could be interpreted as an imported Greek Revival element. However, this tradition is also common in Mexico and most countries that shared in the inheritance of Renaissance traditions. Consequently, its appearance in Hispanic California probably represents the convergence of similar Hispanic and American styles. The same might be said for the detailing of interior ceilings. Exposed joists with beaded edges, which were the norm in Hispanic California, were typical of both Mexican and American vernacular design.[14] However, the larger American houses of the mid-nineteenth century would be expected to have their joists concealed with a plaster ceiling. Plaster cornices and ceilings, although often undatable, do appear on some Hispanic buildings in California.

The second-story porches mentioned previously are another example of an architectural trait that was shared by both Americans and Hispanics. Americans arrived in California with knowledge of multitiered verandas or porches, including those that encircled two or more facades. The most famous examples, the plantation houses of the American South, were contemporary with the Monterey style buildings in California. As in Hispanic cultures, American porches served as a social and climatic buffer between the exterior and the interior. They also promoted circulation between rooms, though a typical Anglo-American house would be served by hallways and interior stairs as well.

American carpentry methods are indeed evident on the surviving two-story porches built in Hispanic California. While similar narrow porch posts with chamfered edges are used by vernacular builders in both Mexico and the United States, the vast majority of such posts in California are not capped by the wooden bracket, or *zapata,* that is a ubiquitous feature on porch posts throughout the Hispanic world (see Figs. 1 and 4). This does represent a departure from Hispanic tradition, but it is a minor one; nonetheless it signifies a willingness on the part of Hispanic patrons to accept construction patterns imported by American laborers.

Probably the most significant American contribution to California's domestic architecture was the compact, nonlinear plan, with several rooms arranged around a central hall, as seen in the Thomas Larkin house in Monterey (Fig. 5) or the Guadalupe Rancho adobe in Santa Barbara County.[15] Not surprisingly, these double-pile plans feature many more internal connections than do Hispanic houses. More significantly, they are not as aggressive as the Hispanic houses in their inclusion of the out-of-doors as living space. Rather, they are more closed and inward-looking. Americans have also been credited with introducing symmetry in window and door openings to the facades of some adobe houses.[16] As noted earlier, vernacular Mexican dwellings are usually unconstrained by symmetry.

Most of the American architectural elements that

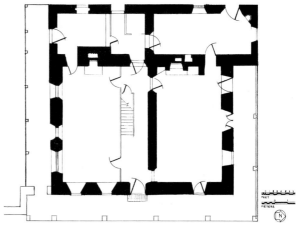

Fig. 5. Plan of the Thomas Larkin house, Monterey, California, 1835–1837. (Drawing by Edward B. Byrne after the Historic American Buildings Survey)

Fig. 6. The Thomas Larkin house was located on one of the principal streets of early Monterey.

appeared in Hispanic California are commonly believed to have been first introduced at the Larkin house in Monterey, hence the term *Monterey style* (Fig. 6). This building has become an icon in the annals of the state's architectural heritage, and it is frequently declared to be the seminal building of the Monterey style. It was erected between 1835 and 1837 by Thomas O. Larkin, a wealthy merchant who was the American consul in California. The Larkin-inspired Monterey style has long been treated as a reflection of the increasing American dominance in the economic and cultural life of the territory, a visible manifestation of the American hegemony that would inevitably lead to annexation.[17]

Larkin's supposed role as architectural innovator seems to stem from the fact that he erected one of the first documented two-story adobe houses in Hispanic California. Larkin left a detailed record of the erection of his house, describing the materials and the non-Hispanic carpenters he employed.[18] But the building was unusual for features other than its height alone; its double-pile plan, central hall, fireplaces, and plastered ceilings were all new. Of course, second-story porches or balconies would have been a departure in a territory where second stories had not yet been seen on secular buildings. Together, these elements have appeared to historians as clear evidence of the wholesale arrival of a new architectural style.

Recently, David Gebhard became the first historian to publish an account critical of this traditional view of the Monterey style. Gebhard successfully challenges the primacy of the Larkin house by documenting the construction of several other similar buildings that were contemporary or perhaps slightly earlier than Larkin's building. More important, Gebhard questions the belief that these buildings were as American as has been claimed. Instead, Gebhard posits that the most prominent features of these buildings—their porches and balconies—are largely derived from an eclectic tradition that developed in the Caribbean, one that combines French and British, as well as Spanish and American, elements. It is known that a number of American immigrants, including Larkin, traveled through the Caribbean on their way to California, and Gebhard uses this fact to explain the diffusion of a Caribbean building type to California. To support this contention, Gebhard uses illustrations of buildings in the Caribbean with similar porches. However, his analysis relies almost entirely on simple visual comparisons, without a thorough investigation of the potential Hispanic contributions. A detailed examination of the Monterey style buildings, particularly with reference to their

plans and their use of space, makes it clear that these buildings are inherently Hispanic in their conception.[19]

As we have seen, the taste for multistory verandas is common to the United States and the Caribbean, as well as to Mexico. But does this necessarily mean that the California builders availed themselves of these various traditions to create a hybrid of Hispanic and American ideas or some kind of regional variation on an international Caribbean style? Probably not, for the vernacular building traditions of Spain and Mexico provide more logical Hispanic models for the derivation of the Monterey style. Studies of vernacular architecture in Spain and its New World colonies have revealed a breathtaking variety of vernacular designs. This rich building tradition provided the Spanish colonists with a great number of design solutions to the conditions they encountered in the Western Hemisphere. One would search in vain for a single or dominant house type or construction method that could characterize Spanish domestic architecture. Yet within certain regions of Spain and Latin America, there are buildings whose plans and details show a clear affinity to the Monterey style in California.[20]

The absence of American influence is evidenced by a closer inspection of the cantilevered balconies on the facades of a number of Monterey-style buildings (Fig. 7). The cantilevered balconies have been interpreted as a Hispanic "substitution" for the more "customary" double veranda.[21] Yet the widespread popularity of such wooden balconies

Fig. 7. José Castro adobe, San Juan Bautista, California, ca. 1840–1841. The Castro adobe faces San Juan Bautista's central plaza.

Fig. 8. House on Federico Tena Street, Pátzcuaro, Michoacán, Mexico, early to mid-nineteenth century. The central *zaguán* (passageway) provides access to an enclosed rear courtyard. The rear facade features a cantilevered balcony similar to the one on the front.

in Spain and Latin America implies that the Hispanic Californians were consciously following their own traditions, rather than creating adaptations to imported American patterns (Fig. 8).

Gebhard's hypothesis of a possible Caribbean source for the Monterey style is not as easy to dismiss. Porches and balconies in the French and British colonies often bear a close resemblance to the buildings of California. Yet such features are equally characteristic of the Spanish colonies in the area. Architectural studies of the Spanish colonies in Cuba, Florida, Venezuela, and Colombia have documented early buildings with an obvious relationship to those later built in California.[22] More to the point, these Caribbean buildings clearly reflect established building patterns in Spain. Though French vernacular buildings might provide similar design solutions, it was certainly unnecessary for the Spanish colonists to employ them. Spain was the first European power to explore and colonize the region, and it remained the dominant culture in the Caribbean into the nineteenth century. If there was a mixing of European design influences in the Caribbean, it was surely one that relied most heavily on Spanish models.

Further evidence for the Hispanic nature of these

buildings is provided by a comparison with structures found in the Mexican state of Michoacán. Located in the interior region of central Mexico, halfway between Mexico City and Guadalajara, Michoacán is noted for its forests, which permitted a greater use of lumber in its architecture than is common in more arid regions of the country. In this Mexican state, there are balconies and porches whose forms and details are very similar to those surviving in territorial California (whose residents exploited the nearby redwood groves for similar ends).[23] A large house in Pátzcuaro, Michoacán (Fig. 9), features a two-story linear plan with an encircling two-story porch and low hip roof that are remarkably similar to the Sánchez adobe in Pacifica or the Blue Wing Inn in Sonoma (see Fig. 1). There is no explicit historical documentation to link the buildings in Michoacán with those in California, for statistical studies of the patterns of Mexican migration to California in this period are incomplete. However, the Monterey style buildings of California and their counterparts in Michoacán provide evidence of the continuing and widespread application of certain Spanish building traditions.

The most dramatic confirmation of the Hispanic source of these California buildings lies less in their particular design motifs than in their overall proxemic qualities. While there is, undeniably, a superficial relationship between the facades of California buildings and those of a variety of cultural groups, the plans and siting of these buildings demonstrate that the Hispanics were drawing upon their own particular traditions. Most of the documented Monterey style buildings maintain the Hispanic single-file arrangement of exterior-orientated rooms. This significant, basic, and enduring quality distinguishes these buildings from their supposed American prototypes. Only rarely do Monterey style houses have double-pile, inwardly focused room arrangements.

The Petaluma adobe, one of the best known of the Monterey style buildings, offers a dramatic example of the central patio previously described,

Fig. 9. House at #47 Jose Ma. Cos, Pátzcuaro, Michoacán, Mexico, early to mid-nineteenth century. This house is located on a hill overlooking central Pátzcuaro.

a form with no domestic equivalent in the United States at that time (Fig. 10). Unfortunately, only the western half of the building survives today. The building was erected as the headquarters of Mariano Vallejo's forty-four-thousand-acre ranch; like many other rural Hispanic buildings, it was placed on a treeless hill that allowed for adequate drainage and the surveillance of the countryside.[24] The building shows obvious affinities with another hacienda (or large agricultural complex) located in Michoacán. This building also features a two-story exterior porch, a completely enclosed courtyard with access provided through a *zaguán,* or wide gate, and two-story wooden porches encircling the courtyard elevations of the house (Fig. 11). The town houses of Pátzcuaro, Michoacán, also feature interior and exterior multistory porches, which are frequently supported by narrow chamfered posts similar to the ones on the California examples.[25] Finally, large rural dwellings can be found in Spain whose form and detailing clearly prefigure the patterns that are evident

in Mexico and California (Fig. 12).

Hispanic single-file houses with a patio and/or porches even proved popular with American immigrants, as can be seen in the Jacob Leese adobe in Sonoma and the Temple house in Long Beach.[26] But should this come as a surprise? While these houses are often named after the male Americans who owned them, it must not be forgotten that nearly all of these men secured their positions in the Mexican territory by marrying prominent Mexican women. Curiously, historians have searched these houses for architectural features that might reflect the American heritage of the husbands, while largely ignoring the influence or desires of their native-born Hispanic wives.[27]

Unlike their American counterparts, Monterey style porches and cantilevered balconies often functioned as the primary circulation spaces between rooms and floors. And many of the Monterey style houses still preserve their exterior staircases and many exterior doors, which is another clear indication of the tenacity of Hispanic atti-

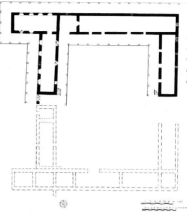

Fig. 10. Petaluma adobe, Petaluma, California, ca. 1834–1844, built as the headquarters of Mariano Vallejo's enormous ranch, plan and view of the central courtyard. Only the western half of the building survives today. Information on the floor plan of the eastern half was gathered through an archaeological investigation. (Drawing by Edward B. Byrne, after California Department of Parks and Recreation, *Petaluma Adobe* [n.p., n.d.], the Historic American Buildings Survey, and Dell Upton)

Fig. 11. Hacienda Chapultepec, near Tzurumutaro, Michoacán, Mexico, early nineteenth century, view of the courtyard serving the residential section of the hacienda. This large rural building also features a second courtyard used for livestock and related agricultural work.

tudes toward circulation and outside space. While some Hispanic houses do adopt central hallways, as can be seen in the José Castro house in San Juan Bautista (Fig. 7), it is possible that at least a few might be converted *zaguanes*.

The distinct Hispanic device of an enclosed open space, observable both in the microcosm of the domestic patio or yard and in the macrocosm of the central civic plaza, is evident throughout the built environment of Mexico and colonial Califor-

Fig. 12. Rural ranch building, Puntallana de la Palma, Canary Islands, Spain, undated. Simple wooden balconies and porches are typical of La Palma. (From Luis Feduchi, *Itinerarios de arquitectura popular española* [Barcelona: Editorial Blume, 1973–1978], 4:443)

nia. Whether urban houses in Los Angeles or haciendas in the countryside, the early Hispanic buildings of California re-created again and again a distinctly Hispanic method of arranging and enclosing domestic space. It seems improbable that the Californians would have turned to a Caribbean hybrid for their balconies, when the buildings in question so obviously follow the other forms and patterns of Hispanic architecture.

If foreign influences were not responsible for the development of the Monterey style houses, what was? A more plausible explanation for the genesis of these buildings can be found by examining the social, economic, and political conditions in California during the 1830s and 1840s. Although this study has focused on the largest houses of Hispanic California, it must be noted that most of the houses erected in the territory were of the simpler one-story type. Unfortunately, very few of these remain standing today.[28] Like the architecture of other eras, the dwellings of the wealthy are the ones that most often survived. Consequently, one might properly ask, where are the dwellings of the

wealthy and powerful in the pre-Larkin period? To answer this, one would need to turn to the missions, for here lay the real material wealth of the territory.

Before Mexico achieved independence in 1821, Spanish laws banning trade with foreign powers had kept California underdeveloped and in economic isolation. After these restrictions were repealed by the new Mexican government, California became a prominent stopping point on the lucrative Chinese and Philippine trade routes. Utilizing cheap Native American labor for their expanding agricultural enterprises, the missions became California's dominant commercial power; and it was with the missions that the lucrative American hide and tallow trade began in the 1820s.[29]

However, the unstable central Mexican government and the economic power of the missions alienated a number of younger Hispanic Californians, including Mariano Vallejo and José Castro, who began to agitate for various political reforms. Most significantly, they lobbied for the secularization or dismemberment of the mission system.

Their efforts came to fruition in 1831, and by 1836 most of the missions' properties had been ceded to private ownership.[30] This period corresponds exactly with the first appearance of the Monterey style. Eventually over eight hundred Californians shared in the carved-up mission ranchos, and those who were particularly well connected profited greatly. Leonard Pitt has observed that secularization "upset class relations, altered ideology and shifted the ownership of enormous wealth. . . . [This] revolutionary social and economic transformation was California's most important event before the discovery of gold."[31] The owners of these newly formed ranchos "evolved into a prosperous ranchero class who, with civil and military authorities, formed an elite."[32] This newly landed gentry also inherited the missions' hide and tallow trade and further expanded it. Exports from California nearly doubled between 1835 and 1841.[33]

This pronounced economic revolution was the real instigator of the dramatic changes in the domestic architecture of California, not Thomas Larkin, other Americans, or ideas from the West Indies. It is not surprising that the Hispanic nouveaux riches of California would desire finer houses in recognition of their elevated status. And it should be expected that they would turn to Hispanic forms for their architecture. It is but a coincidence that secularization allowed the erection of the largest Hispanic dwellings only after the arrival of Americans such as Larkin.

These Monterey style structures were in fact the northernmost representatives of well-established Hispanic building traditions. The Monterey style should be abandoned as a distinct stylistic entity, as these buildings can be interpreted more appropriately as notable examples of the houses of the Mexican landed elite. Together with the smaller single-story houses of the territory, they demonstrate the range of Mexican housing types in a socially stratified society. Certainly some of these structures feature details like mill work and, more rarely, interior staircases and central halls that distinguish them from earlier Mexican models. But these details, which may have been added over time, do not change the Hispanic essence of these buildings.[34]

The traditional exegesis of the Monterey style as an American invention appears to be a belated application of the philosophy of Manifest Destiny. In many instances, the popularity of the Monterey style among the native Hispanic population has been presented as proof of American cultural dominance, or even a desire on the part of leading Hispanics to make California a part of the United States.[35] However, a closer reading of the political and social history of the 1830s and 1840s does not support this position. These houses do not reflect a form of cultural capitulation on the part of Mexican patrons and builders but rather the increasing power, wealth, and self-confidence of the Hispanic upper classes. The territory remained vibrantly Mexican in its spirit and life-style, in spite of trade and intermarriage with Americans.[36] The Hispanic Californians' tolerance of foreigners and their admiration of American technology and political ideals did not lead to a spiritual abandonment of Hispanic building traditions. The final triumph of American architecture would have to await military conquest in 1846 and the subsequent deluge of American immigrants.

III. Buildings and Popular Culture

ELIZABETH COLLINS CROMLEY

A HISTORY OF AMERICAN BEDS AND BEDROOMS

Life in the middle-class American home of the nineteenth and twentieth centuries could hardly have proceeded without the bedroom. Everyone needs to sleep, and most people of this period have preferred to have some privacy while doing it. But the bedroom is also the most unexamined of household spaces, and purposely so, since it represents the private within the privacy of home. This essay will explore the bedroom of the later nineteenth and early twentieth centuries in order to fill in the gap between the word on an architect's plan and the uses and meanings of this room in day-to-day life.

Research for this work has been restricted to published articles and building plans that document middle-class bedrooms. Within those boundaries, some general statements can be made about the spatial location of the bedroom in a house, the role of "privacy," who the occupants of a bedroom are, and how personal character may find expression in the bedroom. Also considered are the ways in which the bedroom has been seen as the site of health concerns and, finally, the bedroom's role in fantasy. None of these issues explains the bedroom fully, but taken together they begin to uncover aspects of its changing meaning in the bourgeois home.[1]

The sleeping aspect of household life is supported by the house's spatial structure; as that structure changes, the locations for sleeping and the relationships between sleeping and other activities change. As the spaces change, so does the name of the room in which the bed is located. *Chamber* often indicates a bedroom but initially meant an inner room, also called a parlor, in which to withdraw from the activities of the traditional hall.[2] Later nineteenth- and twentieth-century house plans often use *chamber* for higher-status bedrooms and *bedroom* for lower-status ones. I will use the term *bedroom* for all sleeping rooms (*sleeping room* indicating function rather than nomenclature) and begin my decoding of the bedroom by looking at changing attitudes toward the space that contains the bed.

In the English or Dutch colonists' house of seventeenth-century America, bedrooms as such were among the missing features. Of course people slept then as now, but where they did it in the house shows our seventeenth-century predecessors to have had a very different conception of how space can be divided. In the hall-parlor plan type of seventeenth-century New England, the hall was the site for cooking and eating, light household production, and a host of other activities done by all the members of the household. The other ground-floor room was the parlor, in which the "best" things, people, and occasions had their places. In the parlor was the best bed; along with it were the best tea table and chairs, the mirror, the tapestry table covering, and other fine-quality possessions of the household. The parlor served as the sleeping place for the heads of the household, since they, like the tea table and mirror, had the most elevated status in this house. This was a world that divided space according to the meaning and value of its contents, not strictly according to the separate functions that it served.[3]

In the well-to-do New England household of the mid-eighteenth century, a clarification of room functions accompanied an expansion in the number of rooms and in the amount of circulation space.[4] Generous passages and stairways created a system of movement through the house. In this era's house we find fully developed bedrooms, with bed curtains, chair seats, and window curtains all made from matching textiles. Canopied beds revived for New England householders some of the authority signified by the hangings on royal beds and the rooflike terminations of pulpits and thrones.

The earlier seventeenth-century merger of activities in the best parlor was reduced in the eighteenth-century bedroom. The use of other spaces in the house for specific activities freed the bedroom of competing uses. Now its inhabitants used the bedroom for daily sleeping and dressing activities, for quiet retirement, and for socializing with their nearest friends and family members. Periodically, at births or deaths, bedrooms hosted more formal receptions. By the eighteenth century, then, a specific room that was focused on the bed and could be called a bedroom had become common in prosperous households, and it continued to be available to the builders of middle-class houses throughout the period we are considering here.

Where a sleeping room should go in relation to other rooms in a house is a complex question. Late twentieth-century house designers tend to gather bedrooms into a group clearly separated from more public activity zones. But in houses of the nineteenth century bedrooms were often linked directly to the public reception rooms. Designs from Gervase Wheeler's 1855 book *Homes for the People* provide examples of houses for rich and poor, set in both urban and rural settings, suggesting preferred bedroom locations. He proposed a two-story addition on the front of an old house in order to give it an up-to-date villa appearance (Fig. 1). On the ground floor are the parlor (labeled room number 2), the dining room (4), and a

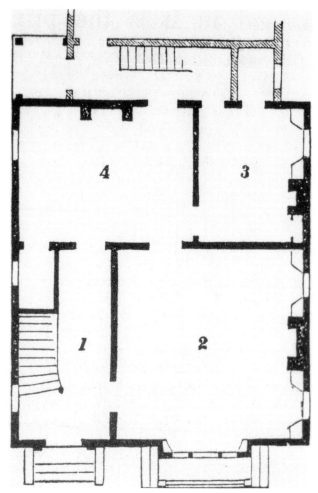

Fig. 1. This plan of an addition to a farmhouse places the bedroom in direct communication with both dining room and a back door. (From Gervase Wheeler, *Homes for the People in Suburb and Country* [1855; rpt. New York: Arno Press, 1972], 387)

bedroom (3). The bedroom has a door communicating with an entry in the old house, a door into the dining room, and, from there, immediate access to the parlor. On the second floor, which Wheeler calls "the chamber floor," there are three large bedrooms for other family members. Third-floor attic and tower spaces provided more potential sleeping spaces for family or servants.[5]

A plan published by Wheeler for a two-story detached cottage with an attic for a suburban or country location (Fig. 2) has a ground-floor center-passage plan with a parlor at the front (labeled room number 5), a sitting room across from it (2), a dining room at the rear (3) that communicates with the kitchen in the wing, and in the corner of the ground floor: a bedroom. This room is linked to the dining room through an entry fitted with built-in drawers and a "wardrobe." This bedroom is also linked to the parlor by one door. Above, on a bedroom floor, are four large family sleeping rooms plus two small ones for children or servants.[6]

Both of these designs provide a separate second floor for the majority of family bedrooms but significantly include a bedroom on the ground floor attached to the most important reception rooms in the house. While a ground-floor bedroom was sometimes appropriated as a guest room, or as a sickroom to save invalids and their caretakers from climbing stairs, often this room belonged to the heads of the household. The master and mistress had their room linked to the principal reception rooms of the house, asserting their authority through spatial location. In general, status decreased with floor level.

Linked reception rooms and master bedrooms became less common in the early twentieth century. The *Delineator,* a magazine specializing in women's fashion and household decoration, held a competition for a three-thousand-dollar house in 1909. The first three prizewinners deployed all their bedrooms on second-story, separate bedroom floors. In the house designed by architect Claude Bragdon of Rochester, the ground floor has a kitchen and dining and living rooms. The bedroom floor has four sleeping rooms: one a servant's room, two bedrooms each marked "child's room," and a third bedroom called "own room."[7] The bedrooms tend to have a single door from a corridor, or at most one other door that links the parents' room with a child's. This plan clarifies room location by function rather than by status of occupant, placing all household members' sleeping rooms together on the second level. The privacy of bed-

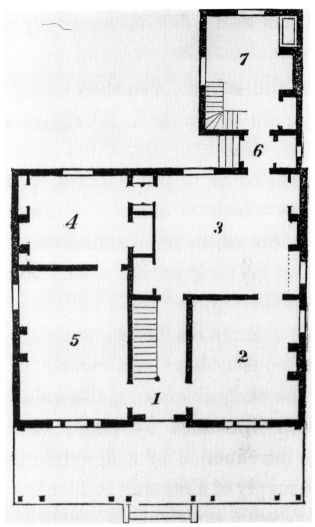

Fig. 2. In the plan of a square cottage the bedroom is linked to the parlor and dining room. (From Wheeler, *Homes for the People,* 322)

room occupants is enhanced as their access from the principal floor of the house is reduced. By the early twentieth century, the category "sleeping zone" prevailed over competing categories such as "servants' zone" and "family zone."

During the same period, problems in locating the bedroom confronted designers of single-floor homes. The plans for early New York City apartment buildings often mix sleeping rooms for the family with the family's other, more social rooms, as seen in Richard Morris Hunt's Stuyvesant Apartments of 1869 (Fig. 3). Here a bedroom is linked to the parlor at the front of the building, while other family bedrooms fall between the dining room and the kitchen to the rear.[8] By the first decade of the twentieth century, apartment designers preferred grouping all family bedrooms together in a sleeping zone, as seen in Israels and Harder's apartment house on Irving Place (Fig. 4), where all reception rooms are grouped at the social end of the plan, and all bedrooms, for both family and servant, are segregated at the other end.

Designers of twentieth-century bungalows, two- and three-family flats, and ranch houses also laid

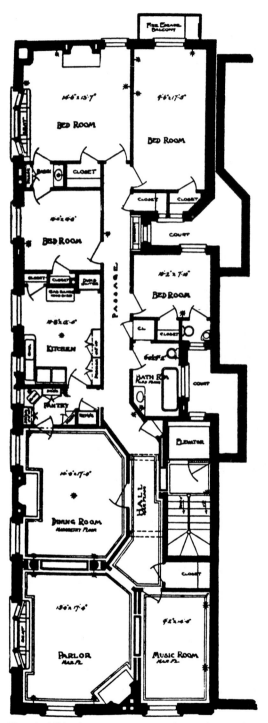

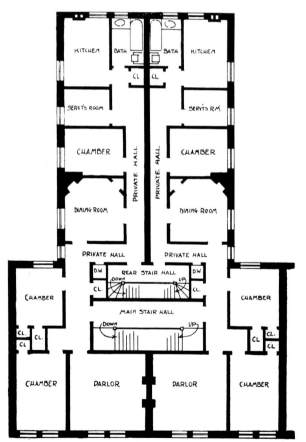

Fig. 3. In the plan of the Stuyvesant Apartments by Richard Morris Hunt, 1869, a chamber is linked to the parlor and given a street view, while lesser bedrooms look onto a light court. The building has since been demolished. (*Architectural Record* 11 [July 1901]: 479)

Fig. 4. All bedrooms are grouped together in the plan of the Irving Place Apartments by Israels and Harder, 1900. (*Architectural Record* 11 [July 1901]: 495)

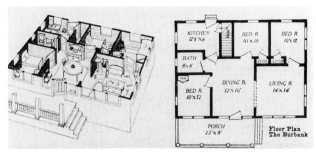

Fig 5. A prefabricated house has all the bedrooms opening directly into the dining and living rooms. (From Aladdin Co., *Redi-Cut Homes* catalog, Bay City Michigan, 1916–1917)

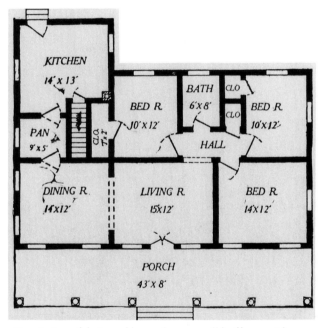

Fig. 6. A prefabricated house has a small buffer corridor protecting the bedrooms from the social areas. (From Aladdin Co., *Redi-Cut Homes* catalog, Bay City Michigan, 1916–1917)

all rooms out on one floor and had to manage the relation of bedrooms to social spaces. Two inexpensive prefabricated Aladdin Redi-Cut houses of 1918–1919 answer the question of the bedroom's relation to other rooms in the house in radically different ways. One has its bedrooms deployed all around the social spaces with doorways opening directly into the living and dining rooms (Fig. 5);

the other has all its bedrooms grouped off a little hallway that completely buffers them from the social spaces (Fig. 6). One plan enhances privacy while the other preserves opportunities for intra-familial surveillance.

Although this history of the spatial location of bedrooms at first seems to indicate a development toward a clarification of rooms' uses, toward a room that is purely a "bedroom," and toward an isolation of all bedrooms in a zone of privacy, the bungalow examples remind us of the complexity of the question. The locations of bedrooms and their spatial relationships to other rooms of the house need further research. One-floor house plans, like two- and three-floor models, show a variety of answers to the problem of bedroom placement, sometimes grouping the bedrooms by their sleeping function, but sometimes locating them in response to other family demands.

While everybody sleeps, different members of the household have different claims to a bed or a room of their own. The bourgeois house of the nineteenth and twentieth centuries typically had at least two if not many more bedrooms, but who got a bedroom of her or his own was an open question. Children were often grouped together and may have had their own single beds but not yet their own bedrooms. Servants, if lucky, were treated the same as children with one bed per servant. Boys and girls old enough to be understood to have individual identities could have their own beds and bedrooms; and even invalids had bedrooms designed for their needs. But one of the things one was likely to lose upon marriage was a room of one's own.

Bedrooms, among all the rooms in a house, are known for their ability to convey *individuality*, noted Ella Church in 1877 in her home-decorating-advice column for the family magazine *Appleton's Journal:* one can tell at a glance the mother's room from the brother's room. In the mother's room one finds an extra large and comfortable bed, an easy chair, and a table—things used for "accommodating numerous inmates." The bachelor's room (the uncle's or brother's) is full of news-papers, pipes, cigar boxes, and photographs of actresses. The young lady's room has muslin flounc-es on everything, usually either pink or blue; the grandmother's room has an old-fashioned four-poster bedstead, three-story bureau, and her favor-ite easy chair. Only in the children's room, with its "snowy-draped" bed for the six-year-old and swinging crib for the two-year-old, are sexes com-bined and individual identity statements blurred.[9]

At the turn of the century, many writers gave the bedroom power to express the Self. "Every oppor-tunity should be given for the development of indi-viduality in a room which is preeminently the corner of the home which is truly home to the occupant, where the taste of no one, either guest or relative, need be considered."[10] The other rooms must reflect the life of the whole family and every-one's various occupations, but the bedroom "is the place for one's personal belongings, those num-berless little things which are such sure indications of individual character and fancy . . . the one room where purely personal preference may be freely exercised."[11]

Of course, the marital bedroom poses a chal-lenge to self-expression. While the modern mar-ried couple's bedroom is almost invariably called the "master" bedroom, most nineteenth- and twen-tieth-century descriptions assume a bias toward the wife's needs, listing dressing tables, mirrors tall enough to see the hem of a dress, and lounges on which to rest during the day as necessary elements in the couple's bedroom. Nineteenth-century de-scriptions often call this room "mother's," even though father slept there too.

In E. C. Gardner's entertaining 1880s book *The House that Jill Built after Jack's Had Proved a Fail-ure,* an uncle of the family espouses the "individu-ality" position in regard to separate bedrooms for husband and wife: "The personality of human be-ings should be respected. The chief object of home is to give each individual a chance for unfettered development. Every soul is a genius at times and feels the necessity of isolation. Especially do we

need to be alone in sleep, and to this end every person in a house is entitled to a separate apart-ment."[12]

Bedrooms test the understanding of the "mother or house-ruler" insofar as she allows each occu-pant some space for self-expression, asserted Can-dace Wheeler in her 1903 book *Principles of Home Decoration.* "Characteristics of the inmate will write themselves unmistakably in the room," Wheeler continued. If you put a college boy in the white and gold bedroom, soon sporting elements and an atmosphere of outdoor life will creep in. "Banners and balls and bats, and emblems of the 'wild thyme' order will color its whiteness. . . . In the same way, girls would change the bare asceticism of a monk's cell into a bower of lilies and roses."[13] Home decorating books advised parents on the proper decorations for the boys and girls of the family. One article suggested making furniture of railroad ties for a boy's room.[14] Girls' rooms had junior dressing tables as well as space for artistic and intellectual development.

What has been represented in these quotes as the expression of individuality was often, instead, an expression constructed out of markers of gen-der roles. This is made clear by the advice of a keeper of a boardinghouse on decorating young men's rooms. What might be seen as "individualiz-ing" in a private setting is revealed to be generic and gender-related in the boardinghouse. This boardinghouse keeper advises that the pictures in a boy's sitting room should be "strong, bordering on frisky," with appropriate images including bull-dogs, baseball players, college scenes, and horses. The pictures in this room should represent "work-aday life—that of a man among men." But in the young man's bedroom should be works "prophetic of his home life. . . . His pictures there should be soft and inspiring like the caress of a good woman. . . . The young man has no mother, sis-ter, wife or child to keep his life sweet and clean, his ideals high and true; the influence of his land-lady" is all he has. So give him an American flag to cultivate his patriotism; hang a madonna in his room, and also a picture of "the Master." "One or two photographs of the mother or best girl should be neatly framed and kept nice—moreover they should be looked at every day."[15]

The sincerity of advice books in urging that each bedroom's occupant have plenty of latitude in self-expression through the choice of objects and furniture must be questioned. All this advice assigns predictable signs of gender to those presumed individuals. All girls should have ruffled dressing tables; all boys need to decorate their rooms with baseball bats. Young men all need to declare their individuality through "frisky" pictures of bulldogs; all mothers' rooms must express nurturance. It seems that the bedroom's decor shapes its occupant into correct gender roles, rather than that the occupant expresses individual taste in shaping the bedroom.

While the bedroom affects psychological health, it has a more overt role in matters of physical health. Sleeping of course is essential to health, but many other health concerns occupied authorities on bedrooms in nineteenth- and twentieth-century literature. Catharine Beecher told her readers how to keep the bedroom dust and bug free in her 1869 *American Woman's Home,* offering recipes for poisoning bedbugs and advice on beating rugs.[16] Many midcentury writers argued against bed curtains, wallpapers, and carpets because they concealed dust and made it impossible to have the bedroom really clean. Metal bed frames had their advocates because bedbugs would not live in their joints as they did in the joints of any wooden bed.

An 1850 article by Harriet Martineau in *Harper's Monthly* gave mock-serious instructions on how to make an unhealthy bedroom: Cover the fireplace up so foul air cannot escape during the night; likewise shut the window. Don't use perforated zinc paneling; if you do, foul air will escape. Close the curtains around your bed; they will be especially effective in containing the "poison vapor bath" if they are of a thick material. Cover yourself with a feather bed so that your skin can't transpire. Likewise wear a tight nightcap.[17] Martineau's con-

cerns centered not on dust and dirt, but on the body's need for fresh air and good air circulation.

The bedroom "is really the most important room in the house by far and far again," advised Dr. Richardson in his home-health magazine articles of 1880.[18] But it is often the room that is least considered in building or furnishing a house. People often turn any unused space, closet, attic, or dressing room into a bedroom, ignoring the true needs of sleepers. Instead he urged designers of houses to make sure the bedroom faced southwest for the best breezes, and he urged sleepers to face east so the body was lined up with the sun's path for greatest health. Health would be protected by locating the bedroom in relation to sun and climate.

By the turn of the century the most pressing health worry had shifted to the prevention of tuberculosis, which experts believed could be combated by means of fresh air. In order to avoid the "Great White Plague," some people even gave up kissing their kin, reported *Scientific American* in 1909. "Fresh air and plenty of it is the best preventive for consumption, the grip, bronchitis, common colds, and pneumonia." The journal even advised using tissue-paper handkerchiefs.[19]

For the early twentieth-century germ-conscious sleeper, fresh air was critical. Popular magazines like the *Ladies' Home Journal* recommended that people build screened-porch sleeping areas just outside their bedrooms (Fig. 7). Patented sleeping bags to use on the porch left only the head exposed, and it was then covered with a hood. Even so, one could get cold going from the warm changing room to the cold outdoor bed.

There were two solutions to this difficulty of keeping the body warm while sleeping in the outdoor air. The window bed extended over the windowsill at night, and the sleeper pulled an awning over his head to protect himself from rain. When above the first floor, however, this method could make one feel in danger of falling, and worse yet, the "bed shows from the outside of the dwelling."[20] The fresh-air tent was more inconspicuous. It fit

Fig. 7. Sleeping porch additions could open from existing bedrooms. (From C. M. D'Enville, "Sleeping Outdoors for Health: Outdoor Sleeping for the Well Man," *Country Life in America* 16 [May 1909]: 43–46)

around the open window and extended inward over the head of the bed and the head of the sleeper (Fig. 8). This tent had a window on the bedroom side so the sleeper could converse with others in the room, and it could be used in a double bed where only one person wanted the air. If the weather was cold, one could use a hood with a shoulder cape that left only the eyes, nose, and mouth exposed to the air.

Although much specialization had gone on within the standard house design, so that many family members had their own rooms where their personalities could be expressed, in sleeping porches they all came together again. A contributor to *Country Life* in 1909 cited an example of a twelve-foot-square sleeping porch used by two adults in a double bed and three strong, healthy children on three cots, all enjoying a bedroom together.[21]

By 1909 outdoor sleeping had become immensely popular, observed a contributor to *Country Life*. A "model house at moderate cost," designed by Ohio architect C. K. Shilling in that year and published in *Country Life*, recognized the new taste for outdoor sleeping and living (Figs. 9 and 10). The dining room and living room each have an outdoor counterpart attached. On the second floor three of the four bedrooms have attached sleeping porches. These have screens in the summer and canvas shields in winter, with floors of reinforced concrete. The outdoor spaces are incorporated under the main house roof and thus do not read as porches but as part of the body of the house.[22]

A Mr. Hoag in the same year described a little wooden house for sleeping out, created as an adjunct to his and his wife's permanent summer cottage. They called it their "sleeping machine" because it produced a lot of sleep. At 8 × 5 feet, it cost $20. The house had a shed roof and flaps that opened up on its south and west sides, lined with mosquito wire. The sleeper's head faced southwest to catch the prevailing breezes. This bedroom had broken entirely free of the house and led a life of its own in the backyard.[23]

Bedrooms may literally break free of houses, but more usually they are places where freedom is found through dreams and fantasies. I conclude with two fantasies of the bedroom. In the first, a journalist of 1902 recollected how mysterious it

Fig. 8. An indoor bed tent covers the sleeper's head, which is exposed to the outside air. (From Katherine Louise Smith, "Indoor Bed Tents," *Scientific American* n.s. 101 [December 1909]: 7)

was to go to bed in her grandmother's huge, canopied, mahogany bedstead; to a child it was so high, and its interior was cavernous and darkened by curtains. She remembered imagining fairies, gnomes, brownies, and angels as inhabiting the space enclosed by the roomlike bed.[24] Hers is a fantasy of pure interiority, where enclosure is so complete that the inhabitant of the bed advances into a world of imagination.

In the second fantasy, a young man recalled his hall bedroom at the top of a city boardinghouse as the site for imaginary travel. Although his room was the size of a closet, it had a skylight controlled by dangling ropes, and through it he could look at the sky and the stars. When he opened the skylight and turned out the gaslight the moon and stars seemed as near as if he were in a meadow in the country. His room was so small and compact he likened it to a ship's cabin, and the muffled city sounds to the sea. When covered in snow the skylight gave a greenish light, and he imagined he was in a cave rather than on a ship, "primitive man in the early wilderness." He says his room possessed a genius for freeing his imagination to such adventures. The temptations of the Hotel St. Regis were nothing to him; he preferred his imaginary voyages in the boardinghouse hall bedroom.[25]

In the cavernous four-poster, the little girl is visited by goblins and angels; in the hall bedroom, the young man sails out toward adventure. Both

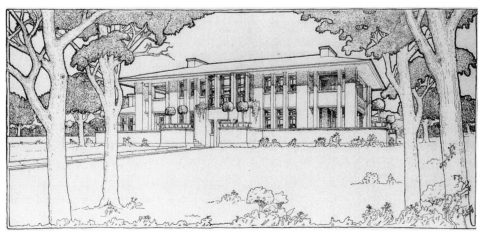

Fig. 9. Elevation of a house designed by C. K. Shilling. (From "A Country Home with Outdoor Sleeping, Living, and Dining Rooms," *Country Life in America* 16 [May 1909]: 71)

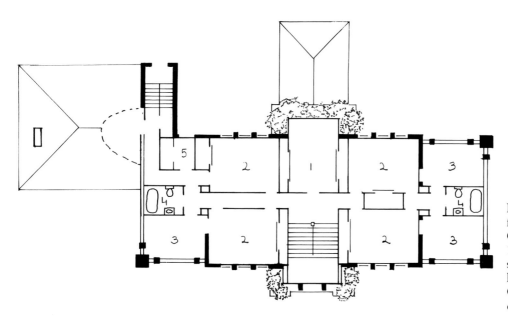

Fig. 10. Second-floor plan for a house designed by C. K. Shilling. Room key: 1. solarium; 2. chamber; 3. sleeping porch; 4. bath; 5. linen closet. (From "A Country Home with Outdoor Rooms," 72)

have their imaginations liberated by their bedrooms. Both fantasies are tied to the particular kinds of beds and bedrooms available at a specific historical moment.[26]

A turn-of-the-century writer speculated, "Perhaps another generation will see the total disappearance of the bedroom proper, and weary individuals, when night falls, will merely sink to rest on the hygienically-covered floor of their library or sitting-room."[27] This has not happened for most of us yet. Instead the bedroom has continued to develop along many of these historical lines into the 1990s, its full participation in the social life of the house always restricted by the bed, yet its pure privacy always compromised by other furnishings—if not a tea table, then a TV. "Personal expression" in the bedroom continues to be dominated by signs of gender. The bedroom continues to serve as a barometer of the ambiguous role of privacy within the family.

LELAND M. ROTH

GETTING THE HOUSES TO THE PEOPLE
EDWARD BOK, THE LADIES' HOME JOURNAL,
AND THE IDEAL HOUSE

At the start of this century, American political progressives fervently believed that social reform was necessary and possible; they set about changing the world around them.[1] Some devoted themselves to reshaping the heavily idealized single-family house, giving it new forms and seeking ways to make such a house available to greater numbers of people. Among the most effective agents in stimulating reform were popular magazines. Some were large-circulation, general magazines that championed a range of causes; others—with more limited circulation—focused specifically on improving house design and interior decoration. This essay surveys the efforts of one magazine—the *Ladies' Home Journal*—to bring about what its editor felt would be a better standard in house design at the turn of the century. Other magazines also aimed at housing reform, among them *House Beautiful* and *The Craftsman,* but none had the impact of the *Ladies' Home Journal.*[2]

During its heyday, the *Ladies' Home Journal* was phenomenally successful. Today the *Journal* has been eclipsed by other women's self-help magazines, yet ninety years ago it reached a massive audience. At its height in 1915, *The Craftsman* had reached a maximum circulation of 22,500, while *House Beautiful* had a run of 45,000 that same year.[3] Most mass-market popular magazines of the period, such as *Collier's* or *Munsey's,* had

circulations of from 400,000 to 700,000. But far surpassing them all, in 1915 the *Ladies' Home Journal* had a circulation of over 1.6 million subscription copies. Hence a bungalow design published in the *Ladies' Home Journal* was seen by far more people than one in *The Craftsman.* One estimate of the reach of the *Ladies' Home Journal* was that in 1903, 20 percent of the entire American population read the magazine, and more than 60 percent of all American women read it.[4] No wonder it was called "the Bible of the American home."[5] Although aimed primarily at women, the *Journal* appealed to a wide readership; for example, government figures indicated the *Journal* was the third most requested magazine among soldiers overseas during World War I.[6] For the middle-class market—the family with an annual income of $1,200 to $2,500—the *Journal* was perhaps the single most effective agent in disseminating ideas regarding improvement in home planning and decoration.[7] Once placed in circulation, these ideas had a widespread effect on popular architecture during the period.

One reason for the unique success of the *Ladies' Home Journal* was its editor, Edward Bok. Although Bok did not actually establish the *Journal,* he was appointed editor in 1889 and he gave it his personal stamp for the next thirty years.[8] Bok took a progressive editorial stance, advocating a number of social, political, and environmental reforms. Theodore Roosevelt is reported to have said that Edward Bok was the only man he knew "who changed, for the better, the architecture of an entire nation."[9] It is a sweeping claim, but it seems fair to say that Bok did indeed exert an exceptional influence. Public campaigns initiated by the *Journal* were, in fact, responsible for the passage of the Federal Food and Drug Act and for a treaty with Great Britain allocating the use of water at Niagara Falls for hydroelectric power.[10]

The pervasive influence of Bok and the *Journal* was the result of several factors, the most basic of which was the magazine's phenomenal reach. The *Journal* began publication in 1883 as a women's supplement in a Philadelphia farm magazine, *Tribune and Farmer*. Within four years the *Journal* had become independent and achieved a circulation of 400,000; at the turn of the century under Bok's leadership circulation had doubled to 800,000, and in 1903 the *Journal* was being mailed to 1 million subscribers. By the time Bok retired in 1919, subscriptions had doubled again to 2 million.[11]

A second factor that set Bok's enterprise apart was that, while his desire was to make the work of professional architects available to readers at minimal cost, he never lost touch with the mainstream tastes of his audience. Bok's architectural program was effective because of its general conservatism. After all, Bok was publishing a popular magazine aimed at the broad middle class, and he tried to provide reform-minded designs that would still appeal to all interests.

The third factor contributing to Bok's success was the long run of his model designs. They appeared in the *Journal* for almost a quarter of a century, from 1896 until Bok's formal retirement in 1919. Only *The Craftsman* and *House Beautiful* carried model house designs on as regular a schedule.

In his autobiography, Edward Bok wrote that he endeavored to make the *Journal* a magazine of "uplift and inspiration," of "light and leading in the women's world." He sought a happy medium, he said, "between shooting over the public's head and shooting too far under it." His standard was to

give his readers the subjects they asked for, but, as he wrote, "invariably on a slightly higher plane, and each year [I] raised the standard a notch."[12]

In traveling across the country to conduct magazine business, Bok was struck by what he viewed as the poor design quality of American residences. "Where they were not positively ugly," he wrote, "they were . . . repellently ornate." He felt that money wasted on useless ornament should be invested on functional planning. Bok's inquiries revealed that home owners hardly ever consulted an architect when building. Bok began to feel, he wrote, "a keen desire to take hold of the small American house and make it architecturally better."[13] In 1896, Bok married his boss's daughter, Mary Louise Curtis; in thinking about where they would live the couple was forced to personally evaluate the current state of American domestic architecture.

The year before, in December 1895, Bok had published his first model house design, "A $3500 Suburban House" (Fig. 1). It was a traditional English Tudoresque design, in keeping with the contemporary Arts and Crafts Movement, by William L. Price, a young Philadelphia architect who was soon to design the Boks' own residence in suburban Merion, Pennsylvania. Bok made no particular demands on his contributing architects as to historic style or appearance, but later he did stipulate that there be cross ventilation and no separate front "parlor," a room he considered useless; instead, there was to be a single living room.[14]

Publication of the Tudoresque house by Price established the format followed in the presentations over the next twenty years. There would be an exterior perspective, an interior perspective (and sometimes two of each), full sets of plans, and perhaps several vignettes, accompanied by a text describing the house, its placement on the lot, landscaping, the interior finishes, and a breakdown of the estimated cost (Fig. 2).

The second house to appear in the *Journal*, in February 1896, was a Georgian colonial design by Cram, Wentworth, and Goodhue of Boston. Cram

Fig. 1. William L. Price, "A $3500 Suburban House," *Ladies' Home Journal* 13 (December 1895): 37.

wrote in his text that this design remedied the "fantastic absurdities" of Queen Anne houses that reflected more the ambitions of speculative builders than the tastes of prospective owners; he believed his design was typically American and well suited to the American suburb. It is difficult to ascertain what these young architects thought they might accomplish by letting Bok publish their drawings. Cram says nothing of this episode in his autobiography, but the text under his name is infused with strong reform sentiments.[15]

Meanwhile, strong criticism was being voiced by the architectural profession and by speculative builders. The architects complained that Bok was diminishing their business through the sale of plan sets, and builders refuted the accuracy of the cost estimates. Bok reported that architects began to refuse requests for plans.[16] In response, Bok followed the first series of eight signed house designs with a second series of nine, running from July 1897 through June 1898, produced by "the *Journal*'s Special Architect." These designs were later collected in a small pocket-size book and pub-

lished in 1898 by the Curtis Publishing Company under the name of William L. Price, the architect who had designed the very first *Journal* house.[17]

To facilitate the construction of the model houses, Bok initiated a program whereby readers could purchase full sets of construction documents for $5.00, a practice adopted by Gustav Stickley, who began selling plans for *Craftsman* houses in 1904. But the advertisements for the sets of plans in the *Journal* also carried the notice that this offer was not intended to compete with the work of architects. Bok hoped that by eliminating architects' fees he could still make it possible for home builders of limited means to have access to good designs. He made clear that his objective was simply "to help our readers to build artistic and comfortable houses."[18] The houses in the second series were projected to cost from $1,000 to $2,500. Also included were three small church plans and a model town house to cost $1,800.

The cost of these houses should be considered in the context of the audience Bok was trying to reach and compared to the cost of a typical single-family

A $3500 SUBURBAN HOUSE

By W. L. Price

IN attempting to adopt any one of the well-defined styles of architecture to American uses it is necessary to put aside at once all thought of exact reproduction; the customs and requirements are so different that what we most admire abroad would make but a sorry year-round home here. More particularly is this true of houses of moderate cost, so that in the accompanying design of a house in the style of the English cottage, many points at variance with English work must be made allowance for.

The charm of the English cottages lies largely in their tile or thatch roofs and low stories set close to the ground—all of which in this country we must abandon at the outset, and, most radical difference of all, we must provide a large, roofed porch in place of their stoop. Then again the unnatural, speculative value of land in the suburbs of all of our cities forces us to build our houses on narrow lots, so that the end of the house is usually toward the road or street, making it still more difficult to follow English precedent.

The choice of site is generally restricted for the same reason, but select, if you can, a lot facing either south or west; in any case the house must be designed to suit the ground, on account of the exposure and also the lay of the land. As to the placing of the rooms, insist first that the dining-room have south and east exposures, giving it the morning sun and sheltering it from the late afternoon sun, which is very annoying when at meals. I make an especial point of the dining-room, as it is, after all, the daily reunion room of the family, and because it is so frequently neglected in the designing of small houses—the very ones in which most care should be exercised that every inch of space be utilized. The hall, if it be more than an entry, may be made a charming reception-room, and thus save the best room, so often sacrificed to the goddess, Fashion, for a living-room or library, which should properly have at least south and west exposures. The stairway, pantry and kitchen will then shelter these rooms from the most severe cold, and while the kitchen must be bright and airy it can well afford to take the colder side of the house. Next to the exposure of the rooms their relation to each other is the most vital point

in a plan. The hall should properly divide the house, and the dining-room and living-room or parlor should not, as a rule, open together, for while it is pleasant at times the noise incident to the preparation and clearing away of meals is something to be avoided if possible.

Entrance from dining-room to kitchen is best had through the pantry, which then answers as serving-room as well, and

The bathroom properly claims much care, not that it may be made gorgeous with tiling and stained glass, nor that it need necessarily be very large, but it must contain good open fixtures with all piping exposed and everything about it cleanable. The large linen-closet across the entry does away with the necessity of any bathroom closet except a small wall-cupboard.

The heating of the house is almost as important as the plumbing in a sanitary way, and unfortunately most of our houses are badly heated. With the heating arrangements usually provided we are compelled to either go cold or breathe incinerated air, mainly because of a heater too small to do the work required of it.

A heater should give, not a little hot air, but a large volume of pure warm air, and it is not necessary to go to the expense of a steam or hot-water plant in the ordinary house to get this result, as a good portable hot-air furnace with a duct for fresh outside air will do the work and do it well, with proper attention, if only it be large enough. It is much more economical, both in coal and wear and tear of furnace, to run a low fire in a large furnace than a forced fire in a small one, and the difference in first cost is not great enough to be considered.

As to lighting, few of our suburbs are without electric light or gas, and if you have the choice by all means use electric light; it is somewhat more costly to put in, but if used with moderate care is not an expensive luxury.

The interior finish should be very simple, as any attempt at elaboration in moderate-cost houses means tawdriness, and good narrow mouldings without corner blocks or gingerbread work of any kind add much to the charm of a room.

The finish of hall, living-room and dining-room may be of chestnut or of red oak—at no great cost if plain, and when stained and finished with wax will be very service-

keeps much of the noise and smell of cooking out of the dining-room. The kitchen should not open directly into the hall for the same reason, but passage from kitchen to hall without going through any other room is very desirable.

The kitchen should be well lighted and ventilated, especially near the range and the sink, and should be so arranged that the work may be readily and easily done.

All the bedrooms should have large windows and sufficient space for bed, bureau, washstand and chairs, as well as good closet room.

The alcove in main bedroom giving access to child's room I have found a very satisfactory arrangement, as it makes communication between the rooms without their opening directly into each other. The closet in this room, large enough to give ample hanging room and shelving, and accommodating a trunk as well, is another great addition to it.

able as it does not show wear. The rest of the house should be finished in white pine, either natural, stained or painted, as the color scheme of the room may require.

For the roof use in preference to anything else cedar shingles unstained, letting them take their own beautiful gray tone, but if you must have stains use only some one of the established makes and avoid the painters' "just as good" substitutes, which are usually just as bad as possible. By combining a little stone work in base, porch, walls and chimneys, with half timber work and plaster, a look of solidity is given that the ordinary frame house does not otherwise possess.

The half timber work should be of two-inch stuff without dressing, as the sawed surface takes a stain well and looks much richer. This should be securely spiked on top of the sheathing. Although not a part of its real construction the plastering or pebble-dashing is done best on grooved plaster-board nailed on to the sheathing, and if properly done makes a warm, tight and cozy house.

The second floor covered with shingles should be at least slightly stained as the shingles on walls are apt to weather badly; never place half timber work above a shingle story as it makes the house top-heavy in appearance.

And now a few words in behalf of the builder and architect: Don't expect your house to be perfect; wood will shrink, plaster will crack more or less, and doors and windows stick; and don't expect them to keep the house in repair. They cannot afford to do more than put it in proper condition when they hand it over to you.

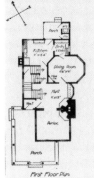

First Floor Plan   Second Floor Plan   Third Floor Plan

Fig. 2. Full-page facsimile of William L. Price, "A $3500 Suburban House."

Fig. 3. William L. Price, "A Model Suburban House," *Ladies' Home Journal* 14 (July 1897): 17.

residence today. Bok endeavored to illustrate houses costing from $1,500 to $7,500 for families whose income was from $1,200 to $2,500; thus, the houses were to cost approximately three times the annual family income. Such absolute dollar amounts look unbelievably low today, but these numbers need to be adjusted for a century of inflation. A house costing $3,500 in 1900 would have cost roughly $198,642 in 1988; in other words, the cost for 1900 must be multiplied by a factor of 56.755. In comparison, the reported cost of the average house during the last quarter of 1988 was $140,400, whereas the average family income in 1988 was $34,017.[19] As of 1988, the average residence cost well over four times the average family income.

The houses of the *Journal*'s second series were especially popular, and there were many orders for sets of plans. Bok noted in July 1898 that five hundred sets had been mailed and at least three hundred houses had already been built. One reader in Brookline, Massachusetts, purchased plans and built a group of twenty-five houses, and seven sets of plans were sent to the United States consul

general for construction in Cairo, Egypt.[20] In June 1898 Bok announced a contest with a prize of $100 for photographs of the best houses built from *Journal* designs. The results were published in June 1899, with the prize going to James A. Richey of Pittsburgh, Pennsylvania, for his house based on the design published in July 1897 (Figs. 3 and 4).[21]

Bok opened the new century by running two concurrent series, the first presenting large suburban residences and the second, model farmhouses. The suburban houses were at the high end of the cost spectrum. Bruce Price's "Georgian House for Seven Thousand Dollars" today would cost roughly $397,236. Price's house provided numerous amenities including a separate library, a sewing room, a conservatory with a skylight, and two servants' rooms. The January 1901 issue included a second house by Ralph Adams Cram. The designer urged that finishes and details of the interior be kept as simple as possible, noting that "the quietest and best effects are obtained by the use of simple materials in broad and simple forms."[22]

Of all the designs published in the *Journal*, cer-

Fig. 4. James A. Richey house, Pittsburgh, Pennsylvania, ca. 1898. *Ladies' Home Journal* 16 (June 1899): 23.

tainly the best known today are the three provided by Chicago architect Frank Lloyd Wright. The first appeared in the series on suburban house design in February 1901. Wright focused especially on the relationship of the house to its context and its physical setting. In the text he described how the extended eaves connected the house to its prairie site.[23] Wright's design was to cost $7,000.

Bok aimed the model farmhouse series, which was designed by Wright's friend the Chicago architect Robert C. Spencer, at the *Journal*'s many loyal rural readers. The first of these designs appeared in October 1900, at the same time as Price's grand colonial house, but costing a somewhat more modest $3,500. Another of Spencer's designs, published in December 1900, was for a northern farmhouse with the rooms arranged in a compact thick-walled stone square, with covered passages leading to the pumphouse, a greenhouse for forcing seedlings, and a barn (Fig. 5). This was followed in January 1901 by Spencer's southern farmhouse with a combination living-dining room having a high ceiling and clerestory lights for ventilation, with the kitchen in a separate connected block.[24] In both these designs Spencer attempted to accommodate his designs to regional conditions and climates.

A half-dozen large Elizabethan and Dutch colonial homes continued the series of suburban house designs, leading to Wright's second submission, "A Small House with 'Lots of Room in It,'" published in July 1901 (Fig. 6). In the text Wright admitted that he had deviated from strict economy to take advantage of light and air.

Beginning in 1901, Bok modified his practice and included a notice with each published design indicating that its architect would furnish a complete set of plans and guarantee the construction cost if the building site was not too distant from a source of building materials available at average

Fig. 5. Robert C. Spencer, "A Northern Farmhouse to Cost $3000," *Ladies' Home Journal* 17 (December 1900): 31.

Fig. 6. Frank Lloyd Wright, "A Small House with 'Lots of Room in It,'" *Ladies' Home Journal* 18 (January 1901): 15.

rates. After mid-1901 the houses tended to be more medieval vernacular in character, and some approached a Tudor style. Among them were designs by architects Elmer Grey of Milwaukee and Wilson Eyre of Philadelphia. The last house of this group was Frank Miles Day's "Sunny House with a Sheltered Garden" of September 1902 (Fig. 7).

Whether reflecting of a shift in Bok's own taste or Bok's perception of his readers' interests, the house designs published in the *Ladies' Home Journal* after 1902 showed an increasing influence of the English Arts and Crafts movement. In several editorials Bok extolled the virtues of William Morris's writings and his beneficial influence on interior design.[25] Morris's influence is visible in the fourth series of houses, designed by Henry Loomis Curtis and published from mid-1903 through January 1905. In September 1903 Loomis offered a pair of small urban houses recalling the steep roofs

and smooth stuccoed wall surfaces of the English Arts and Crafts houses by C. F. A. Voysey.

One of the most interesting manifestations of the *Journal*'s embracing of Arts and Crafts ideals was a series of eight articles that ran from November 1901 through August 1902. In each issue eight pages were devoted to the design of one of the principal rooms of a house—living room, dining room, library, and bedrooms. The designs were by the well-known American Arts and Crafts illustrator and graphic designer Will Bradley.[26] When Bradley published the exterior of his house in the last installment, he presented a full set of plans and a variety of exterior treatments. His preferred exterior had a strong resemblance to contemporary English Arts and Crafts houses by Voysey, but to provide readers a choice Bradley also included Dutch gambrel and half-timbered alternatives. In subsequent years Bradley submitted other designs

Fig. 7. Frank Miles Day, "A Sunny House with a Sheltered Garden," *Ladies' Home Journal* 19 (September 1902): 13.

much more modest in size and cost.

Although after 1904 the model houses in the *Journal* tended more and more toward the Arts and Crafts bungalow or medieval vernacular, a third house by Frank Lloyd Wright appeared in April 1907.[27] This was the most abstract and austere of his three and was designed to be built out of poured concrete. Wright agreed to furnish a complete set of construction documents and supervise building for 10 percent of the cost of the house, or to supply just the drawings for 7.5 percent provided a competent superintendent was engaged and no changes were made in the plans.

After 1907 the *Journal* houses became more conservative in character. Although from time to time various Chicago and Prairie School architects contributed photographs of completed houses, there were no more plans and nothing that approached the originality of Wright's designs. More frequent were double-page spreads of photographs of houses, judged to be of good design, in cities like Detroit or Indianapolis. For example, in August 1910, a two-page spread on Chicago houses included a speculative house built in 1906 in the suburb of Evanston by realtors Quinlan and Tyson following designs by the Chicago firm of Tallmadge and Watson (Fig. 8).[28]

In such photo spreads the name of each designing architect was clearly identified, but plans were no longer offered for sale. For a time after 1908, Bok published the addresses of his architects, in-

Fig. 8. Tallmadge and Watson house for Quinlan and Tyson, Realtors, Evanston, Illinois, 1906. *Ladies' Home Journal* 21 (August 1910): 29.

viting prospective builders to contact the designers directly. Much the same procedure was followed by *House Beautiful,* for the back pages of early issues included a directory of such architects as Frost and Granger and Robert C. Spencer, a frequent early contributor.[29]

After 1908 views of completed residences rather than plans of hypothetical model houses predominated in the *Journal.* Increasingly, these views were of California bungalows, the first article on bungalows having been published in January 1904. In the next decade over thirty-one articles on bungalows appeared, the majority of them contributed by Helen Lukens Gaut of Pasadena. Most of

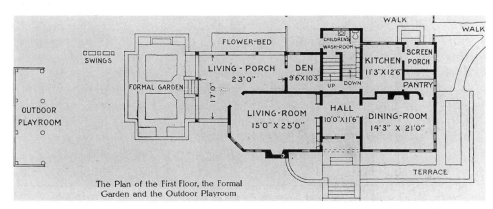

WALK

WALK

FLOWER-BED

SWINGS

CHILDREN'S
WASH-ROOM

KITCHEN
11'3"X12'6"

SCREEN
PORCH

LIVING - PORCH
23'0"

DEN
9'6"X10'3"

FORMAL GARDEN

17'0"

UP   DOWN

PANTRY

OUTDOOR
PLAYROOM

LIVING-ROOM
15'0" X 25'0"

HALL
10'0"X11'6"

DINING-ROOM
14'3" X 21'0"

TERRACE

The Plan of the First Floor, the Formal
Garden and the Outdoor Playroom

Fig. 9. Una Nixson
Hopkins, "A House Built
for Children," *Ladies'
Home Journal* 26 (June
1909): 17. Plan of ground
floor.

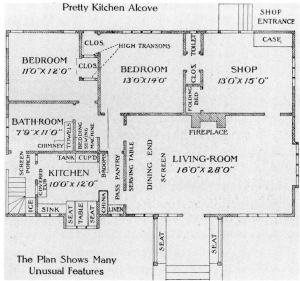

Pretty Kitchen Alcove

SHOP
ENTRANCE

CLOS.

HIGH TRANSOMS

TOILET

CASE

BEDROOM
11'0"X12'0"

CLOS.

BEDROOM
13'0"X14'0"

FOLDING
CLOS.

SHOP
13'0"X15'0"

BED

BATH-ROOM
7'9"X11'0"

CHIMNEY

TOWELS

BEDDING
SEWING
MACHINE

FIREPLACE

SCREEN
PORCH

COVERED

TANK   CUP'D

BROOMS

PASS PANTRY

SERVING TABLE

DINING END

SCREEN

LIVING-ROOM
16'0"X28'0"

KITCHEN
10'0"X12'0"

ICE

SINK

SEAT   TABLE   SEAT

CHINA

LINEN

SEAT

SEAT

The Plan Shows Many
Unusual Features

Fig. 10. Una Nixson Hopkins, "If a Woman Must Earn
Her Living at Home: A House Planned by a Woman to
Meet This Need," *Ladies' Home Journal* 28 (February 15,
1911): 23.

the presentations were one- or two-page photo spreads and included large numbers of bungalows from Pasadena.

Another frequent Pasadena contributor to the *Journal* was Una Nixson Hopkins, who had a particular interest in houses designed to accommodate the special needs of modern women.[30] One example is her piece on "A House Built for Children," which was published in June 1909. This house provided special exterior living and play

areas and a room in which the children could wash and change clothes before entering the rest of the house (Fig. 9).

Mrs. Hopkins seemed especially interested in the problems that single working women faced in obtaining suitable housing. In May 1909 Bok published her article on a shingled bungalow designed for two single working women.[31] The woman who challenged the traditional role of wife and homemaker faced an inhospitable male-dominated world, and although Bok did not strongly advocate single women pursuing careers, his quiet support of changing roles was evident in this and subsequent articles. An article for February 15, 1911, entitled "How the Other Women Live" was filled with scores of examples of modest houses and simple garages, as well as advice in interior design. Several pages were contributed by Helen Lukens Gaut dealing with bungalows, and Mrs. Hopkins had a two-page full-color spread presenting a house she designed for a single woman who wished to earn her living in her home (Fig. 10). The plan provided a large combination living-dining room that could be converted into a recital hall for a piano teacher. In addition, the details were designed to minimize cleaning.

In an article of 1913, Mrs. Hopkins admired the Bowen Court bungalow court complex in Pasadena, designed the year before by Arthur S. Heineman.[32] She praised the way the design made close living comfortable and the fact that the rustic clubhouse at the center provided a pleasant place to sit and sew and enjoy the air.

After 1913 the houses presented in the *Journal* settled into a pattern that continued until Bok retired in 1919. The bungalows lost their distinctly California character and became more generic. In 1914 Carey Edmunds was appointed architectural editor and began to publish Dutch colonial and shingled and stuccoed houses that were hardly distinguishable from those being offered by Sears, Roebuck.[33] Although the *Journal* never ventured into the prefabricated house market, the magazine did offer a number of pamphlets on how to build a house, as well as several plan books. Instead of model houses with plans offered for sale, the *Journal* now carried full-page color advertisements by such leading manufacturers of precut houses as Aladdin, Gordon-Van Tine, and the Southern Pine Association. The *Journal,* nonetheless, continued to focus on moderately priced houses within the reach of those people within the middle-income bracket toward whom Bok had originally aimed.

Whereas Sears, Roebuck has scrupulously maintained its archives, enabling scholars to document virtually every house kit the company ever sold, the records of the *Ladies' Home Journal* have apparently disappeared.[34] Moreover, because the house designs promoted by Bok and his later editors so closely resembled the prevailing speculation-built house, it is difficult to assess the impact the *Journal* had on American middle-class domestic architecture. Robert Winter, an authority on bungalow houses, asserts, however, that Bok was perhaps the single most effective popularizer of the bungalow. The significance of the designs published in the *Journal* is further suggested by the fact that in Hermann von Holst's *Modern American Homes of 1913,* 32 of the 108 plates, or 21 percent, were reprinted by permission from the *Journal.* Another

10 percent of von Holst's plates came from *House Beautiful.*[35]

It is difficult to tell how many of the *Journal* houses were actually built. In February 1916, the magazine ran a four-page spread of photos showing houses built from published plans.[36] Those selected for reproduction were rather plain; there were no Wright houses illustrated, although one adaptation of a Spencer farmhouse was shown. In the text accompanying the photo spread, Bok and Edmunds noted that the prizewinning houses were scattered across the country, from Vermont to California. Altogether, they claimed, 30,000 houses had been built from *Journal* plans. In the same issue, Bok wrote in his editorial that so pervasive were *Journal* houses that every person in the United States probably knew someone who lived in one, a statement typical of his hyperbole but perhaps not altogether an exaggeration. Moreover, Bok claimed that scores of *Journal* houses had been built outside the United States, illustrating five examples.[37]

We will probably never be able to gauge with precision the contribution made by Bok through his housing-reform campaign. Yet *Ladies' Home Journal,* as well as other popular reform-minded magazines, played a significant role in making sensibly designed house plans available to a great number of people in the early years of this century. Perhaps the major role achievement of the magazines and their editors was to reawaken in the mass of Americans the dream of the private house and to prepare them for the appearance of mail-order companies and prefabricated house producers such as Sears, Aladdin, and many others in the years just before and after World War I. It may be that the full measure of the magazines' impact is to be seen more appropriately in the sales of these latter housing companies.

MARY CORBIN SIES

TOWARD A PERFORMANCE THEORY OF THE SUBURBAN IDEAL, 1877–1917

Urban historian Kenneth Jackson has called suburbia "the quintessential physical achievement of the United States . . . more representative of its culture than big cars, tall buildings, or professional football."[1] He may have understated his case. Over the course of the twentieth century, suburbia has also become the quintessential cultural achievement of the United States, so much so that many Americans identify the suburban life-style with the American Dream itself.[2] Americans have come to assume that the ideal form of shelter is the single-family home with a garden and plenty of open space situated in a locally controlled suburban community.[3] For turn-of-the-century suburbanites, that assumption resonated with meaning. The suburban ideal embodied an entire program for modern American living that emerged from a series of vigorous debates underlying the planned, exclusive suburbs of the late nineteenth and early twentieth centuries.[4]

Chronicling those debates and the suburban ideal that resulted from them was the focus of the research on which this essay draws.[5] Two questions helped to structure that research: Why did the suburban residential environment take the form that it did? What meanings did suburbia hold for those who were its creators and original consumers? Those questions led me to reconstruct the community-building process itself in four planned, exclusive suburbs developed between 1877 and 1917.[6] From that research, it became apparent that comprehending the physical environment of the suburban ideal requires an understanding of its cultural meanings and that combining these two tasks presents a formidable challenge. The purpose of this essay is to address that challenge by suggesting a method for recovering the logic of the suburban ideal. The proposed method investigates architectural performances within the larger context of the community-building process, combining extensive documentary research with systematic architectural fieldwork. We begin with a review of the pertinent scholarly literature, followed by a description of the method itself, a very selective illustration of the information it yielded, and some concluding observations about the merits and pitfalls of performance-oriented approaches for vernacular architecture studies.

Historians have focused a good deal of attention on the history of suburban design and development recently. Among architectural historians, the standard treatments concentrate on the formal and regional stylistic origins of certain architect-designed suburban houses. Perhaps the best known of these interpretations is *The Prairie School: Frank Lloyd Wright and His Midwest Contemporaries* (1972) by H. Allen Brooks. Brooks views turn-of-the-century domestic design in the United States as the product of a regional rivalry among professional architects that pitted members of the traditional, academically trained, and largely eastern architectural establishment, who advocated conservative housing styles based upon European precedents, against a revolutionary group of midwestern architects known as the Prairie School, who drew from indigenous sources and aspired to create an original American domestic architecture. According to this interpretation, known as the "siege theory," the more conservative easterners successfully besieged the midwesterners, ostracized them within the profession, and discredited their design solutions with a fashion-conscious upwardly mobile clientele. In this way, America lost its most innovative and promising school of domestic designers at about the onset of World War I.[7]

As an interpretive device for understanding the shape of the turn-of-the-century suburban home, the siege theory has some interesting characteristics. Architects are the dominant players in the scenario; clients are cast as walk-ons who are only recipients of action. Accordingly, the architects' aesthetic judgments are considered the primary determinants of suburban design. Those judgments, however, are both conditioned by and embody social meanings—for example, tensions among architects struggling to establish a professional identity and competition for status among a socially ambitious clientele. What is lacking in the siege theory, though, is a systematic exploration of the social context surrounding the commissioning and designing of houses and any reference whatsoever to the cultural factors that underlie Americans' thinking about "home." Since the house is the most personal of building types and its routine design the least influenced by professional architects, the siege theory presents a very incomplete and one-sided understanding of the logic of suburban design.[8]

But if the siege theorists focus too exclusively on suburban form and neglect matters of context, most urban historians emphasize context at the expense of an analysis of suburban form.[9] This is perplexing since artifacts of the suburban built environment often provide the most potentially articulate body of evidence available to historians

of suburbanization. Recently, however, interdisciplinary scholars have begun to produce histories of suburbia or of the American home that accord artifacts and documentary sources roughly equal value as evidence. For example, in *Borderland* (1988), John Stilgoe examines visual images and a range of documentary descriptions to chronicle the transformation of the suburban landscape between 1820 and 1939, focusing on the aesthetic and philosophical issues underlying the transformation. Scholars of the middle-class American home have drawn from published plans and perspectives and from prescriptive literature for domestic manners and domestic architecture to uncover social values and symbolic meanings embodied in home designs.[10]

More theoretically ambitious is John Archer's effort to "explore how specific features and amenities . . . when physically incorporated into suburban design, served to exemplify and perpetuate specific relations, assumptions, and ideals in Anglo-American culture." In his study of nineteenth-century suburban design throughout the British Commonwealth and the United States, Archer "reads" community plans for their meanings as both reflectors and shapers of the societies that produced them.[11] In *Moralism and the Model Home* (1980), Gwendolyn Wright "elucidate[s] the context in which architects, builders, building workers, reformers and the publics they addressed decided what was appropriate for American homes." Her study of home and landscape designs is the most comprehensive exploration to date of moral and ideological influences on the design of the American middle-class suburban environment at the turn of the century.[12]

These artifact-centered studies are welcome additions to the scholarship on suburbia, but they lean too heavily on published plans and prescriptive literature for their information about the built environment. Those sources convey the stated intentions of designers, developers, and housing reformers, but they do not provide reliable information about how suburban residents experienced their environment and what meanings they attached to its primary features. This is not to suggest that scholars should stop consulting the prescriptive literature, only that they should use it judiciously. Prescriptive literature and books of house plans can be enlightening, but only when the "prescriptions" are compared with what was actually built and how it was used. Research that captures the perspective of the designers and promoters of suburbia, in other words, must be supplemented by research aimed at revealing the building process and the perspective of consumers and inhabitants. What is called for is thorough field research of suburban material culture, field research that seeks the meanings and essential qualities of artifacts within their social and cultural contexts.

These conditions can be met with an ethnographic approach, one that enables the historian to study the suburban built environment as it developed with reference to the activities of real people involved in designing and living in real suburban houses and communities. Historic field research forms the center of the method. Through the close study of records and of artifacts that document the suburban community-building process, one gains precise information about specific suburbs and houses and access to the imaginative universe of those who built and used them. By this means the historian can identify the range of constraints (including formal and aesthetic ones) that shaped suburban design decisions, recognize the social meanings and relationships embedded in particular structures, and probe for the basic cultural complexes that shaped suburbanites' thinking about their homes. An ethnographic approach focused on recovering the process of community-building has an additional advantage. It reveals the dynamic nature of the relationship between suburbanites and their material culture. This enables one, for example, to distinguish between how buildings are designed to be used and how they actually are used, as well as to recognize the ways in which artifacts can both reflect and influence human values and experience.

The success of ethnographic research depends upon the ability to identify appropriate communities for study. Preliminary investigations revealed that the creators, first consumers, and disseminators of the suburban ideal were with very few exceptions members of an identifiable group of new upper-middle-class urban Americans intent upon formalizing their own newfound status and prescribing cultural norms for others. In planned, exclusive suburbs in major metropolitan areas across the nation, they debated and experimented with these ideas beginning in the late 1870s and achieving a rough consensus by the turn of the century. That consensus—what we may call the suburban ideal—in its various guises as model suburb, model home, and model life-style—was later codified (one could even say commodified), mass-produced, and disseminated as the proper standard for modern American living. In using an ethnographic method to comprehend that consensus, the scholar needs to examine the community-building process through which the suburban ideal emerged. The most appropriate community to study, then, was a planned, exclusive suburb created by and for these new suburbanites. There, by examining the experiments that produced the suburban ideal, one has the best chance of recovering the logic of suburban form and reconstructing the complex of meanings that constrained its creation and constituted its appeal. In the research from which this essay is drawn, four planned, exclusive suburbs were chosen for intensive field study: Short Hills, New Jersey; the St. Martin's section of Chestnut Hill, Philadelphia, Pennsylvania; Kenilworth, Illinois; and Lake of the Isles, Minneapolis, Minnesota.

Ethnographic field research at its most basic consists of "an interrogation of one cultural system by another, carried out through the interaction of ethnographer and informant."[13] That interrogation presents an obvious challenge for the historian. Since our informants are usually deceased, we have to reconstruct their thoughts and actions from the records and artifacts they left behind. It is important, therefore, that the historian's choice of evidence, means for sifting it, and schemes for interpreting it respect the qualities and mental constructs of the artifacts and actors studied.

Several historians have found performance models appropriate to their subject matter and useful for grappling with this challenge; their work illustrates the range of strategies that one can devise for "getting inside" an alien historic community. In *The Transformation of Virginia*, Rhys Isaac's dramaturgical model enabled him to determine patterns of authority in eighteenth-century Virginia society and to chronicle how those patterns were challenged and ultimately overthrown. Drawing from written descriptions, Isaac conceptualized key social transactions as "performances" and analyzed their components—settings, props, roles, scripts. By noting changes in the performance patterns, he was able to shed light on changes in the working assumptions of Virginia society between 1740 and 1790. In "Toward a Performance Theory of Vernacular Architecture," Dell Upton adopted Basil Bernstein's theory of restricted and elaborated linguistic codes to probe the meanings and means of transmission of architectural preferences in Tidewater Virginia houses. Upton consulted probate inventories to document architectural performances during a period of stylistic transformation, focusing especially on floor plans and actual uses of rooms. He determined that eighteenth- and nineteenth-century Virginians made their architectural choices deliberately to meet specific cultural or social needs and that vernacular building was "a complex phenomenon, possessed of its own inner logic and cutting across class and economic lines."[14]

Historians interested in recovering the inner logic of the suburban ideal have an advantage over Isaac and Upton because of the relative abundance of evidence remaining from turn-of-the-century planned, exclusive suburbs. Through careful field analysis of the evidence it is possible to reconstruct (some part of) the actual community-building process—to "observe" the development of the suburban residential environment in the process of unfolding. In Short Hills, St. Martin's, Kenilworth, and Lake of the Isles, that process consisted of three parts: (1) a debate regarding the form and content of the ideal residential environment, (2) a period of experimentation that involved the actual creation and adaptation of built forms, followed by (3) a consensus that took the shape of commonly recognized design programs for both the model suburb and the model home. The fieldwork consisted of gathering evidence to assist in reconstructing and understanding those conventions as they appeared with some local variation in each suburb.

Models inevitably oversimplify the phenomena they are employed to describe; the suburban community-building process was messier and more complex than a model of debate, experimentation, and consensus suggests. It helps to recognize that the design process involved several dynamic and interrelated kinds of performances centering on the design decisionmakers, the buildings and landscapes, and the users and inhabitants. Structuring the fieldwork to learn about the community-building process in each case-study suburb required identifying the actors, human and artifactual, whose performances contributed to it. Accordingly, the fieldwork divided into research that provided three perspectives on the process.

The first perspective was that of individual actors. Let us think of the community-building process as a "discourse" and of those persons participating in the process in each suburb as members of a "community of discourse."[15] Fieldwork from this perspective focused on reconstituting the community—identifying the original residents of each house built between the founding of the suburb and 1917, as well as the developers, builders, architects, and any other persons whose contribution to the discourse could be documented or reasonably inferred. The next step was to learn as much as possible about those historical actors—their circumstances, values, life-styles, and, in particular, the ways in which they used and thought about their houses and residential surroundings. The second perspective encompassed the community as a whole; there the fieldwork consisted of recovering each suburb's development history, social geography, social organization, customs, and ambience. The richest sources documenting these two perspectives were photographs, memoirs, scrapbooks, local newspapers, maps, the records of clubs and organizations of local governance, local histories, and published articles on specific residents or residences.

The third perspective concentrated on the artifacts. Here, the field research consisted of documenting and then analyzing the original design of the landscape and of each residence built prior to 1917. The numbers of houses surveyed ranged from 102 constructed between 1877 and 1917 in Short Hills to 432 constructed between 1886 and 1917 in Lake of the Isles. The aim of the fieldwork was to establish the original plans and appearances of the artifacts by comparing original plans and perspectives with blueprints, photographs, other records, and evidence gathered from inspection of the extant houses. Any available information concerning the circumstances of their design and their original uses was gathered as well. Particular attention was paid to spatial organization, room activities, and both interior and exterior expression. The most valuable written sources were drawings, photographs, real estate records, architects' office records, building permits, maps, and local newspapers.

By combining information from all three perspectives, it was possible to discover the major contours of the process of debate, experimentation, and consensus as it unfolded slightly differently in each suburb. Artifactual analysis revealed the design programs that composed the consensus governing the model suburb and model home, and contextual information clarified some of the meanings that the suburban environment held for its constituents. It is difficult to describe with precision the modes of analysis and deliberation that

led to my interpretation of the evidence, but two observations are important to note. First, the exercise of sifting the evidence and drawing conclusions in ethnographic research is, as Rhys Isaac points out, one of "translation," in which the researcher must struggle to remain aware of the distinction between the actors' categories and her own.[16] Second, perceiving the actors' categories so that one can discern the meanings of texts or artifacts or behaviors is very challenging. In the present case, that mental process involved negotiating back and forth between the information contained in the artifact and that generated by the context—balancing stated meanings, apparent experiences, the physical evidence, and their interrelations. To grasp the meanings and uses of the artifacts, one has to refer back to the contextual information concerning the design process. But to comprehend the context, one must return to the artifacts for clues about the cultural constructs shaping the mentalité of the community. The difficulty of these deliberations is a given in research that seeks to understand historical actors in the act of creating and consuming cultural forms.

No method or theory, no matter how clever, can enable the historian to reconstruct the past with certainty. The method outlined here can only produce an interpretation of the suburban ideal that bears partial resemblance to the cultural metaphor that emerged from Short Hills, St. Martin's, Kenilworth, and Lake of the Isles. What we have learned suggests, however, that interpretations that rely exclusively on formal or on contextual analysis have not provided an adequate understanding of the logic or meanings of the suburban ideal. The most dramatic finding of the present research was the remarkable consistency among the design programs emerging simultaneously in all four suburbs. That consistency reflected the homogeneity of the four communities and the similar patterns in their discourse. The suburban ideal manifested in the design program for the model home and model suburb embodied two powerful social goals: the

Fig. 1. Exterior perspective, Sunset Cottage, A. B. Rich residence, Short Hills, New Jersey. Lamb & Rich, architects, 1882. (*American Architect and Building News*, January 7, 1882)

new suburbanites' determination to formalize their own life-style and position in society in a suitable residential setting, and their desire to devise a model environment that might remedy the worst housing conditions and social problems of the city. But the precise form the suburban environment assumed was constrained by a group of deeply felt cultural values, tensions, and beliefs.

It was this set of cultural values and tensions, rather than stylistic considerations or forces emanating from the city, that formed the logic of the suburban ideal and shaped the fundamental principles of the design programs for model homes and suburbs. Field analysis of all of the houses constructed in the four suburbs between 1877 and 1917 revealed, for example, that the design program for the model home embodied at least seven cultural assumptions or beliefs. They are abbreviated as follows: Order/Efficiency, Nature, Technology, Family, Individuality, Community, and Beauty. These seven principles specified the elements that had to be present in any proper dwelling; architects and builders incorporated these requirements into their commissions through a variety of spatial arrangements and choices of style that could accommodate a range of budgets and

local conditions. Let us look briefly at four houses that illustrate the design program for the model suburban home: Sunset Cottage in Short Hills, the McGoodwin residence in St. Martin's, the Sutton residence in Kenilworth, and the Powers residence in Lake of the Isles (Figs. 1–4). These houses vary widely in size, style, and use of progressive design ideas; only two, Sunset Cottage and the Powers residence, are commonly recognized for their architectural merit.[17]

The first principle of the design program for the suburban home was Order or, to use the contemporary term, Efficiency. The new suburbanites considered the efficiently designed home an instrument for engendering healthy, well-adjusted, productive human beings. An efficient home environment was one designed by experts according to rational principles, particularly those of simplicity, utility, structural rationalism, and economy. Floor plans were designed to accommodate a family's needs in a simple, efficient manner by providing five basic first-floor spaces: a living room, hall, dining room, kitchen/service area, and piazza.[18] Regardless of cost, size, style, or date of construction, the houses in Short Hills, St. Martin's, Kenilworth, and Lake of the Isles, with few exceptions,

Fig. 2. Exterior photograph, Robert McGoodwin residence, St. Martin's, Philadelphia, Pennsylvania. Robert McGoodwin, architect, 1913. (*American Architect,* December 29, 1915)

recapitulated this prescription (Figs. 5–8). Their interiors embodied the principle that "great art is commonsense idealized"; furniture, much of it built-in (see Fig. 7), was selected to perform a practical function, and the interior decoration was simple, restrained, and unobtrusive.[19] The model exterior revealed the home's purpose in a straightforward way; chimneys, porches, eaves, window placement, and landscaping formed the primary and unmistakably domestic points of interest.

Residents of planned, exclusive suburbs were environmental determinists; they believed that by harnessing "the primal art of nature and the latest interpretations of science" they could create environments capable of constructively shaping human behavior.[20] Hence, the second assumption of their domestic-design program was that daily exposure to nature's beauty and goodness could rescue urban commuters from the physically and morally debilitating effects of modern urban life. Houses were carefully sited and landscaped to create natural views and offered an abundance of indoor-outdoor spaces: porches, window seats,

Fig. 3. Exterior photograph, F. W. Sutton residence, ca. 1914, Kenilworth, Illinois. George Maher, architect, 1908. (Courtesy Kenilworth Historical Society, Kenilworth, Illinois)

Fig. 4. Exterior photograph, E. L. Powers residence, Lake of the Isles, Minneapolis, Minnesota. Purcell, Feick, & Elmslie, architects, 1910–1911. (*Western Architect,* January 1913)

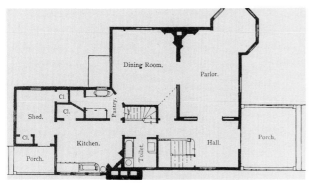

Fig. 5. First-floor plan, Sunset Cottage. (*American Architect and Building News,* January 7, 1882)

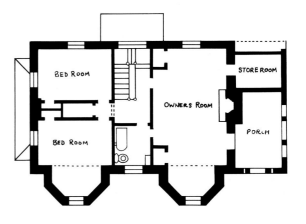

FIRST FLOOR PLAN

SECOND FLOOR PLAN

Fig. 6. First- and second-floor plans, Robert McGoodwin residence. (Anne B. Keating)

terraces, and sleeping porches. Even in Lake of the Isles with its severe winter weather, residents "expect(ed) to live mainly outside"; the Powers residence was typical in fostering contact with the outdoors through features like the glazed sun porch, living room and den window seats, breakfast porch, sleeping porch, and balcony (see Fig. 8).[21] Technology played a central role in the engineering of the ideal home environment as well. The new suburbanites believed that technology possessed nearly limitless potential for ensuring social progress, and they incorporated a dazzling array of improvements in their homes: new construction materials; advances in heating, ventilating, and sanitary technology; new household appliances and gadgets. Kitchens and service areas were highly organized with built-in storage and

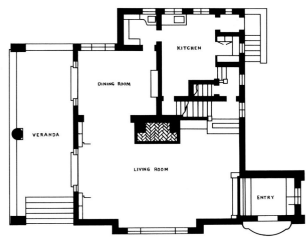

Fig. 7. First-floor plan, F. W. Sutton residence. (Anne B. Keating)

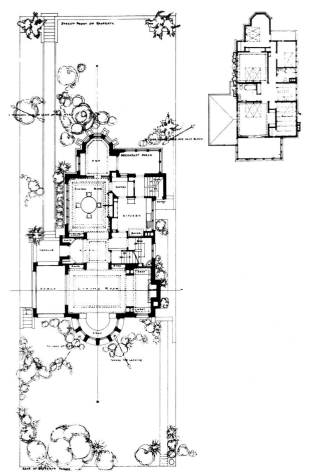

Fig. 8. First- and second-floor plans, E. L. Powers residence. (*Western Architect,* January 1913)

work areas, white walls, and sanitary surfaces. The goal was to employ technology to obtain a therapeutic environment that would guide the inhabitants in the observation of scientific standards of hygiene in their personal habits and household routines.

The model suburban home embodied a careful balance of the values of family, community, and individuality; these formed the fourth, fifth, and sixth principles of the design program. To many suburbanites, the institution of the family seemed gravely threatened by the rapid social and economic changes occurring after the Civil War. To foster family unity, houses were designed around a single gathering space—the living room—which functioned as "the very heart and center of family life."[22] The central feature of the room was a fireplace, sometimes surrounded by an inglenook (see Fig. 8); a fire in the hearth was thought to attract family members and evoke a longing for the comfort and security of the family unit. Proper childrearing was an important focus of the family-centered suburban life-style; in order to encourage individuality and self-discipline, each child was given his own room whenever possible. To compensate for the loss of individual expression that seemed endemic to urban mass society, the suburban home provided a variety of nooks and crannies for privacy, allowed for individual choice in exterior expression, and often featured floor plans tailored to a commissioning family's specific needs. But family unity and individuality were not to be purchased at the price of community involvement; reestablishing communal interaction with likeminded people was an important reason for moving to the suburbs. Accordingly, houses projected a neighborly visage, fences were rare, and floor plans were open and hospitable so that visitors were welcomed immediately into the family spaces without being screened in a reception area and greeted in a parlor.

Underlying the seventh principle in the design program—the desire to build with beauty—was an assumption that "there is no influence so potent upon life as harmonious surroundings." Beauty in the home gratified humankind's aesthetic and spiritual needs and was considered "the privilege of all but the wretchedly poor."[23] Artistic design was cultivated in various ways, with most houses exhibiting a combination of approaches. The McGoodwin residence achieved beauty in a classic manner through simplicity, harmony of outline, and proper proportions. A second approach was to harmonize the dwelling with its natural surroundings, whether the home was sited to take advantage of a felicitous view, like the McGoodwin residence, or embellished with new plantings, like the Sutton residence. A third means for incorporating beauty was through fine craftsmanship, as exemplified in the exterior of Sunset Cottage, whose shingles were graded in colors reflecting the sunset and captured the sensuous nature of a skin stretched to contain a volume of space that characterized the best work of the Shingle style. Both the Powers and Sutton residences achieved a more ambitious expression of beauty through aesthetic unity; they featured ornamental design motifs that were applied throughout their interiors, in decorative glasswork, mantelpieces, and built-in furniture, for example.

The design programs of the suburban ideal addressed the social aspirations of a particular stratum of urban society during a period of intense turmoil in urban development. The raison d'être of the suburban ideal was to rationalize modern life for the new suburbanites and engineer the socialization of everyone else. The entire design process was influenced by deeply ingrained cultural values and tensions that constrained the design choices the new suburbanites would make. Social and cultural factors, then, were the constants influencing the design programs that emerged in Short Hills, St. Martin's, Kenilworth, and Lake of the Isles. Choices of style, material, and finish varied by region and according to local availability, preference, and competence. Historians need to identify both local and national constraints to comprehend the artifacts and learn about the people who interacted with them.

These conclusions point to three additional observations. Although 50 to 80 percent of the houses in the four suburbs were architect-designed (depending upon how loosely or tightly one defines an architect), professional men did not dominate the suburban discourse.[24] It is more accurate to view architects—many of whom, like Robert McGoodwin and Charles Rich of Sunset Cottage, made their homes in these suburbs or ones like them—as fellow members of the social stratum that composed each suburb's community. Although architects brought special skills to the design process, they participated as neighbors who shared similar values and a similar stake in the efficacy of the suburban ideal. Second, analysis of the suburban built environment reinforces Henry Glassie's and Dell Upton's contention that scholars who insist on distinguishing "high" from vernacular architecture often overlook the complex cultural logic underlying buildings of similar type; this seems particularly true with respect to houses. Architect-designed, builder-designed, and mass-produced tract houses in planned, exclusive suburbs, houses of lesser and of greater aesthetic merit, embodied remarkably similar design programs and were the products of similar social aspirations and cultural belief systems. Third, the communities that created the suburban ideal conceptualized a thorough environmental program that encompassed not only the home but also the interior of the home, its yard, and the larger suburban community. Any examination of the suburban ideal must acknowledge the interconnectedness of the suburban landscape.

Every method has its limitations; the performance-oriented ethnographic approach described here is no exception. One of the most serious pitfalls is the danger of reductionism—the tendency to believe that one can explain an artifact by referring to its context as its cause, so to speak. This pitfall is seductive because it offers interpretations that seem so straightforward and easy—but it privileges the context at the expense of the artifacts, a sin just the reverse of that committed in the formal analyses practiced by the siege theorists and criticized earlier. Both texts and contexts must be examined and their dynamic interactions acknowledged for the researcher to perceive the factors that constrain people's design decisions, the meanings that artifacts hold for their various constituents, and the ways that artifacts, in turn, sometimes shape human experiences.[25]

Ethnographic approaches concentrate on observing and understanding the behavior and artifacts of cultural groups. In the present study, the design process that produced the suburban built environment was conceptualized as communal, and suburban houses and landscapes were examined from the perspective of what they had in common instead of what distinguished them from other artifacts. This approach yielded important insights about the suburban ideal—that it was an organic product of socially aggressive communities linked by common circumstances and cultural values. Those insights have been overlooked by architectural historians interested in delineating the unique contributions of individual architects and the artistry of unique buildings. But focusing on the communal discourse and trying to identify all those who participated in it can obscure the precise nature of the contributions of any given individual or segment of the community. Similarly, noting the common principles underlying the design of a group of houses directs attention away from the qualities that may make a given evocation of the suburban ideal special. The historian using an ethnographic method must work to maintain some balance between these perspectives.

Any fieldwork-based method saddles the researcher with the problem of determining whether and to what extent her conclusions apply to phenomena beyond the subject community. It is important to refrain from claiming too much for one's data, but it is also important to avoid claiming too little. Those using fieldwork should make a judicious effort to consider how the "part" they have discovered relates to the "whole" and to link their conclusions to those of similar fieldwork studies. Through this effort we may begin to understand the nature of social relationships in American society and to discuss the ways in which power is manifested and cultural knowledge is transmitted.[26] The suburban ideal, for example, was rife with hegemonic implications, and its cultural impact extended well beyond the gated boundaries of elite suburbs. We need to investigate how this powerful cultural metaphor has influenced the built environment and the lives of a wide range of suburbanites in the United States in the twentieth century. This is partly a question of cultural diffusion, but it just as surely involves a series of investigations of how identifiable groups of Americans of various backgrounds and social classes have interacted with—accepted, resisted, and adapted—basic cultural forms. In addressing these and similar problems, let us continue to develop and refine research strategies that combine and balance investigations of the performance of artifacts, the performance of their creators, and the performance of their consumers.

NOTES

Notes to "Introduction: Toward a New Architectural History," by Thomas Carter and Bernard L. Herman

1. See Camille Wells, ed., *Perspectives in Vernacular Architecture, I* (Annapolis, Md.: Vernacular Architecture Forum, 1982); Camille Wells, ed., *Perspectives in Vernacular Architecture, II* (Columbia: University of Missouri Press, 1986); and Thomas Carter and Bernard L. Herman, eds., *Perspectives in Vernacular Architecture, III* (Columbia: University of Missouri Press, 1989).

2. Eric Mercer, *English Vernacular Houses: A Study of Traditional Farmhouses and Cottages* (London: Her Majesty's Stationery Office, 1975), 1.

3. See Michael Steinitz, "Rethinking Geographical Approaches to the Common House: The Evidence from Eighteenth-Century Massachusetts," in *Perspectives in Vernacular Architecture, III,* ed. Carter and Herman, 16–27.

4. One of the best discussions of the regional qualities of American buildings is found in Dell Upton, "Vernacular Domestic Architecture in Eighteenth-Century Virginia," *Winterthur Portfolio* 17 (Summer/Autumn 1982): 95–120.

5. Henry Glassie, *Folk Housing in Middle Virginia: A Structural Analysis of Historic Artifacts* (Knoxville: University of Tennessee Press, 1975). For a full exegesis of the theories underlying *Folk Housing,* see Henry Glassie, "Structure and Function, Folklore and the Artifact," *Semiotic* 7 (1973): 313–51.

6. Abbott Lowell Cummings, *The Framed Houses of Massachusetts Bay, 1625–1725* (Cambridge: Harvard University Press, 1979). See also Abbott Lowell Cummings, *Rural Household Inventories: Establishing the Names, Uses and Furnishings of Rooms in the Colonial New England Home, 1675–1775* (Boston: Society for the Preservation of New England Antiquities, 1964).

7. See Thomas J. Schlereth, "Material Culture and Cultural Research," in *Material Culture: A Research Guide,* ed. Thomas J. Schlereth (Lawrence: University Press of Kansas, 1985), 1–34; Ian Hodder, *Reading the Past: Current Approaches to Interpretation in Archaeology* (Cambridge: Cambridge University Press, 1986), 77–102, 118–46; and Stephen A. Mrozowski, "Historical Archaeology as Anthropology," *Historical Archaeology* 22 (1988): 18–24.

8. Dell Upton, "The Power of Things: Recent Studies in American Vernacular Architecture," in *Material Culture: A Research Guide,* ed. Schlereth, 58; Camille Wells, "Old Claims and New Demands: Vernacular Architecture Studies Today," in *Perspectives in Vernacular Architecture, II,* ed. Wells, 4.

9. Kenneth L. Ames, "The Stuff of Everyday Life: American Decorative Arts and Household Furnishings," in *Material Culture: A Research Guide,* ed. Schlereth, 85.

10. The preoccupation with the fine points of log architecture is exemplified by the work of geographer Terry Jordan; see his *American Log Buildings: An Old World Heritage* (Chapel Hill: University of North Carolina Press, 1985).

11. George Kubler, *The Shape of Time: Remarks on the History of Things* (New Haven: Yale University Press, 1962), 5–6.

12. Donald Preziosi, *Rethinking Art History: Meditations on a Coy Science* (New Haven: Yale University Press, 1989), 12. See also Robert I. Robert and Theodore K. Rabb, eds., *Art and History: Images and Their Meaning* (Cambridge: Cambridge University Press, 1986), and Elizabeth Blair MacDougall, ed., *The Architectural Historian in America* (Washington, D.C.: National Gallery of Art, 1990).

13. Glassie, *Folk Housing,* 12.

14. See Richard R. Beeman, "The New Social History and the Search for 'Community' in Colonial America," *American Quarterly* 29 (Fall 1977): 422–43; Peter N. Stearns, "The New Social History: An Overview," in *Ordinary People and Everyday Life: Perspectives on the New Social History,* ed. James B. Gardner and George Rolli Adams (Nashville: American Association for State and Local History, 1983), 3–22; and Peter N. Stearns, "Toward a Wider Vision: Trends in Social History," in *The Past Before Us: Contemporary Historical Writing in the United States,*

ed. Michael Kammen (Ithaca: Cornell University Press, 1980), 205–30. An excellent collection of essays defining the varied agendas of the new social history was published as "Historical Studies Today," *Daedalus: Journal of the American Academy of Arts and Sciences,* 100 (Winter 1971).

15. Cary Carson, "Doing History with Material Culture," in *Material Culture and the Study of American Life,* ed. Ian M. G. Quimby (New York: W. W. Norton, 1978), 48.

16. Dell Upton, "Material Culture Studies: A Symposium," *Material Culture* 17 (Summer–Fall 1985): 85–86. See Dell Upton, *Holy Things and Profane: Anglican Parish Churches in Colonial Virginia* (Cambridge: MIT Press, 1986); Bernard L. Herman, *Architecture and Rural Life in Central Delaware, 1700–1900* (Knoxville: University of Tennessee Press, 1987); Thomas C. Hubka, *Big House, Little House, Back House, Barn: The Connected Farm Buildings of New England* (Hanover: University Press of New England, 1984); and Robert Blair St. George, "'Set Thine House in Order': The Domestication of the Yeomanry in Seventeenth-Century New England," in *New England Begins* (Boston: Museum of Fine Art, 1982), 2:159–351.

17. Upton, "Power of Things," 58.

18. Wells, "Old Claims and New Demands," 4.

19. Lawrence W. Levine, *High Brow, Low Brow: The Emergence of Cultural Hierarchy in America* (Cambridge: Harvard University Press, 1989).

Notes to "Carpentry in Northfield, Massachusetts: The Domestic Architecture of Calvin Stearns and Sons, 1799–1856," by J. Ritchie Garrison

1. The author wishes to thank Rosa Johnston and the Northfield Historical Society for their generous assistance with this project and the owners of Northfield's Stearns houses for permission to measure and photograph their buildings. He also thanks Bernard Herman, Rosa Johnston, Greg Nobles, Winifred Rothenberg, Damie Stillman, Kevin Sweeney, and Bryant Tolles, Jr., for reading and commenting on various drafts of this paper. The fieldwork for this research was undertaken during the summers of 1987 and 1989 and was made possible by a General University Research Grant from the University of Delaware. Information on the Nevers house is contained in Calvin Stearns, Daybook, 1811–1813, Northfield Historical Society, Northfield, Mass.; also see Kevin M. Sweeney, "Man-

sion People: Kinship, Class and Architecture in Western Massachusetts in the Mid Eighteenth Century," *Winterthur Portfolio* 19 (Winter 1984): 231–56; William N. Hosley, Jr., "Architecture," in *The Great River: Art and Society of the Connecticut Valley, 1635–1820* (Hartford: Wadsworth Atheneum, 1985), 63–133. Material in this essay appeared in slightly different form in the author's *Landscape and Material Life in Franklin County, Massachusetts, 1770–1869* (Knoxville: University of Tennessee Press, 1991).

2. J. H. Temple and George Sheldon, *History of the Town of Northfield, Massachusetts* (Albany: Joel Munsel, 1875), 539–40; Charles A. Morse, *Warwick, Massachusetts: Biography of a Town* (Cambridge: Dresser, Chapman & Grimes, 1963), 110; all of the Account and Daybooks kept by Calvin and George Stearns are owned by the Northfield Historical Society; Mark Erlich, *With Our Hands: The Story of Carpenters in Massachusetts* (Philadelphia: Temple University Press, 1986), 21–25; scholars have generally paid less attention to carpentry than to cabinetmaking. For other perspectives on joiners in rural New England see Philip Zea, "Rural Craftsmen and Design," in *New England Furniture: The Colonial Era, Selections from the Society for the Preservation of New England Antiquities,* ed. Brock Jobe and Myrna Kaye (Boston: Houghton Mifflin, 1984), 47–72; Robert B. St. George, *The Wrought Covenant: Source Material for the Study of Craftsmanship and Community in Southeastern New England, 1620–1700* (Brockton: Brockton Art Center, 1979); for another perspective see Ann W. Dibble, "Major John Dunlap: The Craftsman and his Community," *Old Time New England* 68 (Winter–Spring 1974): 50–58; Calvin Stearns, Account Book, March 10, 1800.

3. Calvin Stearns, Account Book, December 4, 1800; Hosley, "Architecture," 118–21; William N. Hosley, Jr., "Architecture and Society of the Urban Frontier: Windsor, Vermont, in 1800," in *The Bay and the River, 1600–1900,* ed. Peter Benes, *Annual Proceedings of the Dublin Seminar for New England Folklife* (Boston: Boston University, 1982), 73–86; Jack Quinan, "Asher Benjamin and American Architecture," *Journal of the Society of Architectural Historians* 38 (October 1979): 244–56.

4. For references to the process of tramping see Erlich, *With Our Hands,* 21–25; also see Sean Wilentz, *Chants Democratic: New York City and the Rise of the American Working Class, 1788–1850* (New York: Oxford University Press, 1984), 52.

5. Calvin Stearns, Daybooks, January 2, 1800–December 30, 1805; Elmer D. Keith and William L. Warren, "Peter Banner, Architect, Moves from New Haven to Boston," *Old Time New England* 58 (January–March 1967): 57–76.

6. Harold Kirker, *The Architecture of Charles Bulfinch* (Cambridge: Harvard University Press, 1969), 188–91; Quinan, "Asher Benjamin," 244–56; Calvin Stearns, Daybook, February 1–November 30, 1807.

7. Calvin Stearns, Daybook, February 1–November 30, 1807.

8. Stuart Bruchey, *The Roots of American Economic Growth, 1607–1861* (New York: Harper, 1968), 109–23; Gary M. Walton and James F. Shepherd, *The Economic Rise of Early America* (Cambridge: Cambridge University Press, 1980), 178–200; Curtis P. Nettles, *The Emergence of a National Economy, 1775–1815* (New York: Holt, Rinehart and Winston, 1962); the economic hardship is reflected in the account books. Stearns did plenty of repairs and some minor building, but few people in the region seem to have contemplated building dwellings in the period between 1807 and 1815. Nevers was clearly an exception.

9. Calvin Stearns, Daybook, May 1–September 30, 1820, May 1–September 30, 1838; January 1, 1811–December 31, 1813; building was interrupted by the War of 1812 on several occasions, which accounts for the long delay in finishing the structure.

10. Ibid., April 1–December 31, 1840.

11. Very little systematic research dealing with the fabrication of building elements in rural areas exists, and the Stearns accounts are rather cryptic in the references to sash and doors. On the Murdock house, for example, Stearns recorded on November 14, 1840, that he was making the blinds and two weeks later that Charles was making doors. There are earlier references to work in the shop making sash and doors, but they are seldom more specific. Much of the discussion about these building elements, then, must be inferred by examining the physical evidence.

12. For a discussion of the concept of risk of uncertainty see David Pye, *The Nature and Art of Workmanship* (Cambridge: Cambridge University Press, 1968), 13; Calvin Stearns, Account Book, January 13, 1816–November 2, 1816.

13. Calvin Stearns, Account Book, January 13, 1816–November 2, 1816.

14. Thomas Hubka, *Big House, Little House, Back House, Barn: The Connected Farm Buildings of New England* (Hanover: University Press of New England, 1984), 44–55, 122–28. Hubka's seminal work understates the emergence of the ell as a work space in the eighteenth century. Carpenters were building ells onto the mansion houses of the elite by the 1750s, but they did not become a common addition to middle-class housing until the 1790s. See Sweeney, "Mansion People," 231–56; Stearns charged Mattoon $7.00 on September 1, 1816, "for taking down old house."

15. Dell Upton, "Pattern Books and Professionalism: Aspects of the Transformation of Domestic Architecture in America, 1800–1860," *Winterthur Portfolio* 19 (Summer/ Autumn 1984): 107–50; Henry Glassie, *Folk Housing in Middle Virginia: A Structural Analysis of Historic Artifacts* (Knoxville: University of Tennessee Press, 1975); Thomas Hubka, "Just Folks Designing: Vernacular Designers and the Generation of Form," in *Common Places: Readings in American Vernacular Architecture,* ed. Dell Upton and John Michael Vlach (Athens: University of Georgia Press, 1986), 426–32; Catherine Bishir, "Jacob W. Holt: An American Builder," in *Common Places,* ed. Upton and Vlach, 447–81.

16. For a perspective on this sense of modernity compare the examples depicted in Hosley, "Architecture," 106–32, with Calvin Stearns's house.

17. At the time he built this staircase, Calvin did not own Asher Benjamin's pattern book, which contained instructions for building circular stairs. It is not clear precisely where he learned how to join this type of stairway, but he may have had prior experience when he worked in Boston or observed other carpenters building them. According to Abbott Cummings, the earliest known circular stairs in a domestic building in New England were installed by Asher Benjamin several miles to the southwest in the Colman house in Greenfield in 1797; see Hosley, "Architecture," 120.

18. Basement kitchens were most common on lots with a slope, artificial or natural, and they were more common in coastal areas. Joyce K. Bibber notes that newspaper advertisements in Maine referred to basement kitchens often enough to imply they were not rare, but the surviving evidence does not support this assumption for inland areas. See Bibber, *A Home for Everyman: The Greek Revival and Maine Domestic Architecture* (Lanham: American Association for State and Local History Library and Greater Portland Landmarks, 1989), 44–45, 155–62.

19. George Stearns is mentioned frequently in his father's daybooks. Two letters from him survive, both of them written home to his family while he was teaching school in Wilmington, Del.

20. George A. Stearns, Daybook.

21. Bibber, *A Home for Everyman,* 41–45.

22. All these contracts were listed in George Stearns's account book. The best preserved of this cottage temple form is located in Gill, Mass., across the river from Northfield.

23. For a useful review of the growing literature on preindustrial *mentalité* see Allan Kulikoff, "The Transition to Capitalism in Rural America," *William and Mary Quarterly,* 3d ser., 46:1 (January 1989): 120–44; and Steven Hahn and Jonathan Prude, eds., *The Countryside in the*

Age of Capitalist Transformation (Chapel Hill: University of North Carolina Press, 1985).

24. The evidence for this is contained in his account and daybooks; there were references to communication with his old friend Josiah Oakes about building projects, and on at least one occasion his brother-in-law Augustus Richardson persuaded him to return to Boston to work on a project he had an interest in.

25. The Stearns women seem to have grown accustomed to the absence of their husbands, notwithstanding the ideals espoused by popular literature. See Gwendolyn Wright, *Building the Dream: A Social History of Housing in America* (Cambridge: MIT Press, 1983); Sally McMurray, *Families and Farmhouses in 19th Century America* (New York: Oxford University Press, 1988), ch. 3, 4.

Notes to "Samuel Wilson's Working World: Builders and Buildings in Chester County, Pennsylvania, 1780–1827," by Gabrielle Lanier

1. Dell Upton, "Pattern Books and Professionalism: Aspects of the Transformation of Domestic Architecture in America, 1800–1860," *Winterthur Portfolio* 19 (Summer–Autumn 1984): 107–50. For other studies of the building and designing process, see the preceding article by J. Ritchie Garrison and Catherine W. Bishir, "Jacob W. Holt: An American Builder," *Winterthur Portfolio* 16 (Spring 1981): 1–31.

2. Samuel Wilson, Sadsbury Township stonemason, account book, 3 vols. (1780–1827), Chester County Historical Society, 3:27, 2:9, 2:82, 3:23, 1:100, 1:62.

3. Although Chester County's population doubled in the fifty years between 1790 and 1840, Sadsbury's taxable population followed an even more dramatic trajectory, nearly doubling in half that time. This population growth translated into extensive building activity that eventually involved a wholesale reordering of the colonial Pennsylvania landscape. Triennial tax assessments indicate that the total number of structures in Sadsbury more than doubled between 1796 and 1811. Wilson's accounts reflect the quickening pace of building in this period.

4. See Garrison, "Calvin Stearns," above, and Bishir, "Jacob Holt," 1–31.

5. An inspection of the building materials listed for dwellings in four Chester County townships reveals that stone was the most frequently used building material in 1798. Mean figures for the use of stone for dwellings in these townships hover between 64 and 82 percent. 1798 Direct Tax: Tredyffrin, Sadsbury, Lower Merion and Up-

per Merion Townships, Chester County, Pa.

6. For a discussion of the intertwined relationships of stone, status, and power in the nearby German-settled region, see William Woys Weaver, "The Pennsylvania German House: European Antecedents and New World Forms," *Winterthur Portfolio* 21 (Winter 1986): 243.

7. 1789 Direct Tax, Sadsbury Township.

8. Lucy Simler, "Tenancy in Colonial Pennsylvania: The Case of Chester County," *William and Mary Quarterly* 43:4 (October 1986): 542–69.

9. Charles Thayer, Sadsbury, Pa., to Gabrielle Lanier, November 1986.

10. Samuel Wilson account books, 1:130.

11. Bernard Herman has suggested this link between three-room plans and mill owners. See *Architecture and Rural Life in Central Delaware, 1700–1900* (Knoxville: University of Tennessee Press, 1987), 23–24.

12. In 1784, Wilson and his crew worked for at least six weeks pulling down the old mill walls, clearing and arching a bridge over the tailrace, and rebuilding the dam walls. In 1798, Wilson rebuilt the end of the mill once again. Samuel Wilson account books, 2:10, 1:58.

13. Steven G. Del Sordo, "Eighteenth Century Grist Mills: Some Chester County, Pennsylvania Examples," in *Perspectives in Vernacular Architecture,* ed. Camille Wells (Annapolis, Md: Vernacular Architecture Forum, 1982), 67.

14. Michael Steinitz's research with the 1798 Direct Tax has revealed that the "average" dwelling in eighteenth-century Massachusetts differed considerably from what we might interpret as typical based on material evidence alone. Michael Steinitz, "Rethinking Geographical Approaches to the Common House: The Evidence from Eighteenth-century Massachusetts," in *Perspectives in Vernacular Architecture, III,* ed. Thomas Carter and Bernard L. Herman (Columbia: University of Missouri Press, 1989), 16–26. 1798 Direct Tax, Sadsbury Township.

15. Herman, *Architecture and Rural Life,* 139. See also Garrison, "Calvin Stearns," above.

16. 1796, 1799, 1802 Triennial Tax, Sadsbury Township. 1798 Direct Tax, Sadsbury Township.

17. 1798 Direct Tax, Sadsbury Township.

Notes to "The Social Context of Eighteenth-Century West New Jersey Brick Artisanry," by Michael J. Chiarappa

1. Joshua Evans Diary (1731–1798), Friends' Historical Library, Swarthmore College, Swarthmore, Pa., 7.

2. In this study the phrase *brick artisanry* is used to include both bricklayers and brickmakers. This phrase has emerged from appraisal of the historical documentation and artifactual evidence. As will be demonstrated, this is a valid occupational designation since clarification of the total social dynamic of brick artisanry, in this particular time and context, is the goal of this work. Harry B. and Grace M. Weiss's brief, survey-oriented *Early Brickmaking in New Jersey* (Trenton: New Jersey Agricultural Society, 1966) presented evidence calling for these two occupations to be viewed in their unified social role.

3. The work of Paul Love, "Pattern Brickwork in Southern New Jersey," *Proceedings of the New Jersey Historical Society* 73 (July 1955): 182-208, and Joseph Sickler, *The Old Houses of Salem County* (Salem, N.J.: Sunbeam Press, 1949), was seminal in regard to the documentation and description of these buildings. More recently, Alan Gowans, "The Mansions of Alloways Creek," in *Common Places: Readings in American Vernacular Architecture,* ed. Dell Upton and John Michael Vlach (Athens: University of Georgia Press, 1986), 367-93, has sought a fuller cultural interpretation of these houses in one of the four counties in which they were constructed. Although the number of these houses constructed is remarkable in relation to other areas of the eighteenth-century eastern seaboard, the University of Delaware's Center for Historic Architecture and Engineering quantification of the 1798 Federal Tax List of three Salem County townships by Rebecca Siders and Bernard L. Herman shows what a considerable minority these structures were in relation to those made of frame and log.

4. Richard Neve, *Neve's: The City and Country Purchaser and Builder's Dictionary* (London, 1726; rpt. Newton Abbot, Devon: David and Charles, 1969), 53.

5. Bernard L. Herman, "Kensey Johns and His Carpenters," in *After Ratification: Material Life in Delaware, 1789-1820,* ed. J. Ritchie Garrison, Bernard L. Herman, and Barbara McLean Ward (Newark: Museum Studies Program, University of Delaware, 1988), 65-77, is an eloquent discussion of the interactive nature of building as it concerns all artisans involved and their respective clients. For a thorough look at the total social scheme of craftsman/client relations—people, contracts, and setting—see Louis Chiaramonte, *Craftsman/Client Contracts: Interpersonal Relations in a Newfoundland Fishing Community,* New Social and Economic Studies, 10 (St. Johns: Institute for Social and Economic Research, Memorial University of Newfoundland, 1970). See also Harry B. and Grace M. Weiss, *Trades and Tradesmen of Colonial New Jersey* (Trenton: Past Times Press, 1965).

6. Robert B. St. George, "Fathers, Sons and Identity: Woodworking Artisans in Southeastern New England, 1620-1700," in *The Craftsman in Early America,* ed. Ian

M. G. Quimby (New York: W. W. Norton, 1984), 89-125, and *The Wrought Covenant: Source Material for the Study of Craftsmen and Community in Southeastern New England, 1620-1700* (Brockton, Mass.: Brockton Art Center-Fuller Memorial, 1979) are two excellent studies that address these very issues. See also Carl Bridenbaugh, *The Colonial Craftsman* (Chicago: University of Chicago Press, 1961), 126-27.

7. The term *Weighty Friend* is generally used to designate Quakers who had exceptional wealth and/or a substantial leadership role in their local and monthly meetings. In *Meeting House and Counting House: The Quaker Merchants of Colonial Philadelphia, 1682-1763* (New York: W. W. Norton, 1963), Frederick B. Tolles discusses at length Quaker wealth and hierarchy in the chapter "Quaker Grandees," pp. 109-43. For an in-depth look at how power and hierarchy manifested themselves in monthly meetings, see Susan S. Forbes, "Quaker Tribalism," in *Friends and Neighbors: Group Life in America's First Plural Society,* ed. Michael Zuckerman (Philadelphia: Temple University Press, 1982), 145-73. In any case, these individuals had obviously more than just an incidental relationship with the Quaker culture of the region.

8. Burlington, Gloucester, Salem, and Evesham Monthly Meeting Minutes, Friends' Historical Library, Swarthmore College; Great Egg Harbor/Cape May Monthly Meeting Minutes, Genealogical Society of Pennsylvania, vol. 353, Historical Society of Pennsylvania, Philadelphia; William Wade Hinshaw, *Encyclopedia of American Quaker Genealogy* (Ann Arbor: Edwards Brothers, 1938), vol. 2.

9. Peter O. Wacker, *Land and People: A Cultural Geography of Preindustrial New Jersey* (New Brunswick: Rutgers University Press, 1975), 136, 178, 180-81, 183, 185. Wacker was the first to thoroughly address Quakerism's role in social, cultural, and economic processes in that area during the eighteenth century. See also Thomas Purvis's *Proprietors, Patronage, and Paper Money: Legislative Politics in New Jersey, 1703-1776* (New Brunswick: Rutgers University Press, 1986) and Jean Soderlund's *Quakers and Slavery: A Divided Spirit* (Princeton: Princeton University Press, 1985).

10. Soderlund, *Quakers and Slavery,* 65; Purvis, *Proprietors, Patronage, and Paper Money,* 21; Jack P. Greene, *Pursuits of Happiness: The Social Development of Early Modern British Colonies and the Formation of American Culture* (Chapel Hill: University of North Carolina Press, 1988), 130; Roger T. Trindell, "The Ports of Salem and Greenwich in the Eighteenth Century," *New Jersey History* 86 (Winter 1968): 199-214; James T. Levitt, *For Want of Trade: Shipping and the New Jersey Ports, 1680-1783,* Collections of the New Jersey Historical Society, 17 (Newark: New Jersey Historical Society, 1981).

11. George Fox and William Loddington, *Plantation Work: The Work of This Generation* (London, 1682), quoted in David S. Lovejoy, *Religious Enthusiasm in the New World: Heresy to Revolution* (Cambridge: Harvard University Press, 1985), 116.

12. Carl Raymond Woodward, *Ploughs and Politicks: Charles Read of New Jersey and His Notes on Agriculture, 1715–1774* (New Brunswick: Rutgers University Press, 1941).

13. The best discussion on this process is in Purvis, *Proprietors, Patronage and Paper Money*, 25–49.

14. *New Jersey Archives: Extracts from American Newspapers Relating to New Jersey* (Paterson, N.J., 1895), 12:153.

15. An important interpretation of the symbolic meaning and economic power vested in "Great Houses" with water orientation is presented in Rhys Isaac, *The Transformation of Virginia, 1740–1790* (Chapel Hill: University of North Carolina Press, 1982), 34–42.

16. Barry Levy, *Quakers and the American Family: British Settlement in the Delaware Valley* (New York: Oxford University Press, 1988), 6–15, 25–35.

17. Henry Glassie, *Pattern in the Material Folk Culture of the Eastern United States* (Philadelphia: University of Pennsylvania Press, 1968), 49–53; Peter O. Wacker, "Traditional House and Barn Types: Keys to Acculturation, Past Cultureographic Regions, and Settlement History," *Geoscience and Man* 5 (June 10, 1974): 167. For fuller, regional treatments of Delaware valley Anglo-American building process, see Henry Glassie, "Eighteenth Century Cultural Process in Delaware Valley Folk Building," *Winterthur Portfolio* 7 (1972): 29–57, and Bernard L. Herman, *Architecture and Rural Life in Central Delaware, 1700–1900* (Knoxville: University of Tennessee Press, 1987).

18. N. R. Ewan, *Early Brickmaking in the Colonies* (Camden: Camden County Historical Society, 1970); Harrold E. Gillingham, "Some Early Brickmakers of Philadelphia," *The Pennsylvania Magazine of History and Biography* 53 (1929): 1–27. In addition to bricklaying skills being passed on orally, through families, and in certain shop situations, published manuals on bricklaying practice would have been in circulation. These would have included Neve, *Neve's: The City and Country Purchaser and Builder's Dictionary;* Joseph Moxon, *Mechanick Exercises, or the Doctrine of Handy-Works Applied to the Arts of Smithing, Carpentry, Joinery, Turning, Bricklaying* (London, 1703; rpt. New York: Praeger, 1970); William Leybuorne, *Platform for purchasers, a guide for builders, a mate for measurers* (London, 1685).

19. Barry Levy, "Tender Plants: Quaker Farmers and Children in the Delaware Valley, 1681–1735," *Journal of Family History* 3 (Summer 1978): 116–35.

20. Evans Diary, 4.

21. St. George, *Fathers, Sons, and Identity,* 103–4.

22. Ibid.

23. Harley J. McKee, "Brick and Stone: Handicraft to Machine," in *Building Early America: Contributions toward the History of a Great Industry,* ed. Charles E. Peterson (Radnor, Pa.: Chilton Book Co., 1976), 74; Cornelius C. Vermeule, "Early Transportation in and about New Jersey," *Proceedings of the New Jersey Historical Society* 9 (April 1924): 106–24; Charles S. Boyer, *Old Mills of Camden County* (Camden: Camden County Historical Society, 1962), 30.

24. J. William Frost, *The Quaker Family in Colonial America: A Portrait of the Society of Friends* (New York: St. Martin's Press, 1973), 136–47; Thomas Woody, *Early Quaker Education in Pennsylvania* (New York: Teachers College, Columbia University, 1920), 9–10.

25. Burlington Monthly Meeting Minutes, 11/4/1685, Friends' Historical Library, Swarthmore College, 54.

26. Ibid.

27. George Fox, *Journal,* 2:76; quoted in Woody, *Early Quaker Education,* 9–10. For views of apprentice rebelliousness and social background that Quakers had recently viewed prior to immigrating to the Delaware Valley see Steven R. Smith's "The London Apprentices as Seventeenth-Century Adolescents," *Past and Present* 61 (November 1973): 149–61, and "The Social and Geographical Origins of London Apprentices, 1630–1660," *Guildhall Miscellany* 4 (April 1973): 195–206.

28. Quaker hegemony in Pennsylvania is discussed in Levy, *Quakers and the American Family,* 155–56, 188–89, 256. Territoriality as a humanly conceived method to control people, land, and the entire range of social life is presented in Robert David Sack, *Territoriality: Its Theory and History* (Cambridge: Cambridge University Press, 1986).

29. Direct craftsman/client linkage can be established in the case of James Evans, who died in 1729 owing Richard Woodnutt and Andrew Thompson slightly over fifteen pounds. In all likelihood this was the unpaid portion of his recently constructed pattern-brickwork house. Salem County Wills 529, New Jersey Archives.

30. Tolles, *Meeting House and Counting House,* 89; Balwant Nevaskar, *Capitalists without Capitalism: The Jains of India and the Quakers of the West* (Westport, Conn.: Greenwood, 1971), 133.

31. Salem Monthly Meeting Minutes, November 30, 1698–1699, Friends' Historical Library, Swarthmore College.

32. Aaron Leaming and Jacob Spicer, *The Grants, Concessions and Original Constitutions of the Province of New Jersey* (Philadelphia: W. Bradford, 1758), 456, 458, 472,

490–91, 503–4; *New Jersey Archives,* 3:221.

33. Newton Township Minute Book, 1723–1821, Gloucester County, West New Jersey, Historical Society of Pennsylvania, Philadelphia; Michael C. Batinski, *The New Jersey Assembly, 1738–1775: The Making of a Legislative Community* (Lanham, Md.: University Press of America, 1987), 256–57.

34. The observation of class formation and hegemonic control is more problematic in the eighteenth century since there were not as many signs of overt conflict as in the nineteenth century. E. P. Thompson discusses in "Eighteenth-Century English Society: Class Struggle without Class?," *Social History* 3 (May 1978): 133–65 and "Patrician Society, Plebeian Culture," *Journal of Social History* 7 (Summer 1974): 382–405, how the process was a negotiated, reciprocated one that encompassed all realms of social and economically based cultural expression. The fortuitous position brick artisans operated from, and how they maintained it, is an exceptional story of artisanal power. For further discussion of how craftsmen had to deal with maintenance of craft control, identity, and economic power in the face of capitalist development see Joan Wallach Scott, *The Glassworkers of Carmaux: French Craftsmen and Political Action in a Nineteenth-Century City* (Cambridge: Harvard University Press, 1974).

35. Jack Michel, "In a Manner and Fashion Suitable to Their Degree: A Preliminary Investigation of the Material Culture of Early Pennsylvania," *Working Papers from the Regional Economic History Research Center* 5 (1981): 1–83; Gary Nash, *The Urban Crucible: The Northern Seaports and the Origins of the American Revolution* (Cambridge: Harvard University Press, 1986), 75–76.

36. *New Jersey Archives: Newspaper Extracts,* 24:385.

37. West New Jersey bricklayers Joseph Yard and Jonah Scoggins advertised in the *Pennsylvania Gazette* for runaway indentured servants in 1736 and 1753 respectively, as did brickmaker George Eyre in 1737. Ibid., 11:448–49, 495–96, 19:269–70.

38. Ibid., 24:22; J. Geraint Jenkins, *Traditional Country Craftsmen* (London: Routledge and Kegan Paul, 1978), 159.

39. Soderlund, *Quakers and Slavery,* 69; Purvis, *Proprietors, Patronage, and Paper Money,* 61.

40. Religious specificity in artisanal work is a compelling and practically untouched issue. Frederick B. Tolles, *Quakers and the Atlantic Culture* (New York: Octagon Books, 1980), 83, mentions Quaker dominance of certain trades in Philadelphia in the eighteenth century.

41. This discussion is not meant to imply that Quakers were the only ones practicing the brick trades, just that they were the ones who established its cultural meaning in the area and retained the greatest control of it as an instrument used in the round of social relations. For more on the process by which a particular group establishes the building standard see Fred Kniffen, "Folk Housing: Key to Diffusion," *Annals of the Association of American Geographers* 55 (December 1965): 551. For substantial information on Swedes practicing the brick trades in West New Jersey and further indications of the important relationship between bricklayer and brickmaker see *The Records of the Swedish Lutheran Churches at Raccoon and Penns Neck, 1713–1786,* trans. and comp. Federal Writers Project, State of New Jersey, 1938 (Woodbury, N.J.: Gloucester County Historical Society, 1982).

42. Frost, *The Quaker Family,* 54–55.

43. Burlington and Salem Monthly Meeting Minutes, Friends' Historical Library, Swarthmore College.

44. Salem Monthly Meeting Minutes, 1703–1733, Friends' Historical Library, Swarthmore College.

45. Study of the Federal Direct Tax List of 1798 for Salem County's Lower Alloways, Pittsgrove and Mannington Townships at the University of Delaware's Center for Historic Architecture and Engineering revealed that brick housing made up, respectively, 17.3, 6.9, and 16.7 percent of the total domestic dwellings in each of these townships.

Notes to "Good and Sufficient Language for Building," by Catherine W. Bishir

1. This paper draws extensively on research conducted on North Carolina building practice. Further discussion of this topic may be found in Catherine W. Bishir, Charlotte V. Brown, Carl R. Lounsbury, and Ernest H. Wood, III, *Architects and Builders in North Carolina: A History of the Practice of Building* (Chapel Hill: University of North Carolina Press, 1990).

The author wishes to acknowledge the assistance of Marshall Bullock, Bernard Herman, Carl Lounsbury, Myron Stachiw, and George Stevenson, who located and provided copies of several documents used in this article.

2. Agreement, Macon Whitfield and Richard Gill and Benjamin Ward, February 14, 1774. Bertie County Land Papers, 1736–1819, Archives and Records Section, North Carolina Division of Archives and History, Raleigh. Courtesy of George Stevenson.

3. See Henry Glassie, *Folk Housing in Middle Virginia: A Structural Analysis of Historic Artifacts* (Knoxville: University of Tennessee Press, 1975), and "The Variation of Concepts within Tradition: Barn Building in Otsego County, New York," in *Man and Cultural Heritage: Papers*

in Honor of Fred B. Kniffen, ed. H. J. Walker and W. G. Haag (Baton Rouge: Louisiana State University School of Geoscience, 1974). Thomas Hubka, "Just Folks Designing: Vernacular Designers and the Generation of Form," *Journal of Architectural Education* 32:3 (1979): 27–29; reprinted in *Common Places: Readings in American Vernacular Architecture,* ed. Dell Upton and John Michael Vlach (Athens: University of Georgia Press, 1986), 426–32. Dell Upton, "Toward a Performance Theory of Vernacular Architecture: Early Tidewater Virginia as a Case Study," *Folklore Forum* 12 (1979): 173–98, and "Vernacular Domestic Architecture in Eighteenth Century Virginia," *Winterthur Portfolio* 17 (Summer/Autumn 1982): 95–119. John Michael Vlach, "The Brazilian House in Nigeria: The Emergence of a 20th-Century Vernacular House Type," *Journal of American Folklore* 97:383 (1984): 3–23.

4. For further discussion of such arrangements, see Bishir, Brown, Lounsbury, and Wood, *Architects and Builders in North Carolina,* 38–41, 60–91. For an analysis of a Delaware carpenter's relations with his clients, see Bernard L. Herman, "Kensey Johns and His Carpenters," in *After Ratification: Material Life in Delaware, 1789–1820,* ed. J. Ritchie Garrison, Bernard L. Herman, and Barbara McLean Ward (Newark: Museum Studies Program, University of Delaware, 1988), 65–77. For a study of a builder's relations with his clients, see Catherine W. Bishir, "Jacob W. Holt: An American Builder," *Winterthur Portfolio* 16 (Spring 1981): 1–32.

5. See Louis J. Chiaramonte, *Craftsman-Client Contracts: Interpersonal Relations in a Newfoundland Fishing Community* (St. Johns: Institute of Social and Economic Research, Memorial University of Newfoundland, 1970), for analysis of types of oral contracts between client and craftsman.

6. Berry Davidson, autobiography, undated typescript copy, Alamance County, N.C., Planning Department files, courtesy of Carl Lounsbury. Henry King Burgwyn Diary, March 23, 1841, Archives and Records Section, North Carolina Division of Archives and History.

7. This section of my discussion draws directly upon Upton, "Toward a Performance Theory of Vernacular Architecture," 179–86, which includes extensive discussion of Basil Bernstein, *Class, Codes, and Control,* vol. 1, *Theoretical Studies toward a Sociology of Language* (London: Routledge and Kegan Paul, 1971), 122–36.

8. Upton, "Toward a Performance Theory of Vernacular Architecture," 180.

9. 1483, Gloucester, in L. F. Salzman, *Building in England Down to 1540* (Oxford: Clarendon Press, 1952), 542.

10. Boston: House for John Williams, Building contract, January 24, 1678/1679, Suffolk County Court Records, re-produced in Abbott Lowell Cummings, "Massachusetts Bay Building Documents, 1638–1726," in *Architecture in Colonial Massachusetts* (Boston: Colonial Society of Massachusetts, 1979), 204–5.

11. Agreement between J. F. Gaddy and Thomas Lenoir, January 23, 1860. Lenoir Family Papers, Southern Historical Collection, Wilson Library, University of North Carolina, Chapel Hill.

12. Boston: House for Thomas Robinson, Building contract, August 25 (?), 1660, Lane Family papers, privately owned; reproduced in Cummings, "Massachusetts Bay Building Documents," 203.

13. Contract, Frederick Shelton and others, April 28, 1828, Northampton County Miscellaneous Records, Archives and Records Section, North Carolina Division of Archives and History.

14. See H. M. Colvin, *A Biographical Dictionary of English Architects, 1660–1840* (Cambridge: Harvard University Press, 1954), 6, on the frequent use of existing buildings as models among English builders.

15. 1479, Nottingham, in Salzman, *Building in England,* 541.

16. Marlborough: Parsonage, Building contract, April 5, 1661, reproduced in Cummings, "Massachusetts Bay Building Documents," 216.

17. Agreement between Jacob Brewner and James B. Lindsay and others, November 1842. William Alexander Smith Papers, Duke Manuscript Collection, Perkins Library, Duke University, Durham, N.C.; courtesy of William Erwin.

18. Bill for Dwelling House, 1857, Baskerville Family Papers, Private Collection. Quoted and discussed in Catherine W. Bishir, "Jacob W. Holt," 27–30. Eureka was built for Robert Baskerville; it was to be built in the same style as the house Holt had recently remodeled and expanded for Robert's father, William.

19. Luther Osbourn and Leonard Cozzens, Agreement, February 7, 1849. Worcester County, Mass., Land Records, 443:468, copy courtesy of Myron Stachiw, Old Sturbridge Village.

20. Specifications of a brick house . . . Z. Latimer. Lower Cape Fear Historical Society, Inc., Wilmington, N.C.

21. Stevens Gray and Gilbert Leigh, May 1, 1786, Gray Family Papers, Southern Historical Collection, Wilson Library.

22. Boxford: House for David Peabody, Building contract, April 13, 1726, Peabody-Osgood Papers, Essex Institute, reproduced in Cummings, "Massachusetts Bay Building Documents," 207–8, quote from 208. Presumably Peabody had observed that windows had recently become somewhat larger than in the older houses.

23. Agreement, M. Chambers for John Steele with Elem Sharpe, March 28, 1799, John Steele Collection, Southern Historical Collection. See further discussion of this construction project in Bishir, Brown, Lounsbury, and Wood, *Architects and Builders in North Carolina,* 69–70.

24. Agreement between Burton and Holmes and C. C. Chickering, March 22, 1848, Worcester County, Mass., Land Records, 440:370, courtesy of Myron Stachiw, Old Sturbridge Village. William Ranlett's *The Architect* was a popular architectural book published by William H. Graham in 2 volumes (1847–1849).

25. Contract for the house at 229 West Bank St., Salisbury, N.C., copy from files of James Brawley, Salisbury.

26. Cummings, "Massachusetts Bay Building Documents," 204–7. See also the 1680 case of John Bateman of Boston and carpenter Robert Tafft, where Bateman insisted that Tafft had not satisfactorily completed his contract of August 20, 1679, to build the frame of a house, and Bateman defended his actions. Ibid., 197–99. Herman, "Kensey Johns and His Carpenters," 68, cites the detailed specifications (ca. 1790) for the John Dickinson house in New Castle, Del., and the subsequent court case over misunderstandings between builders and client.

Notes to "Explicit Rules, Implicit Rules, and Formal Variation in Vernacular Building," by Howard Davis

1. Ernst Gombrich, "The Beauty of Old Towns," *Architectural Association Journal* 80 (April 1965): 293–97; Christopher Alexander, *The Timeless Way of Building* (New York: Oxford University Press, 1979). In this work, Alexander sees *patterns* as culturally understood, repeatable relationships in the built world that provide for observable similarities among different buildings.

2. Henry Glassie, *Folk Housing in Middle Virginia: A Structural Analysis of Historic Artifacts* (Knoxville: University of Tennessee Press, 1975), 36, 38. But even Glassie recognizes, however briefly, the phenomenon described in this essay: "Houses that look the same turn out to be different in small ways. A window conceptually in the exact center of a wall may be, in fact, a few inches one way or the other. When the architectural competence directs that a door be placed symmetrically, the carpenter's actual performance generally results in a door that appears to be symmetrically positioned; but when the tape measure is consulted it reveals that his performance only closely approximated the directives within his unconscious design ability. This constant minor variation in real phenomena

blurs the clarity of the surface, confusing him who would be a copyist, confounding him who would simplistically account for cultural processes" (67–68).

3. *Dicker v. Popham* (1890) 63 L.T. 379.

4. Howard Davis, "The Future of Ancient Lights," *Journal of Architectural and Planning Research* 6:2 (Summer 1989): 132–53.

5. *Symonds v. Seaborne* (1625).

6. *Senior v. Pawson* (1866) L.R. 3 Eq. 330; *Higgins. v. Betts* (1905) 2. Ch. 210.

7. *Att. Gen. v. Doughty* (1788) 2 Ves. Sen. 453.

8. *Clarke v. Clark* (1865) 1 Ch. App. 16.

9. *Clifford v. Holt* (1899) 1 Ch. 698.

10. *Cherrington v. Abney* (1709) 2 Vern. 646; *Aynsley v. Glover* (1874) L.R. 18 Eq. 551.

11. *Dickinson v. Harbottle* (1873) 28 L.T. 186; *Robson v. Whittingham* (1866) 1 Ch. App. 442.

12. *Fishmongers' Co. v. East India Co.* (1752) 1 Dick. 163; *Colls v. Home & Colonial Stores* (1904) 73 L.J. Ch. 484 (italics mine); *Ough v. King* (1967) 1 W.R.R. 1547.

13. *William Cory & Son Ltd. v. City of London Real Property Co. Ltd,* quoted in supplement to Bryan Anstey and Michael Chavasse, *The Right to Light* (London: Estates Gazette, 1966).

14. Morton Horwitz, *The Transformation of American Law* (Cambridge: Harvard University Press, 1977), 4.

15. *Parker v. Foote* (1838) 19 Wend. 309.

16. *Lawrence v. Horton* (1890) 59 L.J. Ch. 440.

17. Delissa Joseph, "Building Heights and Ancient Lights," *Journal of the Royal Institute of British Architects* 30:15 (June 16, 1923): 477–88.

18. For examples of such contracts see L. F. Salzman, *Building in England Down to 1540* (Oxford: Oxford University Press, 1952), and also North American works such as Peter N. Moogk, *Building a House in New France* (Toronto: McClelland and Stewart, 1977).

Notes to "Exploring the Role of Women in the Creation of Vernacular Architecture," by Rebecca Sample Bernstein and Carolyn Torma

1. Flora Doran, interview with Rebecca Sample Bernstein, Custer County, S.D., June 20, 1988.

2. Lillian Rantapaa, interview with Carolyn Torma, Lead, S.D., August 16, 1984.

3. Sally McMurry, "Women in the American Vernacular Landscape," *Material Culture* 20:1 (Spring 1989): 1, 37, 38, 41.

4. Emily French, *Emily: The Diary of a Hard-worked

Woman, ed. Janet Lecompte (Lincoln: University of Nebraska Press, 1987), 7.

5. Elizabeth Hampsten, *Read This Only to Yourself: The Private Writings of Midwestern Women, 1880–1910* (Bloomington: Indiana University Press, 1982).

6. Will G. Robinson, ed., "Daughters of Dakota Biographies," *Department of History Collections, South Dakota* 31 (1966): 18–457.

7. Norman Stearns, interview with Rebecca Sample Bernstein, Custer County, S.D., June 24, 1988.

8. David Murphy, "Building in Clay on the Central Plains: Time, Place, Ethnicity" (paper delivered at the Missouri Valley History Conference, Omaha, Nebr., March 8, 1984). See also David Murphy, "Building in Clay on the Central Plains," in *Perspectives in Vernacular Architecture, III,* ed. Thomas Carter and Bernard L. Herman (Columbia: University of Missouri Press, 1989), 74–85.

9. Glenda Riley, "Farm Women's Roles in the Agricultural Development of South Dakota," *South Dakota History* 13:1–2 (Spring/Summer 1983): 88.

10. Walker D. Wyman, comp., *Frontier Woman: The Life of a Woman Homesteader on the Dakota Frontier* (River Falls: University of Wisconsin–River Falls, 1972), 1–2.

11. Glenda Riley, *The Female Frontier: A Comparative View of Women on the Prairie and the Plains* (Lawrence: University Press of Kansas, 1988), 22.

12. Mrs. Harriet Ward, interview with Rebecca Sample Bernstein, Custer, S.D., July 8, 1988.

13. Wyman, comp., *Frontier Woman,* 95–100.

14. Anna Langhorne Waltz, "West River Pioneer: A Woman's Story, 1911–1915, Part One," *South Dakota History* 17:1 (Spring 1987): 49; "West River Pioneer: A Woman's Story, 1911–1915, Part Two," *South Dakota History* 17:2 (Summer 1987): 148–49.

15. Anette Atkins, "The Dynamics of Family Life in 19th Century Minnesota" (paper delivered at the Annual History Conference of the Minnesota Historical Society, St. Paul, Minn., November 18, 1989).

16. Riley, "Farm Women's Roles in South Dakota," 87. For statistics on Minnesota women homesteaders, see Anne B. Webb, "Women Farmers on the Frontier," *Minnesota History* 50:4 (Winter 1986): 135.

17. Glenda Riley, ed., "Proving Up: The Memoir of 'Girl Homesteader' Martha Stoecker Norby," *South Dakota History* 16:1 (Spring 1986): 6.

18. Robinson, "Daughters of Dakota," 239.

19. Ibid., 288–89.

20. Mary W. M. Hargreaves, "Homesteading and Homemaking on the Plains: A Review," *Agricultural History* 157 (April 1973): 158.

21. Robinson, "Daughters of Dakota," 69.

22. Ibid., 217.

23. Ibid., 251.

24. Ibid., 307.

25. Mary W. M. Hargreaves, "Women in the Agricultural Settlement of the Northern Plains," *Agricultural History* 50:1 (January 1976): 186.

26. Eva Larson, interview with Carolyn Torma, Frederick, S.D., June 2, 1984.

27. Maurice Nelson, interview with Carolyn Torma, Clay County, S.D., September 2, 1987.

28. Riley, *The Female Frontier,* 3.

29. Joanna L. Stratton, *Pioneer Women: Voices from the Kansas Frontier* (New York: Simon and Schuster, 1982), 50–51.

30. Charles E. Martin, *Hollybush: Folk Building and Social Change in an Appalachian Community* (Knoxville: University of Tennessee Press, 1984), 16, 28.

31. Peter N. Moogk, *Building a House in New France: An Account of the Perplexities of Client and Craftsmen in Early Canada* (Toronto: McClelland and Stewart, 1977), 60, 80, 94, 117.

32. This study has been too limited to address two additional yet highly significant variables: Were the experiences of rural and urban women different? Did the frontier era of the midcontinent present a unique set of circumstances for women?

Notes to "The Evolution of a Vernacular Tradition," by Jay Edwards

1. James J. Parsons, *San Andrés and Providencia: English-Speaking Islands in the Western Caribbean* (Berkeley and Los Angeles: University of California Publications in Geography), 12:1 (1956): 18.

2. Jay D. Edwards, "African Influences on the English of San Andrés Island, Colombia," in *Pidgins and Creoles: Current Trends and Prospects,* ed. David DeCamp and Ian Hancock (Washington, D.C.: Georgetown University Press, 1974), 1–26.

3. Only on Providencia, a culturally related neighboring island, have hurricanes been a source of serious destruction; that of 1940 damaged or destroyed 410 houses. The vernacular tradition also embraces the Corn Islands (Mangales) of Nicaragua.

4. Lt. José del Rio, "Descripción topográfica de las yslas de San Andrés, Providencia, O Santa Catalina, Mangales, Grande y Chico, sus situaciones, y proyecciones, sus puertos, población, temperamento, suelo, cosechas, y pesca" (a report to the King of Spain), *Revista del Archivo Nacional* (Bogotá, 1793): 15–18.

5. Parsons, *San Andrés and Providencia,* 29; Loren C. Turnage, *Island Heritage: A Baptist View of the History of San Andrés and Providencia* (Cali, Colombia: Historical Commission of the Colombia Baptist Mission, 1975), 19–32.

6. "A Commercial Agency of the United States of America at San Andrés, Colombia," dispatch of December 31, 1873. Dispatches from United States Consuls in San Andrés 1870–1878. Washington, D.C., National Archives micro-copy #T-554.

7. Parsons, *San Andrés and Providencia,* 38.

8. The simple box frame was exposed to view in the interior; the exterior was covered with clapboards. The roof was supported by pairs of rafters joined together at their peaks and stiffened by collar beams. No roof ridge was employed. The roof was covered with cedar shakes (later corrugated iron sheeting) and was pitched at 45 to 55 degrees.

9. Even today, after more than a century of elaboration, a strong tendency toward shared form persists everywhere in the island. What I shall refer to as the *base module* was a single-story rectangular building of modest proportions. It was generally capped with a gabled roof. At first, most houses were laid out with the typical British colonial asymmetrical "room-and-hall" plan—two rooms only. The near-square "hall" functioned as the all-purpose living room, the narrower "room" as the master bedroom. On the early houses the eaves extended very little past the wall—perhaps an inch or two. Full-length porches, universally called "piazzas" in the Western Caribbean, were not much used in the earliest decades.

10. Jay D. Edwards, "The Evolution of Vernacular Architecture in the Western Caribbean," in *Cultural Traditions and Caribbean Identity: The Question of Patrimony,* ed. Jeffrey K. Wilkerson (Gainesville: University of Florida Center for Latin American Studies, 1980), 291–339.

11. Ibid., 302, 317–18; J. M. Jenkins, "Ground Rules of Welsh Houses: A Primary Analysis," *Folk Life* 5 (1967): 65–91; Arthur J. Lawton, "The Ground Rules of Folk Architecture," *Pennsylvania Folklife* 23:1 (Fall 1973): 13–19; Henry Glassie, *Folk Housing in Middle Virginia: A Structural Analysis of Historic Artifacts* (Knoxville: University of Tennessee Press, 1975), 19–26.

12. I hypothesize that this difference resulted from the difference in the availability of architectural models at the time of initial vernacular expansion. In Barbados, big-house polite domestic architecture in the 1660–1700 period was dominated by Jacobean styling, typically characterized by double or triple truss roofs (for example, Drax Hall and St. Nicholas Abbey). In isolated San Andrés there was a dearth of larger models. This permitted a style of expansion in the years 1865–1900 dominated entirely by

the values and perceived needs of the local West Indian vernacular builders. The pattern proved to be conservative and incremental, rather than being based on a multiplication of established units.

13. Perhaps because the long, narrow "halls" (sitting rooms) they created conflicted with the dominant aesthetic for nearly square proportions.

14. Small porches protecting the front doors were generally not used on San Andrés houses. They are not expansions in the sense used here.

15. Linzale Brandt or his father (see introductory quote).

16. The Loft Piazza (MLA2/MLB2) expansion is dependent on two previous expansions. It requires an MF1 front piazza-rear shed and either an MLB1 or an MLA1 dormer expansion. The system of loft expansion had become integrated into the larger system of external expansion, resulting in a fully integrated multistory system of external expansion. It was not very long after the turn of the twentieth century that the ML2 house had become the standard of elegance in the countryside of San Andrés. Both very small and very large houses could be built in the ML2 form.

17. For example, the interesting house in Fig. 18 is an MB2 (enclosed), MF2 (enclosed) d1, MLB2-S (enclosed), with a nontraditional shed expansion on its left side, a nontraditional enclosure of its second-story piazza, and a nontraditional stairway in front. In these respects this building might be termed "ungrammatical."

18. The author wishes to thank Bernard Herman for his valuable comments on this paper.

Notes to "Pitched Roofs over Flat: The Emergence of a New Building Tradition in Hispanic New Mexico," by Chris Wilson

1. This article is adapted in part from Chris Wilson and David Kammer, *Community and Continuity: The History, Architecture and Cultural Landscape of La Tierra Amarilla* (Santa Fe: New Mexico Historic Preservation Division, 1989). That book, the historic building survey on which it is based, and the plans reproduced here were funded in part by the Historic Preservation Division, Office of Cultural Affairs, State of New Mexico. My thanks for helpful suggestions go to Robert Torrez, David Kammer, Margaret Purser, and Thomas Carter.

2. Richard Nostrand, "The Century of Hispano Expansion," *New Mexico Historical Review* 62:4 (October 1987): 361–67. The question of the existence of a secondary Spanish cultural hearth in north-central New Mexico has been the subject of spirited debate. The controversy

was initiated by Richard Nostrand, "The Hispano Home-land in 1900," *Annals of the Association of American Geographers* (*AAAG*) 70:3 (September 1980): 382–96. It attracted an extended rebuttal: J. M. Blaut and Antonio Rios-Bustamante, "Commentary on Nostrand's 'Hispanos' and Their 'Homeland,'" *AAAG* 74:1 (1984): 157–64, and a number of other commentaries, replies and rejoinders in *AAAG* 71:2 (June 1981): 280–83; 74:1 (1984): 164–71.

3. Eric C. Wolf, *Europe and the People without History* (Berkeley: University of California Press, 1982), ix.

4. J. B. Jackson, "First Comes the House," *Landscape* 9:2 (Winter 1959–1960): 26–32; Bainbridge Bunting, *Taos Adobes: Spanish Colonial and Territorial Architecture of the Taos Valley* (Santa Fe: Museum of New Mexico Press, 1964) and *Early Architecture in New Mexico* (Albuquerque: University of New Mexico Press, 1976); Chris Wilson, "When a Room Is the Hall," *Mass* 2 (Summer 1984): 17–23.

5. Jackson, "First Comes the House," 28–29; Wilson, "When a Room," 19–20.

6. A. W. Conway, "A Northern New Mexico House-Type," *Landscape* 1:2 (1951): 20–21; Jackson, "First Comes the House"; Bunting, *Taos Adobes* and *Early Architecture*; Wilson, "When a Room"; Beverly Spears, *American Adobes: Rural Houses of Northern New Mexico* (Albuquerque: University of New Mexico Press, 1986).

7. The installation was known as Camp Plummer ca. 1866–1868 and Fort Lowell ca. 1868–1869. Robert Torrez, "The Tierra Amarilla," 9–10, in *La Tierra Amarilla: The People of the Chama Valley*, ed. Anselmo Arellano (Tierra Amarilla, N.M.: Chama Valley Schools, 1978); Jerry L. Williams, *New Mexico in Maps* (Albuquerque: University of New Mexico Press, 1986), 11–13; D. Mortimer Lee, "Camp Plummer, New Mexico, December 31st, 1867," plan, Records of the Office of Quartermaster General, Consolidated Correspondence File, Camp Plummer, N.M., Record Group no. 92, National Archives, Washington, D.C.; D. Mortimer Lee, "Camp Plummer, New Mexico, July 1st, 1868," aerial view, General File, National Archive, Washington, D.C.

8. Bunting, *Early Architecture*, 5, 90, 98; Wilson, "When a Room," 19; Agnesa L. Reeve, *From Hacienda to Bungalow* (Albuquerque: University of New Mexico Press, 1988), 53–72; Chris Wilson et al., *The South Central New Mexico Regional Overview* (Santa Fe: Historic Preservation Division, 1989), 128–30.

9. Henry Glassie, "Eighteenth Century Cultural Process in Delaware Valley Folk Building," *Winterthur Portfolio* 7 (1972): 29–57; Virginia McAlester and Lee McAlester, *A Field Guide to American Houses* (New York: Alfred A. Knopf, 1984), 139–45; Thomas Carter and Peter Goss,

Utah's Historic Architecture, 1847–1940 (Salt Lake City: University of Utah Press, 1988), 26–27; Bunting, *Early Architecture*, 90–92, Wilson, "When a Room," 19–20.

10. McAlester and McAlester, *Field Guide*, 198–203; Vincent Scully, *The Shingle Style and the Stick Style*, rev. ed. (New Haven: Yale University Press, 1971), fig. 16, pp. xxiii-lix.

11. At first, Tierra Amarilla's most important connection with the outside, European-American world was the Old Spanish Trail, down the Chama River to Abiquiu and Santa Fe. But from the first settlements, trails out of Tierra Amarilla through the San Luis valley were used by annual parties of buffalo hunters from Tierra Amarilla on their way to the plains. When the railroad reached Trinidad and Pueblo, Colo., in the early 1870s, the freight roads that developed over these early trails became the most direct connection to outside products. When the Denver and Rio Grande Railroad passed through the San Luis valley to reach Chama, N.M., in 1880, the orientation of Tierra Amarilla toward Colorado was strengthened. Only with the construction of a state highway during the 1930s from Abiquiu to Tierra Amarilla did the focus shift back toward other New Mexico communities.

12. Nicholas G. Morgan, "Mormon Colonization in the San Luis Valley," *Colorado Magazine* 27:4 (October 1950): 269–93; Richard Sherlock, "Mormon Migration and Settlement after 1875," *Journal of Mormon History* 2 (1975): 53–68; *The Mormons: 100 Years in the San Luis Valley of Colorado*, ed. Carleton Q. Anderson et al. (n.p.: La Jara Stake, 1983).

13. Thomas Carter, "Building Zion: Folk Architecture in the Mormon Settlements of Utah's Sanpete Valley, 1849–1890" (Ph.D. diss., Indiana University, 1984); Richard Francaviglia, *The Mormon Landscape* (New York: AMS Press, 1978), 16–20; Richard C. Poulsen, "Stone Buildings of Beaver City," *Utah Historical Quarterly* (*UHQ*), 43:3 (Fall 1975): 278–84; Teddy Griffith, "A Heritage of Stone in Willard," *UHQ* 43:2 (Summer 1975): 286–300; Thomas Carter, "'The Best of Its Kind and Grade': Rebuilding the Sanpete Valley, 1890–1910," *UHQ* 54:1 (Winter 1986): 88–112; McAlester and McAlester, *Field Guide*, 202–3; Carter and Goss, *Utah's Historic Architecture*, 16, 21–3.

14. The presence of Juan and Maria Luz Truillo, Mormon converts, apparently from Tierra Amarilla, among the first group of settlers at Manasa suggests direct contact. Morgan, "Mormon Colonization," 286; United State Census, "Census Enumerator Sheets for Rio Arriba County, New Mexico, 1870" microfilm, Special Collections, University of New Mexico Library, Tierra Amarilla, precinct no. 16, sheets 6–7.

15. Francaviglia, *Mormon Landscape*, 6–7, 57; *La Tierra Amarilla*, ed. Arellano, 95.

16. *The Mormons,* ed. Anderson et al., 82–85; Morgan, "Mormon Colonization," 283–84; Richard H. Jackson, "The Use of Adobe in the Mormon Cultural Region," *Journal of Cultural Geography* 1:2 (1980): 82–95.

17. For a plan of the Palace of the Governors, Santa Fe, see Hugh Morrison, *Early American Architecture* (New York: Oxford University Press, 1952), 186. For a late eighteenth-century residence in Mexico City with a two-room-deep portion see Ignacio Gonzales-Polo, *El Palicio de los Conde de Santiago* (Mexico City: Departamento del Distrito Federal, 1983), pl. 15. Nearly all the residences in Mexico City and the state of Chihuahua, immediately south of New Mexico, documented in the early 1980s federal survey of historic buildings have single files of rooms; for a double file example see Instituto Nacional de Anthropologia e Historia, *Catalogo Nacional de Monumentos Historicos Inmuebles, Estado de Chihuahua* (Mexico City: author, 1986), building number 08032001-0040.

18. Bunting, *Early Architecture,* 60–63, and *Taos Adobes,* 23–27; A. W. Conway, "Southwest Colonial Farms," *Landscape* 1:1 (1951): 6–9

19. Adrian Praetzellis et al., "Artifacts as Symbols of Identity: An Example from Sacramento's Gold Rush Era Chinese Community," in *Living in Cities: Current Research in Urban Archeology,* ed. Edward Staski (n.p.: Society for Historic Archeology, 1987), 38–47.

20. William deBuys, *Enchantment and Exploitation: The Life and Hard Times of a New Mexico Mountain Range* (Albuquerque: University of New Mexico Press, 1985), 204–6.

21. While a conclusion so full of "suggests," "perhapses," and "may well haves" is less than satisfying, only further study of other aspects of culture and of economic class structure in Tierra Amarilla can yield more definitive answers to the meaning of the area's architecture. David Felton and Peter D. Schulz in *The Diaz Collection: Material Culture and Social Change in Mid-Nineteenth-Century Monterey,* California Archeological Reports 23 (Sacramento: California Department of Parks and Recreation, 1983), employ an interrelated analysis of archaeological artifacts, census enumerator sheets, and period accounts of individual and group political attitudes to address similar questions of ethnic and class identity.

Notes to "The Cycle of Transformations in Schaefferstown, Pennsylvania, Houses," by Charles Bergengren

1. The impact of cultural source areas or "hearths" on subsequent character of a region is discussed in Fred Knif-

fen, "Folk Housing: Key to Diffusion," *Annals of the Association of American Geographers* 55 (December 1965): 549–77; reprinted in *Common Places: Readings in American Vernacular Architecture,* ed. Dell Upton and John Michael Vlach (Athens: University of Georgia Press, 1986), 3–26. The story of German settlement in the Tulpehocken may be found in William Henry Egle, *History of the Counties of Dauphin and Lebanon, in the Commonwealth of Pennsylvania: Biographical and Genealogical* (Philadelphia: Everts and Peck, 1883; rpt. Evansville, Ind.: Unigraphic, 1977), and Lucy Forney Bittinger, *The Germans in Colonial Times* (New York: Russell and Russell, 1901), 76–90.

2. Robert C. Bucher, "The Swiss Bankhouse in Pennsylvania," *Pennsylvania Folklife* 28:2 (Winter 1968–1969): 2–11, prominently features the Alexander Schaeffer house.

3. Henry Glassie, "Vernacular Architecture and Society," *Material Culture* 16:1 (1984): 4–24; "Eighteenth Century Cultural Process in the Delaware Valley," *Winterthur Portfolio* 7 (1972): 6–57; *Folk Housing in Middle Virginia: A Structural Analysis of Historical Artifacts* (Knoxville: University of Tennessee Press, 1975); and James Deetz, *In Small Things Forgotten: The Archeology of Early American Life* (Garden City: Doubleday, 1977).

4. Inasmuch as this finding forms the end of my dissertation, the present paper constitutes a radical condensation or summary of it.

5. In this study, all buildings built with traditional heavy framed, log, or stone construction within a slightly gerrymandered one-mile orbit of the town of Schaefferstown were approached. Field notes for measured drawings of at least the ground-floor plan were taken in every house I gained access to built before 1850. Previous studies of the common German *flurkuchen* house type include Robert C. Bucher, "The Continental Log House" *Pennsylvania Folklife* 12:4 (Summer 1962): 14–19; Henry Glassie, "A Central Chimney Continental Log House," *Pennsylvania Folklife* 18:2 (Winter 1968–1969): 32–39. The house type was first named *flurkuchenhaus* in American literature by John Milner in "Germanic Architecture in the New World," *Journal of the Society of Architectural Historians* 34:4 (December 1975): 299. The term has been picked up by Edward Chappell in "Acculturation in the Shenandoah Valley: Rhenish House in the Massanuten Settlement," in *Common Places,* ed. Upton and Vlach, 27–57.

6. The most common variant is a partition at the rear of the chimney, forming a small buttery at the far end of the *kuche.* This fourth ground-floor room is usually found on the larger examples of the *flurkuchen* type—the Herr house in Lancaster County and Fort Egypt in Virginia's Shenandoah valley are famous examples. See Robert Barakat, "The Herr and Zeller Houses," *Pennsylvania Folklife*

21:4 (Summer 1972): 2–22, and Chappell, "Acculturation in the Shenandoah Valley." The uses to which the rooms of the Pennsylvania German house were put are discussed in Scott T. Swank, *The Arts of the Pennsylvania Germans* (Winterthur, Del.: W. W. Norton for the Winterthur Museum, 1983), 35–60, and William Woys Weaver, "The Pennsylvania German House: European Antecedents and New World Forms," *Winterthur Portfolio* 21 (Winter 1986): 254ff. For the proportions of traditional rooms see Arthur J. Lawton, "The Ground Rules of Folk Architecture," *Pennsylvania Folklife* 23:1 (Fall 1973): 13–19.

7. Findings from the drawings of John Richard of Germantown, travelers' accounts, and murder trial chapbooks (which dissect the issue of how the murderer got inside the house in painful detail) have been presented in my "From Murderers to Wandering Wayfarers: The Etiquette of Entry and the Social Implications of House Form in Eighteenth Century Pennsylvania," at the American Folklore Society Meeting, Boston, 1988.

8. Verband Deutscher Architekten und Ingenieur vereine, *Das Bauernhaus im Deutschen Reiche und in seinen Grenzgebieten* (Dresden: Verlag Gerhard Kühtmann, 1906), contains three examples of the *kreuzehaus* type built as a separate dwelling, and no less than twenty-one (with considerable variations) of it as the dwelling part of a housebarn. See for example Folio: Baden #9 (Abb. 5, Herbolzheim); and Bayern #13 (haus Brutscher). See also an urban example illustrated in Weaver, "The Pennsylvania German House," 252.

9. There are four versions of separate dwellings with the *durchgagigen* floor plan in the folios of the Verband Deutscher Architekten, and at least ten such plans were built as parts of housebarns.

10. Such alterations are defined here as those that changed the type of the plan, such as the removal or addition of a massive chimney or a full interior wall; the widening of doors or the insertion of closets do not count as major alterations. These alterations include thirty chimneys removed (77 percent); seventeen walls removed (43 percent, with more than one wall removed in eight cases, or 25 percent); sixteen walls installed (41 percent, and in almost half of these cases the wall was moved more than once). In addition, fourteen houses (37 percent) have had the location of the stairs changed and over half of the remaining number have had their stairs rebuilt or straightened in situ. Eleven houses (28 percent) were expanded lineally to the side; four (10 percent) underwent major conceptual expansions to the rear (with roofs entirely reframed); and twenty-three (59 percent) had a lean-to or "shanty" appended to the rear. Doors and windows shifted position on six facades (15 percent).

11. Henry Glassie, "Eighteenth Century Cultural Process in the Delaware Valley," *Winterthur Portfolio* 7 (1972): 29–57, reprinted in *Common Places*, ed. Upton and Vlach, 394–425.

12. Henry Glassie, *Pattern in the Material Folk Culture of the Eastern United States* (Philadelphia: University of Pennsylvania Press, 1968), 124ff.

13. On five-plate stoves see Henry Chapman Mercer, *The Bible in Iron* (Doylestown, Pa.: Bucks County Historical Society, 1914); on the advantages of the German system of heating rooms with them (compared especially to the English habit of sitting before an open fire) see Benjamin Franklin, *An Account of the Newly Invented Pennsylvanian Fire-Place* (Philadelphia: B. Franklin, 1744; rpt. Boston: G. K. Hall, 1973), and Dr. Benjamin Rush, *An Account of the German Inhabitants of Pennsylvania* (1790), ed. Theodore E. Schmauk and I. D. Rupp (Lancaster: Pennsylvania German Society, 1910).

14. Among other conspicuous activities in the promotion of himself and his wares, Stiegel kept several men employed building an outlandish tower on the edge of town. Local lore persists as to the extravagant parties he held there, arriving to trumpet fanfares (from the top) and departing to cannon blasts. On Stiegel see George L. Heiges, *Henry William Stiegel and His Associates* (Manheim, Pa.: the author, 1948); the existence of the tower itself, if not its legendary form and uses, is confirmed by explicit references to it in the account books of Henry Schaeffer, Records of Purchases at the King George Hotel, Schaefferstown, Lebanon County, Pa., 1762–1773, transcribed and translated by Frederick S. Weiser and Larry M. Neff, *Sources and Documents of the Pennsylvania Germans: X* (Birdsboro: Pennsylvania German Society, 1987), 90, 98, 124.

15. Other researchers have found similar reactions to the central hallway in their areas. If a passage is built for fashionable purposes when there are no real social differences to invoke, then it simply doesn't work as a usable space. Tom Carter found that hallways were not often viable in the small Mormon communities he studied in Utah and even titled one of his essays after the common reaction there: "It Was In the Way, So We Took It Out: Remodeling as Social Commentary," *Material Culture* 19:3 (Fall 1987): 113–25. To judge from the Peter Issaacsen house in Ephraim, San Pete valley, the change could be radical indeed, involving removing or repositioning every element in the interior of the house except one wall of the hallway.

Similarly, Michael Ann Williams found that the only people for whom the hallway worked as a formal space in the mountains of southwestern North Carolina were those who rented out rooms in their houses to tourists, the ultimate outsiders (Michael Ann Williams, "Homeplace:

The Social Use and Meaning of the Folk Dwelling in Southwestern North Carolina" [Ph.D. diss., University of Pennsylvania, 1985], chap. 4, esp. 107–18). For them, the hallway served as a neutral zone between the family and the outlander sectors of the house. But without such an obvious social dichotomy, the hall either was not used or was put to some kind of use at odds with the concept of a passageway. Many simply left the space for storage (somewhat impeding any passage through it), but others filled it with a washstand, mirror, trunk, dresser, and sometimes even a bed. The hallway was then used as a parlor, or even as a bedroom—the very opposite of its original function for passing through.

16. It should be noted that this authentic use of the hall is concentrated in the town's younger (or retired) professionals, whether or not they have long ancestral roots in the town.

17. I am indebted to Jane Eisely for this information.

18. Such double parlors are typical of the classical and empire designs of Charles Bulfinch and even Andrew Jackson Davis, resulting from the widening of the door between the two main rooms (parlor and dining room) in a standard side-passage or "two-thirds Georgian" house. In some cases the wall is replaced completely by a screen of flanking columns; in the Philadelphia house built for Thomas Willig in 1830, the suggestion of separating walls is quite vestigial. Such rooms can be seen in nineteenth-century paintings such as Henry Sargent's *The Dinner Party* and *The Tea Party* (ca. 1820–1825), or Davis's watercolors for the John C. Stevens house (ca. 1830), both published in Edgar Mayhew and Minor Meyers, *A Documentary History of American Interiors, from the Colonial Era to 1915* (New York: Charles Scribner, 1980), fig. 43 and pls. 8–9.

19. For the Amish use of movable furniture to accommodate changing needs from day to day, or even from hour to hour, see Swank, *Arts of the Pennsylvania Germans,* 35ff.

20. *A Correct Account of the Trails of Charles M'Manus, John Hauer, Elizabeth [Shitz] Hauer, Patrick Donagan, Francis Cox and others, for the Murder of Francis Shitz* (Harrisburg: John Wyeth, 1798). Elizabeth Shitz Hauer received one thousand pounds by the will of her father, Peter Shitz, who had died the previous year, but the house was left to her two brothers, with the proviso it should pass to her if they died first. Having frittered away her substantial sum, and actually having tried to scare her brothers to death as well, she and her husband, John Hauer, contracted with some "Irish drifters" to dispense with them. One brother was killed and the other received an ax wound to the bone but survived to live in the house to old age. Interestingly, one can deduce from the trial that the Hauers' own house had recently been enlarged itself, probably making it resemble the Georgianized house they coveted.

Notes to "Slave Villages in the Danish West Indies: Changes of the Late Eighteenth and Early Nineteenth Centuries," by William Chapman

1. Jerome S. Handler and Frederick W. Lange, *Plantation Slavery in Barbados: An Archaeological and Historical Investigation* (Cambridge: Harvard University Pres, 1978); Michael Craton, *Searching for the Invisible Man: Slaves and Plantation Life in Jamaica* (Cambridge: Harvard University Press, 1978). See also Edwin Lascelles and James Colleton et al., "Treatment of Negroes in Barbados, in 1786 and in 1823," *Journal of the Barbados Museum and Historical Society* 2:1 (1934): 23–31; and Elso V. Goveia, *Slave Society in the British Leeward Islands at the End of the Eighteenth Century* (New Haven: Yale University Press, 1969).

2. A good example suggesting independent Virgin Islands evolution is Earl B. Shaw, "The Villages of St. Croix," *Bulletin of the Geographical Society of Philadelphia* 32 (1934): 10–29.

3. Most famously in A. W. Acworth, *Treasure in the Caribbean: A First Study of Georgian Buildings in the Caribbean* (London: Pleiades Books, 1949). See also Richard S. Dunn, *Sugar and Slaves: The Rise of the Planter Class in the English West Indies, 1624–1713* (New York: Norton, 1973), 287–99, for a discussion of early European architectural contributions to West Indian vernacular structures.

4. Waldemar Westergaard, *The Danish West Indies under Company Rule* (New York: Macmillan, 1917); Theodoor and John J. Faris, *The Virgin Islands: Our Possessions and the British Islands* (Philadelphia: Lippincott, 1918); Isaac Dookhan, *A History of the Virgin Islands of the United States* (Epping, Essex: Caribbean Universities Press, 1974). On St. Croix in particular see Florence Lewisohn, *St. Croix under Seven Flags* (Hollywood, Fla.: Dukane Press, 1970).

5. Westergaard, *The Danish West Indies,* and "A St. Croix Map of 1766: with a Note on Its Significance in West Indian Plantation Economy," *Journal of Negro History* (1938): 216–28.

6. Jens Vibaek, "The Golden Age: 1755–1848," in Johannes Bronsted, ed., *Vore Gamle Tropekolonier,* vol. 2, *Dansk Vestindien* (Copenhagen: Alfred Hassings, 1953).

7. Nationalmuseets 3, afdeling. Mus. nr. 2 504/68. See Eva Lawaetz, *The Danish Heritage of the U.S. Virgin Islands* (St. Croix: St. Croix Friends of Denmark Society, 1977), and Inge Mejer Antonsen, "Plantagen Bethlehem på St. Croix i def attende århundrede," *Saertryk af Nation-*

almuseets *Arbejdsmark* (1968), 113-22, for discussions of the Von Meley map.

8. J. L. Carstens, *En Almindelig Beskrivelse om alle de Danske, Americanske eller West-Indiske Ey-Land* [1740s] (Copenhagen: Dansk Vestindisk Folag, 1981), 66, 90. Translation courtesy of Frederik Gjessing. An even earlier description of black dwellings is in an inventory of Fort Christiansfort and its surroundings compiled by Gov. Jorgen Iversen in 1680, filed under Vestindisk-Guineiske Kompaniets Archiv, File No. 522, in the Rigsarkivet, Copenhagen. Cited in Robert de Jongh, Donna de Jongh, and Frederik Gjessing, *Fort Christian Historic Structures Report* (St. Thomas: Department of Conservation and Cultural Affairs, 1982). Interestingly, the earliest wattle-and-daub huts appear to have had their openings at the narrow end, conforming to John Vlach's descriptions of prototypical shot-gun houses ("Shotgun Houses," *Natural History* 86 (1977]: 50–57). Frederik Gjessing suggests this type may have extended into the eighteenth century and in some cases was translated into masonry construction, as at Annaberg estate on St. John. Personal communication, January 22, 1990.

9. P. L. Oxholm, *Plan of Fortet og Byen Frederiksted med omliggende Egne og Strandbreden* (Plan of the Fort and the Town Frederiksted with surrounding areas and the Beach), [ca. 1778], included as plan VIII in P. L. Oxholm's 1780 "Report on the Danish West Indies with a proposal for implementing their defenses, etc.," MS filed under Generaltoldkammer Og Kommercekollegiet 1775–1832, Dokumenter Vedkommende Forsvarsvaesnet Og Fortifikationer i Vestindien in the Rigsarkivet, Copenhagen. Oxholm's early coastal survey was later incorporated into his impressive *Charte over den Danske öe St. Croix i America for fzerdiget i Aaret 1794 og udgivet i Aaret 1799* (completed 1794, published 1799), though with less detail on estate layout. Oxholm's later idealized plantation layout, from which the illustration used in this study is taken, is described in *De Danske Vestindiske Öers Tilstand i Henseende til Population, Culturog Finance-Forfatning i Anledning af nogle Breve fra St. Croix, etc.* (Copenhagen: Johan Frederik Schults, 1797), plan 1, n.p.

10. C. G. A. Oldendorp, *History of the Mission of the Evangelical Brethren on the Caribbean Islands of St. Thomas, St. Croix, and St. John* [1777], ed. Johann Jakob Bossard and trans. Arnold R. Highfield and Vladimir Barac (Ann Arbor: Karoma, 1987), 151, 101

11. Ibid., 221. The most complete description of slave houses is found here as well.

12. Jay Edwards, "The Evolution of Vernacular Architecture in the Western Caribbean" (typescript, Baton Rouge, Louisiana State University, n.d.); Jean-Pierre Sainton, "The Historical Background; A Sketch," in *Kaz An-*

tiye Jan Moun Ka Rete, ed. Jack Berthelot and Martinc Gaume (Pointe-à-Pitre, Guadalupe: Editions Perspectives Creoles, 1982).

13. Elizabeth Righter, "Post-in-Ground Construction: An Example of Acculturation in the Virgin Islands" (typescript, St. Thomas, Dept. of Planning and Natural Resources, 1988).

14. Pamphlet, *The Planter's House: Einar Kirk's 1948 Inventory of St.Croix Great Houses; An Exhibit of Photographs and Drawings* (St. Croix: Florence Williams Public Library, 1987). See also Frederik Gjessing and William McLean, *Historic Buildings of St. Thomas and St. John* (London: Macmillan, 1987), and Pamela Gosner, *Historic Architecture of the Virgin Islands of the United States* (Durham, N.C.: Moore, 1971). Danish West Indian greathouses are also documented in numerous National Register nominations. Historic American Buildings Survey drawings also on file in the Library of Congress are in part published as *Historic Architecture of the Virgin Islands* (Philadelphia: HABS, 1966).

15. Oldendorp, *History of the Mission*, 151.

16. Carl Anthony, "The Big House and the Slave Quarters," *Landscape* 21:1 (1976): 9–15. See also Bernard L. Herman, "Slave Quarters in Virginia: The Persona behind Historic Artifacts," in *The Scope of Historical Archaeology: Essays in Honor of John L. Cotter,* ed. David G. Orr and Daniel G. Crozier (Philadelphia: Department of Anthropology, Temple University, 1984); and Dell Upton, "White and Black Landscapes in Eighteenth-Century Virginia," *Places* 2:2 (1985): 59–72, for the interrelationship of planters and slave architectural ideas.

17. For example: William Chapman and Chad O. Braley, "An Architectural and Archaeological Survey of Orange Grove, a Highland Estate in Westend Quarter, St. Croix, Virgin Islands" (typescript, Athens, Ga., Southeastern Archeological Services, 1989); and "An Archaeological and Architectural Survey of Butler Bay, a Sugar Estate in Northside A Quarter, St. Croix, U.S. Virgin Islands" (typescript, Athens, Ga., Southeastern Archeological Services, 1989). Known villages in St. John are summarized in Betty Ausherman, ed., *St. John Sites Report, 1981–82* (St. Thomas: Virgin Islands Planning Office, 1983).

18. Slob was also known as Body Slob. The origins of the name are unknown. The estate is well documented in photographs. An early sketch showing the estate configuration is also found in *St. Croix, St. Thomas, St. John: Henry Morton, West Indian Sketchbook and Diary, 1843–44* (Copenhagen: Dansk Vestindisk Selskab, 1975).

19. Early illustrations, including an anonymous wash drawing now at the Royal Academy in Copenhagen, dated 1733 and titled *Det senere Christiansted,* show a number

of single residences, similar, interestingly, to houses illustrated in Peter Gordon's famous view of Savannah of exactly the same period. The impact of military designs—probably a major element in Savannah's two-room-plan houses—on colonial Caribbean housing has been noted by Edwards in "The Evolution of Vernacular Architecture in the Western Caribbean," typescript. The St. Croix drawing is reprinted in *The Danish West Indies in Old Pictures* (Copenhagen: Dansk Vestindien Forlag, 1967).

20. For a discussion of early building codes in the Danish West Indies see Ole Svensson, ed., *Three Towns: Conservation and Renewal of Charlotte Amalia, Christiansted, and Frederiksted of the U.S. Virgin Islands* (Copenhagen: Royal Academy of Fine Arts, 1965, 1980).

21. Dates for this and other St. Croix plantations are based on St. Croix Tax Lists, National Archives, Washington, D.C., Record Group 55; Matriculs (ownership lists) in the Rigsarkivet, Copenhagen (available on microfilm); the Rachel Armstrong Colby abstracts, Whim Museum, St. Croix Landmarks Society; and the Virgin Islands Recorder of Deeds, Christiansted. Much of the information on individual slave villages is based on fieldwork conducted between 1979 and 1983, with additional fieldwork in the spring of 1989. Construction of the masonry village at Sprat would appear to coincide with the building of the windmill in 1794. Sprat's growth is documented in the surveyor J. M. Beck's map, *Kort over Eylandet St. Croix udi America af 1754,* and an annotated version of 1766. See Westergaard, "A St. Croix Map of 1766."

22. Lewisohn, *St. Croix under Seven Flags.* "Estate Hogansburg," National Register Nomination (St. Thomas: Virgin Islands Planning office, 1978).

23. R. W. Brunskill, *Illustrated Handbook of Vernacular Architecture* (London: Faber and Faber, 1978). For Tattersall in particular, see Olive Cook, *English Cottages and Farm Houses* (London: Thames and Hudson, 1982), 82–83. Comparable examples of early English terraces are illustrated in Syndrey Robert Jones, *The Village Homes of England* (London: Studio, 1907).

24. Gjessing and Maclean, *Historic Buildings of St. Thomas and St. John;* P. L. Oxholm illustrates residential rows, used to house "Negroes," in his 1780 report on conditions in the islands. See Herbert Olsen, *Customs House Historic Structures Report* (St. Croix: National Park Service, 1961), vol. 1.

25. Shaw, "Villages of St. Croix," 20.

26. All are documented in National Register nominations held by the Virgin Islands Department of Planning and Natural Resources.

27. "Clifton Hill," National Register Nomination (St. Thomas: Virgin Islands Planning Office, 1983).

28. "Castle Coakley," National Register Nomination (St. Thomas: Virgin Islands Planning Office, 1983). The Matriculs for 1803 list the estate as the property of John and Elizabeth Coakley and show a population of 188 slaves and 2 overseers.

29. "The Williams," National Register Nomination (St. Thomas: Virgin Islands Planning Office, 1983).

30. A map produced by John Parsons for the British admiralty and printed in 1856 documents the numerous villages in St. Croix in the early nineteenth century. *St. Croix, West Indies* (London: Hydrographic Office of the Admiralty, 1856).

31. For an overview see Michael Reed, *The Georgian Triumph, 1700-1830* (London: Paladin, 1983); also J. P. Chambers and G. E. Mingay, *The Agricultural Revolution, 1750-1880* (London: Batsford, 1966); and P. Mathias, *The Transformation of England: Essays in the Economic and Social History of England in the Eighteenth Century* (New York: Columbia University Press, 1979).

32. Michael E. Turner, *English Parliamentary Enclosure: Its Historical Geography and Economic History* (Folkestone: Dawson, 1980), and *Enclosures in Britain, 1750-1830* (London: MacMillan, 1984); Reed, *The Georgian Triumph;* R. J. Brown, *The English Country Cottage* (London: Arrow Books, 1979). See also John Martin Robinson, *Georgia Model Farms: A Study of Decorative and Model Farm Buildings in the Age of Improvement, 1700-1846* (Oxford: Clarendon Press, 1983).

33. Sebastiano Serlio, *On Domestic Architecture* (1541–1551), cited and illustrated in Spiro Kostof, *A History of Architecture: Settings and Rituals* (New York: Oxford University Press, 1985), 469.

34. Nathaniel Kent, *Hints to Gentlemen of Landed Property* (London: J. Dodsley, 1775); John Miller, *The Country Gentleman's Architect* (London: J. Taylor, 1789); John Plaw, *Rural Architecture* (London: J. Taylor, 1790). All went through several editions. *The Annals of Agriculture and Other Useful Arts* 20 (1793): n.p.; no plate number.

35. John Wood, *A Series of Plans for Cottages or Habitations of the Labourer either in Husbandry or the Mechanic Arts: Adapted as Well to Towns as to the Country* (London: J. Taylor, 1806), [3]. This work also went through a number of separate printings.

36. J. H. Parry and Philip Sherlock, *A Short History of the West Indies,* 3d ed. (New York: St. Martin's Press, 1985), 142-60. The best insights into "progressive" planter attitudes are in Bryan Edwards, *The History Civil and Commercial of the British Colonies in the West Indies,* 2 vols. (London: John Stockdale, 1794), and Patrick Browne, *The Civil and Natural History of Jamaica* (London: E. White and Sons, 1789). On sugar planting, see Sidney W. Mintz, *Sweetness and Power: The Place of Sugar*

in Modern History (New York: Penguin Books, 1986), and N. Deerr, *The History of Sugar,* 2 vols. (London: Chapman and Hall, 1949–1950).

37. Lewisohn, *St. Croix under Seven Flags,* 220. On the impact of modern technology on the sugar industry see R. W. Beachey, *The British West Indian Sugar Industry in the Late Nineteenth Century* (Oxford: Blackwell, 1957).

38. W. L. Mathieson, *British Slavery and Its Abolition* (London: Longmans, Green, 1926). Following unsuccessful attempts during the late eighteenth century, the act for abolition of the slave trade finally came into law in England in 1808. The Danish government passed a similar act in 1792, but this did not go into effect until 1801; the Danish ban on the slave trade finally went into effect in 1808, coinciding with the British ban.

39. Svend Erik Green-Pedersen, "The Economic Considerations Behind the Danish Abolition of the Negro Slave Trade," in *The Uncommon Market: Essays in the Economic History of the Atlantic Slave Trade,* ed. H. A. Gemery and J. S. Hogendom (New York: Academic Press, 1979).

40. See especially Eugene D. Genovese, *Roll Jordan Roll: The World Slaves Made* (New York: Vintage, 1976), on American planters' rationalization of slavery.

41. "The Report of the Committee of the Legislature appointed to enquire into, and Report on certain Queries relative to the Condition, Treatment, Rights and Privileges of the Negro Population of this Island" ([Rousseau, Dominica]: n.p., 1823), 4. West Indian planters' efforts to combine philanthropy with self-interest are discussed in Gail Saunders, *Slavery in the Bahamas, 1648–1838* (Nassau: Guardian, 1985), and Orlando Patterson, *The Sociology of Slavery: An Analysis of the Origins, Development and Structure of Negro Slave Society in Jamaica* (Rutherford, N.J.: Fairleigh Dickinson University Press, 1967).

42. Westergaard, *The Danish West Indies;* Vibaek, "The Golden Age."

43. P. B. Hatchett, *Statistics Concerning Properties on St. Croix, 1816–1857* (Christiansted, St. Croix: For the Author, 1859); John T. Quin, *Statistics Concerning Sugar Production in St. Croix from 1862–1889* (St. Thomas: Government of the Danish West India Islands, 1892). Relative production in the nineteenth century is discussed at length in Peter Hoxcer Jensen, "From Serfdom to Fireburn and Strike: The History of Black Labor in the Danish West Indies, 1848–1917" (Ph.D. diss., Aarhus University, 1979).

44. Vibaek, "The Golden Age."

45. A fact confirmed by Frederik Gjessing, who has been investigating the Virgin Islands' historic architecture since the late 1950s. Personal communication, January 22, 1990.

46. Building inspectors and engineers were by this period universally trained in architectural methods and conventions. On an early nineteenth-century high-style architect in the islands, see Kjeld De Fine Licht, "Albert Løvmand and His Work in the Former Danish West Indies," *Journal of the Society of Architectural Historians* 21 (1962): 107–15.

47. Dr. Collins, *Practical Rules for the Management and Medical Treatment of Negro Slaves in the Sugar Colonies* (London: Vernor and Hood, 1803), 11, 9–10.

48. Ibid., 116.

49. The estate is also known as Bethlehem Middle Works. "Bethlehem Middle Works," National Register nomination (St. Thomas: Virgin Islands Planning Office, 1985).

Notes to "African-Virginians and the Vernacular Building Tradition in Richmond City, 1790–1860," by Gregg D. Kimball

1. Mechal Sobel, *The World They Made Together: Black and White Values in Eighteenth-Century Virginia* (Princeton: Princeton University Press, 1987), 44–53.

2. Catherine W. Bishir, "Black Builders in Antebellum North Carolina," *North Carolina Historical Review* 61:4 (October 1984): 423.

3. Standard works on slave and free black artisans include James E. Newton and Ronald L. Lewis, eds., *The Other Slaves: Mechanics, Artisans, and Craftsmen* (Boston: G. K. Hall, 1978); Raymond Pinchbeck, *The Virginia Negro Artisan and Tradesman,* University of Virginia (Richmond: William Byrd Press, 1926); Leonard Stavisky, "The Negro Artisan in the South Atlantic States: 1800–1860" (Ph.D. diss., Columbia University, 1958).

4. For interpretations of urban slavery and the free black community see Ira Berlin, *Slaves without Masters: The Free Negro in the Antebellum South* (New York: Pantheon Books, 1974); Leonard P. Curry, *The Free Black in Urban America, 1800–1850: The Shadow of the Dream* (Chicago: University of Chicago Press, 1981); Claudia Dale Goldin, *Urban Slavery in the American South, 1820–1860: A Quantitative History* (Chicago: University of Chicago Press, 1976); Richard Wade, *Slavery in the Cities: The South, 1820–1860* (New York: Oxford University Press, 1964).

5. *Heads of Families at the First Census of the United States taken in the Year 1790, Records of the Enumerations: 1782–1785, Virginia* (Baltimore: Genealogical Publishing, 1966), 111–12, 114.

6. Marianne Buroff Sheldon, "Black-White Relations in Richmond, Virginia, 1782–1820," *Journal of Southern History* 45:1 (February 1979): 34–35. A standard work on

slave hiring is Clement Eaton, "Slave Hiring in the Upper South: A Step Toward Freedom," *Mississippi Valley Historical Review* 46 (1959–1960): 663–78.

7. *Richmond Enquirer,* November 6, 1821. In the same issue see the advertisement for Jim, a rough carpenter from Chesterfield County.

8. *Richmond Enquirer,* August 16, 1822. Drewry is listed in the 1819 Richmond City Directory.

9. Statistics for Winston's apprentices were compiled from printout of Henrico County/Richmond craftsmen provided by the Museum of Early Southern Decorative Arts, hereafter cited as MESDA craftsmen. Manuscript Census of the United States, Henrico County (Richmond City), Va., 1820, Virginia State Library and Archives, Richmond (Microfilm).

10. Indenture dated September 3, 1805, Henrico County Deed Book 7, pp. 290–92, Virginia State Library and Archives (Microfilm).

11. MESDA craftsmen.

12. These statistics, as well as later ones on places of residence by the free black population, were produced from Wm. L. Montague, *The Richmond Directory and Business Advertiser for 1852* (Richmond: J. W. Wood, printer, 1852), section entitled "Free Colored Housekeepers."

13. Goldin, *Urban Slavery,* 21; Manuscript Census of the United States, Henrico County (Richmond City), Va., 1860.

14. This was true well into the twentieth century. See Herbert Northrup, *Organized Labor and the Negro* (New York: Harper & Bros., 1944), 38–45.

15. Berlin, *Slaves without Masters,* 237.

16. Testimonial of John H. Hillyard and H. J. Goddin for Ebenezer Roper, March 19, 1850, and Register of Freedom of Ebenezer Roper, March 10, 1851, Union Burial Ground Society Papers, Virginia State Library and Archives.

17. Randall M. Miller, "The Enemy Within: Some Effects of Foreign Immigrants on Antebellum Southern Cities" *Southern Studies* 24:1 (Spring 1985): 30–53.

18. *Richmond Enquirer,* August 27, 1857, quoted in Goldin, *Urban Slavery,* 31.

19. *Constitution, By-Laws, and Bill of Prices of the Association of Journeymen Stone-Cutters of the City of Richmond. Established 1845* (Richmond, 1850).

20. John T. O'Brien, "Freedom's Ferment: The Reconstruction Experiment in Richmond, Virginia" (typescript in the possession of the author).

21. Ira Berlin and Herbert Gutman, "Natives and Immigrants, Free Men and Slaves: Urban Workingmen in the Antebellum American South," *American Historical Review* 88 (December 1983): 1186. Berlin notes that about a third of free black workers were skilled, as compared to 39 percent of Irish workers and above 80 percent of Germans and northern- and southern-born whites. See *Slaves without Masters,* 220.

22. See marriage of Peter Roper and Maria Skipwith, May 14, 1805, in Ann Waller Reddy and Andrew Lewis Riffe, IV, *Virginia Marriage Bonds: Richmond City, Volume I* (Staunton, Va.: McClure Co., n.d.), 9; Deed from Peter and Margaret Roper to Trustees of the Union Burial Ground Society, March 25, 1847, Henrico County Deed Book 51, pp. 146–57; and Constitution of the Union Burial Ground Society, January 23, 1848, Virginia State Library and Archives.

23. Original members and trustees were found in the Constitution of the Union Burial Ground Society, January 23, 1848. These names were then crossed with *Richmond City and Henrico County, Virginia: 1850 United States Census* (Richmond: Virginia Genealogical Society, 1977), which was also compared with the section entitled "Free Colored Housekeepers" in Montague, *Richmond Directory, 1852,* to determine occupation.

24. Trustees were identified from the First African Baptist Church Minute Book, Virginia State Library and Archives (Microfilm). Color was determined by comparing the list of trustees with *Richmond City: 1850 U.S. Census;* also see John T. O'Brien, "Factory, Church and Community: Blacks in Antebellum Richmond," *Journal of Southern History* 44:4 (November 1978): 526. O'Brien identified twenty-four of the original deacons; eighteen were free, and six were slaves.

25. O'Brien, "Factory, Church and Community," 526.

26. For information on the correlation between profession and property holding, see Luther Porter Jackson, *Free Negro Labor and Property Holding in Virginia, 1830–1860* (New York: D. Appleton-Century, 1942).

27. Ibid., 161–62, 197.

28. Calculated from chart listing professions in Michael Chesson, "Richmond's Black Councilmen, 1871–1896," in *Southern Black Leaders of the Reconstruction Era,* ed. Howard Rabinowitz (Urbana: University of Illinois Press, 1982), 198–99.

29. Samuel Mordecai, *Virginia, especially Richmond, in By-Gone Days . . .* (Richmond: West and Johnson, 1860), 273; Edward C. Carter II, John C. Van Horne, and Charles E. Brownell, eds., *Latrobe's View of America, 1795–1820: Selections from the Watercolors and Sketches* (New Haven: Yale University Press, for the Maryland Historical Society, 1985), 104.

30. Policy 1157, June 17, 1818, vol. 55, Mutual Assurance Society Collection, Virginia State Library and Archives (Microfilm). Vandewall's name is often spelled in other ways, including Vandervall and Vanderwall. I have

been fascinated by Vandewall's extensive involvement with free blacks but have not been able to pinpoint the reason for that involvement. Vandewall's father was a Quaker, a possible source of his connection with blacks. He left the majority of his property in his will to a free black sister and brother.

31. See policies 1156–59, 1169, 1179–82, vol. 55, Mutual Assurance Society Collection.

32. Mary Wingfield Scott, *Old Richmond Neighborhoods* (Richmond: Valentine Museum, 1975), 286. Notes and photographs of this group of cottages occupied by free blacks around 722–736 North Third Street are in the Mary Wingfield Scott Collection, Valentine Museum, Richmond.

33. Sobel, *The World They Made Together,* 103–4, cites Michael L. Nicholls's study of a 1785 survey of Halifax County buildings that found the 16 × 16 foot "cabin" quite common among both whites and blacks. Henry Glassie notes the large number of 16 × 16 foot structures in England as well as the flexibility of dimensions that the one-room square could facilitate in both the New and Old World, in *Folk Housing in Middle Virginia: A Structural Analysis of Historic Artifacts* (Knoxville: University of Tennessee Press, 1975), 117–19.

34. Mary Wingfield Scott, *Houses of Old Richmond* (New York: Bonanza Books, 1950), 34–37.

35. See John Vlach's discussion of rural slave quarters in *Afro-American Traditions in the Decorative Arts* (Cleveland: Cleveland Museum of Art, 1978), 132–38, and Fred B. Kniffen's discussion of double-pen designs such as the dogtrot and saddlebag house in "Folk Housing: Key to Diffusion," in *Common Places: Readings in American Vernacular Architecture,* ed. Dell Upton and John Michael Vlach (Athens: University of Georgia Press, 1986), 3–26.

36. Mutual Assurance Society Policies in the Virginia State Library and Archives give floor plans, materials, and size of buildings, as well as their function. A typical entry indicating the multiple functions of outbuildings is the policy for the Adams–Van Lew house and a two-story brick building containing a "kitchen + servant's rooms," 2311 East Grace Street, October 3, 1838, policy 10755. Specific photographic examples in the Mary Wingfield Scott and Cook Collections, Valentine Museum, Richmond, include the John Marshall house and outbuilding, 402 North 9th Street; the outbuilding of the Robert Howell house, behind 10 South 5th Street, built circa 1850; the John Gentry house and outbuilding, 2718 East Franklin Street, house built 1839, outbuilding built circa 1850 (and still extant). Extant examples of several outbuildings can be seen at the Pace-King house, 205 North Nineteenth Street, built circa 1860; at the Thomas Hardgrove house, 2300 East Grace Street, house built 1849; and behind Linden Row, 100–120

West Franklin Street, eastern end built 1846 (also see Mutual Assurance Society Policy 16296, August 5, 1851).

37. The Valentine Museum's collection contains three views of Griffin's house, taken circa 1940–1950. For comparison, see the illustration of the Moore house in Glassie, *Folk Housing in Middle Virginia,* 76. Scott, *Old Richmond Neighborhoods,* 60. Scott incorrectly identifies Griffin as a shoemaker. Griffin is listed in Montague, *Richmond Directory, 1852,* as a carpenter, at this address.

38. Scott, *Old Richmond Neighborhoods,* 59–60.

39. Henry Glassie, "Eighteenth-Century Cultural Process in Delaware Valley Folk Building," in *Common Places,* ed. Upton and Vlach, 401.

40. For examples of Richmond houses built by free blacks that follow variations of the urban side-hall plan, see photographs of 221–223 West Leigh Street, owned by Catherine Harris and Sophia Hill; 512–514 West Leigh Street, owned by John Jones and James Sabb; 227 West Leigh Street, owned by John Adams; 2418 E. Main Street, owned by John Lewis; and 609 E. Belvidere, owned by John Miller, all in Mary Wingfield Scott Collection. Compare with the two-thirds type illustrated in Glassie, *Folk Housing in Middle Virginia,* 56.

41. Histories of Richmond's African Baptist Churches can be found in *Inventory of the Church Archives of Virginia: Negro Baptist Churches in Richmond* (Richmond: Historical Records Survey of Virginia, Works Projects Administration, 1940). Data on the movement of members from First African to Ebenezer Baptist Church can be found in the First African Baptist Church Minute Book, entries 1856–1858, Virginia State Library and Archives (Microfilm).

42. Jackson, *Free Negro Labor,* 157–58.

43. Scott, *Old Richmond Neighborhoods,* 245–46.

44. Photographs and notes on 827 North Second Street in Mary Wingfield Scott Collection. Will of John E. Ferguson, Circuit Court Will Book 3, 1860, Virginia State Library and Archives (Microfilm). Jackson, *Free Negro Labor,* 157.

45. See, for instance, Charles L. Knight, *Negro Housing in Certain Virginia Cities* (Richmond: William Byrd Press, 1927), and Gustavus A. Weber, *Report on Housing and Living Conditions in Neglected Sections of Richmond* (Richmond: Whitett & Shepperson, 1913), 27, 31, 35, 45.

46. Inventory and will of Amanda Cousins, Richmond City Hustings Court Will Book 20, pp. 254–55, 267–69, 1860, Virginia State Library and Archives (Microfilm).

47. Will of Anna Thacker, Richmond City Hustings Court Will Book 14, pp. 381–82, dated May 4, 1852. For other examples of slave and free black family relationships in Richmond see the will of Abraham Skipwith, Henrico County Will Book 2, p. 585; and the will of Jacob Smith, a

free black carpenter, 1854, Richmond Hustings Court Will Book 16, p. 604. All Virginia State Library and Archives (Microfilm).

Notes to "A Legacy of Coal: The Coal Company Towns of Southwestern Pennsylvania," by Margaret M. Mulrooney

1. Raymond E. Murphy, "The Geography of Mineral Production," in *American Geography: Inventory and Prospect,* ed. Preston James and Clarence Jones (Syracuse: Syracuse University Press, 1954), 286; see also John Aubrey Enman, "The Relationship of Coal Mining and Coke Making to the Distribution of Population Agglomerations in the Connellsville (PA) Beehive Coke Region" (Ph.D diss., University of Pittsburgh, 1962), 7.

2. This essay is condensed from the author's *A Legacy of Coal: The Coal Company Towns of Southwestern Pennsylvania* (Washington, D.C.: HABS/HAER, 1989).

3. *What the Coal Commission Found: An Authoritative Summary by the Staff,* ed. Edward Eyre Hunt, F. G. Tryon, and Joseph H. Willitts (Baltimore: Williams and Wilkins, 1925), 51–52.

4. Leifur Magnusson, U.S. Department of Labor, "Employers' Housing in the United States," *Monthly Labor Review,* no. 5 (Washington, D.C.: Government Printing Office, November 1917), 879.

5. Morris Knowles, *Industrial Housing* (New York: McGraw-Hill, 1920; rpt. Arno Press, 1974), 310; Magnusson, "Employers' Housing," 878–79; "The Company Community in American Coalfields," *New Statesman* 30 (October 15, 1927): 6–7.

6. Knowles, *Industrial Housing,* 50.

7. John Aubrey Enman, "The Shape, Structure, and Form of the Pennsylvania Company Town," *Proceedings of the Pennsylvania Academy of Science* 42 (1968): 870–71; Magnusson, "Employers' Housing," 870–71.

8. U.S. Immigration Commission, *Immigrants in Industries (In Twenty-five Parts), Part I: Bituminous Coal Mining, Volume II* (Washington, D.C.: Government Printing Office, 1911), 74.

9. Leslie H. Allen, *Industrial Housing Problems* (Boston: Aberthaw Construction, 1917), 12.

10. Ibid., 14.

11. *What the Coal Commission Found,* 143.

12. Magnusson, "Employers' Housing," 880–81.

13. Herbert Gutman, *Work, Culture and Society* (New York: Vintage Books, 1977), 40.

14. *What the Coal Commission Found,* 143.

15. Zechariah Chaffee, Jr., "Company Towns in the Soft Coalfields," *Independent* 111 (October 13, 1923): 102–3.

Notes to "Charterville and the Landscape of Social Reform," by Annmarie Adams

1. The author would like to acknowledge the insights of Mark Brack, Margaretta Lovell, Trevor Rowley, Kate Tiller, Dell Upton, and Abigail Van Slyck in the preparation of this paper.

2. The other settlements were Heronsgate or O'Connorville (Hertfordshire), Great Dodford (Worcestershire), and Lowbands and Snigs End (Gloucestershire).

3. Alice May Hadfield has noted that some contemporary records describe eighty, rather than seventy-eight cottages; see *The Chartist Land Company* (Newton Abbot: David and Charles, 1970), 154.

4. Kate Tiller, "Charterville and the Chartist Land Company," *Oxoniensia* 50 (1985): 256; Hadfield, *Chartist Land Company,* 157.

5. Dorothy Thompson, *The Chartists: Popular Politics in the Industrial Revolution* (Aldershot: M. T. Smith, 1984), preface.

6. Hadfield, *Chartist Land Company,* 152.

7. Tiller, "Charterville," 254.

8. Crispin Paine et al., "Working-class Housing in Oxfordshire," *Oxoniensia* 43 (1978): 211; Christopher Doyle was "a power-loom weaver of waterproofs from Manchester." See Hadfield, *Chartist Land Company,* 18.

9. Tiller, "Charterville," 256.

10. Feargus O'Connor, *A Practical Work on the Management of Small Farms,* 3d ed. (Manchester: A. Heywood, 1846), 28, 29.

11. Thompson, *The Chartists,* 303.

12. O'Connor included a cottage plan with a small porch in *Management of Small Farms.* The houses at Charterville, however, were built without porches.

13. Henry Glassie, *Passing the Time in Ballymenone: Culture and History of an Ulster Community* (Philadelphia: University of Pennsylvania Press, 1982), 338.

14. Cited in Tiller, "Charterville," 260.

15. Paine et al., "Working-class Housing," 210.

16. Thompson has described the structure of the Land Plan as participatory and democratic, rather than socialist; see *The Chartists,* 302.

17. George L. Hersey, *High Victorian Gothic: A Study in Associationism* (Baltimore: Johns Hopkins University Press, 1972), 14–19.

18. In the United States, for instance, Thomas Jefferson

saw Palladianism as consistent with a nation of free land-owners who made their livings as farmers. Such architecture could also be interpreted, however, as an affirmation of aristocratic symbols of power and authority over others. For a review of the various interpretations of Jefferson's architecture see Dell Upton, "New Views of the Virginia Landscape," *Virginia Magazine of History and Biography* 96 (October 1988): 451–57.

19. The party was split decisively after the Manchester conference on the Land Plan in 1845. Leaders of the movement saw the plan as a distraction from the central concerns of the movement and as a ploy by O'Connor to attract his own following. See Hadfield, *Chartist Land Company,* 18–19.

20. Tiller, "Charterville," 258.

21. Paine et al., "Working-class Housing," 208.

Notes to "Graeme Park and the Three-cell Plan: A Lost Type in Colonial Architecture," by Mark Reinberger

1. On the mansion as a malthouse see Nancy Wosstroff, "Graeme Park, an Eighteenth Century Country Estate in Horsham, Pennsylvania" (M.A. thesis, University of Delaware, 1958); Charles Harper Smith, "The Keith Estate in Horsham," *Hatboro Public Spirit,* February 18, 1937, and "Sidelights on the History of Graeme Park," *Bulletin of the Historical Society of Montgomery County, Pennsylvania* 4:4 (April 1945): 259. The evidence against the malthouse theory is presented in Martin Jay Rosenblum, R. A. & Associates, "Graeme Park Historic Structures Report" (Philadelphia, 1987), written by the author (hereafter referred to as "HSR"). The most important documents proving that the malthouse and mansion were different buildings are William Rawle, "Diary," *Pennsylvania Magazine of History and Biography* 23 (1899): 533–34; and Direct Tax of 1798 (Federal) Pennsylvania, Montgomery County, Horsham Township, Third Division, Third District, in Records of the Internal Revenue Service, National Archives, Washington, D.C., Record Group 58.

2. Thomas T. Waterman, *The Dwellings of Colonial America* (Chapel Hill: University of North Carolina Press, 1950), 125–26. See also Sigurd Erixon, *Byggnadskultur* (Stockholm: A. Bonnier, 1953), 320.

3. Rosenblum, "HSR," forms the basis for the history and analysis of Graeme Park. Special thanks go to Peter Andrew Copp of Martin Jay Rosenblum, R.A. & Associates for his perceptive observations that helped elucidate Graeme Park's original form, for his appreciation and

insight into the colonial architecture of the Delaware valley, and for his considerable help in all aspects of the research and preparation of this project. He is currently conducting the restoration of Graeme Park.

4. The best secondary source on Keith is Thomas H. Wendel, "The Life and Writings of Sir William Keith" (Ph.D. diss., University of Washington, 1964). Early land records of Graeme Park are in the Philadelphia City Archives and are summarized in Wosstroff, "Graeme Park," and Rosenblum, "HSR."

5. William Keith to Cadwallader Colden, January 9, 1721/22, in *Letters and Papers of Cadwallader Colden* (New York: AMS Press, 1918, 1973), 1:138. Another important early document is a communication of Keith to the Pennsylvania Assembly of early 1722, reprinted in *Pennsylvania Archives,* 8th ser., 2 (1931): 1386.

6. The original of the survey has not been found. Fortunately it was photographed in 1958. The advertisement was in the *American Weekly Mercury,* September 15, 1737.

7. The inventory is reproduced in Wosstroff, "Graeme Park," and Rosenblum, "HSR." See Rosenblum, "HSR," for details on the paint analysis and the complicated transfer of the land from Keith to Graeme.

8. Thomas Graeme to John Penn, July 1, 1755, in manuscripts of the Historical Society of Pennsylvania, Philadelphia.

9. Thomas Graeme to John Penn, November 9, 1746, in Penn Papers, Private Correspondence, 3:63, Historical Society of Pennsylvania. On Graeme's biography more generally, see Wosstroff, "Graeme Park"; Smith, "Keith Estate"; and Rosenblum, "HSR."

10. See Rosenblum, "HSR," 27–29, for references to letters describing the Graeme family's life at Graeme Park.

11. Graeme's inventories and those of his daughter are printed in Wosstroff, "Graeme Park," app. B. Original in Office of Wills, Philadelphia City Hall. Significant inventories from 1778 are printed in *Pennsylvania Archives,* 6th series, 12 (1949): 653, 649; and in *Pennsylvania Magazine of History and Biography* 39 (1915): 294. Another valuable reference in this context is a sale advertisement in the *Pennsylvania Packet and Daily Advertiser,* August 29, 1787.

12. Ann Graeme to Elizabeth Graeme, July 17, 1764, in William J. Buck, *History of Montgomery County* (Philadelphia: Everts & Peck, 1884), 887. Buck's original manuscript material on Graeme Park is in the Chester County Historical Society, West Chester, Pa.

13. Elias Boudinot to Elizabeth Graeme, 1782, printed in Wosstroff, "Graeme Park," 103, n. 20. For other references to the longhouse see Rosenblum, "HSR," 29–30. The 1798 Direct Tax makes clear the distinction between

the tenant house and the much more valuable mansion house. Graeme Park's longhouse represents a very early example of an industrial building being upgraded into a residence, in this case one used at first for friends of the family and later for tenants.

14. The evidence for this partition consists of bridging between floor joists, the function of which was to hold doorposts. With this partition, the former chamber would have had a perfectly symmetrical fireplace wall. Graeme Park retains clear evidence for bellpull systems from two different periods, giving valuable information about room layout, the hierarchy of the house, and how such systems functioned in the late eighteenth century. See Rosenblum, "HSR."

15. The stylistic analysis of stair balusters uses information from Penelope Hartshorne Batchelor, "An Architectural Analysis of Hope Lodge, Whitemarsh, Pennsylvania" (ms., October 1961, available at Independence National Historic Park, Philadelphia).

16. The partition rests awkwardly on a joist below, the studs being irregularly notched as if to accommodate a preexisting situation. Most tellingly, the partition carries a header above that originally was joined to and borne by joists framed into the chimney blocks, and at least one stud of the partition joins to the header in a manner that would have been impossible originally.

17. I would like to thank Robert St. George, Bernard Herman, Orlando Rideout, Alice Schooler, Nancy Van Dolsen, Elizabeth Meg Schaefer, Dell Upton, Henry Glassie, and John J. Snyder, Jr., for assistance in my search for comparative examples.

18. On the English background for the three-cell plan see M. W. Barley, *The English Farmhouse and Cottage* (London: Routledge and Kegan Paul, 1961); Eric Mercer, *The English Vernacular House* (London: Her Majesty's Stationery Office, 1975); and Lyndon F. Cave, *The Smaller English House* (London: Robert Hale, 1981).

19. Mercer, *English Vernacular House,* makes this distinction most definitively.

20. See ibid., 60–61, 64.

21. Henry Glassie observed this point. Telephone conversation with author, December 1989.

22. James Deetz, *In Small Things Forgotten: The Archaeology of Early American Life* (Garden City: Doubleday, 1977), 92–99.

23. Robert Blair St. George, "Bawns and Beliefs: Architecture, Commerce, and the Conversion in Early New England," *Winterthur Portfolio* 25 (Winter 1990): fig. 3. St. George's figure 8 illustrates comparative examples from the west country of England.

24. Cary Carson et al., "Impermanent Architecture in the Southern American Colonies," *Winterthur Portfolio* 16

(Summer/Autumn 1981): 182–83, 194. My starting points for Virginia examples were the articles by Dell Upton and Fraser D. Neiman in *Common Places: Readings in American Vernacular Architecture,* ed. Dell Upton and John Michael Vlach (Athens: University of Georgia Press, 1986).

25. Information on this house kindly given by Bernard Herman.

26. On Greenspring, see Thomas T. Waterman, *Domestic Colonial Architecture of Tidewater Virginia* (New York: Charles Scribner's Sons, 1932), 11–17; *The Mansions of Virginia 1706–1776* (Chapel Hill: University of North Carolina Press, 1946), 19–27; and "From the Society's Collections," *Virginia Magazine of History and Biography* 58 (1950): 227–28; and Louis R. Caywood, "Green Spring Plantation," *Virginia Magazine of History and Biography* 65 (1957): 67–83. Waterman's works also illustrate Fairfield, in Gloucester County, Va., another possibly related seventeenth-century house. However, Fairfield was destroyed, and I am not aware of any archaeology that has determined its plan.

27. Wright's Ferry Mansion is mentioned and illustrated in John J. Snyder, Jr., *Lancaster Architecture, 1719–1927* (Lancaster: Historic Preservation Trust of Lancaster County, 1979), 8. It was also the subject of an unpublished restoration study by Edwin Brumbaugh available at the site. The biographical information on the Wrights came from Elizabeth Meg Schaefer, the curator of Wright's Ferry Mansion, who is currently writing a book on the family and house.

28. Historic American Buildings Survey, PA-1067, 1961. Other information on the house and its builders comes from Kate Hamilton Osborne, *An Historical and Genealogical Account of Andrew Robeson of Scotland, New Jersey, and Pennsylvania and of his Descendants from 1653 to 1916* (Philadelphia: J. B. Lippincott, 1916), 1–20. The dating of this house is problematic. The HABS survey, drawing on a 1957 report by Margaret Bailey Tinkcom of the Philadelphia Historical Commission, dated the house to 1759. However, Tinkcom's report is tentative on the date, quoting an earlier source that said the house was built by 1759. A 1759 account of measuring of stonework was also cited; however, the amount of stonework listed is far too small to represent the original house. Rather, the account could refer to later additions, of which there were several. Further, the account does not specify place, and the Robeson family owned many properties, so the account could refer to another building entirely. It is known that the Robesons, a wealthy family, were living on the site at least as early as 1702, and their mill was operating there by 1693.

29. Other Pennsylvania examples that may have had three-cell plans include the original wing of Chalkley Hall

(built 1723 and now demolished; see Historic American Buildings Survey, PA-110, 1938) and the Emlen house in Whitemarsh, Pennsylvania (1720; see Ray Thompson, *Washington at Whitemarsh* [Fort Washington, Pa.: Bicentennial Press, 1974], 14–15). The Emlen house has been so extensively altered and rebuilt that its original plan cannot be made out with certainty. However, as depicted in the mid-nineteenth century, its exterior form was much like Graeme Park's, and, from what can be observed in the surviving fabric, it can be tentatively suggested that its original plan may have had three rooms with a cross passage.

Another possible example is the Martic Forge Mansion in Marticville, Lancaster County, not far down the Susquehanna River from Columbia. The original portion of this stone house may well have been a single-pile, three-cell house with internal dimensions of 24 × 51 feet. It is traditionally thought to have been built soon after 1737 by Abraham, James, and Thomas Smith, who received a warrant for the land from the Penn family. The Smiths ran an iron furnace at the site and owned thirty-four hundred acres of land in the vicinity. This house is placed in the "tentative" category because several oddities and later renovations make its reading uncertain. Further field research may clarify its original form. I would like to thank Mr. and Mrs. Benjamin Stowe, the owners of the Martic Forge Mansion, for their gracious hospitality in allowing me to investigate their house.

30. John Cowperthwaite moved to Moorestown from Long Island, where his parents were Quaker ministers. John was evidently born in England. Information on the Cowperthwaite house and family was provided by Nan Pillsbury, who undertook research on the house for the Historical Society of Moorestown. My thanks to both her and Elizabeth Volckening, president of the Historical Society, for their help in research and in gaining access to the house.

31. John Milner Associates, "Trevose, the Growden Mansion" (report for the Supervisors of Bensalem Township, 1983, written by Alice Kent Schooler), 9–21, 37.

32. Ibid., 123–27.

33. On this generally see Carl and Jessica Bridenbaugh, *Rebels and Gentlemen: Philadelphia in the Age of Franklin* (New York: Reynal and Hitchcock, 1942), 191–202.

Notes to "Grand Illusions: Decorative Interior Painting in North Carolina," by Laura A. W. Phillips

1. The Flinchum house was demolished by its owners in 1985. Its painted parlor, however, was salvaged and moved to Raleigh by the North Carolina Museum of History for installation in the Folk Life exhibit of the new museum facility, scheduled to open in 1992.

2. No evidence of additional painting was uncovered prior to the demolition of the house, and family tradition does not suggest its presence elsewhere.

3. Sponsored by the State Historic Preservation Office in the North Carolina Division of Archives and History, these surveys have been conducted by staff members and by consultants, including the author.

4. The author's study of North Carolina's decorative interior painting has been funded in part by the North Carolina Museum of History in its effort to develop interpretive materials for the exhibition of the Flinchum parlor. Portions of this essay were published in abbreviated form in Laura A. W. Phillips, "Decorative Painting Study an Outgrowth of Statewide Historical Survey," *North Carolina Historic Preservation Office Newsletter* (Summer 1989): 5–9.

5. Examples have been derived from the author's fieldwork and from the survey files of State Historic Preservation Office. Examples have been recorded on the "North Carolina Decorative Interior Painting Data Form" developed by the author for use with this study. The form is designed for the eventual computerization of the recorded data.

6. It is not yet clear whether this concentration of examples is indicative of distribution patterns or represents the interest level of the surveyors or the comprehensiveness of survey efforts in those counties.

7. Pearl Flinchum Royston, letter to Marion F. Venable, December 14, 1984, Henry Flinchum House file, Surry County files, Survey and Planning Branch, State Historic Preservation Office, Raleigh, N.C.

8. Laura A. W. Phillips, "Rutherfordton House Plays Role in Painting Mystery," *North Carolina Preservation* 75 (Spring/Summer 1989): 17. A chronological descriptive listing of newspaper advertisements for house and ornamental painters in North Carolina, dated 1788 through 1840, is provided in James H. Craig, *The Arts and Crafts in North Carolina, 1699–1840* (Winston-Salem: Museum of Early Southern Decorative Arts, 1965), 95–106.

9. Rodney Barfield, "North Carolina Black Material Culture: A Research Opportunity," *North Carolina Folklore Journal* 27:2 (November 1979): 62, 66; Andrew Steele House file, Stokes County files, Survey and Planning Branch, State Historic Preservation Office.

10. Information on Edward Zoeller was supplied by Catherine W. Bishir. Marshall Bullock also provided several newspaper articles (from Tarboro newspapers of the 1850s to the 1870s) pertaining to Zoeller's work as a fresco painter.

11. Laura A. W. Phillips, National Register nomination for William Carter House, Surry County, N.C., November 1, 1989.

12. Stephen Johnson House file, Wilkes County files, Survey and Planning Branch, State Historic Preservation Office.

13. Interestingly, the Damascus Methodist Church in Lumpkin, Georgia, and the Calhoun-Perry house in Chireno, Texas, not only have smoked ceilings but are closely related in a variety of other ways to a small group of North Carolina houses with stenciled painting.

14. Phillips, "Rutherforton House Plays Role," 17.

15. Waterloo file, Duplin County files, Survey and Planning Branch, State Historic Preservation Office.

16. Reich-Strupe-Butner House file, Forsyth County files, State Historic Preservation Office.

17. Archibald Taylor House file, Franklin County files, State Historic Preservation Office.

Notes to "Domestic Architecture in Hispanic California: The Monterey Style Reconsidered," by Mark L. Brack

1. David Gebhard provides a superb historiographic analysis of the Monterey style in "The Monterey Tradition: History Reordered," *New Mexico Studies in the Fine Arts* 7 (1982): 14–19.

The author would like to acknowledge the valuable assistance provided by the following individuals in the research and preparation of this study: Dell Upton, John Mader, Esperanza Ramirez Romero, Edgar Lopez, Edward B. Byrne, and Eric Sandweiss. A Graduate Humanities Research Grant from the University of California at Berkeley enabled the author to do field research in Mexico.

2. Harold Kirker, *California's Architectural Frontier* (Santa Barbara: Peregrine Smith, 1973), 16, 18, 19. The attribution of the Monterey style to Yankee influences is so popular that it appears in virtually every interpretive or commemorative program associated with these sites. Kirker has further developed this theme by suggesting that marriages between prominent Hispanic families and immigrant Yankees help to explain the diffusion of the Monterey style ("The Role of Hispanic Kinships in Popularizing the Monterey Style, 1836–1846," *Journal of the Society of Architectural Historians* 43 [October 1984]: 250–55). The California buildings chosen to illustrate this essay were considered by Kirker to be among the preeminent examples of the Monterey style in the state.

3. *American* is used in this essay to refer to those qualities or characteristics that represent the dominant cultural patterns of the United States during this period.

4. Richard Henry Dana, *Two Years before the Mast* (1840, rpt.: Boston: Houghton Mifflin, 1911), 69, 99.

5. For the significance of the flat roof in Mexican domestic architecture see Robert C. West, "The Flat-Roofed Folk Dwelling of Rural Mexico," in *Geoscience and Man,* ed. H. J. Walker and W. G. Haag (Baton Rouge: School of Geoscience, Louisiana State University, 1974), 5:111–32. For early views of Hispanic California see John Reps, *The Making of Urban America* (Princeton: Princeton University Press, 1965), 52–53, and Elizabeth Egenhoff, ed., *Fabricas* (San Francisco: State of California, Division of Mines, 1952).

6. Alfred Robinson, *Life in California* (1846; rpt. New York: De Capo Press, 1969), 11. For additional information on the construction and appearance of early Hispanic houses in California see J. N. Bowman. "Adobe Houses in the San Francisco Bay Region," *Geologic Guidebook of the San Francisco Bay Counties,* bulletin 154 (San Francisco: State of California Division of Mines, 1951); James Delgado and Christopher Wade, *How California Adobes Were Built into the 1830's* (San Jose: Smith-McKay Printing, 1978); Helen Giffen, *Casas and Courtyards* (Oakland: Biobooks, 1955) and "Some Two-story Adobe Houses of Old California," *Quarterly Historical Society of Southern California* 20:1 (March 1938): 4–21; Donald Hannaford and Revel Edwards, *Spanish Colonial or Adobe Architecture in California, 1800–1850* (New York: Architectural Book Publishing, 1931); George Hendry and J. N. Bowman, "The Spanish and Mexican Adobes and Other Buildings of the San Francisco Bay Counties, 1776 to about 1850" (typescript, Bancroft Library, University of California at Berkeley, 1940–1945); and Marion Parks, "In Pursuit of Vanished Days," *Historical Society of Southern California* 14 (1928–1929): 6–63, 134–204.

7. The author's observations on the plans of the Hispanic California houses are derived from visits to surviving sites and examinations of published drawings, including those prepared by the Historic American Buildings Survey from the 1930s to the 1960s and reprinted in David DeLong, ed., *Historic American Buildings, California* (New York: Garland, 1980), vols. 1–4.

8. Leonard Pitt, *The Decline of the Californios* (Berkeley: University of California Press, 1966), 11; Christopher Wilson, "When a Room Is a Hall," *Mass* 2 (Summer 1984): 19; Robert Adams, *The Architecture and Art of Early Hispanic Colorado* (Boulder: Colorado Associated University Press, 1974), 37.

9. George Kubler has written, "In Mexico as in Spain, the urban courtyard or patio plan was associated with the

privileges of wealth" (*Mexican Architecture of the Sixteenth Century* [Westport, Conn.: Greenwood Press, 1972], 188). Wilson also notes in "When a Room Is a Hall" that the terms *placita* and *plazuela* are used to describe the courtyards found in the Hispanic houses of New Mexico.

10. This requirement is set forth in ordinance 115 of the Laws of the Indies; see Dora P. Crouch, Daniel J. Garr, and Axel Mundigo, *Spanish City Planning in North America* (Cambridge: MIT Press, 1982), 14.

11. See James B. Alexander, *Sonoma Valley Legacy* (Sonoma: Sonoma Valley Historical Society, 1986); Robert D. Parmelee, *Pioneer Sonoma* (Sonoma: Sonoma Index Tribune, 1972); Egenhoff, ed., *Fabricas;* and Reps, *The Making of Urban America.*

12. Bainbridge Bunting attributed the introduction of double-hung sash windows in New Mexico to Americans as well in *Early Architecture of New Mexico* (Albuquerque: University of New Mexico Press, 1976), 88. Early accounts of Hispanic California note that glass was uncommon due to its expense, so that windows, particularly in poorer houses, were left open or were covered with wooden shutters, wood or metal bars, or oiled paper; see T. J. Farnham, *Life, Adventures and Travels in California* (New York: Nafis and Cornish, 1849), 108–9; and Jose Fernandez, "Casas de California" (dictated manuscript, Bancroft Library, University of California at Berkeley, 1874), 166–67.

13. Those who claim the province had no fireplaces or chimneys include Hubert Howe Bancroft, *California Pastoral, 1769–1848* (San Francisco: History Company, 1888), 401; Dana, *Two Years before the Mast,* 100; and Sir George Simpson, *Narrative of a Voyage to California Ports in 1841–1842* (rpt. San Francisco: Private Press of Thomas Russell, 1930), 61, 68. However, a resident of California during the period in question, Jose Fernandez, notes in his memoirs ("Casas de California," 166–67), that the Monterey style *cuartel* or barracks erected in Monterey in 1840 had four chimneys. William Butler's archaeological survey of an early house in Los Angeles ("The Avila Adobe: The Determination of Architectural Change," *Historical Archaeology* 7 [1973]: 36–38) discovered traces of a Hispanic corner fireplace in a room dated to ca. 1818.

14. George Garrison and George Rustay, *Mexican Houses* (New York: Architectural Book Publishing, 1930), xi.

15. The Guadalupe Rancho adobe is illustrated in DeLong, ed., *Historic American Buildings, California,* 1:228.

16. Kirker, "Role of Hispanic Kinships," 251.

17. Ibid., 250, 254, 255. See also Alexander, *Sonoma Valley Legacy,* 4. In his article, Kirker also says the Monterey style "imposed upon almost every inhabited part of the province visual evidence of Yankee ingenuity, comfort, convenience, and power" (250).

18. Robert Parker, "Building the Larkin House," *California Historical Society Quarterly* 16:4 (December 1937): 320–35.

19. David Gebhard, "Some Additional Observations of California's Monterey Tradition," *Journal of the Society of Architectural Historians* 46 (June 1987): 157–70. In his first article on the subject, "The Monterey Tradition," Gebhard gives substantial credit to Hispanic sources as inspiration for the Monterey style porches. In "Some Additional Observations" he gives less consideration to available Hispanic influences and concentrates on examining the potential contributions of non-Hispanic cultures in the Caribbean and American South.

20. See Luis Feduchi, *Itinerarios de arquitectura popular española* (Barcelona: Editorial Blume, 1973–1978), vols. 1–4; and Carlos Flores, *Arquitectura popular española* (Madrid: Aguilar, 1974), vols. 1–4. Both series offer beautifully illustrated surveys of Spanish vernacular architecture. The Spanish regions and provinces of Santander, Toledo, Extremadura, Andalucia, and the Canary Islands feature buildings whose forms, details, and materials are similar to those found in California.

21. Kirker, "Role of Hispanic Kinships," 254, and Trent Sanford, *The Architecture of the Southwest* (New York: W. W. Norton, 1950), 239. A comprehensive inventory of Monterey style buildings (standing and/or demolished) has never been prepared, making exact quantitative comparisons impossible at this time. However, evidence of one Monterey style building that no longer survives suggests that Monterey style features might have appeared in California several years before the significant immigration of American merchants. Casa de la Materna near Pajaro in Monterey County was built by the Vallejo family and had an undocumented construction date of 1824. Photographs of the deteriorated building show cantilevered balconies on one and perhaps two elevations. See Donald Johnson, *Lost Adobes of Monterey County* (Monterey: Monterey County Archaeological Society, 1973), 12–13, and *Ranchos of Monterey County* (Monterey: Monterey County Archaeological Society, 1978), 13.

22. See Albert Manucy, *The Houses of St. Augustine* (St. Augustine: St. Augustine Historical Society, 1962); Mariana Patiño de Borda, *Monuments nacionales de Colombia* (Bogotá: Instituto Columbiano de Cultura, 1983); Graziano Gasparini, *La casa colonial venezolona* (Caracas: Centro Estudiantes de Arquitectura, Universidad Central de Venezuela, 1962); and Joaquin E. Weiss, *La arquitectura colonial cubana* (Havana: Instituto Cubano del Libro, 1972), vols. 1–2.

23. See Esperanza Ramírez Romero, *Catálogo de mon-*

umentos y sitios de Pátzcuaro y Región Lacustre: Premier tomo, Pátzcuaro (Morelia, Mexico: Universidad Michoacana de San Nicolás de Hidalgo, 1986); and Manuel Toussaint, Pátzcuaro (Mexico City: Imprenta Universitaria, 1942). The timber porches and balconies of Mexico are also featured in Garrison and Rustay, *Mexican Houses;* Louis LaBeaume and William Papin, *The Picturesque Architecture of Mexico* (New York: Architectural Book Publishing, 1915); Francisco Javier Lopez Morales, *Arquitectura vernácula en México* (Mexico City: Editorial Trillas, 1987); Trent E. Sanford, *The Story of Architecture in Mexico* (New York: W. W. Norton, 1947); and Virginia Shipway and Warren Shipway, *The Mexican House, Old and New* (New York: Architectural Book Publishing, 1960). The buildings from Michoacán illustrated here unfortunately are not dated exactly. However, the publications on Pátzcuaro listed above describe similar buildings dating to the late eighteenth and early nineteenth centuries. Weiss, *La Arquitectura colonial cubana,* illustrates even earlier Cuban buildings, some dating to the seventeenth and eighteenth centuries with plans and wooden porches and balconies resembling those in California. Regarding the use of redwood in California, see *The Diary of Faxon Dean Atherton, 1836–1839,* ed. Doyce Nunis (San Francisco: California Historical Society, 1964), 75; Sherwood D. Burgess, "Lumbering in Hispanic California," *California Historical Society Quarterly* 41:3 (September 1962): 237–48; and John Woolfenden and Amelie Elkinton Cooper, *Juan Bautista Rogers Cooper* (Pacific Grove, Calif.: Boxwood Press, 1983), 63–64.

24. California Department of Parks and Recreation, *Petaluma Adobe* (n.p, n.d.); and Woodrow J. Hansen, *The Search for Authority in California* (Oakland: Biobooks, 1960), 21.

25. See Romero, *Catalogo de monumentos y sitios: Pátzcuaro.*

26. The Temple house (Rancho Los Cerritos) is illustrated in DeLong, ed., *Historic American Buildings, California,* 1:99. The Leese adobe is illustrated in Alexander, *Sonoma Valley Legacy,* 32, 36.

27. Kirker claimed, without documentation, that it became the "ambition" of Hispanic California women to "follow Mrs. Larkin's example of living in . . . an American house" ("Role of Kinships," 10).

28. Kirker, *California's Architectural Frontier,* 15, 16.

29. Robinson, *Life in California,* v.

30. Pitt, *Decline of the Californios,* 2, 3; Hansen, *Search for Authority in California,* 20.

31. Pitt, *Decline of the Californios,* 7–8.

32. Hansen, *Search for Authority in California,* 20.

33. Jessie D. Francis, "An Economic and Social History of Mexican California, 1822–1846" (Ph.D. diss., University of California, Berkeley, 1936), 2:731.

34. In an analogous case of cultural confrontation, John Michael Vlach noted that the early American immigrants to the hispanicized Rio Grande valley of Texas in the 1840s and 1850s "found themselves in the role of cultural modifiers rather than creators" who largely adapted or adopted "Mexican cultural traits" ("Borders and Cultural Landscapes," in *An Exploration of a Common Legacy: The Proceedings,* ed. Marlene Elizabeth Heck [Austin: Texas Historical Commission, 1978], 9).

35. Kirker, *California's Architectural Frontier,* 16, and "Roll of Kinships," 254–55. Mariano Vallejo's feelings concerning American hegemony are difficult to determine, as the accounts of his statements, attitudes, and actions are often contradictory. José Castro led armed opposition to the American forces and was so embittered by the conquest that he never became an American citizen and later moved to Sonora, Mexico.

36. Pitt, *Decline of the Californios,* 23–25.

Notes to "A History of American Beds and Bedrooms," by Elizabeth Collins Cromley

1. I would like to thank the Office of Advanced Studies, Winterthur Museum, Winterthur, Del., for a Forman Fellowship under which much of this research was done. I also want to thank my student assistant, Don O'Leary, for preliminary bibliographic research and Thomas Carter for comments on an earlier version of this paper. Some of this material appears in my Banham memorial lecture, "Sleeping Around," *Journal of Design History* 3 (1990): 1–17. This essay is an effort to make sense out of research that is still incomplete and that will result in a book-length study of the bedroom.

2. Dell Upton, "Vernacular Domestic Architecture in Eighteenth Century Virginia," in *Common Places: Readings in American Vernacular Architecture,* ed. Dell Upton and John Michael Vlach (Athens: University of Georgia Press, 1986), 317.

3. Abbott Lowell Cummings, "Inside the Massachusetts House," in *Common Places,* ed. Upton and Vlach, 219–39.

4. According to David H. Flaherty, *Privacy in Colonial New England* (Charlottesville: University of Virginia Press, 1972), 39–40, the numbers of rooms in houses in Essex County, Mass., between 1638 and 1664 were: 3 or more rooms in 65 percent of houses, 4 or more rooms in 45 percent, 5 or more rooms in 22 percent, and an average of 3.3 rooms per house. In Suffolk County, Mass., between

1675 and 1775 the average number of rooms was: 1675–1699, 4.3 rooms; 1700–1749, 5.7 rooms; 1750–1775, 6.0 rooms. But for the poor, a one-room house was all they could afford.

5. Gervase Wheeler, *Homes for the People in Suburb and Country* (1855; rpt. New York: Arno Press, 1972), 389–91.

6. Ibid., 321–27.

7. *Delineator's Prize $3000 House* (New York: B. W. Dodge, 1909), 26.

8. For room relationships in apartments, see Cromley, *Alone Together: A History of New York's Early Apartments* (Ithaca: Cornell University Press, 1990). While apartments like the Stuyvesant had as many rooms as two-story houses, the grouping of parlor, dining room, and bedroom at the front of the apartment is reminiscent of the room relationships in eighteenth-century one-story houses, identified by Dell Upton as the "social molecule" in "Vernacular Domestic Architecture," 323.

9. Ella Rodman Church, "How to Furnish a House," *Appleton's Journal*, n.s. 2 (February 1877): 160. Kathy Peiss in a paper given at the "Gender and Material Culture" conference, Winterthur Museum, November 1989, reported that pink and blue were specifically gendered in the mid-nineteenth century: pink for boys (a strong, assertive color), and blue for girls.

10. Martha A. Cutler. "Hygienic Bedrooms," *Harper's Bazaar* 41 (January 1907): 80–81.

11. "The Bedroom and Its Individuality," *Craftsman* 9 (February 1906): 695–96.

12. E. C. Gardner, *The House that Jill Built after Jack's Had Proved a Failure* (New York: Fords, Howard and Hulbert, 1882), 246–47.

13. Candace Wheeler, *Principles of Home Decoration* (New York: Doubleday, Page, 1903), 61.

14. C. B. Walker, "Railroad Tie Furniture to Furnish a Boy's Den," *Women's Home Companion* 32 (October 1905): 48.

15. Tekla Grenfell, "Renting Rooms to Young Men: How I Have Successfully Done It for Years," *Ladies' Home Journal* 25 (September 1908): 24

16. Catharine Beecher and Harriet Beecher Stowe, *American Woman's Home* (New York: J. B. Ford & Co., 1869), 369–71, 377.

17. Harriet Martineau, "How to Make Home Unhealthy," *Harper's New Monthly Magazine* 1 (June–November 1850): 618–19.

18. B. W. Richardson, "Health at Home," *Appleton's Journal*, n.s. 8 (April 1880): 314.

19. Katherine Louise Smith, "Indoor Bed Tents," *Scientific American*, n.s. 101 (December 1909): 423.

20. Ibid., 416.

21. C. M. D'Enville, "Sleeping Outdoors for Health:

Outdoor Sleeping for the Well Man," *Country Life in America* 16 (May 1909): 43–46.

22. C. K. Shilling, "A Country Home with Outdoor Sleeping, Living, and Dining Rooms," *Country Life in America* 16 (May 1909): 71–72.

23. C. G. Hoag, "Sleeping Outdoors for Health: Part VI. A Sleeping Machine," *Country Life in America* 16 (May 1909): 102.

24. M. MacLean Helliwell, ed., "Woman's Sphere," *Canadian Magazine* 20 (1902–1903): 281.

25. "The Contributors' Club: Cave-Dwellers, or the Hall Bedroom," *Atlantic Monthly* 96 (July–December 1905): 574–75.

26. Sexual fantasies and sexual practices are noticeably missing from this account. I will include this aspect of the bedroom in a future publication, pending further research.

27. Helliwell, "Woman's Sphere," 283.

Notes to "Getting the Houses to the People: Edward Bok, The Ladies' Home Journal, *and the Ideal House," by Leland M. Roth*

1. The literature on Progressive reform is extensive. For a basic introduction see Samuel P. Hays, *The Response to Industrialism, 1885–1914* (Chicago: University of Chicago Press, 1957); Richard Hofstadter, *The Age of Reform* (New York: Random House, 1955); Christopher Lasch, *The New Radicalism in America, 1889–1963* (New York: Random House, 1965); David E. Shi, *The Simple Life: Plain Living and High Thinking in American Culture* (New York: Oxford University Press, 1985); Robert H. Wiebe, *The Search for Order, 1877–1920* (New York: Hill & Wang, 1967). For reform in housing design see Clifford E. Clark, Jr., *The American Family Home, 1800–1960* (Chapel Hill: University of North Carolina Press, 1986); David Handlin, *The American Home: Architecture and Society, 1815–1915* (Boston: Little, Brown, 1979); Gwendolyn Wright, *Moralism and the Model Home: Domestic Architecture and Cultural Conflict in Chicago, 1873–1913* (Chicago: University of Chicago Press, 1980) and *Building the Dream: A Social History of Housing in America* (New York: Pantheon Books, 1981).

This research grew out of my earlier work on McKim, Mead & White, particularly the alleged request that White design a house for the *Ladies' Home Journal*. I passed this line of research to a student, Ellen E. Frances, and it resulted in her "Progressivism and the American House: Architecture as an Agent of Social Reform" (M.A. thesis, University of Oregon, 1982). At the time we were unaware of Alice M. Bowsher, "Edward Bok's Attempt to Promote

Good Design in the Suburbs: An Analysis of Architecture Illustrated in the *Ladies' Home Journal*" (M.A. thesis, University of Virginia, 1977).

2. The most detailed and comparative history of the magazines discussed here is found in the last three volumes of Luther Frank Mott, *A History of American Magazines* (Cambridge: Harvard University Press, 1957–1968). For Gustav Stickley's *The Craftsman* see John C. Freeman, *The Forgotten Rebel: Gustav Stickley and His Craftsman Mission Furniture* (Watkins Glen, N.Y.: Century House, 1966); Cheryl Robertson, "House and Home in the Arts and Crafts Era: Reforms for Simpler Living," in *"The Art That Is Life": The Arts and Crafts Movement in America, 1875–1920,* ed. W. Kaplan (Boston: Museum of Fine Arts, 1987), 336–57; Barry Sanders, ed., *The Craftsman: An Anthology* (Santa Barbara: Peregrine Smith, 1978); and Mary A. Smith, *Gustav Stickley, the Craftsman* (Syracuse: Syracuse University Press, 1983).

3. Mott cites circulation figures for all the magazines he discusses; for the most part these come from trade journals such as N. W. Ayer & Sons, *American Newspaper Annual and Directory* (Philadelphia). The volume for 1915 provides these figures: *Architectural Record,* 11,300; *American Architecture,* 3,604; *House Beautiful,* 45,000; *House and Garden,* 24,208; *The Craftsman,* 22,500; *Ladies' Home Journal,* 1,606,263.

4. This optimistic estimate is given by the *Journal* editor, Edward Bok, in an editorial in the February 1903 issue, p. 16. Circulation figures for that month had just reached the million mark. Bok's figures on readership were based on a survey conducted in several cities across the country to determine the extent to which copies were passed on to nonsubscribers. The impact of the *Journal* by 1919, when subscriptions had increased by another .6 million, would have been proportionately greater.

5. This phrase is used in James P. Wood, *The Curtis Magazines* (New York: Ronald Press, 1971), vii.

6. Edward Bok, *The Americanization of Edward Bok* (New York: Charles Scribner's Sons, 1920), 393.

7. This specific target market, and the related group with incomes of $3,000 to $5,000, is identified in the Curtis Publishing Company, Condensed Report of the 1915 Advertising Conference. This typescript, in the Charles Coolidge Parlin Papers, University of Pennsylvania Library, is quoted in Salme H. Steinberg, *Reformer in the Marketplace: Edward W. Bok and* The Ladies' Home Journal (Baton Rouge: Louisiana State University Press, 1979), 6–7.

8. For Edward Bok's impact on the development of the *Journal* see Mott, *History of American Magazines,* 4:536–55; Steinberg, *Reformer;* and Wood, *Curtis Magazines,* 3–90. Bok gives his own account in two autobiogra-

phies: *The Americanization of Edward Bok* and *Twice Thirty* (New York: Charles Scribner's Sons, 1925). A useful survey is also provided in John M. Brown, ed., *The Ladies' Home Journal Treasury* (New York: Simon and Schuster, 1956), xi- xviii.

9. Bok, *Americanization,* 249–50.

10. For the impact of the *Journal* in affecting reform see Steinberg, *Reformer.*

11. Mott, *History of American Magazines,* 4:536–45.

12. Bok, *Americanization,* 163, 165.

13. Ibid., 238.

14. Ibid., 241. The injunction against separate parlors must have come after the first few house designs had been published, since several of them do have distinct parlors.

15. Ralph Adams Cram, "A $5000 Colonial House," *Ladies' Home Journal (LHJ)* 13 (February 1896): 17; Cram, *My Life in Architecture* (Boston: Little, Brown, 1936).

16. Bok, *Americanization,* 241. The opposition of the profession surfaced again in 1919 when *LHJ* attempted to revive the practice of selling house plans for one dollar to help solve the post–World War I housing shortage. The American Institute of Architects viewed such proposals with disdain, believing that an offer so cheap "belittled the value of the article sold and therefore . . . architectural service" (AIA *Octagon* 2 [1930]: 22). For the opposition of the profession to the dissemination of inexpensive house plans see Alan Gowans, *The Comfortable House: North American Suburban Architecture, 1890–1930* (Cambridge: MIT Press, 1986), 63–67.

17. William L. Price, *Model Houses for Little Money* (Philadelphia: Curtis Publishing, 1898). In the next decade *LHJ* published two additional books of house designs and plans, one on garden design, two on home financing, one on fireplace construction, four on housekeeping, six on social etiquette, eight on clothes and sewing, plus several others on support activities for servicemen (this list was published a month before the armistice, *LHJ* 35 [October 1918]: 142).

18. The first offer to sell plans, as well as the description of Bok's objectives, accompanied the presentation of "A Model Suburban House" by the *Journal*'s Special Architect, *LHJ* 14 (July 1897): 17.

19. The average national construction index has been generated monthly by the *Engineering News-Record (ENR)* since 1913. The index for September 8, 1988, was 4534.94 (with 1913 being 100), or a ratio of approximately 45.35 to 1. Other studies derived from the *ENR* indexes indicate that from 1900 to 1913 building costs rose 25.15 percent, so that the *ENR* index needs to be multiplied by 1.2515 to compare building costs between 1900 and 1988. See Miles L. Colean and Robinson Newcomb, *Stabilizing Construc-*

tion (New York: McGraw-Hill, 1952), app. N, table 4, 238–40. For a detailed explanation of the origin and use of the *ENR* cost index, see *ENR* 143 (September 1, 1949): 398–431. The figures for average house cost and family income for 1988 come from U.S. Department of Commerce, Bureau of the Census, *Current Construction Reports, New One-Family Houses Sold and For Sale,* September 1989, Table 11, and *Current Population Reports, Consumer Income,* October 1989, p. 23.

20. *LHJ* 15 (June 1898): 26 and (July 1898): 27. Bok notes the twenty-five houses built by the unidentified Brookline reader in *Americanization,* 241.

21. *LHJ* 15 (June 1898): 26 and 16 (June 1899): 23.

22. *LHJ* 18 (January 1901): 15.

23. Frank Lloyd Wright, "A Home in a Prairie Town," *LHJ* 18 (February 1901): 17.

24. Robert C. Spencer, Jr., "A Good Farmhouse for $3500," *LHJ* 17 (October 1900): 21; "A Northern Farmhouse to Cost $3000," *LHJ* 18 (December 1900): 31; "A Southern Farmhouse to Cost $3000," *LHJ* 18 (January 1901): 23. On the life and work of Robert Clossen Spencer, Jr. (1865–1953), see H. Allen Brooks, *The Prairie School: Frank Lloyd Wright and His Midwest Contemporaries* (Toronto: University of Toronto Press, 1972), and Wright, *Moralism.*

25. An example appeared in Bok's editorial page, *LHJ* 20 (January 1903): 16. During the same time, the *Journal's* midwest counterpart, *House Beautiful,* published essays on Morris's Arts and Crafts designs, with illustrated articles on the houses of C. F. A. Voysey and Edwin Lutyens.

26. For Will Bradley see Kaplan, *"The Art That Is Life."*

27. Frank Lloyd Wright, "A Fireproof House for $5000," *LHJ* 24 (April 1907): 24.

28. "Good-Taste Homes of Chicago Folks," *LHJ* 27 (August 1910): 28–29. Other Prairie School architects represented in the photo spread included Robert C. Spencer, Jr., George Maher, Charles E. White, Myron Hunt, and Dwight H. Perkins. For Tallmadge and Watson see Brooks, *The Prairie School.*

29. For example, see *House Beautiful* 11 (January 1902), xxv.

30. On the bungalow and its spread across the country see Clay Lancaster, *The American Bungalow: 1880–1930* (New York: Abbeville Press, 1985), and Robert Winter, *The California Bungalow* (Los Angeles: Hennessey and Ingalls, 1980). Although both Gaut and Hopkins are mentioned in Winter, *California Bungalow,* 27, little is known about them. Both women were frequent contributors to *The Craftsman,* and Hopkins contributed even more frequently to *House Beautiful.* She also published a pulp romance novel set in Pasadena, in which the bungalows exert a therapeutic effect: *A Winter Romance in Poppyland* (Boston: Richard G. Badger, 1911).

31. *LHJ* 26 (May 1909): 50–51.

32. Una Nixson Hopkins, "A Picturesque Court of 30 Bungalows," *LHJ* 30 (April 1913): 99. See also Winter, *California Bungalow,* and Lancaster, *American Bungalow,* 148–49.

33. See Katherine Cole Stevenson and H. Ward Jandl, *Houses by Mail: A Guide to Houses from Sears, Roebuck and Company* (Washington, D.C.: Preservation Press, 1986).

34. *LHJ* was published for more than seven decades by the Curtis Publishing Company. In the late 1960s the highly successful Curtis enterprise began to disintegrate. This sad tale is told in detail in Matthew J. Culligan, *The Curtis-Culligan Story* (New York: Crown, 1970); Otto Friedrich, *Decline and Fall* (New York: Harper & Row, 1970); and Joseph C. Goulden, *The Curtis Caper* (New York: G. P. Putnam's Sons, 1965). Since then the *Journal* has been transferred, sold, and resold six times; with each corporate reorganization and relocation, the interest in the history of the magazine and its pivotal social impact early in this century diminished. A conversation in 1985 with Li Dwork, a longtime employee and director of reader services for *LHJ,* revealed that virtually all the company papers had been discarded. Even the Bok papers on loan to the Pennsylvania Historical Society, and used by Steinberg in writing *Reformer in the Marketplace,* were withdrawn and can no longer be located.

35. Winter, *California Bungalow,* 27. Hermann von Holst, *Modern American Homes* (Chicago: American Technical Society, 1913); reprinted as *Country and Suburban Homes of the Prairie School Period* (New York: Dover, 1982). The large number of *House Beautiful* plates in von Holst's book may also be due to the fact the magazine was published in Chicago, von Holst's own center of operations.

36. "Some Ladies' Home Journal Houses," *LHJ* 33 (February 1916): 29–32.

37. "They Live in Ladies' Home Journal Houses: Here are Five Successfully Erected in Foreign Countries," *LHJ* 33 (March 1916): 1. In comparison, by 1939 Sears is said to have provided 100,000 houses, over a period of thirty-one years; see Stevenson & Jandl, *Houses for Sale,* 19.

Notes to "Toward a Performance Theory of the Suburban Ideal, 1877–1917" by Mary Corbin Sies

1. Kenneth T. Jackson, *Crabgrass Frontier: The Suburbanization of the United States* (New York: Oxford University Press, 1985), 4.

2. According to U.S. Bureau of the Census figures, in 1980, 43.4 percent of the population was living in a suburban location (up from 37.2 percent in 1970), compared to 27.4 percent living in central cities and 27.2 percent living in rural areas; John F. Long, *Population Deconcentration in the U.S.* (Washington, D.C.: U.S. Bureau of the Census, Special Demographic Analysis, CDS-81-5, November 1981), 65. Recent Harris polls indicate the continuing appeal of the suburban ideal; see "Be It Ever So Humble, There's No Place Like a Three-Bedroom Home," *Gainesville Sun,* December 20, 1987.

3. Carol Aronovici, "Housing and the Housing Problem," *Annals of the American Academy* 51 (January 1914): 3.

4. Architectural historians discussing the professional design of the American suburban home begin their accounts anywhere from 1869—the founding date of Riverside, Ill.—to 1880 and are unanimous in asserting that World War I marked a watershed in suburban design. See Gwendolyn Wright, *Moralism and the Model Home: Domestic Architecture and Cultural Conflict in Chicago, 1873–1913* (Chicago: University of Chicago Press, 1980) and *Building the Dream: A Social History of Housing in America* (New York: Pantheon Books, 1981), chs. 6, 9; Alan Gowans, *Images of American Living* (New York: Harper & Row, 1976), 395–417; Walter Creese, *Crowning of the American Landscape* (Princeton: Princeton University Press, 1985); Leonard K. Eaton, *Two Chicago Architects and Their Clients* (Cambridge: MIT Press, 1969); H. Allen Brooks, *The Prairie School: Frank Lloyd Wright and His Midwest Contemporaries* (New York: Norton, 1972). For the contemporary view see *Annals of the American Academy* 51 (January 1914).

5. See Mary Corbin Sies, "American Country House Architecture in Context: The Suburban Ideal of Living in the East and Midwest, 1877–1917" (Ph.D. diss., University of Michigan, 1987).

6. I use the term *community-building process* instead of *design process* to convey that a wide range of persons—not just design professionals—participated in the decisions that produced planned, exclusive suburbs.

7. Brooks, *Prairie School.* See also Eaton, *Two Chicago Architects,* and Gowans, *Images of American Living.* Two more recent works that carry forward the east vs. west dichotomy are Alan Gowans, *The Comfortable House: North American Suburban Architecture, 1890–1930* (Cambridge: MIT Press, 1986), and Richard Guy Wilson, "American Arts and Crafts Architecture" in *The Art That Is Life,* ed. Wendy Kaplan (Boston: Museum of Fine Arts, 1987), 101–37.

8. Dell Upton, "Pattern Books and Professionalism: Aspects of the Transformation of Domestic Architecture in America, 1800–1860," *Winterthur Portfolio* 19 (Summer/ Autumn 1984): 114; Henry Glassie, "Eighteenth-Century Cultural Process in Delaware Valley Folk Building," in *Common Places: Readings in American Vernacular Architecture,* ed. Dell Upton and John Michael Vlach (Athens: University of Georgia Press, 1986), 407.

9. Most urban historians interpret the process of suburbanization in terms of forces originating in the city such as transportation innovations, racial discrimination, population growth, and class conflict. For the most penetrating studies see Jackson, *Crabgrass Frontier;* Sam Bass Warner, *Streetcar Suburbs* (Cambridge: MIT Press, 1962); Matthew Edel, Elliott Sclar, and Daniel Luria, *Shaky Palaces* (New York: Columbia University Press, 1984). For strong interpretations that focus on the suburban community-building process itself but without extensive analysis of the built environment see Henry Binford, *The First Suburbs* (Chicago: University of Chicago Press, 1985); Michael Ebner, *Creating Chicago's North Shore* (Chicago: University of Chicago Press, 1988); Robert Fishman, *Bourgeois Utopias* (New York: Basic, 1987); and Marc Weiss, *Rise of the Community Builders* (New York: Columbia University Press, 1987).

10. John Stilgoe, *Borderland: Origins of the American Suburb, 1820–1939* (New Haven: Yale University Press, 1988). See also David Handlin, *The American Home* (Boston: Little, Brown, 1979); Clifford Clark, Jr., *The American Family Home* (Chapel Hill: University of North Carolina Press, 1986); and Colleen McDannell's carefully documented *The Christian Home in Victorian America, 1840–1900* (Bloomington: Indiana University Press, 1986), which underscores the often neglected religious dimension of the American home.

11. John Archer, "Ideology and Aspiration: Individualism, the Middle Class, and the Genesis of the Anglo-American Suburb," *Journal of Urban History* 14 (February 1988): 215, and "Country and City in the American Romantic Suburb," *Journal of the Society of Architectural Historians* 42 (May 1983): 139–56.

12. Wright, *Moralism and the Model Home,* 6.

13. Janice Radway, *Reading the Romance* (Chapel Hill: University of North Carolina Press, 1984), 9. For a helpful discussion of ethnographic fieldwork see John Caughey, "The Ethnography of Everyday Life: Theories and Methods for American Culture Studies," *American Quarterly* 34 (Bibliography 1982): 222–43.

14. Rhys Isaac, *The Transformation of Virginia, 1740–1790* (New York: Norton, 1988); Dell Upton, "Toward a Performance Theory of Vernacular Architecture: Early Tidewater Virginia as a Case Study," *Folklore Forum* 12 (1979): 173–96 (190). See also Henry Glassie, *Folk Housing in Middle Virginia: A Structural Analysis of Historic Artifacts* (Knoxville: University of Tennessee Press, 1975), chs. 2–3.

15. On communities of discourse see David A. Hollinger, "Historians and the Discourse of Intellectuals," in *New Directions in American Intellectual History,* ed. John Higham and Paul Conkin (Baltimore: Johns Hopkins University Press, 1979), 42–63.

16. Isaac, *Transformation of Virginia,* 324.

17. For a full analysis of the suburban design programs emerging in planned, exclusive suburbs see Sies, "American Country House Architecture in Context." For a brief analysis of the design program of the model suburban home see Mary Corbin Sies, "'God's Very Kingdom on the Earth': The Design Program for the American Suburban Home, 1877–1917," in *Modern Architecture in America: Visions and Revisions,* ed. Richard Guy Wilson and Sidney K. Robinson (Ames: Iowa State University Press, 1991), 2–31.

18. When budget allowed, the next room generally provided was a den or study for the head of household.

19. George Bertrand, "Architecture," *Western Architect* 2:2 (1903): 14; Bertrand was a resident and architect of several houses in Lake of the Isles, Minneapolis.

20. E. P. Powell, *The Country Home* (New York: McClure, Phillips, 1904), 9.

21. Florence E. Parker, "The Ideal Country House," *Western Architect* 1:1 (1902): 15.

22. Harold D. Eberlein, "A House at St. Martin's," *American Homes and Gardens* 8 (December 1911): 430.

23. Candace Wheeler, *Principles of Home Decoration* (New York: Doubleday, 1908), 227; Alfred Mathews, "Short Hills, New Jersey," in *History of Essex and Hudson Counties* (Philadelphia: Everts and Peck, 1884), 3.

24. In my documentation of buildings in all four suburbs, I found no female architects of record.

25. John E. Toews, "Intellectual History after the Linguistic Turn: The Autonomy of Meaning and the Irreducibility of Experience," *American Historical Review* 92 (October 1990): 879–907.

26. Several scholars have emphasized the need to address these issues. See, for example, Thomas Bender, "Wholes and Parts: The Need for Synthesis in American History," *Journal of American History* 73 (June 1986): 120–36; Dell Upton, "The Power of Things," *American Quarterly* 35 (Bibliography 1983): 262–79; Simon Bronner, "Art, Performance, and Praxis," *Western Folklore* 47 (April 1988): 75–101. For an excellent discussion of these issues with reference to American domestic pottery see Paul Mullins, "A Problematic for the Research of Domestic Pottery Production and Consumption" (seminar paper, University of Maryland, Department of Anthropology, 1989). For an excellent study exemplifying these suggestions, see Dell Upton, *Holy Things and Profane: Anglican Parish Churches in Colonial Virginia* (Cambridge: MIT Press, 1986).

ABOUT THE CONTRIBUTORS

Annmarie Adams teaches design and architectural history at the School of Architecture, McGill University, Montreal. She received a Master of Architecture degree from the University of California at Berkeley, where she is currently a Ph.D. candidate in architectural history. Her dissertation is entitled "Architecture in the Family Way: The Nineteenth-Century English Homescape and the Design of Motherhood."

Charles Bergengren was given a mainstream Protestant upbringing in the visually austere but intellectually liberal Congregational church of New England (not far removed from the Protestant culture he studies in Pennsylvania). After studying art history at Oberlin, he moved to New York City where the music of John Cage and the theater of Richard Foreman (with whom he performed for five years) were major influences; nevertheless he finished his degree in art history and anthropology at CUNY. This led to graduate degrees in folklore at the University of Pennsylvania, specializing in material culture with Henry Glassie. His dissertation (1988) is on the architecture of the Pennsylvania Germans.

Rebecca Sample Bernstein developed her interest in women and domestic architecture with her thesis on the architectural and social dimensions of household use. In 1988 she received her M.A. in historic preservation planning from Cornell University. Her 1983 B.A. in the history of art is also from Cornell. Currently a preservation consultant in Madison, Wisconsin, she previously worked for the South Dakota Preservation Center as a historic

sites surveyor and for the Comstock Historic District Commission in Nevada as the staff preservationist. Her research work continues in the area of women's influences on domestic architecture.

Catherine W. Bishir, a previous contributor to *Perspectives,* is architectural survey coordinator for the North Carolina State Historic Preservation Office. Her many books and articles include *North Carolina Architecture* and, with Charlotte Brown, Carl Lounsbury, and Ernest Wood, *Architects and Builders in North Carolina: A History of the Practice of Building.* One of the founders of the Vernacular Architecture Forum, she has served as a member of the board and as first vice-president.

Mark L. Brack received a B.A. in environmental planning from the University of California at Santa Cruz and an M.S. in historic preservation from the University of Vermont. He has done architectural surveys in Vermont and California and formerly served as architectural historian for the Washington State Office of Archeology and Historic Preservation. He is currently a Ph.D. candidate in architectural history at the University of California at Berkeley, where he is working on a dissertation entitled "The Nature of Architecture: The Rustic Tradition in Anglo-American Architecture." He also co-authored, with James Delgado, the Historic American Buildings Survey Report "Presidio of San Francisco: National Historic Landmark District."

Thomas Carter teaches in the Graduate School of Architecture at the University of Utah. His main interest lies in the vernacular architecture of the American West, and he is currently editing a multi-volume monograph series on the building traditions of that region.

William Chapman is assistant professor in the Historic Preservation Section, School of Environmental Design, University of Georgia. Chapman holds a doctorate in anthropology from Oxford and an M.S. in historic preservation from Columbia. He worked for five years in the Virgin Islands, as architectural historian for the government of the Virgin Islands. Much of the fieldwork for his paper was conducted then and on subsequent trips to the islands. A former Fulbright Scholar (Italy, 1985), Chapman is interested in the broader issues of settlement and urbanism, particularly in the Caribbean. Most recently he has participated in an in-depth study of post-Hurricane Hugo damages in the Caribbean and coastal United States for the National Trust for Historic Preservation.

Michael J. Chiarappa has a B.A. in history from Ursinus College and an M.A. in folklore and folklife from the University of Pennsylvania. He is currently a Ph.D. candidate in folklore and folklife at the University of Pennsylvania. He has worked as a folklife researcher for the McKissick Museum of the University of South Carolina. Currently, he is doing research for the Philadelphia Maritime Museum, focusing on the architectural, shipbuilding, and fishery practices of the Delaware Bay oystering industry and its communities.

Elizabeth Collins Cromley is an architectural historian with a special interest in popular and vernacular American architecture. She came to SUNY at Buffalo's department of architecture in 1980 after teaching art and architectural history at the City College of New York and Bronx Community College. She has a B.A. from the University of Pennsylvania and an M.A. from New York University's Institute of Fine Arts. She was a Graduate Fellow

at the Institute for Architecture and Urban Studies in New York and received her Ph.D. in 1982 from the City University of New York Graduate School. Her work, published in various professional and scholarly journals and books, includes articles on resort architecture, popular housing, parks, and artifact design. She was awarded a postdoctoral research grant from the National Endowment for the Humanities to do work at the Winterthur Museum in American design, resulting in the book *Alone Together: A History of New York's Early Apartments*. In 1990 she was again an NEH Fellow, working on the history of domestic space.

Howard Davis holds degrees in physics from The Cooper Union and Northwestern University and in architecture from the University of California, Berkeley. He is currently associate professor of architecture at the University of Oregon, where he teaches design studios and courses in architectural theory and vernacular architecture. His current research is concerned with the building process and its relationship to the detailed forms taken by vernacular buildings. He has done professional work in housing and settlement planning and is coauthor, with Christopher Alexander and others, of *The Production of Houses*.

Jay Edwards received his Ph.D. in Anthropology from Tulane University. He is an associate professor of anthropology at Louisiana State University, where he teaches courses in anthropology, folklore, and vernacular architecture. He has conducted field research and surveys of vernacular architecture on twelve islands of the West Indies, in Normandy, Quebec, Missouri, England, and Louisiana. He is the author of *Louisiana's Remarkable French Vernacular Architecture, 1700–1900* and "The Complex Origins of the American Domestic Piazza-Veranda-Gallery," published in *Material Culture*.

J. Ritchie Garrison holds an M.A. and Ph.D. in American civilization from the University of Pennsylvania, an M.A. from the Cooperstown Graduate Programs, and a B.A. from Bates College. From 1976 to 1985 he was director of education at Historic Deerfield, Inc. Since then he has been assistant director of the Museum Studies Program and assistant professor of history at the University of Delaware. He has co-edited *After Ratification: Material Life in Delaware, 1789–1820,* with Bernard Herman and Barbara McLean Ward, and is the author of *Landscape and Material Life in Franklin County, Massachusetts, 1770–1820,* to be published in 1991 by the University of Tennessee Press.

Bernard L. Herman is associate director of the Center for Historic Architecture and Engineering at the University of Delaware, where he also is an associate professor in the College of Urban Affairs and Public Policy and in the department of history. His books include *Architecture and Rural Life in Central Delaware, 1700–1900, A Land and Life Remembered: Americo-Liberian Folk Architecture* (with Svend Holsoe and Max Belcher), and *The Stolen House: Material Culture and Metaphor in the Early Republic.*

Gregg D. Kimball is curator of books and manuscripts at the Valentine Museum in Richmond, Virginia, and received an M.A. in history and an M.L.S. degree from the University of Maryland, College Park. He has developed several exhibitions at the Valentine Museum, co-curating *In Bondage and Freedom: Antebellum Black Life in Richmond, Virginia* with Marie Tyler-McGraw and recently curating *Jim Crow: Racism and Reaction in the New South: Richmond, 1865–1940.* He is currently working on an overview of Richmond's working class from 1865 to 1920.

Gabrielle Lanier received a B.A. in fine arts from the University of Pennsylvania and an M.A. from the Winterthur Program in early American culture at the University of Delaware. She is currently a Ph.D. candidate in the history of American civi-

lization program at the University of Delaware and works at the university's Center for Historic Architecture and Engineering.

Margaret M. Mulrooney received her B.A. from the University of Delaware in 1987 after completing a self-designed program in historic preservation. After graduation she worked for two years as a historian for the Historic American Buildings Survey/Historic American Engineering Division of the National Park Service in Washington, D.C. During this time she researched and wrote *A Legacy of Coal: The Coal Company Towns of Southwestern Pennsylvania* under the auspices of the American Industrial Heritage Project at the Historic American Buildings Survey. She is currently pursuing her doctorate in American Studies at the College of William and Mary.

Laura A. W. Phillips holds a B.A. in history and art history from the University of South Alabama and an M.A. in art history from Tulane University. Formerly an architectural historian with the Louisiana State Historic Preservation Office, she has served since 1978 as a consulting architectural historian in North Carolina, where her work has included numerous architectural surveys, National Register nominations, and other preservation projects. She is the author of *Reidsville, North Carolina: An Inventory of Historic and Architectural Resources; Simple Treasures: The Architectural Legacy of Surry County;* and, with Kirk F. Mohney, *From Tavern to Town: The Architectural History of Hickory, North Carolina.*

Mark Reinberger holds a B.A. from the University of Virginia and an M.A. and Ph.D. from Cornell University. He is currently an architectural historian with Martin Jay Rosenblum, R.A. and Associates in Philadelphia, for whom he has conducted reports on several colonial houses of the Delaware valley. He also teaches at Drexel University.

Leland M. Roth received a B.A. in architecture from the University of Illinois–Urbana, followed by an M.Phil. and Ph.D. in art and architectural history from Yale University. His early research resulted in a series of books on the architecture of McKim, Mead & White culminating in *McKim, Mead & White, Architects,* as well as such general studies as *A Concise History of American Architecture* and *America Builds,* an annotated anthology of source documents. His present research has focused on such topics as industrial communities, industrial housing, and the role of the print mass-media in influencing housing design reform.

Mary Corbin Seis holds a Ph.D. in American studies from the University of Michigan. She is currently an assistant professor in the department of American studies at the University of Maryland, College Park, where she teaches courses in material culture studies and cultural history. For her doctoral research, she studied the social, cultural, and architectural history of planned, exclusive American suburbs in the late nineteenth and early twentieth centuries; her dissertation was awarded the Ralph Henry Gabriel prize of the American Studies Association (co-winner) in 1988.

Carolyn Torma has an M.A. in American studies from Emory University and a B.A. from the University of Michigan She is currently a Bush Fellow in the College of Urban Affairs at the University of Delaware. Over the past sixteen years, she has worked for state preservation offices in Michigan, Kentucky, and South Dakota. A strong interest in public education led to a 1984 film produced with Michael Koop and titled *Folk Building of the South Dakota German Russians* as well as to a course focused on rural workers' housing, community planning, ethnic architecture, and South Dakota architects.

Chris Wilson, an adjunct assistant professor of architecture and planning at the University of New Mexico and member of the board of directors of the Vernacular Architecture Forum, also works as a consultant to government agencies on historic preservation and planning issues. In addition to an interest in vernacular architecture and cultural landscape, Wilson has made a particular study of the interrelation of picturesque eclecticism, the historic preservation movement, tradition making, tourism, and modern cultural identity.

INDEX